D0931495

Culture Wars in Brazil

CULTURE WARS IN BRAZIL

Daryle Williams

The First Vargas Regime, 1930–1945

Duke University Press

Durham & London

2001

© 2001 Duke University Press

All rights reserved

Printed in the United States of America on acid-free paper ∞

Designed by C. H. Westmoreland

Typeset in Dante by Tseng Information Systems, Inc.

Library of Congress Cataloging-in-Publication Data appear

on the last printed page of this book.

TO JAMES

Contents

Figures

Tables

Abbreviations

Archives

AAA	Archives of American Art
AHI	Arquivo Histórico do Itamaratí
AMPOP	Arquivo Municipal da Prefeitura de Ouro Preto
AN	Arquivo Nacional, Rio de Janeiro
ANTT	Arquivos Nacionais—Torre do Tombo
CPDOC	Centro de Pesquisa e Documentação da História Contemporânea do Brasil/Fundação Getúlio Vargas
IPHAN	Instituto do Patrimônio Histórico e Artístico Nacional
LC-AHC	Library of Congress, Archive of Hispanic Culture
MCM	Museus Castro Maya
MHN	Museu Histórico Nacional
MI	Museu Imperial
MIOP	Museu da Inconfidência
NYPL	New York Public Library

Institutions

DIP	Departamento da Imprensa e Propaganda (Department of Press and Propaganda)
DNI	Departamento Nacional de Informações (National Department of Information)
DNP	Departamento Nacional de Propaganda (National Department of Propaganda)
DOP	Departamento Oficial de Publicidade (Official Department of Publicity)

DPDC   Departamento de Propaganda e Difusão Cultural
       (Department of Propaganda and Cultural Diffusion)
ENBA   Escola Nacional de Belas Artes
       (National School of Fine Arts)
IMN   Inspetoria dos Monumentos Nacionais
       (National Monuments Inspection Service)
IHGB   Instituto Histórico e Geográfico Brasileiro
       (Brazilian Historical and Geographic Institute)
INCE   Instituto Nacional do Cinema Educativo
       (National Institute of Educational Film)
INL   Instituto Nacional do Livro
       (National Book Institute)
MES   Ministério da Educação e Saúde
       (Ministry of Education and Health)
MESP   Ministério da Educação e Saúde Pública
       (Ministry of Education and Public Health)
MHN   Museu Histórico Nacional
       (National Historical Museum)
MJNI   Ministério da Justiça e Negócios Interiores
       (Ministry of Justice and Internal Affairs)
MNBA   Museu Nacional de Belas Artes
       (National Museum of Fine Arts)
MOMA   Museum of Modern Art, New York
MTIC   Ministério do Trabalho, Indústria e Comércio
       (Ministry of Labor, Industry, and Commerce)
SPHAN Serviço do Patrimônio Histórico e Artístico Nacional
       (National Historical and Artistic Patrimony Service)
SRE   Serviço da Radiodifusão Educativa
       (Educational Radio Broadcasting Service)
TSF   Tribunal Supremo Federal
       (Supreme Federal Tribunal)
TSN   Tribunal de Segurança Nacional
       (National Security Tribunal)

Political Parties

AIB   Ação Integralista Brasileira
(Brazilian Integralist Action)

ANL   Aliança Nacional Libertadora
(National Liberation Alliance)

PSD   Partido Social Democrático
(Social Democratic Party)

PTB   Partido Trabalhista Brasileiro
(Brazilian Labor Party)

UDN   União Democrática Nacional
(National Democratic Union)

Publications

AMHN   *Anais do Museu Histórico Nacional*

AMNBA   *Anuário do Museu Nacional de Belas Artes*

AMI   *Anuário do Museu Imperial*

DHBB   *Dicionário Histórico-Biográfico Brasileiro, 1930–1984,* 4 vols. (1984)

NPB   Getúlio Vargas, *A Nova Política do Brasil,* 11 vols. (1938–1947)

States

AL   Alagoas

AM   Amazonas

BA   Bahia

CE   Ceará

DF   Distrito Federal

ES   Espírito Santo

GB   Guanabara

GO   Goiás

MA   Maranhão

MT   Mato Grosso

MG   Minas Gerais

PA   Pará

PB   Paraíba

PR	Paraná
PE	Pernambuco
PI	Piauí
RJ	Rio de Janeiro
RN	Rio Grande do Norte
RS	Rio Grande do Sul
SC	Santa Catarina
SP	São Paulo
SE	Sergipe

Preface

This book is about a certain type of cultural conflict — culture wars — fought in Brazil between October 1930 and October 1945, a period commonly known as the first Vargas regime. In the following pages, I argue that the contentious politicking over the administration, content, and meaning of a national culture specifically marked as *Brazilian* was endemic to the authoritarian-nationalist politics associated with the populist dictator Getúlio Vargas (1883–1954). In these culture wars, bureaucrats, artists, intellectuals, critics, and everyday citizens competed against one another and the state for control of *brasilidade,* an intangible but highly coveted sense of Brazilianness. These culture wars shaped the cultural and political landscapes of the first Vargas regime as state centered, nationalist, and contested. These wars fueled the double process of state building and canon formation that defined Brazilian political culture (*cultura política*) and cultural policies (*política cultural*) in the middle decades of the twentieth century.

This book explains how the cultural politics of the first Vargas regime simultaneously drew on the unconventional and dynamic expressions of *modernismo* (modernism) that have come to be celebrated in Brazil and abroad as the quintessential markers of twentieth-century Brazilianness, alongside the conservative aesthetics of traditionalism and academicism that rooted Brazilian culture in its colonial and nineteenth-century pasts. This study locates the substance and meaning of cultural conflict over the past, present, and future of Brazilian culture within the political and cultural tensions of republican Brazil. The book concludes with an argument that the culture wars of the first Vargas regime were powerful enough to influence national and international imaginaries of Brazilianness well beyond the fall of the Estado Novo dictatorship in 1945.

Following a brief introduction to the metaphors of war that developed during the first half-century of republican rule, chapter 1 situates the concept of "culture wars" within the history and historiography of canon formation, state building, and cultural nationalism. Chapter 2 surveys the Brazilian cultural landscape in the period preceding Getúlio Vargas's rise to power, noting how cultural politicking developed between the 1808 transfer of the Portuguese Court to Brazil and the overthrow of the First Republic in 1930. Chapter 3 turns to the period after the Revolution of 1930, when culture wars periodically erupted within a state trying to become regulator, patron, and censor of a national culture. Together, chapters 2 and 3 explore the politics of "cultural management" in a period stretching from the early institutional initiatives of Dom João VI through the fall of the Estado Novo dictatorship (1937–1945). Chapters 4–6 examine three arenas of cultural conflict—the national historical and artistic patrimony, federal museums, and foreign expositions—where various political and cultural actors fought to give meaning to a national culture regulated, but never fully controlled, by federal cultural management. The conclusion surveys Brazil's cultural landscape in the immediate wake of the Estado Novo—a landscape conquered by the state and marked by memorials of Brazilianness, where hegemonic claims to brasilidade remained elusive.

The biographical appendix provides essential background information on various figures under consideration. Bringing together profiles of familiar and obscure names in the history of Brazilian culture, the appendix will be useful for specialists and newcomers alike. It has proved to be impossible, however, to profile each and every cultural personality of the Vargas era. It has proved to be equally impossible to present an exhaustive overview of the myriad cultural movements and artifacts that evoke the visual, ideological, and architectural languages of Brazilianness produced in the 1920s, 1930s, and 1940s. Fernando de Azevedo's *A Cultura Brasileira* (1943; English trans., *Brazilian Culture,* 1950) remains the single most encyclopedic work on Brazilian letters, arts, and sciences in the period prior to 1940.[1] A handful of specialized works, cited in the bibliography, address the institutional histories of cultural and educational policy-making bodies active during the Vargas era, as well as the various "isms" of nineteenth- and twentieth-century Brazilian cultural history.[2]

What follows is an interdisciplinary exploration into Brazilian culture in which close readings of the politics of culture illuminate the larger politics of cultural authority, memory, and state building. My approach is not intended to diminish the need to carefully plot the successes and failures of individual personalities, ideas, and movements within their respective political and cultural fields. I could not discount the extreme value of formal analysis in understanding the power of cultural artifacts. Instead, I write as a political historian of culture who has surveyed a wide range of personalities, sites, objects, and institutions in search of the reasons why the echoes of a hard-fought war for State and Nation might still be heard today.

Acknowledgments

The idea for *Culture Wars in Brazil* took off in the fall of 1987, deep in the bowels of Princeton's Firestone Library, where I and a few other intrepid souls braved Peter T. Johnson's Latin American Studies research methods course. My interest in Brazilian cultural history took root in the briefest of assignments on the primary source of my choice, a suicide letter written by Brazilian dictator-populist Getúlio Vargas in 1954. My fascination with Brazilian culture under Vargas has not since abated. I thank Peter and Ben Ross Schneider for mentoring me through the early stages of my work on the Vargas era. I also thank John Wirth, the late Fred Bowser, and the late Karin Van den Dool for shepherding this project through graduate school at Stanford. Fred and Karin are greatly missed.

This book took its present form in 1997, when I returned to Brazil as a Fulbright Junior Scholar. I am forever indebted to the Fulbright Commission, which has played an instrumental role in my intellectual and professional development. I am equally grateful for the institutional support extended by the Museu Histórico Nacional, the Centro de Pesquisa e Documentação da História Contemporânea do Brasil/Fundação Getúlio Vargas, and the Programa de Pós-Gradução em História Social at the Instituto de Filosofia e Ciências Sociais/Universidade Federal do Rio de Janeiro. All three institutions lent much-appreciated support throughout my field research.

Back in the United States, the Department of History at the University of California, San Diego, and the Ford Foundation Postdoctoral Fellowship Program for Minorities supported a year of writing in 1998. The sunsets over La Jolla brightened many an afternoon spent writing. Dain Borges merits a special word of thanks for his generous support and incisive comments during my stay at UCSD.

Many colleagues at the University of Maryland have been behind this project since I arrived at College Park in 1994. I am most grateful for their support. My special thanks to Jim Gilbert and Phyllis Peres for reading drafts of the manuscript, and to Rebecca Allahyari, Elsa Barkley Brown, Ira Berlin, Bill Bravman, James Brooks, Clare Lyons, Robyn Muncy, the late Marie Perinbam, Leslie Rowland, and Rob Wright for being such great colleagues and friends. I also thank the University of Maryland's Department of History, College of Arts and Humanities, and General Research Board for supporting portions of my field research, write-up, and illustration reproduction costs.

I must extend some special words of indebtedness and thanks to individuals who have come to the rescue in moments of need. Vera de Alencar, Jean Coffey, João Cândido Portinari, Barbara Tenenbaum, and Vera Bottrel Tostes played instrumental roles in securing access to several illustrations when labor strikes in Brazil and the United States threatened to delay my completion date. My editor at Duke University Press, Valerie Millholland, consistently proved herself to be an extremely kind and understanding advocate, especially in the final stretch, when seemingly endless revisions and grand jury service had exhausted my patience.

My Brazilian and *brasilianista* friends constantly remind me that I chose the right place to study and the right people to study with. I extend my best to Desmond Arias, Peter Beattie, Antonio Claudio de Carvalho, Flávio di Cola, Jerry Dávila, Noah Elkin, Keila Grinberg, Anne Hanley, Marguerite Harrison, Tom Jordan, Carlos Kessel, Paulo Knauss, Hendrik Kraay, Marisa Leal, Jeffrey Lesser, Flávio Limoncic, Luciana Lopez, Bryan McCann, Ligia Mefano, Rita Monteiro Moriconi, Ignez Neidu, Shawn Smallman, Nilza Waldeck, Barbara Weinstein, Erica Windler, and Joel Wolfe. José Neves Bittencourt, researcher at the Museu Histórico Nacional, remains a great friend and interlocutor. To the many other friends and colleagues whom I have met making the journey back and forth to Brazil, *obrigado*.

I close with more thanks to my best friend Jackie Scott, to my mother Barbara Cash, grandmother Blanche Catrabone, and the other members of my family. They all remain close to my heart, even when we are thousands of miles apart. Finally, I thank James Rostron, my caring partner, who has endured more long-distance phone calls and lonely nights than he deserves.

Introduction

On 15 November 1889, the Emperor Pedro II of Brazil received word that a handful of high-ranking military officers had joined ranks with disgruntled civilian elites to proclaim the Republic. Under direct orders from Field Marshal Manoel Deodoro da Fonseca (1827–1892) to seek immediate exile, the emperor quickly assembled the imperial family and set sail for Europe. The deposed monarch soon discovered that Fonseca had issued a ban on all members of the House of Bragança. Pedro quietly resigned himself to his new fate as persona non grata in his Brazilian homeland, greatly diminishing the prospects that those still loyal to the Bragan-ças might mount a monarchist resistance to the new regime. The second and last Brazilian emperor would be dead within two years, making restoration of the monarchy all the more improbable. The republicans were clearly relieved to see the empire (1822–1889) pass without bloodshed or civil disturbance.

The consolidation of republican rule proved much more contentious, because Fonseca, named chief of the Provisional Government, and his civilian allies failed to reach consensus over the character of the new political order. Relations between the field marshal and the republicans were especially tense regarding the question of military rights, a sore spot among the political elite well before November 1889. The civilian-military alliance proved itself to be unable to resolve other disputes over states' rights, constitutional law, and presidential powers, while dissident factions openly revolted against the young republic. In the first half-decade of republican rule, federal troops had to put down a separatist rebellion in Rio Grande do Sul and a monarchist naval mutiny off the coast of the capital. By 1896, in the arid backlands (*os sertões*) of the northeastern state of Bahia, federal troops

1   Brazil, 1938. Adapted from Instituto Brasileiro de Geografia e Estatística, *Brazil, 1938: A New Survey of Brazilian Life* (Rio de Janeiro: Serviço Gráfico do Instituto Brasileiro de Geografia e Estatística, 1939).

launched a brutal campaign against a community of impoverished agriculturists and religious pilgrims who rejected the republic's secular political authority.[1] The bitter struggle resulted in the total annihilation of the settlement on the Vasa-Barris River known as Canudos. Later immortalized by Euclides da Cunha, in his monumental *Os Sertões,* the conflagration at Canudos became a defining moment in Brazilian republicanism, making warfare part of the lexicon of state building and nationhood.

Less epic, but nonetheless violent, clashes over the meaning of republicanism persisted into the twentieth century. In the capital, the Revolt of the Vaccine (1904) and the Revolt of the Whip (1910) brought into sharp relief the latent violence in defining state authority, citizenship, and racial power under republicanism. In the South, along the Paraná-Santa Catarina border, a millenarian movement at Contestado (1912–1915) provoked a bloody conflict over the expansion of market relations that were coveted by the landowning elite who supported the republic. In each episode, state violence purged the republic of its internal demons, or so it appeared. The severity of these official responses to social and political protest produced a political culture of republicanism that invoked the principles of classical liberalism, but sharply limited regional autonomy, political freedoms, and civil citizenship. The federalist constitution enacted in 1891 provided that all states were equal and self-governing, but in reality the economically powerful states of São Paulo, Minas Gerais, and Rio de Janeiro used the federal government and the national army to discipline regional elites from the smaller or poorer states. The Constitution of 1891 provided for equality before the law, but in truth, full citizens were secular, educated white men whose material and social status was built on republican party membership, literacy, private property, and the regional export economies. Much of the remainder of society bore the ignoble label *os bestializados* (the bestialized).² Local police forces treated them as such.

By the time the republic completed its second decade, the frequency of open rebellion had diminished. The most powerful regional oligarchies, best personified by the landowning elite from the states of São Paulo and Minas Gerais, maintained order through fixed elections, backroom deals, and a delicate balance of repression and co-optation. The selective appropriation of bourgeois European values reinforced the oligarchs' claim to manage a society largely miscegenated and poor. To be sure, labor radicalism, the pressing "social question," rural banditry, and disquiet among junior military officers and the emergent middle classes continued to test the notion of "Order and Progress," a phrase emblazoned on the national flag. The home, street, and workplace were sites of intense struggles for hegemonic control. Nevertheless, the republican oligarchies carried off the image that they had mastered the forces of enlightened civilization necessary to triumph over barbarism.

The *pax republicana* was broken in 1929, when President Washington Luiz (Pereira de Sousa), a member of the São Paulo oligarchy, threw his support behind a fellow *paulista,* Julio Prestes (de Albuquerque), in the presidential elections of 1930. Luiz clearly had every right to nominate his successor, but his choice upset competing regional oligarchs, who expected the president to nominate a candidate from the state of Minas Gerais. The successional dispute, in conjunction with the severe crisis in the export economy brought on by the stockmarket crash of 1929, strained oligarchical liberalism to the breaking point. Unwilling to support Luiz's handpicked successor, elites from Minas, Rio Grande do Sul, and Paraíba turned to Getúlio Dornelles Vargas, governor of Rio Grande do Sul and former minister of the treasury. With the support of a new political party, the Aliança Liberal (Liberal Alliance), Vargas launched an opposition bid for the presidency on a reformist platform, which drew its strength from disgruntled regional elites and a heterogeneous coalition of reform-minded military officers, urban liberals, and industrialists. Vargas's calls for political reform, economic stabilization, and *renovação* (renewal) resonated with many. The widespread popularity of the Aliança's platform strongly suggested the oligarchical political culture of the First Republic was in the throes of crisis.

To the frustration of Vargas's supporters, the insurgent popularity of the Aliança Liberal was not sufficient to defeat the political machine behind Julio Prestes and the old-line republican party establishment. The paulista handily defeated Vargas in the March 1930 election. Vargas's supporters claimed voting fraud, while the defeated *gaúcho* (native of Rio Grande do Sul) made a commitment to respect the electoral returns. President Luiz, in the meantime, began preparations to transfer the presidency to Prestes.

The national political scene turned restless again in late July 1930, when João Pessoa, vice-presidential candidate on the defeated Aliança Liberal ticket, was shot and killed by a rival from his home state of Paraíba. The motive for the shooting was clearly local, but Pessoa's allies assigned blamed to the federal government. Still eager to unseat President Luiz, Vargas's supporters in the armed forces quickly made plans to topple the elected government. The armed insurrection that began October 3 in Rio Grande do Sul and Minas and quickly spread to the Northeast was brief. Once it became clear that Luiz would be unable to maintain support among the loyalist troops, a military junta deposed the president. Luiz's fall opened up the opportunity for Vargas's forces to move onto the capital. Sweeping into Rio during the last week of October, the insurgents suspended the federalist Constitution of 1891, closed Congress, and dashed all hopes that president-elect Prestes would assume office. A uniformed Vargas arrived in Rio on October 31 to the ovation of the masses and no small number of armed troops. When Vargas entered the Presidential Palace to become chief of the Provisional Government, he set a precedent, to be repeated on numerous occasions throughout the twentieth century: extraconstitutional measures, including threats of civil war, were legitimate tools for resolving political crises among elites.

Vargas's initial victory did not guarantee the oligarchs' unconditional surrender. Thus, the rebel troops searched out war trophies to symbolize the end of an old order. Taking the capital, the rebels hitched their horses to the Obelisk at the end of Avenida Rio Branco, claiming ownership of Rio's quintessential monument of the bourgeois republic. Elsewhere, military parades took possession of the civic spaces formerly controlled by the fallen republican elite. On November 19, Flag Day, Vargas presented the National Historical Museum (Museu Histórico Nacional; MHN) with a flag used in the recent civil war.[3] The following month, the MHN accepted an armband used by the triumphant rebel troops in a military parade of November 15 (not uncoincidentally, the anniversary of the republic).[4] These artifacts entered an institution that prided itself on the collection of war trophies seized in other armed conflicts of nationhood. The insurgents' greatest prize was President Luiz himself, who was imprisoned in a military fort before being sent into exile. In short order, the Vargas coalition transfigured the coup of 1930 into a Revolution, remaking the First Republic (1889–1930, also known as the Old Republic) into the ancien régime and the post–1930 regime into a purifying force of redemption.

In his frustrated presidential campaign, Vargas spoke of a reformed state that would not shy away from the demands of protecting and promoting national interests. Once in power — and dispensing with the democratic legislative process — Vargas and his regional allies quickly set out to expand and strengthen the federal government. Preexisting federal agencies received additional powers to set controls on agricultural production, exchange rates, and commodity prices. New federal agencies coordinated national policies in education, health, labor relations, industrial policy, and commerce. The state assumed a more conciliatory attitude toward labor by extending certain protections to Brazilian workers in private industry and the civil service. Literate women won the vote, reflecting the Vargas regime's willingness to expand the number of avenues through which state and civil society might interact.

The Vargas regime initially justified these unusual measures as necessary to manage the economic crisis and to reform atrophied political institutions. The call to emergency measures gradually gave way to an emergent political culture built around an interventionist state, which sought to establish a palpable presence in the home, schoolroom, hospital, and work-place. Vargas and his advisors presented the expansion of federal powers as necessary to expand political and economic opportunities and to prevent the return to oligarchical liberalism. By the late 1930s, the regime justified its continuation in office, even at the expense of the democratic reforms originally supported by the Aliança Liberal, as necessary to guarantee that the promises of the Revolution of 1930 would be fulfilled. Incrementally, Vargas replaced the liberal-oligarchical political culture of the First Repub-lic with a nationalist-authoritarian political culture that endured until the mid-1980s.

Civil unrest was a leitmotiv in these tumultuous years following the armed phase of the Revolution of 1930. In 1932, a civil war broke out in São Paulo, provoked by regional demands that the Vargas regime meet its commitment to reinstate constitutional law. Defeated on the battlefield, the paulistas still managed to pressure Vargas into accepting the forma-tion of a Constituent Assembly. The assembly completed its work in early 1934, and the return to constitutional rule followed soon after. Legalists were saddened to see that ratification of the new constitution and the re-turn to popular elections would not guarantee social or political peace. In November 1935, leftist soldiers quartered in the Northeast and Rio mutinied in hopes of inciting a popular uprising against the landholding elite. The central government responded to the so-called *Intentona Comunista* with ferocity, quickly putting down the rebellion. The state of siege and anti-leftist purges that followed the failed uprising circumscribed all demo-cratic institutions. The presidential elections slated for 1938 neared under the specter of state violence. In early November 1937, Vargas's military ad-visors fabricated evidence of another communist insurgency as a pretext for suspending the presidential elections and instituting an authoritarian-nationalist regime. According to Vargas, the *Estado Novo* (New State) an-nounced on November 10 was supposed to restore to the Brazilian people an organic political culture that had been corrupted by liberalism during the First Republic and threatened by communism in the constitutional period. This Estado Novo was built on the state's real and implied use of violence against any and all threats to the nation.

Metaphors and monuments of war were ubiquitous under the Estado Novo. In the interior, federal troops, technicians, and settlers were sent on a "march" to conquer the West. In the capital, the federal government erected monuments to the military heroism of nineteenth-century warriors Admiral Joaquim Marques Tamandaré (1807–1897) and Marshal Deodoro da Fonseca, as well as government troops martyred at the Retreat at Laguna (1867) and the Intentona Comunista (1935).[5] The state coordinated a *Campanha da Borracha* (Rubber Campaign) to help stimulate rubber production. In conjunction with the Rockefeller Foundation, the federal government organized an army of sanitation workers and public information campaigns in an attack on tropical and venereal diseases. Civil engineers and public health officials looked to the Baixada Fluminense, a particularly unhealthy region located to the north of the federal capital, as a battleground against misery and underdevelopment. In the interior of the Northeast, bounty hunters pursued a guerrilla war against *cangaceiros* (outlaws) in hopes of stamping out the scourges of rural banditry and bossism. In 1939, the most notorious of the rural bandits, Lampião (Virgolino Ferreira da Silva), was captured and decapitated. His head, which remained on public display in Salvador da Bahia for three decades, was yet another prize in the regime's war against internal disorder.

War in the most conventional sense had a marked impact upon Brazil under Vargas. In the early 1930s, Brazilian diplomats helped broker an end to the Chaco War (1932–1935) out of fear that the armed conflict between Bolivia and Paraguay might threaten Brazilian territory. The Constitutionalist Revolution of 1932 was a civil war replete with armored tanks, trenches, and dead war heroes. Rising geopolitical tensions in the Atlantic region were also felt in Brazil, as the Vargas regime cautiously negotiated a position of equidistance between Nazi Germany and the Western democracies. The arrival of Jewish refugees fleeing persecution in Europe and fears of Nazi infiltration among German immigrant communities in the Brazilian South were continual reminders that instability in Europe could have a direct impact on Brazilian national security. With the outbreak of the Second World War in 1939, the Vargas regime grew closer to the United States, which offered economic concessions in exchange for Brazilian neutrality. When Brazilian merchant marine vessels fell under Nazi attack in 1942, the Vargas state formally signed onto the Allied cause. Now at war against Germany and Italy, the national military complex grew significantly through the expansion of the domestic arms industry and the installation of a huge U.S. airbase near Natal, Rio Grande do Norte. Northeastern Brazil became an Allied fortress readied against a possible German attack on the South Atlantic. In July 1944, 25,000 Brazilian troops joined the Allies, fighting alongside U.S. troops in the liberation of Italy. Inaccurate in their

2 Third Congresso de Brasilidade, Rio de Janeiro, 1943. During the second half of the Estado Novo, the Centro Carioca, a private patriotic association with strong ties to the leaders of the Vargas regime, sponsored an annual Congresso de Brasilidade (Conference on Brazilianness). The November 1943 Congress focused on Brazil's recent entrance into the Second World War. The posters in the upper row read "*Brasilidade* is the Religion of Courage and Energy in Defending Brazil and her Material and Spiritual Patrimony." Courtesy of AN-Fundo Agência Nacional.

characterization of an all-white Brazilian army, broadsides published by the state and private patriotic leagues such as the Centro Carioca still reminded Brazilians that they were a people at war.

Far from these explicitly militarized zones, the international war resulted in an increased workday in the factories of São Paulo, food and energy shortages, and civil-defense preparations. The wartime economy institutionalized a number of changes in industrial relations, increasing state penetration into central planning and labor relations. Meanwhile, Hollywood films, newsreels, civic ceremonies, civil-defense drills, and boy scouting staged the European and Pacific front lines on Brazilian soil.

One of the paradoxes of Vargas's early years in power was how the diminutive gaúcho cultivated violence and was fundamentally shaped by

3 Youth Parade, Dia da Raça, Rio de Janeiro, 3 September 1944. In the same year in which 25,000 Brazilian troops departed for the European war front, an estimated 30,000 Brazilian youth prepared for battle in the streets of Rio de Janeiro in celebration of the "Day of the Race." Courtesy of AN-Fundo Agência Nacional.

war, yet preferred to promote an image of peace. As a civilian chief of the Provisional Government (1930–1934), president (1934–1937), and president-dictator (1937–1945), Vargas consistently presented himself as the affable, almost avuncular, chief of state. Vargas burst onto the national stage as a uniformed officer in October 1930, but he would wear civilian clothes for the rest of his political career. With the exception of the ministers of defense and security, the presidential cabinet was made up of civilians trained in law, medicine, engineering, and other liberal professions. State policy promoted social harmony and class collaboration, rather than conflict. State-sponsored civic culture ritualized collective action, social peace, and national integration.

But public images of peace and harmony could be deceiving. On the morning of 29 November 1937, Vargas presided over the symbolic attack upon the political culture of federalism, watching as the flags of all Brazilian states were ritually burned in a pyre mounted along Rio's Russell

Beach. The infamous *Queima das Bandeiras* (Burning of the Flags) was not merely a celebration of national unity, but rather an assault upon regional autonomy, individual rights, and political liberties. When Vargas's civilian, military, and ecclesiastical allies watched the symbols of regional sovereignty go up in flames, they lent their support to the state's attack upon elements of Brazilian society deemed threatening. Unbending regional elites, communists, liberal republicans, Jews, and unacculturated immigrants would bear the brunt of a broader assault on groups that did not conform to the regime's vision of Brazilian society. The Estado Novo anticipated a militarized technology of internal surveillance, policing, repression, and countersubversion that took on horrid proportions during the military regime of 1964–1985.

When the politics of warfare began to falter in mid-1945, Vargas faced the grim reality that his political base was not strong enough to support a civilian presidency organized around the politics of a sustained peace. Early in 1945, the dictator made a public pledge to step down at the end of the Second World War. But this commitment to redemocratization was suspect, and Vargas quietly explored the possibility of remaining in office until a new constitution could be drafted. In the streets of Rio, a popular political mobilization called *queremismo,* so-named because its working-class adherents wanted (*querer* = to want) Vargas to remain in office, gave the dictator a popular voice to reconsider stepping down. With the subtle encouragement of presidential operatives, the *queremistas* staged a series of public rallies calling for a constitutional convention with Vargas in the presidency. The president's disingenuous commitment to a transparent transition to democracy undermined his political legitimacy, which was already shaken by the contradiction of sending troops to fight totalitarianism abroad while maintaining a dictatorship at home. Once an ally of the dictatorship, the Army High Command threw its support behind a democratic transition. Rather than see queremismo turn into an unmanageable political mobilization from below, the generals forced Vargas from office on 29 October 1945.[6] Vargas departed the Presidential Palace just as he had entered—in a *golpe de estado.*

The material and symbolic repercussions of war echoed again during the second Vargas regime (1951–1954), when Vargas returned to the presidency as a democratically elected president. In the second term, a combination of economic instability, cold war polarization, and a botched political assassination attempt against a rival of the president cut short Vargas's bid to lead a populist state. Staring down another military coup, Vargas forever changed the nature of Brazilian politics on the night of 24 August 1954, by turning a firearm on himself. The suicide letter — doctored by allies before reaching the press — dripped with images of bloodletting, combat, and self-sacrificing valor.[7] When the news of Vargas's suicide became public, a grieving mob rushed to the Presidential Palace, while others combed the streets of the capital, setting fire to newspaper offices associated with the president's critics. A truly spectacular reversal of fortune followed: the one-time dictator, mired in a political scandal that he himself characterized as a "sea of mud," was transfigured into a national martyr felled on the battle-field by sinister national and international forces, whereas Carlos Lacerda, a champion of liberal democracy, who was nearly shot dead for his vocal opposition to the Vargas administration, fled into exile.[8]

One of the many ironies of Vargas's suicide was that the enigmatic states-man ended his life surrounded by an aura of a battle-hardened soldier, when he was, in fact, a poor candidate for a pantheon of republican heroes built around soldier-statesmen. Vargas may have come from a family with a distinguished military record, but his military experience amounted to little more than a brief stint as a midlevel officer in a regional infantry division based in Rio Grande do Sul. When geopolitical tensions between Bra-zil and Bolivia heated up in 1903, Vargas traveled to the western state of Mato Grosso, ready to defend Brazilian territory. The "Acre Question" was resolved peacefully, denying the gaúcho the bragging rights to combat ex-perience. Vargas left military service in late 1903, on a medical discharge allegedly granted under false pretense.[9] He subsequently became a civilian lawyer, and soon thereafter a politician, not to return to military fatigues until the armed phase of the Revolution of 1930. By then, he maintained close contact with officers and infantrymen, while still managing to remain far from the front lines.[10] Vargas did not travel to Rio until his position had been secured by the capitulation of President Luiz. Not once during the civil war did he find himself in the line of fire.

Vargas, a wealthy male landowner, educated as a lawyer, who entered politics through state party machines, had a political biography that began much the same as that of the civilian bacharéis (degreed liberal profes-sionals) who controlled the oligarchical parties during the First Republic. While Vargas was closely allied with the military, he was never of the mili-tary. At the height of the Estado Novo dictatorship, Vargas cut the figure of a well-heeled civilian who wore suits — and even casual wear — in public.

He never assumed the public persona of a military dictator. His stout frame and affable sense of humor were far from the commanding fiery profiles cut by the first two presidents of the republic, Deodoro da Fonseca and "Iron Marshal" Floriano Peixoto (1839–1895). By the end of his life, Vargas had invented himself as a beleaguered "Father of the Poor," not an old general ready to fade away. Yet, paradoxically, when Vargas took his "first step on the road to eternity [to] leave life to enter History," he left as a warrior. Indeed, Vargas and his era were built around the metaphor of war.

1

The Vargas Era and Culture Wars

At the height of the authoritarian Estado Novo, the infamous Department of Press and Propaganda published an essay, written by Oswaldo Teixeira, director of the National Museum of Fine Arts and well-known painter, which acclaimed Getúlio Vargas as a peer to Cósimo de Médici, the wealthy fifteenth-century banker who helped make Florence into the political and cultural epicenter of the Italian Renaissance. Crediting the Revolution of 1930 and the Vargas state with rescuing Brazilian society from a descent into cultural confusion and political disorder, Teixeira portrayed Vargas as a modern-day Renaissance prince. "Getúlio Vargas is the only President who has confronted the full range of problems facing Brazil with a clear, optimistic, and brilliant vision, guided by tranquillity, equilibrium, and the truest principles of Brazilianness [*com os mais sadios princípios de brasilidade*]," declared Teixeira.[1]

Teixeira was not alone in praising Vargas for a national cultural renewal. In 1940, the arts column of the regime's highbrow political review, *Cultura Política,* observed that the president's goodwill had afforded Brazilian artists the kind of official support that could be bitterly contested elsewhere. "The 'conquests' [of state patronage] won in other countries, typically granted only in the most dramatic and dire of circumstances, have come to Brazilian artists as goodwill gifts from the Chief of State," exclaimed the journal.[2] Even Gustavo Capanema, the influential minister of education and health and Vargas's closest advisor on subjects concerning official cultural programming, credited the president-dictator with the cultural gains won since 1930. At the March 1943 inauguration of the Imperial Museum, Capanema praised Vargas for his role in the flowering of Brazilian arts and letters, echoing Teixeira's earlier remarks in characterizing the chief of state as a peer of Pericles, Augustus, and Louis XIV — "great men who have filled History with the fanfare, honor, and joy of the human spirit."[3]

The image of a national cultural flowering cultivated by Vargas was very alluring, but in truth, the minister of education managed federal cultural policy, bestowing personal and institutional favors on some of the most important cultural figures of the 1930s and 1940s. It was the minister who actually changed the nature of cultural policy making. Vargas's interests in cultural patronage were generally limited to ceremonial galas, inaugurations, and civic parades. He rarely took a proactive stance in cultural matters. Looking back at the first Vargas regime, Carlos Drummond de Andrade, Capanema's chief of staff, stated bluntly, "Vargas could not care less [for cultural programming] . . . . Capanema's accomplishments, which today are credited to Getúlio, were merely tolerated by the President. . . . His great concern was signing papers and making politics." [4] As the *mineiro* poet suggests, the cultural renovação that took place after 1930 must be credited to the initiatives coordinated through the Ministry of Education, not the Presidential Palace. Vargas clearly knew this, but he never disavowed the perception that he was a savior, protector, and patron of Brazilian culture.

Several developments in the evolution of public administration and federal policy making bolstered the image that the Vargas regime, if not Vargas personally, was dedicated to a national cultural renaissance. Thanks to Capanema, the regime fully integrated cultural programming into the lexicon and practice of federal power, making Brazilian culture a charge of the state. Federal culture managers—an entirely new category of civil servant—directed a remarkable amount of energy toward the stimulation, proliferation, and officialization of cultural activities deemed expressive of a national ethos. A systematic approach to cultural management created or expanded nearly two dozen federal institutions tending to the performing and visual arts, historical preservation, museums, letters, and civic culture. Significant federal expenditure accompanied this institutionalization of cultural management and patronage. In addition to the investment of financial and administrative capital into the cultural arena, the federal government plowed substantial amounts of symbolic capital into the patronage of the national cultural patrimony.

Praised by high-ranking culture managers, the state's investment in culture faced opposition from many camps. For critics of Vargas-era cultural policies, censorship, political repression, social control, and cultural authoritarianism fueled the regime's thirst for managing a national cultural renewal. To their critics, federal culture managers, and most especially Vargas, were not humanists, but rather brutal thought police. In 1942, for example, the leftist U.S. publisher Samuel Putnam (1892–1950) spoke out for several Brazilian authors, including prominent novelists Jorge Amado and Graciliano Ramos, who had been silenced through the federal government's proclivity for harrassing intellectuals and literary figures deemed a threat to the regime's political and cultural supremacy. Relaying what would surely have been censored in Brazil, Putnam cited a 1941 speech Amado delivered while in exile in Argentina in which the Bahian novelist denounced the Vargas regime for its draconian cultural policies of mind-control and cultural repression. In a thinly veiled allusion to cultural policies implemented by the German National Socialists, Putnam characterized the Vargas regime's program of cultural management as *kulturkrieg*.[5] Teixeira's Cósimo had been transfigured into a book-burning Savanarola.

The paradox is that the same state that persecuted left-wing intellectuals as threats to Brazilian culture, while patronizing conservative artists such as Oswaldo Teixeira, exhibited a high tolerance for cultural nonconformists who questioned the political and cultural establishment. Rather than censure the iconoclastic vanguard collectively known as the *movimento modernista* (modernist movement), the Vargas regime absorbed modernist artists and modernist projects into federal cultural management. Modernist literary figures including Mário de Andrade, Carlos Drummond de Andrade, and even novelist Graciliano Ramos (imprisoned during the Estado Novo for his leftist political sympathies) gravitated toward the federal government. With the cover of state support, these figures wielded considerable influence in defining and administering Brazil's cultural identities during the 1930s and 1940s.

Modernist architecture—disparaged by conservatives in Brazil and abroad as communistic, ugly, and wholly unnational—made its biggest strides in Vargas-era Brazil *because* of state sponsorship. Self-consciously "Brazilian" architecture, exemplified in the neocolonial movement, was certainly tolerated by the Vargas state. Local adaptations to the stolid federalist style favored by American New Dealers, the neoimperial architecture favored by European totalitarian states, and the *indigenista* public art commissioned by the postrevolutionary Mexican state would also be found in state architecture in Brazil. Nevertheless, the Vargas regime tolerated, and at times embraced, the importation of the principles of modernist architecture promoted by the International Congress of Modern Architecture and its charismatic leader Le Corbusier. The signature building of the Estado Novo, celebrated within Brazil and abroad as the pinnacle of cultural change in Brazil, was the Ministry of Education and Health, a modernist skyscraper whose design was literally taken out of Le Corbusier's sketch-books. At times, the official architecture of the Vargas regime seemed at direct odds with the regime's clearly stated war on communism, interna-tionalism, and other "threats" to the nation. Official cultural policy making under Vargas was obviously more complex, paradoxical, and contradictory than Teixeira and Putnam might admit.

As a rhetorical device, the bipolarity of Vargas as culture-maker/culture-destroyer is powerful. As an explanatory model, the dichotomy collapses under scrutiny. A political history of culture that looks at the institutional growth, programmatic advances, and aesthetic contradictions of state-sponsored culture during the first Vargas regime is necessary. This politi-cal history must decenter Vargas, who received the credit for much of the cultural underwriting/repression but in reality played a supporting role in the articulation and implementation of cultural policy making. This political history of culture must examine the complexities of politics within cultural production. It must expose internal divisions within the state. It must demonstrate the connections and disjunctures between offi-cial cultural policy and the modes of cultural production and consumption present outside of the state. Finally, the political history of culture must ex-plain how and why the Vargas regime successfully helped create a mosaic of modern Brazilian culture—graced by Ouro Preto, Cândido Portinari's *Café*, Jean-Baptiste Debret's watercolors, the uncompromisingly modern-ist steel-and-glass skyscraper juxtaposed against lush tropical foliage, and the nostalgic memories for Dom Pedro II—that remained forever ill-at-ease with itself and with state intervention.

Writing a political history of Brazilian culture during the Vargas regime is a daunting challenge. The North American *brasilianistas* (Brazilianists) who pioneered the political history of the Vargas era in the late 1960s passed over the politics of culture when assessing the construction of politi-cal power during the Vargas era.[6] E. Bradford Burns, Ludwig Lauerhauss, and Thomas Skidmore examined the ideologies of nationalism, but stuck mainly to intellectual history.[7] The iconoclast Richard Morse looked at the internal ethos and aesthetic genealogies of Brazilianness, but remained largely uninterested in the "on-the-ground" politics of culture.[8] When North American literary critics and art historians took up the cultural his-tory of the Vargas era, they were largely uninterested in the state. In 1967, for example, literary critic Jean Franco published a wonderful overview of

Latin American modernism, dedicating a considerable number of pages to the Brazilian literary avant-garde.[9] The Vargas state is incidental to Franco's study, despite the fact that many titans in the modernist canon—Carlos Drummond de Andrade, Mário de Andrade, Augusto Meyer, and Graciliano Ramos—all maintained intimate contacts with the Vargas state. Similar observations can be made for the work of John Nist, whose 1967 survey of modernism queries whether modernism died in 1930, rather than face head-on how modernism matured under state tutelage following the Revolution of 1930.[10] English-language audiences of the late 1960s and 1970s went largely unaware of the intimate nature of culture and politics under Vargas.

The silences were not mere North American oversights. Numerous factors inhibited Brazilian scholars of the 1960s and 1970s from looking too closely at the politics of culture under Vargas. First, the politics of military dictatorship reinforced the connection between official culture and the culture of repression. Histories too critical of state cultural policies could possibly run afoul of state censors. Less critical histories ran the risk of censure from an academic and cultural establishment that was justifiably suspicious of the cultural machinations of a repressive state. The second factor came from within the state itself, as the federal cultural apparatus created under Vargas verged on collapse in the late 1960s. In 1970, the National Historical Museum—one of the institutions most favored by the Vargas regime—was literally falling to pieces. The Serviço do Patrimônio Histórico e Artístico Nacional, created in 1937, had ossified into an understaffed, underfunded state agency that treated cultural patrimony much like a stuffed animal. The decomposition of the documentary, material, and technical artifacts of Vargas-era cultural management nearly damned the history of that management to oblivion. The third and final obstacle surrounded the dynamics of Brazilian cultural criticism, which exalted a triumphalist history of modernism that largely ignored the state.[11] Wilson Martins's widely read history of modernism, updated in 1969 and later translated into English, makes little of modernism and the state.[12] In 1974, João Luiz Lafetá identified an ideological shift in modernism circa 1930, as the modernists turned from aesthetic to political questions.[13] Unfortunately, the study failed to explore the place of public policy in this shift. For these authors, the modernist canon existed outside of state politics.

A paucity of primary source materials posed significant barriers to the reconstruction of the politics of culture of the 1930s and 1940s. The Brazilian National Archives, sadly, received little documentation related to state cultural policy during the Vargas era. Few of the federal secretariats, foundations, and institutes managing culture in the 1970s and 1980s maintained institutional archives dating back to the first Vargas regime. The papers of most major cultural figures of the period remained in personal collections. Most problematic of all was the fact that the institutional archive of the Ministry of Education and Health, the most important regulatory agency in cultural management during the Vargas era, was in the possession of Gustavo Capanema, while the institutional archive for the other major federal agency responsible for cultural regulation, the Department of Press and Propaganda, had disappeared. Without access to these archives, historians were unable to write close histories of the politics of state-sponsored culture.

After 1979, the normalization of an incremental process of political liberalization known as *abertura,* combined with changes in archival management, presented new opportunities for a more systematic recovery of the cultural politicking of the Vargas regime. Social scientists looked at the cultural policies of the 1970s in relation to the antecedents of the 1940s.[14] In 1984, the well-known literary critic Antonio Cândido made a brief survey of the impact of the Revolution of 1930 on Brazilian culture, noting the process of routinization of cultural renewal that accompanied the regime change.[15] Historians studied ideological currents, educational policy, and propaganda. Finally, a heterogeneous group of social scientists and designers affiliated with the Centro Nacional de Referência Cultural rethought federal cultural policy, revisiting the history of state cultural management to see the paths not taken in the state's institutional relationship to cultural patrimony.[16]

Changes in archive management enabled historians to pursue new themes in the history of culture under Vargas. In a process that could be painfully slow and inefficient, most federal agencies began to organize their institutional memory. (This study draws heavily on institutional archives organized in the 1980s and 1990s.) The single-most important development in archive management came from outside the state, at the Centro de Pesquisa e Documentação da História Contemporânea do Brasil (CPDOC), a subdivision of the Fundação Getúlio Vargas in Rio de Janeiro. Created in 1973, this research institution had by the late 1970s revolutionized Brazilian historical research by collecting and cataloguing the papers and oral histories of many of the most important figures of the Vargas era, including Vargas, Oswaldo Aranha, and Gustavo Capanema. The research team and publication series coordinated by CPDOC gave the history of the Vargas regime an institutional foundation unequalled in any other field in Brazilian history.

A team of Brazilian social scientists led by Simon Schwartzman was the first to make use of the CPDOC archives to recover the history of federal cultural management during the first Vargas regime.[17] *Tempos de Capanema* (1984), a collaborative study based on the preliminary organization of the Capanema archive, still stands as the most complete study on the confluence of culture and politics during the Vargas era.[18] In its pathbreaking use of the former minister's "personal" archive, the study brought to light the lively cultural politicking that surrounded the influential minister from Pitangui, Minas Gerais. Schwartzman's team set a high standard for a number of subsequent studies that have analyzed the cultural world created by Capanema and his interlocutors.

The most dramatic reappraisal of culture under Vargas came in 1979, when sociologist Sérgio Miceli published a study of intellectuals and the elite (*classes dirigentes*) in the 1920s–1940s.[19] Creatively researched and theoretically innovative, Miceli's work introduced an epistemological framework capable of describing the relationship between culture and the state. Miceli was especially attuned to the state's role as an employer that provides intellectuals with the material and symbolic resources to engage in cultural (and political) creativity. Pierre Bourdieu's theories of the "field of cultural production" and economy of symbolic exchange loomed large. Plotting the professional and intellectual lives of some of the most prominent figures in the Brazilian cultural canon, Miceli demonstrated how the same canon had been conditioned by employment and patronage opportunities that opened up during the Vargas era. This approach proved controversial, with critics taking exception to the suggestion that the protagonists of the modernist movement used a repressive state as a mechanism for professional and aesthetic advancement. Antonio Cândido questioned Miceli's research.[20] The controversy, in turn, inspired a number of new works on intellectuals and the state, cultural policy, and canon formation.[21] The political culture of cultural policy making became a hot topic.

Like Miceli's and Bourdieu's Brazilian(ist) interpreters, I am drawn to the argument that cultural production and consumption must be plotted within a sociological framework that makes accommodations for politicking and power differentials. U.S. literary critic Randal Johnson has provided the most expressive framework for understanding the politics of culture in Vargas-era Brazil, arguing with respect to literary production that cultural practices "are neither totally autonomous nor entirely self-contained, nor simply 'reflective' of social structure, but rather constitute dynamic systems or networks of social relations that are intimately bound up with frequently subtle relations of authority and power."[22] Following Johnson, a charismatic model of cultural production, grounded in individual profiles of genius, inadequately explains how culture is actually produced and regulated. Cultural authority is a product of politicized social and institutional relations.[23] Culture actors compete for control of the mechanisms regulating the cultural field (for example, patronage, criticism, commercial markets, legislation) because these mechanisms rank individual styles, works, and figures. Cultural artifacts (for example, a book, a painting, a building, a theory, a symbol, a personality) are produced within a system of stratified power that gives status and meaning to all artifacts and their producers, but not equally. Institutional ties and social relations matter just as much as aesthetic quality. Johnson's theory, which owes much to Miceli, Bourdieu, Edward Said, and others, does not wholly discount the idea of artistic genius and the sublime. Rather, it makes genius a product of its political and cultural ecology.

Johnson and others have rightly suggested that scholars must be cautious in directly applying Bourdieu's theories to Brazil. The fields of cultural production, power, and class in pre-1945 Brazil were too coterminous to make the same case for Brazil that Bourdieu makes for nineteenth-century France, where the regulatory mechanisms of the literary field were increasingly distinct from the political and economic fields. In Brazil, the regulating powers of the cultural field could not stray too far from the political field. To my reading, the distance between the humanities (a large subset of the field of cultural production) and the state (a large subset of the field of power) actually closes in the 1930s and 1940s, as various cultural actors sought out institutional, legal, and bureaucratic aides within the state to help manage their position within the humanities. The state, in turn, sought out cultural actors to promote state interests, which included state tutelage of the arts. Cultural and political authority were dually regulated by mechanisms of the cultural field (professional associations, publishing houses, foreign and domestic critics, public opinion) and mechanisms of the state proper (federal ministries, museums, the civil service, laws, and so forth).

If a theory of autonomous fields makes for a poor fit with the history of the first Vargas regime, Bourdieu's concept that the cultural field is a "field of struggles" remains extremely useful. During the first Vargas regime, prominent political figures, cultural figures, and federal institutions incessantly fought over the rights to cultural patronage and management. Within the state, cultural patronage could border on a zero-sum game, in which gains made by one state agency came at the expense of another. The confrontations between various state agencies internally divided the federal government and weakened the state's leverage in cultural management. Outside the state, prominent cultural figures and aesthetic positions fought for cultural hegemony, or at the least, a competitive advantage. The metaphor of a field of struggles seems entirely appropriate in characterizing a historical process in which competing interests assume oppositional, relative positions to win the moral and political capital necessary to shape the terrain in which culture is produced, consumed, and understood.

My interest in federal cultural patronage naturally leads to a consideration of the contested cultures of nationalism, because the "national" came up again and again in the cultural politicking of the first Vargas regime. At stake in the culture wars was not just the definition of good and bad art, but rather the consecration of good and bad *Brazilian* art and the enthronement of dominant cultural brokers willing to protect and defend their cultural positions in the name of protecting national culture. Bourdieu seeks to describe a field of struggles that ultimately directs its occupants toward an autonomous field in which "pure art" and the "pure gaze" constitute the rules of engagement. In Brazil, I see a different picture, where the language of nationalism muddies the purity of art and gaze. Real differences over aesthetics cannot be discounted. Universal categories of good and bad art should not be dismissed out of hand. However, the antagonisms over cultural politicking seem to be part and parcel of a campaign to control the subjective "imagination" of a national community, where the claim to national pedigree trumps any extranational claim to universal genius or enlightened viewership.

The reference to the national imagination is, of course, borrowed from Benedict Anderson, who treats nationalism as a complex cultural enterprise pursued by elites who speak and act as if fictive national communities actually exist, to see that over time fiction can turn into real emotive, political, and linguistic realities for large groups of people who may live within a shared political space, but who can never know one another personally. The study of the imaginative capabilities and the imaginary (image-based and fictive) elements of nationalist elites, and its insights into the invention of nations, appears highly consistent with Brazilian studies. Anderson himself makes several allusions to Brazil in the revised version of *Imagined Communities* (1991).[24] Unfortunately, Anderson confines his Brazilian remarks to the nineteenth century, when the Portuguese Court, fleeing Napoleon, struck an unusual deal with the local "creole pioneers" to "imagine" an independent Brazilian Empire. Although Anderson fixes New World nationalism in the nineteenth century, I argue that the Brazilian case begs an examination of the twentieth century, when cultural nationalism explodes beyond the limited number of creole elites to engulf an expanding state and expanding client base of culture managers and culture consumers.

If Anderson's imagined communities help to identify the mental worlds of nationalism, a third concept — culture wars — provides the tools necessary to explore the actual forums and the local politics of the national imaginary. "Culture wars" entered into the U.S. cultural lexicon in the late 1980s, when the United States experienced a series of acrimonious debates that conflated party politics, art, sexual politics, religion, and state powers.[25] The first flash point was a retrospective exhibition in honor of the U.S. photographer Robert Mapplethorpe (1946–1989) planned for Washington's Corcoran Gallery in the summer of 1989. The planned exhibition, *Robert Mapplethorpe: The Perfect Moment,* was to be partially funded by the National Endowment for the Arts, an independent funding agency that distributes federal money for various art projects. The second flash point was an interpretative exhibition, scheduled for 1995, about the *Enola Gay* and the 6 August 1945 atomic bombing of Hiroshima. The venue was the National Museum of Air and Space, a branch of the Smithsonian Institution.[26]

Quite unexpectedly, both exhibits were thrust to the center of public debate about morality, good and bad art, and patriotic and revisionist history. In the Mapplethorpe case, the exhibit at the Corcoran was cancelled in a firestorm of protest about public decency and state censorship. At issue were a handful of erotic photographs that struck conservatives as immoral and obscene. Supporters of the cancelled exhibit staged a counter-exhibit outside the Corcoran, showing the photographs deemed indecent and unworthy of public support. In the meantime, congressional committees met to debate whether the National Endowment for the Arts should lose its funding in retribution for its original support of the Mapplethorpe exhibit. In Ohio courts, the director of the Cincinnati Contemporary Art

Center was put on trial for obscenity after authorizing a local showing of the Mapplethorpe retrospective.

The *Enola Gay* exhibit provoked its own firestorm of controversy, hotly debated in the press, universities, and the halls of Congress. At the center of the controversy were the narrative texts that were to accompany the exhibit, which veterans' groups found unjustifiably critical of President Harry Truman's decision to use atomic weapons in lieu of a conventional land-and-sea assault on Japan. The restored plane did indeed go on public display at the National Museum of Air and Space in commemoration of the fiftieth anniversary of the bombing of Hiroshima and the end of the Second World War, but the watered-down exhibit seen by the public said relatively little about the airship's place in the death and injury of tens of thousands of Japanese civilians and the dawn of atomic warfare. The exhibit said even less about the plane's place in the contested battles for U.S. identity and memory. So powerful were the Mapplethorpe and *Enola Gay* controversies that they continue to shape museum politics.

At face value, these controversies were not really culture wars, but rather disagreements about museum display and interpretation. After all, the academic and museum establishment, demagogic politicians, veterans' associations, the politically mobilized Christian Right, hyperbolic talk radio announcers, and pressure groups were *ostensibly* in disagreement over the content of museum exhibits. Given the preexisting disagreements among these groups, why else would they devote so much attention to two museum exhibits? But as is well-known, the divisive controversies engulfing each exhibit went *far* beyond the internalist politics of museum management. The fight over the Mapplethorpe exhibit was not about the appropriateness of public sponsorship for controversial art, but about the place of the homosexual and the homoerotic image (even if it was just a calla lily) in the public view. The opposing sides debated whether America's official visual culture could make room for Mapplethorpe as an *American* interpreter of *American* culture. The fight over the exhibition of the *Enola Gay* at Air and Space was not about the appropriate tone of object-grouping, labeling, and lighting—the stock-and-trade of museum management—in a historical exhibition. Had these been the main points of contention, the lengthy revision process should have corrected disagreements about the material, social, and textual content of the exhibition. The controversy endured, rather, because of America's (and the world's) conflicted readings of atomic warfare, the unresolved relationship between the United States and Asian peoples, and the lingering suspicions between the generation of the Great Depression and the Second World War and the generation of the Vietnam War and the Civil Rights Movement.

What made the *Enola Gay* and Mapplethorpe exhibits "culture wars," and what makes the term "culture wars" useful for my purposes here, was the fight for nationhood taking place within state-sponsored cultural venues. The imprimatur of state patronage—no matter how indirect, or how symbolic—pits competing constituencies against one another for control of objects and exhibition spaces that they claim to harbor and protect the national ethos. The objects need not be controversial. Consider, again, Mapplethorpe's beautifully rendered calla lilies. The venue need not be known as a battleground. The National Museum of Air and Space had been the Smithsonian Institution's jewel before the controversies surrounding the *Enola Gay*. At issue is the way in which official patronage can set the stage for bitter disagreement over the meaning of national identity and the appropriate use of public resources. At these moments of disagreement, culture wars arise. The term *culture wars,* then, seems eminently useful for understanding the poetics, geopolitics, and imagery of culture during Vargas era, when the struggle for controlling national identity was fought over objects, images, and locales that the central state presented as carriers of brasilidade.

There are undoubtedly many pitfalls to bringing "culture wars" to Brazilian history. Anyone familiar with the United States will be sadly disappointed to find that the social scope of cultural warfare in Brazil was limited to a small fraction of a population that exceeded forty million in 1940. The multiplicity of cultural combatants in North America's culture wars is missing in the Brazilian case. For the majority of the first Vargas regime, federal and state legislatures were shuttered, denying the opportunity to examine parliamentary debates over cultural policy making. From 1937 through 1945, federal censors regularly interfered in print media and radio, limiting opportunities for dissenters and demagogues to use the newspapers and airwaves to stir up popular resentment against certain culture projects. Small in number and largely marginalized from the process of cultural management, Brazil's civic associations, religious organizations, and professional groups played minor roles in cultural politics. With some limited exceptions, such as residents of historic urban centers who expressed opposition to certain restrictions imposed by historical preservation, there is little evidence that Brazil's culture wars enlisted a large volunteer army. This differs from the contemporary U.S. context, where culture wars bring a broad cross-section of "combatants" to square off in our schools, workplaces, legislative chambers, radio call-in programs, and local cultural institutions.

The limited social nature of cultural warfare does not discount the importance of the culture war, especially in relation to the crucial process of state formation taking place under Vargas. Although the culture wars of the Vargas era were most often confined to the cultural elite, the wars helped shape political and cultural power for all Brazilian society. The competition for control of increased state resources destined for culture stoked larger tensions about the role of the Brazilian state in a modernizing society. The competition for access to state patronage stoked larger tensions about the content of the cultural canon. Even if the supply of state funding was inexhaustible, which it most certainly was not, the combatants of the Vargas era were compelled to fight for state resources, because these resources conferred upon the victors the legitimacy to use the state in the definition of national culture at home and abroad. Victory in the battle for state resources guaranteed privileged access to the sites of the nationalist imaginary, which, in turn, transformed cultural positions into political power and cultural artifacts into national icons.

The problem is that no one faction attained hegemony. The state was internally divided, with the Ministry of Education ferociously guarding its cultural powers against an encroaching Ministry of Justice and the Department of Press and Propaganda. No single faction located outside of the state won the unchallenged ability to manage, patronize, and control cultural production. When the Estado Novo fell in October 1945, the modernists had won the moral and political power to shape the national debate on the arts, architecture, and letters, but this was an incomplete victory. The modernists' erstwhile opponents, situated within the state and without, continued to control certain sites intimately associated with the management of Brazilian national identity. Critics in Brazil and abroad were not in agreement about the essence of Brazilian culture. The first Vargas regime ended in 1945 with a state that held great influence in managing brasilidade. But this was a state that remained internally divided in a society that was internally divided, despite all myths of a cultural and political vocation for compromise and harmony.

2

Cultural Management before 1930

Cultural management — an institutionalized, administrative relationship between the state and culture — can be traced back to the dramatic events of late 1807, when Queen Maria I of Portugal, her son Prince Regent João, and 15,000 subjects fled to Brazil, just hours before Lisbon was overrun by the armies of Napoleon Bonaparte.[1] When the royal family arrived in Rio de Janeiro in January 1808, the nobles quickly discovered that the Court would have to reverse restrictive colonial regulations regarding cultural production if the capital of the viceroyalty was actually going to serve as the temporary seat of the Portuguese Empire. Royal decrees immediately rescinded long-standing prohibitions against printing presses and free trade, which had deliberately hindered the growth of "enlightened" civilization on the western shores of the Luso-Atlantic. Fleeing Portugal to avoid the revolutionary ideas carried by Napoleon, the Portuguese Crown brought enlightened reformism to colonial Brazil.

To be sure, some of the building blocks of enlightenment were already present in late-colonial Brazil. A select handful of elite men studied at the University of Coimbra in Portugal, returning to Brazil to shape the colony's intellectual milieu. The regular and secular clergy were the colony's ecclesiastic intelligentsia. Learned societies, princely collections, schools, hospitals, and military installations funded by royal, ecclesiastic, and private patrons were the institutional homes for scholarly thought, scientific experimentation, artistic expression, and technological innovation in Portuguese America. Rio de Janeiro's Casa de História Natural (Natural History House, more commonly known as the Casa dos Pássaros, or House of Birds), founded by viceregal decree in 1784, was a notable example of colonial Brazil's integration into the encyclopedic tradition at a time when the publications of the philosophes were on the Index of subversive works.[2] A series of antiregalist conspiracies that broke out in the last quarter of the eighteenth century, led by the Inconfidência Mineira of 1789 and the Tailors' Conspiracy of 1798, explicitly drew upon the ideas of liberty and reason closely associated with European enlightened thinkers. In putting down these challenges to the colonial order, the imperial state confronted the reality that notions of self-determination, natural rights, trade liberalization, and direct observation had already taken root in Brazil.

The newly arrived Braganças still found Brazil lacking a cultural infrastructure befitting a European court, even if it was a court of refugees. The prince regent therefore initiated a number of measures to enlighten Portuguese America. Between 1808 and 1818, Rio gained a royal press, library, botanical garden, and museum. The Crown revoked standing prohibitions on institutions of higher learning in the colony. As Portuguese America made the transition from the jewel in the crown of the Portuguese Empire to the head actually wearing the crown, the prince regent ensured that the Court could look to a cultural infrastructure that looked more metropolitan than colonial. These royal measures to bring to Brazil *as luzes* (the lights, to be understood as a metaphor for enlightened civilization) resonated throughout nineteenth- and twentieth-century Brazilian history. In 1943, nearly one hundred and fifty years after the arrival of the Portuguese Court, the paulista educator Fernando de Azevedo remarked in his monumental *A Cultura Brasileira,* "It is with the installation of the Portuguese court in Brazil that, broadly speaking, the history of our culture begins for, until this time, one cannot find anything but sporadic manifestations of exceptional figures, educated in Portugal and under foreign influence." [3]

The establishment of an artistic and scientific infrastructure worthy of a European court was a special preoccupation of advisors to the Crown. In 1816, one year after Brazil had been elevated to cokingdom status by João VI, the new king accepted a proposal to sponsor a group of French artists and master artisans—they themselves refugeed by Napoleon's fall from power—to come to Brazil to establish a royal academy dedicated to the visual arts, manual trades, and architecture.[4] Led by Joachin Lebreton, a French art critic who previously directed the Louvre Museum, the French Artistic Mission arrived in Rio on 26 March 1816. Five months later, D. João authorized the creation of the Escola Real de Ciências, Artes e Ofícios (Royal School of the Sciences, Arts, and Trades). The French neoclassical tradition took root in America. In 1817, Princess Leopoldina, bride to the royal heir Prince Pedro, arrived in Brazil with an Austro-Bavarian scientific mission that began to redefine scientific inquiry in Portuguese America, institutionalizing direct observation, collection, and in-country publication (a cultural practice nearly impossible before the arrival of the Portuguese

Court) on a range of subjects related to the natural sciences, cartography, and ethnography.

These royally sanctioned missions were fundamental to the institution-alization of a new form of cultural management, which placed the royal government at the center of cultural patronage. The missions were equally important for instituting a hierarchy of cultural clientelism, which privi-leged a small group of non-Brazilians who had won the Crown's favor. An outsider such as Jean-Baptiste Debret, history painter to the French Artistic Mission of 1816, could exercise such an influential role in cultural imagery surrounding the royal family because the king favored Frenchmen over native Brazilians. The Acclamation of D. João VI, celebrated on 6 Febru-ary 1818, and other grand pageants organized by Debret and his colleagues earned the Frenchmen access to the royal protections needed to outlast local opposition to the imposition of neoclassicism. The French had no natural cultural authority in Portuguese America. Rather, their authority was won in a politicized environment built around networks of patronage that radiated outward from the king.

Protected by the Crown, foreigners still faced incessant partisan politics at Court. Soon after the Bourbons were restored to the French throne, the French ambassador to the Portuguese Court petitioned to have Lebreton apprehended for his past allegiances with Napoleon Bonaparte (who, the ambassador pointed out, had originally forced the Braganças to flee to Bra-zil). Lebreton successfully avoided arrest, only to discover that ethnic ten-sions between Portuguese, Brazilian, and Continental artists undermined the success of the mission's aim to disseminate luzes. Following Lebreton's death in 1819, anti-French interests at Court slowed the remaining French-men's attempts to institutionalize the instruction of a neoclassical tradi-tion more secular and rational than the cultural norms characteristic of Luso-Brazilian aesthetics. Brazilian artists and master artisans versed in the conventions of Luso-Brazilian arts and architecture, which were making an independent, though gradual, transition from the baroque to the neo-classical, resisted efforts to make Court-appointed disciples of French neo-classicism the official style-brokers for an independent Brazilian Empire proclaimed by Dom Pedro I, son of João VI, on 7 September 1822. The Por-tuguese artists at Court were equally hostile to the Frenchmen. Opposition to the French mission delayed by a decade the formal opening of the Im-perial Academy of Fine Arts, which the mission members had been asked to establish in 1816.[5] Given these less-than-ideal working conditions, several

4 Jean-Baptiste Debret, *Acclamation of D. João VI*. 1818, watercolor on paper, 23 × 30.5 cms. As history painter to the French Artistic Mission, Debret was both organizer and memorialist for major events in the life of the Braganças, including the 1818 Acclamation of D. João VI. Courtesy of Museus Castro Maya.

members of the mission had either died or returned to Europe well before the Imperial Academy was fully operational.

Ethnic conflict within state-sponsored cultural institutions diminished during the final years of the First Reign (1822–1831), when Dom Pedro I redoubled his personal protection over the beleaguered Frenchmen, and the Regency (1831–1840), when the remaining members of the French mission began to cultivate a self-sustaining client network among immigrant and native artists and artisans. The expanded opportunities for royal patronage that accompanied the 1840 Acclamation of Dom Pedro II, son of D. Pedro I, further diffused conflict. Well before he reached twenty years of age, the young emperor cultivated the image of the enlightened monarch and cultured gentleman. Pedro actively patronized the most important cultural institutions of the Second Reign (1840–1889), paying special attention to the Instituto Histórico e Geográfico Brasileiro (IHGB, f. 1838). Beginning in 1845, the emperor set aside a small portion of funds allocated to the imperial household to support his favorite artists, writers, and composers. The most coveted of the emperor's favors was a travel grant, the Prêmio de Viagem, a travel grant given to artists whose works received top honors at the art salons, as well as other figures who attracted the emperor's broad cultural and scientific interests. Official cultural policy under the empire was largely a win-win arrangement in which the practitioners of high culture could win state support in exchange for honoring the Crown with highly nationalistic works of romantic art and literature, while the monarch doled out sinecures as proof of his enlightened stewardship of the national cultural arena.[6]

The symbolic capital traded in imperial patronage far outweighed the actual monetary outlays, because the emperor's direct support for his "pensioners" represented a small fraction of the Imperial Household's annual budget.[7] The imperial state never equaled the protoindustrial cultural complex built by European states in the nineteenth century. Brazil's Imperial Academy of Fine Arts, for example, was a poor cousin to the French École des Beaux-Arts. In truth, the cultural establishment in nineteenth-century Brazil was dependent upon European academies, which provided training to promising Brazilian artists. The economy of cultural patronage was such that the recipients of royal patronage were clients of the Brazilian state, which itself was a client of European institutions. Cultural patronage remained, nonetheless, a central component of state building during the Brazilian Empire, affording the emperor the opportunity to cultivate the image of an enlightened monarch and providing the state privileged access to talented figures in the arts and letters who were willing to glorify the monarchy and aristocracy in exchange for official support.[8] Figures such as historical painter Vitor Meireles (de Lima) and sculptor Francisco Chaves Pinheiro (1822–1887) led a cohort of state-sponsored artists who created the monuments to nationhood upon which the imperial state imagined a nation called Brazil. Statuary depicting a noble emperor and gargantuan historical paintings idealizing the great battles of the Paraguayan War (1865–1870) were the indispensable props of statecraft in a political culture in which the vast majority of the population faced enormous obstacles to claiming the rights of citizenship.

Ironically, Pedro II would discover that royal patronage to the arts was a double-edged sword. Those cultural figures not fortunate enough to win royal support were forced to build their cultural personae outside the empire's official institutions. As these figures gained larger audiences among the small, but expanding, urban literate classes, they questioned the necessity of state patronage as a gateway to cultural acclaim. When the influential art critic Luís Gonzaga Duque (1863–1911) assumed a critical stance toward the academic art supported by the imperial state, other intellectuals could take heart in calls to break free from the cultural establishment. Politicians could be equally critical of imperial patronage. Critics of the monarchy questioned the emperor's cultural indulgences at those key moments when the Brazilian nation, socially circumscribed as it was, confronted the daunting challenge of maintaining social order and economic progress against an uncertain future to be shaped by the abolition of slavery, the rise of republicanism, and a possible successional crisis. Caricaturists of the 1870s and 1880s frequently poked fun at Dom Pedro, suggesting that the emperor preferred painting and cultural tourism to the pressing affairs of state.[9]

When the bloodless coup of 15 November 1889 sent the Braganças into exile and replaced the monarchy with a republic, the prospects for a continuation of the type of cultural patronage associated with Pedro II diminished rapidly. The art world split into the so-called moderns, advocates of incremental reforms in official art instruction, and the "positivists," who called for the outright abolition of the Imperial Academy.[10] Within a year of the Proclamation of the Republic, Benjamin Constant, the intellectual mentor of Brazilian republicanism and first minister of the interior, forced Vitor Meireles and other clients of the imperial state into retirement. For a time, it appeared that the new republican government might completely do away with the Imperial Academy, renamed the National School of Fine Arts, or any of the other institutions of cultural management so closely associated with the imperial state.

The decentralized political system codified in the Constitution of 1891 and refined in the federalist politics known as the *política dos governadores* further limited the republican government's need for national cultural institutions. The federal legislature continued to provide annual subsidies to the IHGB and the new Brazilian Academy of Letters (ABL, f. 1897), but neither institution could count on the federal government as imperial institutions had. Federal ministries continued to sponsor expositions, civic ceremonies, and art salons, but the political utility of such events was unclear. The republican elite were undoubtedly obsessed with civilizing Brazil, just as their imperial predecessors had been. The urban and social transforma-

5 Francisco Chaves Pinheiro, *Statue of Dom Pedro II.* 1870, plaster, 225 cm. During the Second Reign, bronze castings of Chaves Pinheiro's imposing statue of Emperor D. Pedro II as monarch-general popularized a monumental, noble, and virile image of the Brazilian Empire. Courtesy of Museu Histórico Nacional/Banco Safra.

6 Vitor Meireles, *Batalha Naval do Riachuelo*. 1882–1883, oil on canvas, 400 × 800 cm. Monumental in size and theme, *Batalha Naval do Riachuelo* represented the apogee of state-commissioned history painting in the years following Brazil's victory in the Paraguayan War (1865–1870). One of the most prominent academic painters of his time, Meireles traveled to the site of the conflict to help infuse the painting with historical accuracy. At the same time, academic convention and the highly racist politics of memory operative in the empire afforded Meireles the freedom to distort key historical aspects of the battle, diminishing the presence of a large number of Afro-Brazilians in the Brazilian naval forces. Courtesy of Museu Histórico Nacional/Banco Safra.

tions brought to downtown Rio de Janeiro during the first decade of the twentieth century were the ultimate symbol of elite aspirations to improve Brazilian culture.[11] Nevertheless, in civilizing the Brazilian republic in the image of turn-of-the-century Paris, the political and cultural elite seemed uninterested in making the state into the nation's premier cultural patron.

The moderate levels of state investment in cultural patronage encouraged the cultural field at the turn of the twentieth century to distance itself from the central state. In 1897, the most celebrated cultural figure of the early republic, author (Joaquim Maria) Machado de Assis (1839–1908), went so far as to call upon the nation's intelligentsia to seek refuge in an ivory tower, far removed from the self-compromising messiness of politics.[12] Although Machado had been a civil servant during the empire and many of his colleagues at the Brazilian Academy of Letters were politically active, the call for self-isolationism encouraged the cultural elite to turn away from state employment in the construction of a national culture.

Vanguard movements emerging outside the academy provided additional opportunities for aesthetic and political autonomy. With print capitalism and transatlantic transportation bringing the European vanguard to Brazil — Marinetti's *Futurist Manifesto* (1909) appeared in Salvador da Bahia shortly after it was first published in Paris — Brazil's cultural elite were aware that European cultural figures toyed with the idea of a complete overthrow of a cultural establishment built by the bourgeois state. Although Marinetti would have limited influence in Brazil, the message and media of the vanguard manifesto would later become a vehicle to express frustration with official culture of all stripes.

As a rule, the republican political and cultural establishment managed to limit the challenge posed by independent-minded academics as well as iconoclasts. In the first instance, the state remained one of the largest and most reliable sources of employment. Most intellectuals found it hard to sacrifice economic livelihood for aesthetic independence.[13] Thus, state patronage rendered Machado's republic of letters more ideal than reality. In the latter instance, the academy itself helped to contain the avant-garde. When vanguard movements threatened to penetrate the thick walls erected by the cultural establishment, the *acadêmicos* generally managed to domesticate the iconoclastic original. As art critic Carlos Zillio has suggested, a peculiar sociology of Brazilian art in the late nineteenth and early twentieth centuries compelled Brazilian artists to tame anticonventional movements.[14]

Take the case of impressionist painting: The enfant terrible of French academic painting in the 1870s and 1880s, impressionism came to Brazilian art circles only after 1910. The winners of the Prêmio de Viagem who studied in France at the turn of the century would have been quite familiar with the impressionist style and its dramatic history, but none bothered to bring impressionism back to Brazil until impressionism had ceased to lead the French avant-garde.[15] When impressionism finally managed to cross the Atlantic, the movement had lost much of its stylistic specificity, connoting anything from Manet's preimpressionism to Seurat's pointillism. By the time impressionism became popular in Brazil, it was taken up by the ultraestablishment National School of Fine Arts, not some Brazilian version of the Salon des Refusés. The Brazilian academy produced some fine artists who painted in the impressionist style, led by Georgina and Lucílio de Albuquerque. However, the social and political context of impressionism had been tamed in the Atlantic passage.

Those cultural figures who chose to make a radical break from convention, as well as those who assumed a direct engagement with politics, sailed rough waters. Nicolau Sevcenko has demonstrated that writers who actively participated in the political debates of the First Republic risked political and aesthetic ostracism. Sevcenko singles out Euclides da Cunha (1866–1909), author of the classic *Os Sertões* (1902), and (Afonso Henriques de) Lima Barreto (1881–1922), the mulatto author of numerous literary works of social satire, as figures marginalized from the cultural and political establishments precisely because of their politicized writing, as well as their ignoble social backgrounds.[16]

Those artists who embraced the avant-garde faced equally precarious circumstances. Anita Malfatti, a first-generation Brazilian from São Paulo who circulated among the German and U.S. avant-garde in the 1910s, painfully discovered that entrenched cultural figures could be highly critical of the practitioners of new styles. Late in 1917, soon after returning to São Paulo from an extended stay in New York, Malfatti agreed to exhibit the works she had completed abroad. Malfatti's electric color, distorted perspectives, and bold brushstrokes influenced by German Expressionism, fauvism, and open-air painting were initially well received by a small number of critics and collectors who viewed the show. The critical and commercial success soured, though, when José Bento Monteiro Lobato, one of the most well-known authors of the period, wrote a harsh review in the afternoon edition of *O Estado de São Paulo,* arguing that Malfatti's many talents were overwhelmed by stylistic choices suggestive of mental disturbance.[17] Although a young and energetic group of intellectuals, including Mário de Andrade and Oswald de Andrade, immediately came to Malfatti's defense, the damage had been done. Instead of joining the emergent modernist movement as a foot soldier, Malfatti became its protomartyr. Monteiro Lobato's infamous query "Paranoia or Mystification?" stuck. Malfatti's shockingly beautiful paintings, including *O Homem Amarelo* (1916), were successfully integrated into a modernist canon, but the artist personally suffered, never fully regaining the self-confidence seen in works exhibited in 1917. The Malfatti episode was a cautionary tale for painters who wished to challenge convention. It was also a demonstration that outsiders without patrons would find it difficult to become insiders.

1922 and Beyond

The year 1922, the one-hundredth anniversary of Brazilian independence, was a watershed in a changing landscape of culture and politics. Notably, within the arts and letters, the foundation of Machado's ivory tower began to erode as the changing social profile of the intellectual class and the rise of new cultural practices, institutions, and ideas undermined the viability of an intellectual class isolated from society. With urbanization, foreign immigration, and industrialization transforming urban areas, radically so in the case of São Paulo, the medieval image of the scholar-in-the-turret became antiquated. As new forms of political expression, including syndicalism, suffrage movements, and reformist party politics, began to appeal to the working and middle classes, which did not have a place in the political machine run by the republican parties, and new forms of cultural expression, including popular literature, cinema, sports, recorded music, and *automobilismo,* proliferated, a younger generation of intellectuals found it hard to resist the impulse to take part in the changing cultural and political landscape. While the cultural establishment in Rio and the state capitals continued to cultivate a measured distance from politics, more independent-minded intellectuals of various ideological persuasions explored the political nature of cultural expression.

The regional republican parties controlling the national state and economy expressed little concern for the disquiet in the cultural arena. They, instead, turned toward celebrating the political culture of bourgeois republicanism. The International Exposition of the Centennial of Brazilian Independence, inaugurated in Rio on 7 September 1922, trumpeted the success of the civilizational achievements of the republic. President Epitácio Pessoa opened the exposition with a demonstration of wireless radio, a medium that could extend modernity across vast expanses at the speed of sound. The exposition pavilions, built on land once occupied by the venerable Castelo Hill, showcased the march of progress in the areas of public administration, ranching and farming, industry, and commerce. The presence of numerous foreign missions reassured Brazil's oligarchs that the Brazilian republic had joined the international concert of nations. The corporate pavilions of General Electric and Brahma brewers demonstrated the conquests of industry in a nation principally known for its agricultural ex-

7 Centennial Exposition, Rio de Janeiro, 1922. A spectacle of light and wonder, the Centennial Exposition imagined a century of progress and civilization, set within the architectural idiom of neocolonialism. Courtesy of LC-AHC.

ports. The exposition left its 3.6 million visitors with a vision of a modern, civilized society coming of age.

The artwork assembled for the centennial exposition fell in line with this celebration of progress. That year's salon exhibited several works commissioned by the federal government, which fondly and proudly looked back upon moments leading up to independence. The most important of these nostalgic-memorial paintings was Georgina de Albuquerque's *Primeira Sessão do Conselho do Estado* (*First Session of the Council of State*), a large canvas depicting the moment in early September 1822 in which Princess Leopoldina, wife to Prince Pedro, and José Bonifácio de Andrada, the "Patriarch of Brazilian Independence," discuss how best to advise the prince regent on the question of independence from Portugal (see Plate 1). As a historical text, the painting documented the quiet, interior moments leading up to Pedro's Cry of Independence. In stark contrast to Pedro Américo's defiant *Grito de Ipiranga* (1886), Albuquerque's independence was a highly domesticated act, won on its reasoned merits rather than inflamed passions. The memory of independence turned on evolution, not rupture.

8 Large Industries Pavilion, Centennial Exposition. Arquimedes Memória's design for the Large Industries pavilion took an eighteenth-century munitions depot and added decorative adornments evocative of Luso-Brazilian colonial architecture. Once the Centennial Exposition ended, the neocolonial edifice became the permanent home of the National Historical Museum. *Ilustração Brasileira* (7 September 1922 issue).

As a piece of art, *Primeira Sessão do Conselho do Estado* reinforced the idea of gradual transitions toward greater civilization. Typical of much of her work, Albuquerque used the commission to harmonize the conventions of academic portraiture, beautifully captured in the faces and body-positioning of Leopoldina and José Bonifácio, with neoimpressionism, present in the plays of light, color, and brushstroke seen in the background. The history of these two artistic traditions would not suggest such a harmonious pairing. Albuquerque, nevertheless, chose to demonstrate how the arts in Brazil could serve as a model for incremental, domesticated transitions toward political and cultural maturity.

The architectural language of Brazilian civilization endorsed by the republican oligarchy reinforced the image of a gradualist, domesticated approach to national development. In a rebuke of previous expositions where the Brazilian pavilions consciously mimicked French or British tastes, the federal pavilions built in 1922 sported *o estylo neo-colonial*. Stone archways, whitewashed stucco, blue-and-white glazed tiles, red-tiled roofs, and other adornments typical of colonial architecture graced most federal pavilions, transforming the exposition grounds into an oversized, illuminated version of the central squares built by the Portuguese in Rio and Salvador da Bahia. The disfavor once heaped upon architectural styles evocative of the colonial past appeared to have ended. Now the state embraced an architectural language that drew deeply upon the Luso-Brazilian colonial past. In designing the industrial pavilion, the successful Brazilian architect Arquimedes Memória dressed up an eighteenth-century munitions depot with neocolonial adornments to prove that a modern industrial society could maintain a structural and aesthetic relationship with its forebears. The official version of Brazilian culture put on in Rio declared to the world that the Brazilian nation no longer needed to ape belle époque Paris to earn its place in the world system. Modernity conferred the privilege of reconnecting the national culture to the baroque churches, colonial fortifications, and baronial sugar mansions built during the foundational moment of Brazilian civilization.

Not all Brazilians were so eager to celebrate the achievements of the civilized republic, no matter how nationalistic or reverent of national traditions it appeared to be. Novelist Lima Barreto offered a withering critique of the centennial commemorations, which he claimed had completely failed to stir up a popular sense of patriotism or appreciation for the past.[18] In the meantime, the centennial year's presidential election was marred by bitter divisions between the republican oligarchies. The Brazilian Communist Party, founded earlier in the year, openly questioned the civilization of the bourgeois state. In Rio, midlevel army officers, dismayed by the way in which the promise of liberal republicanism had been corrupted by class interests and mimesis, launched the first of a series of rebellions against their superiors and the larger system of republican governance. Easily repressed in 1922, the *tenentes* (literally, lieutenants, though some rebels held other ranks) would later return to take up arms against a political and economic system that they warned provided neither the order nor the progress promised by earlier generations of republicans.[19] For many, the spectacle of progress on display at the centennial exposition was just a mirage.

The most significant cultural response to the bourgeois vision of nationhood came from São Paulo, the once-sleepy mule station that had exploded into an urban-commercial-industrial metropolis. In February 1922, Marinette and Paulo Prado, heirs to one of the region's great coffee fortunes, provided financial and political support for a week-long exhibition of new art that the event's idealizer, *carioca* artist Emiliano Di Cavalcanti, hoped could bring together artistic figures and intellectuals working outside of the narrow confines of the academy. With a certain irony, the link between Di Cavalcanti and the Prados was made through José Pereira da Graça Aranha, a founding member of the Brazilian Academy of Letters who had recently turned against the academic tradition that he had helped institutionalize.[20]

Held in the lobby of São Paulo's Municipal Theater, the participants in "Modern Art Week" launched a frontal assault upon the type of faux modernity cultivated by the regional oligarchies who controlled the national purse strings and the *acadêmicos* who controlled the cultural establishment in Rio. The week-long series of art exhibitions, musical performances, literary readings, and cultural polemics lashed out at the bourgeois establishment, mocking the formal conventions that dominated literature, architecture, and the visual arts. The week's three "festivals" offered bold, sometimes shocking, visions of the plasticity of language and paint, the plurality of Brazil's musical traditions, the speed of technological change, and the new living and working spaces that would come to define modern life in the second century of independence.

Graça Aranha, one of the best-selling authors of the First Republic who had grown disaffected with the linguistic formalism defended at the Brazilian Academy of Letters, set the iconoclastic mood for the week in his inaugural speech, which rejected academic tradition in favor of an artistic expression that allowed the artist the freedom "to uncover nature by following one's own liberated sentiment . . . free to create and manifest his dream, those intimate fantasies untethered by rules. May the canon and the law be replaced by absolute liberty." Graça Aranha's speech reveled in the prospect that the more conventional members of the audience, whom he labeled *retardatários,* would reject the artwork hanging in the Teatro Municipal. The author spoke as if the quicker the conservatives reacted, the better the new art would seem. Heaping praise upon the "aesthetic remodeling" seen in the works of composer Heitor Villa-Lobos, sculptor Vítor Brecheret, and painter Anita Malfatti, the *acadêmico*-turned-*modernista* called upon the younger artists in attendance to see the event as "not some mere renaissance of an art which does not exist [but] the birth of art in Brazil." [21]

Subsequent speeches delivered by the futurist poet Menotti del Picchia (1892–1988) and poet-ethnographer Mário de Andrade proposed even more violent breaks with the formalism of the past.[22] Andrade was only twenty-eight years old in 1922 and had yet to publish his first major work of modernist poetry *Cidade Desvairada* (Engl. *Hallucinated City*). Nevertheless, the future "pope" of Brazilian modernism took poetic formalism head-on, calling upon his audience to reject the burdensome rules and absurd decorativism of poetry produced by *passadistas* in favor of "Free verse/Free rhyme/Victory of the dictionary" in technique and "the Substitution of the Intellectual Order for the Subconscious Order/Speed and Synthesis/Poliphonism" in aesthetics.[23]

Although Graça Aranha's place as the pied piper of Brazilian modernism would be challenged subsequently by participants and critics of the modernist movement, he correctly predicted that the paulista cultural establishment would be scandalized by the unconventional art on display in the lobby of the conventional Municipal Theater. The painter Anita Malfatti, herself a victim of a bruising fight over the early stages of Brazilian modernism, reported that Mário de Andrade had to outwit hecklers circulating within the theater, lest his manifesto toward a new aesthetic of freedom, expression, and poetic beauty be drowned out by boos.[24] Members of the audience unsympathetic to the modernist insurgents still managed to mock Malfatti's garish color palette, the impressionistic music of Heitor Villa-Lobos, and Brecheret's smooth, elongated sculptures. Amidst all the sound and fury, São Paulo's Modern Art Week was a preview of a looming battle for brasilidade.

The cultural establishment in Rio was initially unimpressed by the scandals in São Paulo. Modernity had its place in Rio, but the principals and propositions most closely associated with modernism were mainly paulista.[25] Still, 1922 signified a paradigm shift: cultural figures throughout Brazil had a green light to explore alternatives to the cultural heritage of colonialism and mimesis that continued to shape cultural development one century after independence. In their novels, journals, poetry, painting, and sculpture, the post-1922 modernists sought to revive and *Brazilianize* Brazilian culture through dynamic and unscripted combinations of region and nation, tradition and modernity, Europe and the New World, order with chaos. In 1928, Oswald de Andrade issued the most radical of the modernist manifestos, the *Manifesto Antropófago* (*Cannibalist Manifesto*), which used the metaphor of the Amerindian cannibal to visualize the process of cultural empowerment through the consumption of the outsider. According to Richard Morse, this aesthetic of "cannibalism recognized both the nutritive property of European culture and a transformative process of appropriation."[26]

The experimental, radical aesthetics that now define the pioneering phase of Brazilian modernism produced mixed results. Oswald de Andrade's cannibalistic metaphors could not appeal to all interested in change. What became collectively known as the "modernist movement" was really several movements, characterized by a plethora of manifestos, speeches, meetings, and short-lived journals, all of which approached modernity from distinct vantage points. The "regionalist" subcurrent of the tradition-bound, underdeveloped Northeast had relatively little to share with the modernists in São Paulo who reveled in a vertigo of speeding cars, soaring skyscrapers, and iconoclasm. The *modernistas mineiros,* drawn to the baroque heritage of the state of Minas Gerais, were far less obsessed with the futurist city. They, instead, looked for the cultural essence of a regional identity grounded in the Luso-baroque. The *verde-amarelistas,* so named for their appropriation of the colors of the Brazilian flag, were the most explicitly nationalistic, adopting indigenous symbols as a shield against the contaminating influences of foreign aesthetics and ideologies. However, their political conservatism distanced them from Oswald de Andrade and the other left-leaning paulistas.

Modernismo was, in short, just as heterogeneous as the culture that it was trying to renew. Perhaps the only commonality uniting all subcurrents of the modernist movement was the participants' initial distance from state patronage. The Modern Art Week was funded through the private initiative of wealthy patrons, and private monies funded other regional subcurrents of modernism, if they were funded at all. Antistatism was an undercurrent in modernist production precisely because the cultural institutions protected by the state, such as the National School of Fine Arts, were hostile to modernism. The relationship between modernism and the state would change significantly under Vargas, when figures such as Mário de Andrade accepted state commissions and modernism assumed an *institutionalized* form within the state apparatus.[27] Prior to the Revolution of 1930, the renewal envisioned by the modernists was of little use for the republican state.

As the modernists tried to express a new vision of Brazil that embraced the new, traditionalists made their own claims to Brazilianness, arguing that modernization threatened to wipe away what remained of a truly Brazilian cultural heritage. The loss of traditional architecture, compounded by the proliferation of "eclectic" styles imported from abroad, was especially troubling to figures such as José Mariano, a physician-turned-maecenas who emerged as one of the most vocal critics of the march of bourgeois progress, eclecticism, and modernism. Witness to the demolition of religious and civil edifices built during the colonial period, and the construction of transportation arteries, public parks, and residential and commercial zones signifying modernity, Mariano sponsored architectural and artistic surveys of the architectural legacy left by the Portuguese colonizer and mulatto artisan in hopes of stimulating interest in a nativist cultural heritage movement.[28] Mariano distributed his own funds to sponsor promising architectural projects designed in "traditional" styles inspired by the past. He even took the unusual step of calling upon the federal government to devote public funds toward the cataloguing and preservation of important monuments.[29]

Historical architecture was not the only *tradição* whose loss conservative intellectuals lamented. As early as 1912, Gustavo Barroso, a folklorist and journalist from Ceará who later become a leading figure in the protofascist movement known as Integralism, argued that a modernizing Brazil lacked a *Culto da Saudade* (Cult of Nostalgia) that venerated the past. Barroso was particularly preoccupied with the disappearance or sale of historical artifacts once used by military leaders and nineteenth-century nobles amidst the march of technological progress and urbanization. In 1922, after lobbying for a decade for a national museum that would protect military and other historical artifacts, Barroso convinced President Epitácio Pessoa to authorize the creation of Brazil's first National Historical Museum. The idea of a national historical museum had circulated among intellectuals and historians well before Pessoa's move, but the passage of the centennial of Brazilian independence brought together the political and civic forces necessary for the federal government to take a definitive step toward creating a permanent temple of national memory.[30] Amidst the fanfare of the Centennial Exposition, Barroso proudly opened two small galleries filled with a hodgepodge of objects, personal effects, coins, paintings, and armaments primarily associated with prominent figures of the empire.

Ricardo Severo, a Portuguese-born engineer who worked with a prominent architectural and construction firm in São Paulo, joined Mariano and Barroso in arguing that modernity threatened to erase the vestiges of a traditional society that Brazil desperately needed in order to know itself. Doubly preoccupied with the loss of the architectural legacy of colonial Brazil, which was under full assault in the urban core of São Paulo, as well as the proliferation of imported architectural styles within urban neighborhoods with high concentrations of immigrants, Severo saw *arte tradicional* as the quintessential signifier of national identity. Recognizing that it was impossible to protect traditional art in toto, Severo became one of the most important figures to incorporate echoes of traditional art into contemporary architecture. If Barroso argued that the preservation of historical objects was a precondition for a cult of nostalgia, Severo called upon his fellow architects to look to the colonial church and *sobrado* (elite residence) for inspiration for a new type of modern architecture that harmonized past and present. Severo's idealized world of whitewashed stucco and glazed tiles quickly proliferated in new residential constructions in São Paulo and Rio, making *neocolonialismo* one of the most important aesthetic movements of the 1920s and 1930s. The fact that the architects of neocolonial projects amalgamated disparate elements of Ibero-American colonial architecture, spiced with heavy doses of the California Mission style lifted from Hollywood films and imported magazines, to create a "Brazilian" architectural style and material culture that had never really existed had little negative impact on the commercial success of neocolonial aesthetics.[31]

It may seem counterintuitive that the modernists would join conservatives in seeking inspiration in the beauties of colonial architecture. The modernists were, after all, nicknamed *futuristas* (although most rejected comparisons to Marinetti after the Italian poet embraced fascism). In their search for an architectural language for cultural renewal, the modernists often looked not to Severo's neocolonial projects, but rather to the designs of Giorgi Warchavchik, the first architect to demonstrate to Brazilians that a house could be a "machine for living." The radical notion that the house should be modeled on a machine came from Le Corbusier, the Swiss-French apostle of modernist architecture whose *Plan Voisin* (1925) envisioned leveling several historic quarters of Paris to make room for rationalized urban spaces for living, working, commerce, and transportation. Le Corbusier's *Radiant City* (1933), a plan developed after the *Plan Voisin* proved unfeasible, represented the apogee of the early modernist idealism, where radical urban renewal would rid modern society of all traces of the past.[32] Given the thoroughly forward-looking genealogy of modernist architecture, it seems a paradox that Brazil's modernists might seek inspiration in colonial architecture. Nonetheless, the same group who sought cultural redemption in the machine also came to embrace Brazil's preindustrial, underdeveloped past.

The modernists rehearsed their incipient appreciation for colonial ar-

chitecture during Holy Week 1924, when the poet-novelist Oswald de Andrade, painter Tarsila do Amaral, and Mário de Andrade accompanied
the French symbolist poet Blaise Cendrars (1887–1961) on an excursion
by train to the old mining towns of Ouro Preto, São João del Rey, Tiradentes, Diamantina, and Congonhas do Campo. In São João, the modernists attended Easter Sunday celebrations in one of the town's magnificent baroque churches. In Ouro Preto, where nearly every vista contains at
least one church tower, Cendrars admired the glorious vestiges of Brazil's
Golden Age. In Congonhas, the group climbed the steps in front of the Santuário do Bom Jesus de Matosinhos and marveled at the impressive soapstone and wooden sculptures carved by the mulatto sculptor Aleijadinho.

This so-called *caravana modernista* (modernist caravan) became a foundational moment in the Brazilian avant-garde, where the young artists
found the grammar, if not the precise syntax, of Brazilian modernism.
The Pau-Brasil (Brazilwood) movement, initiated by Oswald de Andrade's
Manifesto Pau-Brasil (1924), was directly inspired by the trip to Minas and the
discovery of a colorful, exotic, almost primordial Brazil.[33] Certain poems
in *Pau-Brasil* (1925), a book of poetry written by Oswald and illustrated
by Tarsila, read as nostalgic elegies to a gilded past revived in short, stac-
cato prose.

The poem *Ocaso* (End, or Sunset), which fittingly closes out the book
of poetry inspired by the trip to Minas, captures the sense of loss and the
wonderment that the paulistas and their French guest experienced during
their caravana:

Ocaso	End
No anfiteatro das montanhas	In the amphitheater made of mountains
Os profetas do Aleijadinho	The prophets of Aleijadinho
Monumentalizam a paisagem	Turn the landscape into monuments
As cúpulas brancas dos Passos	The side chapels' white domes
E os cocares revirados das palmeiras	And the palms' upturned plumes
São degraus da arte do meu país	These are the steps of my nation's art
Onde ninguém mais subiu	No one has reached such heights since
Bíblia de pedra-sabão	Bible in soapstone
Banhada no ouro das Minas	Gilded in the gold of *Minas*[34]

Tarsila do Amaral would be equally kind to Brazil's Golden Age, finding
in Minas the visual motifs, including church towers and palm trees, that

9 Santuário de Bom Jesus de Matosinhos, Congonhas do Campo, *c.* 1942. This church and its surrounding soapstone sculptures were inspirational to the caravana modernista of 1924. Courtesy of LC-AHC.

appear prominently in the sketches and easel paintings produced during her Brazilwood phase (1924–1926).

The significance of the modernist caravan grew even after Tarsila and Oswald turned to a much more radical aesthetic of cannibalism. Tarsila and Oswald partially attributed their fascination with the idea of ingesting the adversary to a chance encounter in the town of Tiradentes, when the travelers met up with a manual laborer imprisoned for murder. The dramatic part of the prisoner's (apocryphal?) story—the part that resonated among the idealizers of the *Cannibalist Manifesto* (1928)—was that the laborer claimed to have eaten his rival's heart.[35] Cendrars, Andrade, and Tarsila would take this horrid, exhilarating image of devouring one's enemy to invent an aesthetic that allowed the modern Brazilian, following the lead of the native cannibals who terrorized the Portuguese friars and inspired Michel de Montaigne to write *On Cannibals* (1580), to consume his European rival, transforming the taboo of cannibalism into a sacred act of self-actualizing liberation.[36] The modernist caravan quietly set the stage for many felicitous, but contested, readings of Brazil's historical patrimony. In the years following 1924, the modernists celebrated the journey to Minas as an act of rediscovery. The stark contrast between industrializing São Paulo and historic Minas afforded the modernists the opportunity to look to a cultural past that had not yet been erased in the chaotic, frenetic urban life celebrated in Mário de Andrade's *Hallucinated City.*

Ironically, the modernists may have neglected to see how historic Minas could lay claim to modernity at the expense of, not in conjunction with, the past celebrated by the members of the modernist caravan of 1924. In São João del Rey, one of the few mining centers to survive the end of the gold cycle, locals tried to show their visitors the town's newer buildings. The modernists chose instead to focus their attention on the town's historical quarter.[37] The tensions between a modernist renewal that needed to maintain a "lost" past in order to understand modernity, and a local renewal that wanted modernity at the expense of the past, set the stage for later conflicts between preservationists and locals. In short time, the modernists would have to turn to the federal state to ensure that Minas remained ready to be "(re)discovered" by the rest of Brazil for the remainder of the twentieth century and beyond.

The modernists were not alone in living in modern cities and thinking nostalgically upon the past. The traditionalists Ricardo Severo, José Mariano, and Gustavo Barroso circulated among the same chaotic cities celebrated by Oswald, Tarsila, and Mário de Andrade. These traditionalists, all natives of regions located far from Andrade's hallucinated city, did not seek out evidence of a national past safely dislocated in space and time. To the contrary, the traditionalists were horrified by the interventions into historic neighborhoods they witnessed on a daily basis in larger cities. These traditionalists were especially fond of the baroque period, which was treated as the point at which European culture became Brazilian culture.[38] This admiration and nostalgia for the achievements of the eighteenth century germinated not from a conscious attempt to overlook the violent confrontation between the past and present/Europe and Brazil, nor from some bucolic idealism that tried to resurrect a preindustrial society immunized from the maladies of the modern city.[39] These traditionalists, instead, wanted to ensure that modernity constantly looked backward, to remind an urbanizing society that Brazil was a product of a noble experiment of Luso-Catholic colonialism. The battle for the past waged by these traditionalists against the modernists and against modernization would become a key point of cultural and political conflict once the Vargas regime took on the task of protecting national patrimony and making foundational myths out of the colonial past.

Cultural Management on the Eve of the Revolution of 1930

On the eve of the Revolution of 1930, modernism played an increasingly large role in an expanding literary, artistic, and consumer marketplace. Cultural figures throughout the country articulated regional variants of the visions of Brazilianness unleashed in São Paulo in 1922. In Rio and São Paulo, the modernist city celebrated by Mário de Andrade and criticized by Gustavo Barroso was a reality. Modern painting became increasingly common in art galleries and private collections. Literary journals and the commercial press brimmed with the modernist visual aesthetic. Product design, interior decor, and the decorative arts incorporated a modernist look that drew from art deco and Bauhaus. The 1920s came to a close with the construction of Warchavchik's Casa Modernista, a private residence built in the Pacembú neighborhood of São Paulo. More than 20,000 people came to see the Russian-born, Italian-trained architect's interpretation of the much-discussed notion that the home should be a machine and that landscape design should be Brazilian in content and form.[40]

The traditionalists kept pace with the modernists in trying to redefine the aesthetic and institutional foundation for cultural renewal. The neo-colonial style advocated by Ricardo Severo and José Mariano became a common feature of private residences and major public buildings, especially in the upscale neighborhoods of São Paulo. Rio's Escola Normal, the premier educational institution for the capital's teacher corps, was built in the style of an oversized Jesuit college, sealing an ideological and architectural relationship between the education of future generations and the veneration of past ones. In 1930, Mariano addressed the Fourth Pan-American Congress of Architects, assembled in Rio, urging the attendees to follow Rio's lead and adopt the neocolonial style for all public schools throughout the Americas. For Mariano, neocolonial architecture gave North and South Americans the aesthetic language to dream of a noble colonial past and the armaments to protect the youths of the Americas from the incursions of eclecticism, futurism, and crass modernism. The congress closed

10 Ministry of Education and Health Building, Rio de Janeiro, 1940–1945. The world's first skyscraper to integrate fully the principles of the "new architecture" established by the Swiss-French modernist Le Corbusier, the Ministry of Education and Health headquarters, designed by a team of Brazilian architects including Lucio Costa and Oscar Niemeyer, was a symbol and a lightning-rod of cultural renewal during the first Vargas regime. Courtesy of CPDOC-GC.

with a lavish party at Mariano's private residence, the Solar do Monjope, where the conference attendees saw firsthand one of the most spectacular neocolonial residences ever built in Brazil.

The state's official cultural institutions played a circumscribed role in the national cultural life in the waning years of the Old Republic. Established institutions, including the Brazilian Academy of Letters, the IHGB, and the National School of Fine Arts continued to consecrate figures who mastered the formal conventions of the academy. They provided the conservative standard by which others could judge the success of renewal. More recent

11 Vargas Joins the Brazilian Academy of Letters, 29 December 1943. Vargas's admission into the venerable Brazilian Academy of Letters symbolized the regime's interest in cultural management. Ironically, Vargas took only a passing interest in the day-to-day politics of cultural management. Courtesy of AN-Fundo Agência Nacional.

arrivals to the institutional landscape, including the Museu Histórico and the Casa Ruy Barbosa, straddled the divide between research centers and temples to fallen heroes. The central state still could not count on one single agency to coordinate cultural policy, and there were many republicans who continued to make the case that the state should not be in the business of managing culture. Official culture was not precisely a private affair, but it was not an affair of state as it had been during the empire, or as it would become after 1930.

The cultural landscape outlined above reveals that the Revolution of 1930 did not invent the question of cultural renewal and modernity. Rather, the newly empowered Vargas regime inherited a rhetorical and ideological climate of renovação in which the central state could assume a starring role. Cultural management quickly emerged as a federal prerogative in the wake of the Revolution of 1930. By 1939, the Vargas regime had created an interconnected network of institutions charged with managing culture. The new headquarters for the Ministry of Education were under construction in Rio, symbolizing the regime's determination to create a permanent, monumental presence in the politics of culture.

When Vargas became a member of the Brazilian Academy of Letters in 1943, he observed that the nation's intelligentsia had abandoned Machado's ivory tower to join the politicians and liberal professionals in a national cultural renewal, stating "only in the third decade of this century have we reached that necessary symbiosis between men of thought and men of action." Vargas cautioned that academies and academics need not lead the vanguard in art and culture, nor remain completely isolated in the rearguard. Instead, he envisioned a cultural landscape in which the establishment would "actively manage trends, ideas, and values, to elevate the intellectual life of the country to a higher plane, giving it a positive direction, force, and creative balance." [41] In joining the nation's most important literary academy, Vargas was well aware that the federal government could provide the institutional positions for intellectuals, artists, and civil servants to help manage the nation's cultural development. To borrow a term used by Sérgio Miceli, Vargas knew that cultural management could be the state's *negócio oficial* (official business), transacted through a partnership of state institutions, intellectuals, public policy, and the icons of cultural nationalism.[42] Vargas knew this because the regime instituted in November 1930 had made cultural management its official business.

3

Cultural Management, 1930–1945

The Vargas regime's reliance upon an expanding network of federal agencies charged with cultural management reflected a keen awareness among politicians, educators, artists, intellectuals, and everyday citizens that managing culture could be a powerful weapon in managing Brazilianness. Under the stewardship of a small number of political and cultural elites, many hailing from the state of Minas Gerais, the Vargas regime built a network of federal institutions of cultural management that acted as sentinels in the larger struggle to control brasilidade. These institutions were exemplars of the sometimes paternalist, typically authoritarian, and invariably nationalist process of state and nation building that characterizes modern Brazilian political history.[1]

It is no coincidence that presidents Fernando Collor de Melo (1990–1992) and Fernando Henrique Cardoso (1995–) proposed drastic reforms to the federal government's institutional relationship to culture in hope of reversing the patterns of state building established under Vargas. In their zeal to reform, or even eliminate, the central state's investment in cultural management, Presidents Collor and Cardoso discovered that it would be difficult, if not impossible, to wholly divorce the state from cultural policy making. On the one hand, an institutional relationship to the cultural field has proven itself to be indispensable to making claims to representing the nation's interests. No matter how "modern" the president, the national state needs its own institutions of cultural management in order to invoke the national. On the other hand, the institutions of cultural management built during the Vargas era proved resilient in the face of reform because they could draw upon a long history of conflict with adversaries within the state and in civil society. During the Vargas era, federal institutions of cultural management proved unable to completely reconcile their internal differences over what agencies should manage culture and how. They failed to establish hegemonic controls over civil society's understanding of good and appropriate national culture, in large part because civil society expressed displeasure or disinterest in federal cultural programming. Nevertheless, the network of federal cultural policy-making institutions founded during the first Vargas regime built itself into the bedrock of Brazilian culture and state power. Even when these institutions acted as their own worst enemies, they helped the Vargas regime and all subsequent federal administrations lay claim to managing brasilidade.

Cultural Reform c. 1930

Vargas's 1930 presidential platform included provisions for the creation of several new federal agencies to coordinate educational, health, and labor policy at the national level. Within ten days of becoming chief of the Provisional Government, Vargas authorized the creation of the Ministry of Education and Public Health (MESP) and the Ministry of Labor, Industry, and Commerce. Together, these two ministries were at the vanguard of the regime's reformist campaign to undo a federalist system that had left education, health care, labor relations, industrial policy, and cultural policy making to regional oligarchies and private interests. Vargas invited Francisco Campos, the secretary of the interior for the state of Minas Gerais and confidant of mineiro kingpin Olegário Maciel, to direct the new education ministry. Like most figures who joined Vargas's cabinet in 1930, Campos offered Vargas key political connections to the regional power brokers who had helped guarantee Vargas's rise to power. Campos, like Vargas, exhibited a deep commitment to strengthening the central state at the expense of regional autonomy. Sharply critical of the liberal machine politics that controlled his home state before the Revolution of 1930, Campos made education and health reform a wedge issue to distinguish public administration of the revolutionary regime from the political culture of the First Republic.[2]

At his swearing-in ceremony, Campos declared the recent revolution to be an unprecedented opportunity to change fundamentally Brazilian society through the elevation of national health and educational standards (*sanear e educar o Brasil*).[3] Rejecting four decades of social engineering informed by pessimistic theories of racial and climatological degeneracy, Campos's brief words implied that state policy could reverse an endemic pattern of malnutrition, poor health, and cultural incoherence through inclusive public policy.[4] In practice, educational and health reforms constantly struggled between the optimistic ideals of education reformers and hygienists and the more exclusionary, pessimistic policies advocated by racial theorists, criminologists, and medical authorities. Perfecting the Brazilian race would be a project riddled with conflict.[5] This did not inhibit the minister from focusing his energies on developing an institutional apparatus capable of managing educational and health policy at a national level.

In January 1931, the ministry acquired its definitive administrative structure, which divided into four departments (Instruction, Public Health, Public Assistance, and Experimental Medicine), two inspection agencies (Professional and Technical Instruction, Water and Sewage), two museums (Museu Nacional and Museu Histórico Nacional), and the National Observatory, the National Library, and the Casa Ruy Barbosa.[6] When Campos stepped down from his ministerial post in 1932, a package of administrative reforms, collectively known as the Reforma Campos, had established the Ministry of Education as the gatekeeper for a cluster of educational, health, scientific, and cultural institutions that embraced the responsibility for managing the national mind and body.[7]

Reforms in education and culture could be quite contentious, especially when ideological and personnel changes did not sit well with groups with vested interests in maintaining the status quo, irrespective of the Revolution of 1930. With new directors being appointed to the government's most important posts in the fine arts, architecture, music, libraries, and historical heritage, the entrenched cultural establishment had just as much to lose as the republican oligarchs overthrown in 1930. The most explosive opposition to reform came at the venerable National School of Fine Arts (ENBA), a direct heir to the original cultural institutions founded by D. João VI. Working on the recommendation of Rodrigo Melo Franco de Andrade, a mineiro journalist, lawyer, and cultural critic whom Campos brought to Rio to serve as chief of staff, Campos appointed Lucio Costa, a promising young architect born in France to Brazilian parents, to devise a structural and pedagogical reform of the nation's visual and architectural sensibilities. This was a tall order, as the ENBA was a redoubt of Brazil's most conservative artists who ferociously protected the academic tradition established in the nineteenth century. Costa's appointment ignited a bitter conflict at the school, making the federal culture apparatus a battleground in an emerging pattern of culture warfare that would mark cultural and politics during the first Vargas regime.

12 National School of Fine Arts, Rio de Janeiro. The National School of Fine Arts, pictured here in the early 1940s when much of the building had been taken over by the National Museum of Fine Arts, was a cultural bellwether of sorts. During the belle époque, the school was a bastion of elite francophile culture. In 1930, the school became a site for an intense struggle over the future of art instruction. In the 1940s, the school became a fortress for academic artists who resisted the rise of modernism. Courtesy of LC-AHC.

Young and energetic, Costa was undoubtedly qualified to lead Brazil's most traditional art academy into the postrevolutionary period. An ENBA graduate, Costa was well versed in the conventions of academic art and architecture that had been taught at the academy since the Second Reign; he had experience with newer styles in Brazilian art and architecture, including neocolonialism. Costa was equally familiar with the avant-garde, acting as the self-appointed propagandist for the "new architecture" associated with International Congress of Modern Architecture. Costa's artistic knowledge encompassed past, present, and future.

Instead of universal praise, Costa's appointment incited hostile dissent. Neocolonialist José Mariano openly questioned how a devotee of Le Corbusier could direct an institution as venerable as the National School of Fine Arts. Why, Mariano asked, did Costa reject neocolonialism, an aesthetic style the young architect had once studied under Mariano's patronage, when neocolonialism offered the happiest of compromises between tradition and modernity. According to Mariano, Brazil need not overthrow its Luso-Catholic roots in order to prove its modernity. Modern materials and construction techniques could easily be adapted to ensure that the national past could resist the forces of material progress and internationalization and still be modern. Deeply stung by the loss of his former student, Mariano questioned how Costa could betray cultural nationalism.

In his defense of modernism, Costa argued that the Brazilian arts desperately needed to rid themselves of the decayed conventions of academic art and the false cultural genealogies of neocolonialism. What Brazil needed, he argued, was to embrace technologies and aesthetics adequate to the demands of the machine age. Tradition would not be overthrown. Rather, it would be preserved as tradition. Modernity, by contrast, would be the motivating force of a modern age. In order to achieve this goal, Costa put forward a plan to reform the ENBA curriculum, opening up the possibility of integrating "new" art and architecture into the established program of study. Costa invited several modernists to take part in reforming artistic education, including German painter Leo Putz, Brazilian sculptor Celso Antônio, and architects Alexander Buddeus and Giorgi Warchavchik. For the first time since modernism had become a force in Brazilian arts, the students enrolled at the most important art school would be given the opportunity to study the principles of modern art and architecture.

The coincidence of the Revolution of 1930 and the reform of art education at the ENBA was not lost on the modernists. Sculptor Celso Antônio saw Costa's choices as wholly in keeping with the aesthetic and political changes brought on by the revolution, arguing, "Brazil's intellectual vanguard has come to support the revolutionary movement, because the revolution affords us a vast field upon which new ideas can be sowed. Costa's move, coming from within the halls of official power, will revolutionize the intellectual core of the visual arts. We have before us an enjoined commitment to search for the paths which will make Brazil a great country." [8] Once at odds with officialdom, the modernists were now seeking a place within the state.

If Costa's nomination irritated conservatives such as Mariano, the prospect that modernists such as Antônio, whose works had been rejected for the National Salon of 1927, would be carrying out curricular reform provoked a violent backlash from ENBA faculty members and their allies. Warchavchik, high on the success of the audacious Casa Modernista, was precisely the kind of avant-garde architect whom the academics wanted to keep out of the ENBA. Within the school, conservative professors railed against the newcomers. Elsewhere, the São Paulo Institute of Architects sent a seventeen-page report to Francisco Campos, asking the minister to protect the population from "the hallucinations of cubist painting, the naiveté of sculptures depicting distorted figures, and the so-called 'machines for living' offered up by the self-styled vanguard of architecture." [9] José Mariano took to the press, severely criticizing Costa's new colleagues and labeling the modernists promoters of "Jewish, communist architecture" bent on destroying national traditions. [10] (The poisonous conflation of anticommunism and anti-Semitism would be a hallmark of Mariano's antimodernism—similar to antimodernist invectives heard in totalitarian states in Europe.) [11]

Costa chose to answer his challengers point for point. His counterattack blasted Mariano for his commitment to "the infinite folly of false architecture," which employed a pastiche of colonial elements to invent "traditional" architecture with tragic results. Costa characterized the most celebrated example of neocolonial architecture, Rio's Escola Normal, as a stuffed animal, which simulated life without actually living. Costa argued that modern social and economic relations created the conditions in which modern architecture had become a necessity rather than a luxury of aesthetes. The young architect pledged to bring to the National School of Fine Arts a new vision of art and architecture that embraced the technological and aesthetic demands of the modern world, respected the traditional as tradition, and avoided, at all costs, the attempt to pass off the modern as the past. Calling himself a "cadet," Costa reluctantly counseled his former mentor to cease his melodramatic attempts to undermine the important work to be done at the ENBA.[12] With the overthrow of the Old Republic still fresh in the nation's political memory, the ENBA became a new battleground for a culture war over the content and form of renewal promised by the revolution.

Tensions resurfaced when several dozen nonacademic paintings and sculptures were exhibited at the thirty-eighth Salão Nacional de Belas Artes, held at the ENBA in September 1931. Since 1840, the National Salon had been the premier exhibition space for academic art. Innovation had always been possible at the salon, but within parameters established by the salon juries, which were dominated by ENBA professors who themselves were typically prizewinners at earlier salons. For the academics, the national salon continued to confer status on individuals who could master the techniques and forms taught at the ENBA. A prize won at the salon was an entryway to critical acclaim, public and private commissions, and for a select few, state-subsidized tours of study in Europe. Yet for the modernists, such as Pernambucan poet Manuel Bandeira, the event had degenerated into "a grotesque gallery where one merely goes to be humored."[13]

Modernists such as Bandeira were certainly pleased by a change in the rules for the 1931 salon that allowed entries that did not fit academic conventions. For the first time, the National Salon exhibited pioneers of the modernist movement, including Anita Malfatti, Emiliano Di Cavalcanti, and Vítor Brecheret, as well as painters whose work had become synonymous with the post–1922 vanguard, including Tarsila do Amaral, Cicero Dias, and Ismael Nery. In order to reinforce the image of reform and renewal, the modern works hung individually mounted on unadorned panels covered in burlap. This display strategy helped enhance the viewer's ability to appreciate an individual artist's exploration of his or her chosen subject, without the visual interference of other paintings or ornate framing. The academic paintings hung in the more traditional salon style — mounted in elaborate frames, hung closely together and several rows high.[14]

Proponents of modernist art, including Mário de Andrade, Manuel Bandeira, and a young paulista painter recently returned from a two-year European tour, Cândido Portinari, spoke in defense of the reform underway at the ENBA. Art critics favorable to modernist art suggested that the modernists were revolutionizing Brazilian art just as the tenentes were revolutionizing Brazilian politics. Proponents of modern art made direct connections between the Revolution of 1930, with its promise of political renewal, and the arrival of the modernists in the National Salon, with its promise of cultural renewal. Defenders of academic art were far less enthused. The antimodernist backlash against the so-called *Salão Revolucionário* reached the point where the traditionalists succeeded in forcing Costa from office. ENBA students sympathetic to reform went on strike, effectively closing the school for several months. The academics still prevailed, quickly reasserting the primacy of academic conventions in the school's curriculum and expositions. Arquimedes Memória, a politically conservative ENBA-trained architect closely linked to the eclectic school, which the modernists disparaged, replaced the embattled Costa.

Costa's forced departure and the retrenchment of the old guard came as a loss for individuals such as Bandeira and Portinari who looked to the reforms at the National School of Fine Arts as a way in which to change the meaning of Brazilian culture by changing the institutional relationship between the cultural establishment and the cultural field. This was, in fact, a double loss for the reformers, as Rodrigo Melo Franco de Andrade, the chief of staff who had cultivated close ties to the modernist camp well before joining Francisco Campos in educational reform, left federal service at the same time that Costa found himself under siege at the ENBA. Would the reforms in state organization brought on by the Revolution of 1930 still translate into cultural reform?

The interconnected battles over state building, curricular reform, and the admission criteria at the National Salon of Fine Arts delineate the terms of an acrid debate about the content and direction of cultural management in the immediate aftermath of the regime change of 1930. To be sure, the comparative merits of academicism versus modernism, traditionalism versus the avant-garde were the pretext for debate. But the larger cause of the fight was the state's place in a brave new world inaugurated by the revolution. The controversies of 1930–1931 begged the question whether official cultural institutions could impose ideological or aesthetic litmus tests to individuals and projects that received state sponsorship. Equally troubling was the content of cultural management. Could the *National* School of Fine Arts embrace art forms that had shallow Brazilian roots? Could the state be associated with art forms that the protectors of tradition proclaimed to be degenerate, or the thin edge of a Bolshevist conspiracy? Could the modernists, conversely, participate in the renovação promised by the revolution when the "revolutionary" state continued to protect ultraconservatives?

The furor over Costa's tenure at the ENBA was a clear indication that once-neglected state cultural institutions might become battlegrounds for a looming culture war over the foundations of national cultural production and the allocation of state power. Unlike the 1920s, when cultural debate was contained outside of the state, culture warfare was migrating into the central state, shaping the manner in which the state apparatus operated internally. Neither modernists, traditionalists, nor academics were willing to let competing camps control the strategic apparatus of cultural management. Rather, each camp wanted to use the state to promote its own political and aesthetic agenda, deeply weaving the state into the politics of culture, just as the state itself was formulating a systematic approach to cultural policy making.

"The Critical Years" Revisited:
Cultural Management, 1934–1939

The Brazilian state's systematic, institutional approach to cultural management took definitive form during a key period in Brazilian political history, once called "the critical years," when the democratic political system codified in the Constitution of 1934 strained to accommodate opposing factions, ultimately falling victim to an authoritarian coup in November 1937.[15] Hopes ran high for a strengthening of liberal democracy after the new constitution took effect on 16 July 1934, and Vargas was elected, albeit indirectly, to a one-term presidency. The new constitution promised to democratize Brazilian republicanism. Important liberalizing provisions included the constitutional guarantee of women's enfranchisement, the protection of civil liberties, and the extension of state protections to various occupational groups, including unionized workers. Liberal reformers hoped that the return to constitutional rule would create a foundation for a strong national political system, which still managed to return to the states powers that had been seized by the federal government after the Revolution of 1930. The paulistas, sworn enemies of the Vargas regime in 1932, looked to governor Armando Salles de Oliveira (1887–1945), in anticipation of bringing the presidency back to São Paulo through honest elections. Leftists

13 Gustavo Capanema, 1935. The young minister of education and health from Pitangui, Minas Gerais, delivers a radio address just as educational radio became a point of contention among competing cultural managers in the Vargas regime. Courtesy of CPDOC-GC.

gravitated toward the Aliança Nacional Libertadora (ANL), a popular front movement seeking a systematic reform of Brazil's highly inequitable social and economic relations.

One of the most significant newcomers to the national political scene in this period was a thirty-two-year-old mineiro, Gustavo Capanema, who assumed the top post at the Ministry of Education and Public Health days after the new constitution went into effect. Educated in law, Capanema came to federal government from Pitangui, a small town in central Minas. Prior to coming to Rio, Capanema had spent his early adulthood employed as an instructor of child psychology and a municipal councilman before rising to be secretary of the interior in Minas and state interventor. Like his predecessors Francisco Campos and Washington Pires, Capanema had been seasoned in the regional political machine of Minas Gerais before coming to Rio. Capanema owed much to fellow mineiros, who helped broker the deal between Vargas, state kingpins, and prominent Catholic activists to bring a third mineiro to head the Ministry of Education.

The young minister brought many assets to a regime trying to adapt to the new democratic political culture proscribed by the Constitution of 1934. As a founding member of the Legião de Outubro, a short-lived paramilitary movement that operated in Minas after the Revolution of 1930, Capanema was familiar with the appeal of social mobilization and militarization. As a former educator with direct experience in educational reform, Capanema saw the public educational apparatus as a vehicle for social and cultural transformation—an ideology well suited for an expanding state seeking new vehicles for social education and control. As a former state secretary and interventor, Capanema had direct experience with administration. As an intimate of the modernistas mineiros who gathered at cafés on the Rua da Bahia near the governor's palace in Belo Horizonte, Capanema knew where to turn when looking for allies in state-managed cultural renewal. And, finally, as an intimate of key members of the Catholic revivalist movement, Capanema had the ear of social conservatives who agreed to support the Vargas regime in exchange for guarantees that the expanding state would uphold Christian morality and religious education.[16] Thus, the reformist spirit brought by Capanema was a complex one—clientelistic, pragmatic, ideologically ecumenical, moralizing, and statist.

Inexperience in federal politics did not inhibit Capanema from quickly assuming a proactive stance toward expanding the scope of the ministry's powers. In an unfinished memorandum drafted in 1935, Capanema outlined the Ministry of Education's responsibilities: "Under the provisions laid out in the constitution [of 1934], the mission of the Ministry of Education, and the government as a whole, can be summed up in one word: culture. Or perhaps better stated, national culture."[17] Contemplating the idea that the ministry be renamed the Ministry of National Culture, the young minister set out to turn his administration into the regulator of Brazilian culture.[18]

The administrative reform proposed by Capanema in October 1935 and legalized on 13 January 1937 was central to the minister's claim that his primary responsibility was the improvement of Brazilian culture. Although Capanema would be unable to convince Vargas to include the word "culture" in the formal name of the Ministry of Education and Health (MES), the construction of an extensive network of federal cultural institutions subordinate to the education ministry made Capanema the de facto minister of culture (see table 1). Building upon the presence of older cultural institutions established in the nineteenth century, including the National Library, National Observatory, and the National Museum, Capanema shepherded an organizational reform through Congress, which created the National Historical and Artistic Patrimony Service, the National Museum of Fine Arts, the National Theater Service, the Educational Radio Broadcasting Service, the National Institute of Educational Cinema, and the Instituto Cairú, an agency charged with the publication of the *Enciclopédia Brasileira*. By the end of 1937, the Brazilian federal government was fully equipped to manage a broad range of cultural activities.

At the same time that Capanema busied himself with state building, the liberal tenets codified in the Constitution of 1934 strained to expand the bases of political participation. Extremists on the right began to push Vargas and the armed forces toward a crackdown on democratic rule. Early victims of state repression included the popular front ANL, closed down in July 1935. By November of the same year, a small group of left-wing military officers upset by the closure of the ANL and the rising strength of the semifascist Integralist movement coordinated a mutiny in military garrisons in Natal, Recife, and Rio. Failing to rally popular support, the rebels were quickly taken by loyalist troops. Right-wing hardliners in the armed forces, in collaboration with civilian conservatives and a growing number of political police, seized upon the failed revolt as a pretext to declare a state of siege. Thus began the definitive turn away from the liberal constitutionalism promised in 1934. Capanema's role in the regime's turn to the right was minor, but the minister still saw fit to structure cultural management around the ideas of anticommunist, statist nationalism that bolstered the rise of right-wing politics.

The erosion of liberal constitutional rule, amidst a rising tide of political extremism and anticommunist paranoia, culminated in a bloodless coup announced the night of 10 November 1937. Vargas took to the radio waves and announced a state of siege, which included the suspension of Congress, the cancellation of the presidential elections scheduled for January 1938, and the replacement of the Constitution of 1934 with a corporatist constitution written by former Minister of Education Francisco Campos, who returned to the federal state as the minister of justice and internal affairs.

Table 1 Federal Institutions of Cultural Management, 1930–1945
(Date of Foundation and Director)

MINISTÉRIO DA EDUCAÇÃO E SAÚDE*

	1930	Francisco Campos (1930–1932)
		Washington Ferreira Pires (1932–1934)
		Gustavo Capanema (1934–1945)
Conselho Nacional de Cultura	1938 †	Ronald Porchat

EDUCATIONAL RADIO AND FILM

Serviço de Radiodifusão Educativa	1937 ‡	Edgard Roquette-Pinto (1936–1943)
		Fernando Tude de Souza (1943–?)
Instituto Nacional do Cinema Educativo	1937 ‡	Edgard Roquette-Pinto (1936–1947)

HISTORICAL AND ARTISTIC PATRIMONY

Escola Nacional de Belas Artes	1891	Lucio Costa (1930–1931)
		Arquimedes Memória (1931–1937)
		Lucílio de Albuquerque (1937–1938)
		Augusto Bracet (1938–1948)
Museu Histórico Nacional	1922	Gustavo Barroso (1922–1930)
		Rodolfo Garcia (1930–1932)
		Gustavo Barroso (1932–1959)
Inspetoria dos Monumentos Nacionais	1934	Gustavo Barroso (1934–1937)
Serviço do Patrimônio Histórico e Artístico Nacional	1937 ‡	Rodrigo Melo Franco de Andrade (1936–1967)
Museu Nacional de Belas Artes	1937	Oswaldo Teixeira (1937–1961)
Museu da Inconfidência	1938	Raimundo Otávio de Trinidade (1940–1959?)
Museu Imperial	1940	Alcindo Sodré (1940–1952)
Museu das Missões	1940	
Museu do Ouro	1945	Antônio Joaquim de Almeida (1945–?)

LIBRARIES AND PUBLISHING

| Biblioteca Nacional | 1810 | Rodolfo Garcia (1932–1945) |
| Instituto Nacional do Livro | 1937 ‡ | Augusto Meyer (1937–1966) |

PERFORMING ARTS

Serviço Nacional do Teatro	1937 ‡	Abadie Faria Rosa (1936–1945)
Escola Nacional de Música	1841	Antônio de Sá Perreira (1938–1946)
Conservatório Nacional do Canto Orfeônico	1942	Heitor Villa-Lobos (1942–1957)

Table 1   Continued

OTHER

Museu Nacional	1818	Edgard Roquette-Pinto (1926–1935)
		Alberto Betim Paes Leme (1935–1937)
		Heloisa Alberto Torres (1937–1955)
Observatório Nacional	1827	Sebastião Sodré da Gama (1930–1951)
Casa Rui Barbosa	1928	Various
Conselho Nacional dos Símbolos Nacionais	1939	Pery Constant Beviloaqua (1939–1940)

MINISTÉRIO DA JUSTIÇA E NEGÓCIOS INTERIORES

	1891	Vicente Rao (1934–1936)
		Francisco Campos (1932; 1937–1942)
		Alexandre Marcondes Filho (1943–1945)
Departamento Oficial de Publicidade	1931	Antônio Rodrigues de Sales Filho (1931–1934)
Departamento de Propaganda e Difusão Cultural	1934	Lourival Fontes (1934–1938)
Departamento Nacional de Propaganda	1938	Lourival Fontes (1938–1939)
Departamento Nacional de Informações	1945	

DEPARTAMENTO DE IMPRENSA E PROPAGANDA

	1939	Lourival Fontes (1939–1942)
		Antônio José Coelho dos Reis (1942–1943)
		Amílcar Dutra de Menezes (1943–1945)

Note: Table includes federal agencies whose primary responsibility by legal mandate and by actual practice was cultural management. Not included are federal agencies that indirectly dealt with cultural management, including the Ministry of Labor and the Conselho de Imigração e Colonização, among others.

*Created 14 November 1930 as Ministry of Education and Public Health. Renamed Ministry of Education and Health in ministerial reform of 13 January 1937.

†The Conselho Nacional de Cultura was created by Decree-Law 526, issued 1 July 1938. Formal announcement of the council's membership was delayed until 10 October 1940. In reality, the council never fulfilled its legal mandate.

‡Federal agencies that functioned on a provisional basis prior to official creation on 13 January 1937.

Deeply invested in an ideology of conservative, state-led renewal, Vargas became president of a "New State" committed to the completion of the political and cultural renovation initiated with the Revolution of 1930.

The ideological polarization that accompanied the golpe of 1937 encouraged conservatives to advocate direct federal intervention into the cultural arena. Ideologues from the right, including Francisco Oliveira Vianna and Azevedo Amaral, joined authoritarians working within the federal bureaucracy, including fascist-sympathizer and Director of the Department of Propaganda and Cultural Diffusion Lourival Fontes, to direct state resources toward cultural change. These ideologues specifically targeted the political culture of orthodox liberalism, which they saw as an ideological import ill-suited to Brazil's organic political culture. For conservatives, the golpe provided the opportunity to undo the political culture of liberalism that, they argued, had severed Brazilian society and the Brazilian citizen into the legal and the real Brazil—o Brasil legal/o Brasil real—where legal institutions such as suffrage had been used by cynical, self-serving oligarchs bent on denying Brazilians the enjoyment of their true cultural heritage. The Revolution of 1930 and the Estado Novo were corrective measures, then, designed to reunite the legal and the real. Although the precise nature of Brasil real remained vague, conservatives called for a central state that could manage a cultural renaissance from above, where liberal laws would be held in abeyance.[19]

The institutional implications of the turn to the right were profound. With most forms of mass consumption, including the press and radio, declared to be of "public utility," the federal government gained remarkable access to the mass media. Journalists, film distributors, radio announcers, and musicians had to negotiate within a new institutional environment in which federal and local agencies threatened sanction or closure for private enterprises that strayed from the type of cultural programming deemed appropriate for the new regime. Federal intervention was not limited to the mass media. Article 128 of the Constitution of 1937 explicitly conferred upon the state the responsibility "to contribute, through direct and indirect means, to the stimulus and development of individual and collective initiatives, with preference given to the foundation of artistic, scientific, and educational institutions." The supporters of the Estado Novo gave legal justification for turning state institutions into vehicles for creating an improved, virtuous, and organic Brazilian culture.

As suggested, the number and scope of federal institutions of cultural

14 Interior of the Ministry of Education Pavilion, Exposição do Estado Novo, Rio de Janeiro, December 1938. The Exposição do Estado Novo helped popularize the Ministry of Education's legal and institutional claims to cultural management. In this display, cultural management is given equal importance to health, education, and public assistance. Courtesy of CPDOC-GC.

management created or expanded during these "critical years" is impressive. Not since the early nineteenth century had the central state taken such an expansive attitude toward cultural management. Eager to extend the ministry of education's institutional reach further, in July 1938 Capanema successfully lobbied Vargas to approve a Conselho Nacional de Cultura (National Culture Council, CNC), to "coordinate all activities dealing with cultural development undertaken directly or indirectly by the Ministry of Education and Health." [20] The measure was highly significant in that "cultural development" (*desenvolvimento cultural*) was legally and formally defined to encompass: (a) philosophical, scientific, and literary production; (b) art appreciation; (c) preservation of cultural patrimony; (d) intellectual exchange; (e) the mass media (books, radio, theater, cinema); (f) patriotic

Table 2   Annual Expenditures by Federal Government and Ministry of
Education, 1931–1937 and 1938–1944

CONTOS	1931	1937	GROWTH RATE
Federal	1,944,116	4,013,330	106%
MESP	104,831	241,682	130%
	1938	1944	GROWTH RATE
Federal	4,729,244	7,323,258	55%
MES	265,551	608,271	129%

Note: The figures for total federal expenditure differ slightly from figures appearing in the
Anuário Estatístico.
Source: CPDOC-GCf 36.05.28 Doc. V-11, "Quadro comparativo dos índices de crescimento
das despesas da União e do MES nos anos 1931 e 1937 e os anos 1938 e 1944," Joaquim
Bittencourt Fernandes de Sá, director general of Departamento da Administração/MES
to Capanema, 29 September 1945.

and humanitarian causes; (g) civic education; (h) physical education; and
(i) recreation.[21] Although the decree-law made no mention of popular culture—a strong indication of Capanema's reluctance to manage cultural
practices that originated in rural areas and the popular classes—culture
had attained a legal-administrative structure on par with other branches
of public administration. The Ministry of Education made much of its extended reach at the Exposição do Estado Novo, a grand national exposition
held to commemorate the first year of Estado Novo rule.

Significant financial investment accompanied the institutionalization of
cultural management. Even when one takes into account the recurrent
complaints of underfunding, federal outlays for education, health, and culture were fast-growing areas in the federal budget. Table 2 demonstrates
that the Ministry of Education's growth rate for the period 1931–1937 exceeded the rate of growth for the entire federal budget by 24 percentage
points, and under the Estado Novo, the difference in growth rates would be
even more pronounced, approaching 75 percentage points, for the period
1938–1945. Unfortunately, the figures for federal expenditures on cultural
management are incomplete, but available data indicate that federal expenditure toward education and culture combined grew by 262 percent for
the period 1932–1943.[22] If outlays for the Department of Press and Propaganda are included, one can see that the Vargas regime devoted significant
resources to cultural management (see table 3).

Table 3   Budget of the Department of Press and Propaganda versus Ministry of Education Expenditures on Education and Culture, 1940–1945

CONTOS	DIP	MES
1940	6,578	150,090
1941	9,573	158,250
1942	11,437	162,711
1943	14,537	160,724
1944	13,591	N/A
1945	5,583	N/A

Sources: Brazil, Ministério da Fazenda, Contadoria Geral da República, *Balanço Geral da União* (1940), 93; (1941), 104; (1942), 127; (1943), 107; (1944), 125; (1945), 234; *Anuário Estatístico do Brasil* (1939/1940), 1146; (1941/1945), 457.

As the Estado Novo matured, federal cultural management became the wedge issue that Campos envisioned for educational and health reforms in 1930. According to conservative ideologues, active cultural management was proof that the Vargas regime was fulfilling a commitment to cure the national culture of the damage inflicted by the liberals prior to 1930. An editorial published in the July 1938 issue of the *Revista do Serviço Público* summed up the historical, functional, and ideological place of federal cultural management under the Estado Novo:

> The era has ended in which state intervention into a nation's culture was believed to amount to nothing. A false and empty liberalism once denounced any State initiative as an invasion into territory which should be exclusively reserved for free intellectual initiative. . . . Only an imbecile would now be capable of defending this position, which is unsustainable in today's world. Those nations that do not demonstrate active consciousness of their unique characteristics will find it difficult to survive this tempestuous era in which we live. No aspect of national life can be left at the margins of state action, as the State is the sole entity capable of imprinting upon each citizen a truly nationalist mark.
>
> Cultural development merits the highest level of attention from those in power, as it is the linchpin to real and lasting national progress. . . .[23]

According to the civil service reformers who wrote for the *Revista do Serviço Público,* efficient and orderly public administration would guarantee that cultural management met the lofty goals of national improvement.

These same reformers also recognized that an institutionalized approach to cultural management might be adversely affected by the inefficiency and lethargy that afflicted other areas of public administration. The editorial cited above warned, "Surely, government action must be coordinated in a careful manner, such that positive results are made. Excessive regulation may produce the opposite results. Cultural management is incompatible with mere bureaucratic procedures devoid of creativity." As predicted, cultural management could indeed fall victim to the inefficiencies of public administration. However, the full scope of inefficiency and mismanagement would not become apparent until after the fall of the Estado Novo, when annual funding began to stagnate. In the pioneering days of cultural management, a much greater drag on efficiency was political infighting among various state agencies. Tensions *within* the state added another dimension to cultural management, as the functionality and objectives of cultural policy making were subject not merely to negotiations between state and society, but also within the state proper.

Interministerial tensions were acute in the mid-to-late 1930s, as the Ministries of Education and Justice sought control of the federal cultural apparatus. As early as 1932, the two ministries squared off over jurisdictional questions related to government regulation of the motion picture industry. From then on, interministerial battles became an integral part of state regulation, shaping not just individual policies but also the nature of cultural management, ultimately limiting the overall effectiveness of federal policy making.

One of the best documented fights over cultural management, with significant repercussions for state-sponsored cultural programming, centered on "educational" cinema and radio. Both radio and cinema had attracted the interests of reformers since the late 1910s, when anthropologist and radio pioneer Edgard Roquette-Pinto proposed that the burgeoning media could help raise Brazil's dismal educational standards at relatively low costs.[24] By the 1930s, Roquette-Pinto was joined by liberal educational reformers associated with the Escola Nova movement to promote the educational possibilities of film and radio. These liberals tended to see in film and radio the potential to reach large numbers of undereducated adults living across wide geographic areas. In a break from the text-bound educational policy in place since the nineteenth century, Roquette-Pinto was also impressed by the potential to educate through the senses.[25] Even conservatives such as Jonathas Serrano, a professor of history at the prestigious

Colégio Dom Pedro II, also rallied around the cause of educational cinema, seeing film as a medium for instilling Catholic values.[26] For all interested parties, both film and radio were treated as vehicles for cultural improvement in the face of undereducation, moral laxity, and an unruly private market.

If the desire to improve national educational and moral standards was the driving force behind state-sponsored educational cinema within Brazil, then the worldwide increase in the powers of central states, combined with the parallel growth of political and propagandistic radio programming and filmmaking, must also be considered influential in the genesis of educational filmmaking in Brazil. The Capanema archive clearly indicates that the minister and other state figures kept current with developments in European cinema, where "educational" film had become an important part of education and civic nationalism in totalitarian and democratic regimes established after the First World War. In 1937, Capanema reviewed a detailed assessment of the German Ministries of Propaganda, Science, Education, and Public Instruction, as well as state-run educational filmmaking agencies in Italy and France.[27] The information helped the minister and his aides formulate plans for a federal institute that could produce, distribute, and store educational film, as well as publish a monthly review about educational film.[28]

Fearful that the unchecked growth of commercial film and radio threatened to erode moral and educational standards, in 1936 Capanema called upon Vargas to create a federal film institute.[29] Capanema left his intentions slightly ambiguous regarding whether he envisioned the agency's responsibilities as purely educational (that is, the production of educational film materials for distribution to educational establishments), or if he was also trying to reestablish the power to censor commercial film. (The ministry censored commercial film releases between 1932 and 1934, before losing the power to the Department of Propaganda and Cultural Diffusion, DPDC.) In either case, the planned Institute for Educational Cinema was to establish a firm federal foothold at the juncture of education, morality, and mass media. Soon after Vargas gave his initial approval, Capanema invited Edgard Roquette-Pinto to serve as director. The agency's first edited film was released on 26 May 1936.[30] Formal legislative approval for what was officially named the Instituto Nacional do Cinema Educativo (National Institute of Educational Cinema, or INCE) came in the ministerial reform of January 1937.

Although the INCE certainly found some of its inspiration in the film institutes created under European authoritarian states, the agency consciously differentiated itself from its German and Italian counterparts. This can be undoubtedly attributed to the pedagogical and ideological orientation of Roquette-Pinto, who viewed educational cinema as an auxiliary tool to public instruction rather than propaganda. Top culture managers at the Ministry of Education, including Capanema and Roquette-Pinto, were not categorically opposed to borrowing some of the bureaucratic features of foreign cultural institutions, but they shied away from proposals explicitly modeled after totalitarian states. And, even if Capanema or Roquette-Pinto had wanted the INCE to become a more explicitly politicized branch of the state, the agency faced several structural constraints that hampered any attempt to position the INCE as a tool of political engineering, including limited funding, low-level technology, and restricted audiences.[31] The mere fact that early releases were silent and used 16-millimeter film unsuitable for commercial film houses effectively blocked any hopes of transforming the INCE into an agency of mass persuasion.

The lack of the trappings of propagandistic filmmaking did not necessarily mean that educational cinema provided purely "educational" images, devoid of ideological content. The INCE played a key role in the dissemination of images recorded at patriotic, proregime civic ceremonies. The agency's first release with a soundtrack documented the celebration of the 1936 Dia da Pátria (Independence Day) in the national capital. The grand civic pageants enacted in Rio would be standard fare for the 223 films released during the first Vargas regime. Even the most uninterested moviegoer would recognize that these ceremonies were neither politically neutral nor explicitly educational. Educational film was entirely consistent with the cult of personality and the cult of the state promoted by the Estado Novo regime. The INCE also produced patriotic dramatic films, including the classic *O descobrimento do Brasil* (The Discovery of Brazil, 1937), which brought together the talents of pioneer filmmaker Humberto Mauro and modernist composer Heitor Villa-Lobos in a cinematic recreation of Pero Vaz de Caminha's narrative of the momentous encounter between Pedro Álvarez Cabral and the Tupi in April 1500. The resonance of these dramatic releases was undoubtedly enhanced by official cultural nationalism.

Certain structural factors shaped the administrative choices made by the INCE. Just as important was the competitive administrative environment within the state, which structured and ultimately limited educational filmmaking during the first Vargas regime. With the Ministry of Education making modest gains in educational film, the Ministry of Justice went about building its own institutional network of cultural management, including filmmaking. The state of siege following the Intentona Comunista of November 1935 was a great boon for the ministry of justice, which used the suspension of political liberties to build a critical mass of judicial, policing, and censorial institutions that could exert direct influence on culture. The most notable gains at Justice were made in the areas of censorship and propaganda making. Although Education shied away from these two areas, the precise administrative boundaries between the educational and the propagandistic were always unclear, making for an increasingly tense relationship between the two ministries over who would manage Brazilian culture and how.

On the eve of the Estado Novo, the stage had been set for a showdown between the Ministry of Education and the increasingly hard-line Ministry of Justice, because both ministries fought for a controlling interest in the federal government's institutional and technological investment in mass media. Education remained committed to its self-proclaimed "educational" role in creating healthy, moral, and enlightened Brazilians, while Justice sought to protect Brazilian culture against the scourges of internal and external threats and to promote the rituals of patriotism. A memo written by Capanema in July 1937 illustrates the rising tensions between the two ministries at the twilight of liberal constitutional rule. In an internal memo on federal administrative reform, Capanema returned to an idea originally put forth in 1935 and proposed that the recently reorganized Ministry of Education and Health be renamed the Ministry of Culture.[32] This proposal echoed Capanema's established views that the responsibilities of the Ministry of Education and Health were cultural in nature, aimed at the harmonious formation of the Brazilian mind, body, and spirit. Capanema reasoned that education and health were part of a larger category of culture; therefore the name of the federal ministry responsible for education and health should reflect its overarching cultural mandate. Implied in this proposal was the notion that the concept of "culture" had become part of the world of managed state institutions and competent civil servants that had to function outside of the democratic political process. Culture became a national problem in need of careful bureaucratic-technocratic solutions, not party politics. The question, then, was which branch of government would control cultural management.

15 Vargas Announces the Estado Novo, 10 November 1937. This famous photo depicts Vargas, surrounded by the members of his cabinet and military advisors, proclaiming the authoritarian-nationalist New State. As the Estado Novo took shape, various state agencies fought for control of cultural management. Courtesy of CPDOC-GV.

The minister was well aware that the Ministry of Education was but one of several federal organs that sought to manage bodies, minds, spirits, and souls. The Ministry of Justice was a known threat. The Ministries of Labor and Justice, as well as the Army, directly competed with the Ministry of Education for cultural hegemony over urban-industrial bodies. With schools, the armed forces, and state-sponsored unions each vying for the power to socialize new citizens (youths, unionized workers, rural-to-urban migrants, women), Capanema saw in a Ministry of Culture the ability to mold the nation *latu sensu*.

In a more tactical sense, Capanema also realized that should his request be granted, a Ministry of Culture would be able to protect, if not expand, the state's institutional control over a wide spectrum of cultural activities that included traditional outlets of "high art" and learned culture as well

as the burgeoning culture industries found in Rio and São Paulo. Concluding the July 1937 memo, Capanema made a proposal that hinted at the
impending battle over which federal organs would control Brazilian culture when he boldly suggested that oversight responsibilities for film and
radio transfered to the Department of Propaganda and Cultural Diffusion
in 1934 be returned to the Ministry of Education. This was one of the few
instances in which Capanema tried to appropriate administrative powers
exercised by the Ministry of Justice. The tactic failed, but the minister's
thinking was highly suggestive of the strategic warfare for the management
of culture taking place in the months preceding the proclamation of the
Estado Novo.

In practice, almost none of the specifics of the proposal to transform the
Ministry of Education into the Ministry of Culture were implemented. In
the period 1937–1940, the MES strengthened its role as a prominent patron
of cultural initiatives through the cultural institutions legally established
in the ministerial reform of 13 January 1937. Capanema also convened several standing committees on cultural issues and cultivated a good working
relationship with a wide range of figures in Brazilian letters, arts, and sciences to assist in the formulation and coordination of ministerial strategies
toward cultural management.[33] But, the MES never gained control of the
DPDC's bureaucracy and personnel. The golpe of 10 November 1937 effectively blocked any subsequent MES attempts to assume responsibilities from
other federal agencies, as Justice and the DPDC took the offensive against
internal subversion through a combination of political-judicial repression
and political-cultural propaganda. By 1938, the National Department of
Propaganda (DNP), created in 1938 to replace the DPDC, was effectively immune to any challenges from other federal organs. By December 1939, the
infamous Department of Press and Propaganda, successor to the DNP, took
the offensive against the MES. Attacks on the Ministry of Education ranged
from the proposed transfer of the Ministry of Education's radio station to
the creation of a National Culture Council to compete with the one already
answering to the Minister of Education.[34]

In the interim, the tensions between Education and Justice continued
unabated over the question of control of state-sponsored radio programming. At stake was control of the technology capable of penetrating large
geographic expanses, severe socioeconomic disparities, and private spaces
previously immune to a strong governmental presence. With cultural patronage and policy making assuming a prominent role in ministerial ac-

tivities of the Ministries of Education and Justice, the power to make significant inroads into the areas of mass media and technology was a highly contested and coveted prize within the federal bureaucratic structure.

Already aware that the ministry's educational filmmaking institute was in the sights of the Ministry of Justice, Capanema proposed that Vargas authorize the transformation of the Educational Radio Broadcasting Service (Serviço de Radiodifusão Educativa, SRE), which had operated as an appendage to the INCE since 1936, into an autonomous administrative entity called the National Educational Radio Broadcasting Service (Serviço Nacional de Radiodifusão Educativa, SNRE).[35] The new agency would maintain its original charge of educational radio, as well as assume the additional power to administer the compulsory broadcast of a daily ten-minute program of educational texts supplied by the Ministry of Education to all licensed radio broadcasters.[36] With the number of radio receivers growing at a dizzying pace, Capanema hoped to use radio to extend the campaign to form educated minds, bodies, and spirits into private homes and public squares. This proposal met with stiff resistance from the Ministry of Justice, which countered that it should retain the exclusive power to control obligatory radio broadcasts. Francisco Campos asserted that Justice, not Education, should administer the federal government's sole radio broadcast station, Rádio MES. Campos saw the station as a key tool in the campaign to ferret out sources of potential opposition to the young Estado Novo through the aggressive use of antisubversive/pronationalist radio programming.

Unwilling to see Justice gain control of Rádio MES, Capanema submitted a modified proposal to Vargas, which substituted school broadcasting (*radiodifusão escolar*) for educational broadcasting (*radiodifusão educativa*). The acronyms of the SNRE*ducativa* and the SNRE*scolar* would remain unchanged, but the agency's mission would be strictly "educational." In his revised proposal to Vargas, Capanema wrote:

> [In the international field of educational radio] Brazil cannot fall behind. It is essential that we introduce radio into all institutions of primary, secondary, higher, and professional education, be they day schools or night schools. And through this powerful instrument we must establish some form of spiritual communion among our educational establishments. Given the fact that the difficulties of great distances and uneven population distribution conspire to make our schools into isolated units, each possessing its own standards and

way of thinking, radio is the sole medium by which to achieve this commu-
nion of spirit.

The proposal to transfer [Rádio MES] to the Ministry of Justice seems incon-
venient because above all else, Justice does not need it. What Justice should do
is avail itself to all radio broadcasters operating in the country. . . . Laws should
determine which hours should be given to the programming from the Department of Propaganda [*sic*]—programming which should be interspersed
between musical programming, much like commercial advertisements. . . .

If Justice were to use solely one station for daily and nightly propaganda
broadcasts, the fatal result will be that that station would lose all of its listening public, because everyone, including those friendly to the government,
will change the station. If Justice is set on having its own station, it should be
a short-wave one, intended for broadcasts to foreign countries.[37]

Capanema's letter to the chief of state indicates that within the internal bureaucratic culture of the Estado Novo regime, and amidst the overall
authoritarian turn of Brazilian political culture, the Ministry of Education
was struggling to maintain its autonomy from other branches of government. A successful raid of Rádio MES could lead to additional raids upon
other elements of the ministry's bureaucratic structure exhibiting some
form of explicit political/propagandistic utility. In response to these attacks, Education reiterated the "educational" posture that it would aggressively defend until the fall of the Estado Novo. In this posture, Capanema
described initiatives like educational radio and film as inherently instructive, designed to spread a common language and cultural system across
wide geographic and socioeconomic expanses. Capanema framed this educational view of ministerial activities in contrast to the political objectives
of the Ministry of Justice. In a clever rhetorical move, Capanema also defended MES control over Rádio MES for purely operational reasons, asserting that Justice's insertion into mass media necessitated universal market
penetration. The use of a single station for propagandistic purposes would
prove ineffective in reaching a national audience uninterested in propaganda. Educational radio, by contrast, would meet the needs and desires
of countless numbers of uneducated or undereducated Brazilians yearning for access to some form of educational opportunity. Capanema treated
educational radio as essential for national and spiritual growth, whereas
propagandistic/political radio was a discretionary commodity that had to
be marketed correctly, lest the listening audience simply tune out. (There

is evidence to indicate that Capanema was largely correct on the second allegation.)

In this particular battle, Capanema was successful in maintaining his ministerial prerogative. In early May 1938, the Federal Civil Service Council agreed that the originally proposed nomenclature, Serviço Nacional de Radiodifusão Educativa, should be retained in keeping with administrative naming practices at other MES services. Council President Luiz Simões Lopes denied Justice's request for control of Rádio MES, stating the SNRE's responsibilities were "essentially educational." [38]

The decision to keep Rádio MES under Education's control did not deter Justice and other agencies from trying to wrest control of other cultural decision-making bodies under the control of the Ministry of Education, particularly after the proclamation of the Estado Novo. In 1942, several years after control of Rádio MES had been definitively awarded to the SRE, Department of Press and Propaganda Director Lourival Fontes tried once again to convince Vargas to transfer control of the SRE, as well as the INCE and filmmaking offices at the Ministry of Agriculture, to the DIP. [39] Once again, the top level of the state bureaucracy rejected this proposal.

Capanema and the ministerial apparatus that he headed were generally successful in casting the responsibilities of the MES in nonpartisan, cultural or educational language that elevated the MES above the political concerns of antisubversion, counterintelligence, and political propaganda that concerned Campos and Fontes, among others. However, the creation of the Department of Press and Propaganda in December 1939 ensured that the promotional activities of the MES would be placed in an uneasy, sometimes confrontational, alliance with the censorial DIP until late in the Estado Novo. Throughout the Estado Novo, the two organs expressed their mutual suspicions as they also went about regulating a cultural milieu marked by claims to modernism, patriotism, historicism, and authoritarianism.

The administrative battles of 1937–1939 illuminate pivotal moments in the internal politicking that accompanied the proclamation of the Estado Novo. In an authoritarian state that presented a public image of unity and harmony, the state was divided against itself, pitting advocates of cultural management as a form of educational reform against those who saw cultural management as a tool for social control. Unable to agree on the responsibilities of various state agencies, cultural managers at Justice and Education still found consensus over the state's obligation to manage culture. Infighting limited the success of federal cultural management, but it did not diminish the fact that cultural management had indeed become an official state responsibility, supported by a wide range of cultural and political interests.

The Politics of Being a Culture Manager

At the height of the Estado Novo, the Vargas regime counted on a cadre of conservative authors who enthusiastically supported the turn to the authoritarian state. Top public posts went to conservative ideologues such as Minister of Justice Francisco Campos, legal advisor to the Ministry of Labor Oliveira Vianna, DIP Director Lourival Fontes, Director of the São Paulo State Department of Press and Propaganda Cassiano Ricardo, and Menotti del Picchia, editor-in-chief of the proregime newspaper *A Noite*. Midlevel posts went to a broad range of minor intellectuals and ideologues who supported the conservative tenets of the Estado Novo. Renovação opened many doors for conservatives.

Moderates and liberals also gravitated to state service. Between 1934 and 1939, Capanema convinced some of the most important figures in the modernist movement to take on paid and unpaid positions in the expanding network of federal cultural institutions. Mineiros Carlos Drummond de Andrade and Rodrigo Melo Franco de Andrade served as Capanema's chief of staff and the director of the Serviço do Patrimônio Histórico e Artístico Nacional, respectively. Gaúcho poet Augusto Meyer took the position of director of the Instituto Nacional do Livro. Heitor Villa-Lobos acted as director of the Superintendência de Educação Musical e Artística. Modernist poet-author-critic Mário de Andrade was a loyal consultant and interlocutor to the minister of education. All of these figures used the state apparatus to visualize a modern Brazil.

Modernists with strong leftist convictions were often deeply troubled by their direct participation in an authoritarian state. In 1936, Drummond tendered a letter of resignation after Capanema invited Tristão de Ataíde, an antileftist Catholic revivalist and close advisor to the minister, to speak to the ministerial staff about communism. Capanema chose not to accept the resignation—an act suggestive of the minister's willingness to patronize culture managers drawn from a wide ideological spectrum as long as they remained loyal to the minister's public policies.[40] Drummond's decision to remain in the ministry is also telling. Intellectuals with leftist inclinations could find a place within the state, even when confronted with figures and ideas they could not support.

Capanema was the linchpin to this ideologically heterodox, pragmatic system of political affiliation, clientelism, public service, and patronage. Although the mineiro had few direct ties to the coalition that swept into power in November 1930, he made the most of his connections to key figures who supported Vargas during the provisional government, including the first minister of education, Francisco Campos. By the time Capanema reached the federal government in 1934, he had broken with Campos over ideological differences. The schoolteacher from Pitangui would still manage to sit alongside his former mentor in the presidential cabinet and collaborate with the conservative minister of justice on matters of civic culture and state security. A tireless and gifted administrator, Capanema capitalized on his post to cultivate a broad network of clients who did not let the absence of liberal institutions dampen their enthusiasm for state action. Navigating regional politics in Minas, high politics in the Presidential Palace, mundane politics in the ministerial suite, and cultural politics in museum galleries, newspaper columns, historical cities, and ateliers, Capanema counted upon the assistance of authoritarians, reformists, and leftists situated within and outside the state. This unusual combination of political acumen, ideological flexibility, and intimacy with the national intelligentsia and political elite, including Vargas, put the minister in a privileged position to manage federal policies intended to improve the population, empower the central state, and satisfy multiform demands for renewal.[41]

Capanema was inflexible on one point: he had no intention of making the Ministry of Education into a Brazilian version of cultural, educational, and propaganda ministries found in totalitarian Europe. The minister consistently balked at the suggestion that the Ministry of Education explicitly sponsor cultural programs modeled upon the cultural politics of Europe's totalitarian or fascist regimes. In early 1938, for example, when Nazi sympathizers Joint Chief of Staff Pedro Góes Monteiro and Federal District Chief of Police Filinto Müller exercised significant influence within the government, Capanema rejected the proposal made by the acclaimed stage actor Procópio Ferreira that the Ministry of Education use theater as a means of state propaganda.[42] In defending his position, the minister reiterated his support of federally funded theater, but eschewed the explicit linkage between state funding and political indoctrination found in the Soviet Union.

Capanema never rejected the authoritarian state outright, but he consistently did reject the attempt to consciously make the Estado Novo in the image of totalitarian states abroad.

Perhaps because of Capanema's opposition to totalitarianism, intellectuals associated with the moderate and left-wing political movements of the early 1930s somehow managed to make their peace with the Vargas regime. Moderates, including Mário de Andrade and Rodrigo Melo Franco de Andrade, and future Communist Party members, including Oscar Niemeyer, Carlos Drummond de Andrade, and Cândido Portinari, accepted employment or commissions from the state at the same time that state-sponsored repression of the left was at it harshest. Against a backdrop of authoritarianism and official antileftism, those intellectuals who made their peace with public employment used the state apparatus to manage culture and guarantee a certain degree of institutional patronage and aesthetic freedom. Culture managers and clients of the state, the left-leaning modernistas from Minas Gerais — Carlos Drummond de Andrade, Rodrigo Melo Franco de Andrade, and others — used the authoritarian Estado Novo to transform a regional variant of the modernist movement into a national project.[43]

In his pioneering study of intellectuals and the dominant classes during the 1920s, 1930s, and 1940s, Sérgio Miceli argued that the nationalist ideal allowed left-wing intellectuals to serve an authoritarian state without betraying their ideological convictions. The state provided intellectuals with sustenance and cultural capital. In turn, they provided administrative and intellectual services with the idea that they were working for the nation, rather than a dictatorial state. Miceli writes, "These co-opted intellectuals defined themselves as spokespersons from all of society. . . . Seeing themselves as responsible for the administration of the nation's cultural assets, they placed themselves in a position to assume the work of preservation, diffusion, and manipulation of this heritage, working to celebrate authors and works which could be of use in this cause."[44]

In August 1939, Carlos Drummond de Andrade, one of the most prominent left-wing intellectuals to accept a position in the state, proffered a more aesthetic interpretation of the place of the intellectual in cultural management. In an interview granted to the Rio literary review, *Dom Casmurro,* Capanema's chief of staff asked whether intellectuals who accepted state patronage were mere mouthpieces for an "official" art. Answering his own rhetorical question, Drummond asserted that his fellow intellectuals produced "Brazilian" art.[45] This was a project of aesthetic nationalism, not state propaganda. Tellingly, the poet's listing of intellectuals working for the Ministry of Education did not include any conservatives, belying the fact that Drummond's take on aesthetic nationalism was refracted through a left-wing ideological orientation that nonetheless had made its peace with a right-wing state.

Miceli is convincing in arguing that a nationalist ideal allowed left-of-center modernists to work within an authoritarian state without automatically compromising their political convictions for the sake of winning cultural capital. Miceli notes that several intellectuals who worked for the Estado Novo, including Drummond, came to state employment having already attained social and intellectual stature. These individuals did not need the state to create and perpetuate their aesthetic legitimacy. This argument seems to work well for analyzing the intellectual's relationship to the state. The state's relationship to the cultural field is more complicated, because an authoritarian state helped shape the parameters under which cultural agents functioned. Drummond's silence on the presence of conservatives within the inner circles of state cultural managers indicates that the left-wing was highly sensitive to the fact that the state extended its protection not solely to the vanguard. The modernists who sought patronage and positions from the federal government were not authoritarians. Nonetheless, they knowingly worked under an authoritarian state that made the entire project of cultural management possible.

Managing Culture at the Height of the Estado Novo

With Capanema and Francisco Campos sharing aspirations for the administrative power to renew national culture, cultural management widened the gap between the Ministries of Education and Justice. Certain administrative areas, such as museums and historical preservation, went to Education unchallenged. The Ministry of Justice controlled other areas, including censorship and countersubversion. In the middle, the state's relationship to mass media and national symbols remained the contested ground upon which Education and Justice acted out their particular visions for renovação.

The competitive environment of cultural management took on increased complexity in 1939, when Vargas authorized the transformation of the Departamento Nacional de Propaganda (successor to the DPDC) into a full-fledged state propaganda agency, known as the Departamento de Imprensa e Propaganda (Department of Press and Propaganda, DIP). Unlike its institutional predecessors that answered to the Ministry of Justice, the DIP was under the direct supervision of the president. Answering directly to Vargas, the DIP exercised administrative powers approximating a ministry. As it weighed in on the preexisting interministerial culture wars, the DIP bolstered policies of cultural authoritarianism, in its censorship and antisubversive activities, as well as policies of cultural nationalism, in its promotion of the national cultural patrimony of heroes, rituals, and values. The disappearance of the DIP's permanent archives will forever complicate a full understanding of the internal politics of culture during the Vargas regime. One can know very little about the tensions *within* the DIP over the administration of culture.[46] Nevertheless, the creation of an official propaganda ministry compounded ongoing tensions in managing culture.

The 27 December 1939 presidential decree authorizing the DIP capped five years of institutional developments in the area of cultural management at the Ministry of Justice. With the creation of the DIP, Justice relinquished much of the day-to-day responsibilities of cultural management formerly performed by the DPDC and turned its attentions to the suppression of political and cultural subversion through an institutional apparatus of systematic surveillance, justice, and incarceration. As Justice restricted its presence in the cultural arena, the DIP greatly expanded the federal government's role in the cultural arena in the areas of mass media, cultural expression, propaganda, and civic culture.

Organized into five divisions (propaganda, cinema and theater, radio, tourism, and press), the DIP centralized the propaganda, publicity, and public relations activities of *all* federal agencies and assumed control of all state censorship of the press, cinema, radio, and theater. Lourival Fontes accompanied the DNP's reorganization into the DIP, becoming general director.[47] The DIP performed a wide array of services in both promoting Vargas and the Estado Novo regime and censoring their detractors. By 1941, the agency exerted influence in nearly all aspects of cultural production and political discourse, including film (through its newsreel series, *Cine Jornal Brasileiro,* and a handful of film shorts), radio (through the nightly program, *Hora do Brasil*), publishing (through press releases and press censorship, as well as the publication of numerous monographs, pamphlets, and journals, including *Cultura Política* and *Estudos e Conferências*), and civic culture.

Similar to the Ministry of Education, the DIP placed itself at the center of Brazil's cultural intelligentsia by securing the occasional-to-permanent collaboration of a wide range of intellectuals, social scientists, and novelists, including Cassiano Ricardo, Almir de Andrade, Azevedo Amaral, Gilberto Freyre, and even Graciliano Ramos. By late 1940, the activities of the federal DIP, housed in the headquarters of the disbanded national Congress, were extended to the state level through a series of state-level DIPs.[48] In these various capacities, the DIP performed many of the most important functions of *estadonovista* public administration.

Although the DIP's propagandistic intentions were never hidden, its cultural interventions was emblematic of the way in which an authoritarian state could use cultural management as a cover for a political crackdown on potential threats to the regime. The DIP's *Cine Jornal Brasileiro* was an exemplary cultural artifact that blended repressive political and cultural messages into an attractive product readily available through the mass media. The *Cine Jornal* first appeared following the institution of the Estado Novo, when the Departamento Nacional de Propaganda began to raise dramatically the production values of state-sponsored film and propaganda.[49] The DNP initially contracted out its filmmaking activities to a private interest, Cinédia, for the production of the first 127 editions of the *Cine Jornal*. When the DIP assumed the DNP's cultural apparatus in December 1939, it began to contract its own cameramen, many of them lured away from Cinédia, and production facilities to produce, direct, film, and distribute the newsreel. By 1940, the DIP assumed total directorial and artistic control of the first newsreel to be regularly produced and distributed in Brazil by Brazilian media interests.[50] (The fact that this innovative media actor was also a government entity reveals much about the forces that expanded the Brazilian cultural market during the crucial years between 1930 and 1945.) The importance of the *Cine Jornal* is underscored by the fact that the DIP's film releases comprised the largest percentage of domestically produced films released in the Brazilian market at a time when domestic production averaged just 7.6 feature-length films per year, whereas foreign-produced releases of the same category averaged nearly four hundred.[51] Even in the face of persistent problems with distribution and audience disinterest in the newsreels, the DIP strove to bridge the major disparities between Brazilian and foreign interests in the national film market.[52]

The *Cine Jornal* offered carefully crafted, optimistic visions of Brazil and its progress under Vargas rule. The newsreels glossed over the details of

Vargas-era public policy, letting seductive images and orchestration develop the visual texture of state-sponsored political culture. These newsreels were important venues through which culture managers showed to Brazil's movie-going audiences that their nation was indeed in the throes of dynamic political and administrative modernization, economic diversification, and cultural renewal. The newsreels imagined the fruits of modernization without a hint of conflict within the state or in society. Compulsory screenings certainly helped to guarantee that movie-goers were exposed to an imagined Brazil that contained no conflict, no misery, no setbacks, and no culture wars, even if this was a fiction of a repressive regime.[53]

Those Brazilians interested in the contested invention of brasilidade under the Estado Novo need not have looked farther than the regime itself, where the content of radio programming was a topic of endless debate. In the debate over the content and meaning of radio programming, the federal state weighed in heavily, trying to regulate private radio markets through broadcasting licenses, regulations of commercial advertising, and programming quotas. At stake was the state's ability to manage Brazilian culture through a medium dominated by the private market, the emergent culture industries, and popular culture. The state proved itself to be quite capable in managing certain aspects of radio programming, especially through the manipulative use of laws granting the federal government regulatory powers over broadcasting concessions. Managing content and cultural reception proved much more difficult, because private commercial interests and popular tastes consistently outwitted federal interventions.

The preponderance of musical programming on commercial radio was not, in and of itself, cause for worry among state culture managers. It was the type of music most commonly heard that bothered cultural managers at the Ministry of Education and the Department of Press and Propaganda. Samba and other musical forms born in the bohemian demimonde and impoverished shantytowns of Rio de Janeiro were especially worrisome for state culture managers, who made every effort to transform samba, often maligned for its glorification of the *malandro* (rogue) and use of pulsating sensual rhythms, into musical compositions which extolled the virtues of hard work, moral rectitude, and patriotism. In 1941, Martins Castelo, the DIP's semiregular radio critic, reaffirmed the mandate to "prohibit the release of compositions which employ slang corrosive to the national language and present insipid elegies to *malandragem* [rougery]."[54] In practice, the DIP took a more pragmatic attitude to samba looking to the genre as a vehicle for conveying the message of social and moral uplift. Álvaro Salgado, music critic for the DIP, stated, "Although we find it intolerable that there exist street children prone to all types of mischief, we do not eliminate them from society; we ask for schools for them. What the samba, *marchinha, maxixe, embolada,* and *frevo* need are schools." [55]

Several studies on popular music have demonstrated how the DIP, hoping to "educate" samba, called upon well-known musicians and lyricists to compose samba lyrics that praised the Estado Novo or Vargas for the bounty of gifts that they had bestowed upon the nation. [56] When these compositions hit the airwaves, they helped popularize and commercialize hyperpatriotic lyrics that complemented the Vargas regime's goals of civic renewal and social uplift. With titles such as *Glórias do Brasil!* (Glories of Brazil!), *Salve 19 de Abril!* (Long live April 19! [Vargas's birthday]), and *É Negócio Casar* (It's time to get married), the ideological message for these state-sponsored sambas was not difficult to understand. [57]

Yet, the Vargas regime could never effectively appropriate samba as it had hoped. As a musical genre and social signifier, samba remained a vehicle for resistance to state intervention into cultural production and commercialization. It remained a vehicle for resisting the official versions of renewal. Subverting the DIP's "suggestion" that samba composers desist from glorifying the bohemian life, *sambistas* continued to use popular music to glorify malandragem. Commercial radio stations continued to broadcast all but the most subversive compositions. In the street, state regulations proved largely irrelevant, as lyrics to state-commissioned sambas were subverted by alternative stanzas glorifying malandragem and other symbols of social deviancy. Popular composers who fell outside of the state-regulated cultural industries enjoyed the freedom to make up whatever lyrics they chose.

The state proved equally hapless in its bid to act as mediator in a bitter war over samba fought not by state culture managers, but by sambistas themselves. Bryan McCann demonstrates that throughout the 1930s, sambistas from Rio's lower-middle and working-class white and mixed-race neighborhoods clashed with sambistas from the hillside shantytowns, overwhelmingly populated by Afro-Brazilians. At stake was the control of a musical genre that was increasingly associated with nationality, yet maintained a strong social and political association with marginality. The national character of samba and the sambista, be he a shady malandro or an "honorable" musician, was a leitmotif of these debates.[58] The DIP tried to influence these debates, coaxing musicians to treat samba as a tool for collective social uplift, rather than internal division. Samba did, in the end, attain highly nationalistic overtones. But the tensions between the various practitioners of samba and the contested meanings of samba endured, largely immune to state intervention.

Direct government programming also faced its own problems. The government's nightly radio program first produced in 1931, *Hora do Brasil*, held the potential to have an immense impact on Brazilian culture. Highly doctrinaire authoritarian speeches accompanied apolitical reports on education, commerce, industrial production, and cultural events. Musical programming ran from doggedly nationalistic compositions to broadcasts of symphonic and popular music of Brazilian and foreign composers. The *Hora do Brasil*'s news programming, supplied by press releases from the Agência Nacional, covered a wide range of stories about national and international events.[59] Federal law guaranteed that the *Hora do Brasil* enjoyed broad market exposure by requiring that all licensed radio stations transmit the program at 8:00 P.M. No private radio interest enjoyed a similar 100 percent market share during prime-time evening hours. The DIP also took advantage of the proliferation of loudspeakers in major public squares to mandate the public, open-air broadcast of the *Hora do Brasil* and other recorded programming. The loudspeakers, in conjunction with the rapid rise in the number of radio receivers, ensured that the DIP's radio programming had a broad cultural and political reach within public and private spheres.[60]

Despite the wide market penetration, unpublished and anecdotal evidence strongly indicates that the *Hora do Brasil* was largely a failure. Broadcasters in São Paulo initially refused to retransmit the program, silencing the airwaves during the time allotted for compulsory broadcasts. Radio listeners turned off their radios. Vargas himself was informed by a rather honest civil servant that the *Hora do Brasil* should, in fact, be named the *Hora da Fala Sozinho* (The hour that talks to itself).[61]

Educational radio faced similarly disappointing audience appeal. Rádio MES reached thousands, perhaps tens of thousands, of residents of Rio and beyond without access to public education. The station's programming introduced radio audiences to educational programming, classical music, and news reporting that was unavailable on commercial airwaves. By the end of the Estado Novo, Rádio MES included programming featuring regional and folkloric music, which the service's director described as working to elevate the level of Brazilian popular music as a counterbalance to the purported low level of commercial radio programming.[62] The Serviço de Radiodifusão Educativa still could not reach the audiences imagined by Edgard Roquette-Pinto and Capanema. Educational radio of the 1930s and 1940s, like amateur radio in the 1920s, was more curiosity than cultural carrier.

Fernando Tude de Souza, a well-established journalist who directed the SRE after the service gained administrative autonomy in 1943, laid much of the blame for the agency's disappointments on the constant administrative fighting with the DIP. In the annual report submitted to Capanema in early 1945, Souza complained that a competitive environment that pitted the DIP's Radio Division against the SRE, and pitted both agencies against a commercial radio market uninterested in educational radio, undermined the successes of educational radio in a nation so desperately in need of basic education. After proudly informing Capanema that the SRE never lost control of its radio transmitter to the Ministry of Justice or the DIP, Souza bitterly recounted how judicial and police authorities, rather than educators, set the guidelines for radio promotion and censorship. Souza specifically lambasted the DIP for trying to control what could *not* be said on radio, while the SRE was trying to direct what could and should be said. With echoes of earlier *censura policial* (police censorship) versus *censura cultural* (cultural censorship) debates that framed federal management of commercial cinema in the early 1930s, Souza complained that the agents of order ultimately held more sway than educators in the field of radio broadcasting.[63] According to Souza, radio's potential to educate simultaneously tens of thousands of Brazilians, many with marginal literacy, residing throughout a nation of continental proportions had been squandered on political infighting. Souza was saddened to note that the state had proven to be its own worst enemy in combating the overcommercialization of the mass media.[64] In this formulation, the state had lost the fight for brasilidade.

The Late Estado Novo and Beyond

A key component of state cultural management collapsed on 22 February 1945, when the Rio daily *Correio da Manhã* published an interview with José Américo de Almeida in which the former presidential candidate openly questioned the legitimacy of the Constitution of 1937. Without public explanation, the DIP declined to retaliate against the newspaper. This interview marked the DIP's weakening position vis-à-vis the press and the regime's strong-arm posturing vis-à-vis civil society. As the DIP faced eroding control over the press, it lost legitimacy across a broad spectrum of cultural and political initiatives. By March 1945, Vargas announced that the DIP would be reorganized as an "instrument of the promotion of Brazilian culture," signaling the end of the agency's control over the press. Two months later, the DIP was reorganized into the Departamento Nacional de Informações (National Information Department, DNI).[65] Subordinate to the Ministry of Justice, the DNI was charged with such nonpolitical activities as promoting Brazilian tourism. The creation of the DNI marked the legal end of institutional censorship and political propaganda, and thus began the gradual de-institutionalization of certain avenues of cultural management.

The demise of the DIP was a clear precursor to the demise of the Estado Novo. When the various components of the authoritarian state apparatus gave out, the entire regime fell soon after. A bloodless military coup deposed Vargas on 29 October 1945. The dictator quickly left Rio, heading to his ranch in Rio Grande do Sul. Vargas's closest advisors, including his longtime minister of education, Gustavo Capanema, also left government service.

Of course, the fall of the Estado Novo and the departure of the regime's top elite did not entirely do away with the state apparatus built since 1930. This was particularly true for the agencies of cultural management subordinate to the Ministry of Education, all of which survived the regime transition unscathed. Many of the directors enlisted to build the federal government's cultural apparatus retained their positions. All post–Estado Novo constitutions have mandated that the state protect and promote culture, authorizing the state to maintain institutions of cultural management. Cultural management, virtually unknown at the federal level before 1930, is now a fully recognized area of public policy, thanks to the Vargas regime.

In 1953, the word "culture" would be added to the highest levels of federal bureaucratic nomenclature when the Ministry of Education and Health was split into the Ministry of Education and Culture and the Ministry of Health in 1953. Capanema's 1935 hope that the state would formally embrace cultural management had been fulfilled. The culture wars generated by this embrace in the areas of historical preservation, museum management, and expositions are the subject of the following three chapters.

4

"The Identity Documents of the Brazilian Nation"

THE NATIONAL HISTORICAL AND ARTISTIC PATRIMONY

The authoritarian Estado Novo (1937–1945) was coterminous with the legal and administrative invention of *patrimônio*.[1] When Vargas launched a coup against President Washington Luiz in October 1930, preservation was wholly outside the purview of federal law. Seven years later, Vargas promulgated a decree-law instituting one of the world's most advanced preservationist codes. By the close of the Estado Novo, federal law protected an exemplary collection of cultural treasures, collectively known as the "national historical and artistic patrimony." Nearly half of *all* entries into Brazil's official registry of national heritage, the *Livros do Tombo*, were completed before 1945.[2] The Vargas regime was extremely proud to present itself as a defender of a set of structures and objects that Brazil's most prominent preservationist called "the identity documents of the Brazilian nation."[3]

The history of preservation in Brazil has attracted critical attention since the 1980s, when the Serviço do Patrimônio Histórico e Artístico Nacional (SPHAN) began to write its institutional memory. Highly sympathetic to the accomplishments of the agency's founding director, mineiro Rodrigo Melo Franco de Andrade, the SPHAN's early autobiographies characterized federal preservation under "Dr. Rodrigo" as a *fase heróica* (heroic phase).[4] These same studies described the period subsequent to Andrade's departure from federal service in 1967 as a time of stagnation and decline. Various plans to reform federal preservation policies were predicated, in part, upon a revaluation of the accomplishments of the heroic past. In these readings of the history of preservation, the connection between the SPHAN and the Estado Novo is understood as incidental. The origins of historic preservation, as this story goes, have to be set apart from the history of the authoritarian-nationalist Vargas state.

Alternative readings of the history of preservation, also appearing in the

1980s, present a less nostalgic understanding of the so-called heroic phase. Those critical of early preservation efforts charged that the elitist, Euro-centric politics of preservation associated with Andrade's tenure were ill suited to a nation of tremendous socio-economic and ethnic diversity. A team of ethnographers, anthropologists, and graphic designers associated with the Centro Nacional de Referência Cultural and the Fundação Pró-Memória, two federal organs that rivaled the SPHAN in the late 1970s and early 1980s, were especially critical of the SPHAN's history of elitism. These reformers advocated a break with the aesthetic values and administrative policies institutionalized during the Estado Novo. Elsewhere, the SPHAN's sharpest critics placed the agency squarely within the authoritarian main-stream of the Estado Novo, while moderates within the SPHAN conceded that the systematic identification and legal protection of the nation's core collection of cultural treasures did indeed correspond with the most au-thoritarian phase of the Vargas era.[5] In the face of their critics, defenders of the fase heróica idea continued to assign the success of early preservation efforts to a group of left-of-center intellectuals, architects, and historians who worked under an authoritarian state, yet never supported it.[6]

Against this backdrop of interpretative disagreements, a history of the "heroic phase" of patrimônio histórico e artístico nacional becomes the per-fect vehicle for unlocking the conflicted history of cultural management during the first Vargas regime. In this history, civil servants, intellectu-als, architects, private property holders, antiquarians, municipal interests, and everyday citizens who live in or near historic structures fight over the moral, aesthetic, economic, and administrative meaning of preservation. They fight over state resources. They fight over the law. They fight over the memory sites upon which the Brazilian nation could be ritualized.[7] Ultimately, they fight for brasilidade itself.

The Revolution of 1930 and National "Monuments"

Historical preservation in Brazil was not invented ex nihilo in 1930. In the early years of the republic, a select number of intellectuals, architects, historical associations, and art historians made intermittent calls on the federal government to institute an official policy of preservation.[8] These calls largely went unanswered, but they did establish a certain baseline for preservationist movement that came out of the Revolution of 1930. Of the handful of preservationist initiatives undertaken by the federal government before 1934, the most important prevented the destruction of two eighteenth-century residential structures once occupied by the principals of the Inconfidência Mineira of 1789.[9] This was clearly an isolated event, as other historical properties were ripped down in the name of progress. Federal inattention to historical preservation changed little when the First Republic fell in 1930. If anything, the prospects for federal intervention into historical preservation diminished as the Vargas regime closed the Congress and suspended all pending legislation, including a legislative bill submitted by the Bahian deputy José Wanderley de Araújo Pinho, which outlined a policy of federal preservation. At the same time, Gustavo Barroso and José Mariano, two of the most prominent preservationists of the 1920s and 1930s, found themselves alienated from the new minister of education, Francisco Campos, and his chief of staff, Rodrigo Melo Franco de Andrade. It was entirely possible that the Revolution of 1930 might not have revolutionized historical preservation.

In spite of the inauspicious beginnings, the Vargas regime turned toward preservation as a means to institutionalize and nationalize the revolution. One motivating factor was ideological, because the ascendance of a preservationist spirit was fueled by the regime's attack on liberalism. As the logic of conservative regime ideologues went, liberalism had been ill-suited for Brazilian republicanism, leading to the rule of corrupt oligarchies over a culturally disenfranchised citizenry. In abolishing federalism, electoral politics, and the elevation of the individual over the collective, ideologues read the revolution as a corrective to the misguided policies of the Old Republic. In time, they also targeted a multitude of policies associated with liberalism, including the refusal to devote public funds toward protecting national patrimony. Preservation presented the Vargas regime with an opportunity to distinguish itself from the Old Republic on programmatic as well as ideological grounds.

The first major step toward institutionalizing preservation came in 1933, when prominent political figures from the state of Minas Gerais, including Minister of Education Washington Pires, persuaded Vargas to designate the town of Ouro Preto as a national monument. Formerly known as Vila Rica, Ouro Preto had been founded in 1698 by *bandeirantes* (trailblazers) who had struck out from São Paulo in search of Indian slaves and inadvertently discovered fluvial gold deposits. The discovery of gold in the mountains and streams surrounding Ouro Preto (literally, black gold) sparked a

fevered gold rush, which brought tens of thousands of Portuguese pros-
pectors, enslaved Africans, and free people of color into the provinces of
Minas Gerais and Goiás. In 1720, Vila Rica became capital of the *capitania*
of Minas Gerais, a testament to the town's importance in a mining boom
that peaked at midcentury. In 1789, with gold mining on the decline and
royal taxation on the rise, an antiregalist conspiracy was hatched in Ouro
Preto. The plot to declare an independent republic was betrayed by one
of the conspirators, soon known as *inconfidentes*.[10] The purported leader of
the Inconfidência Mineira, Joaquim José da Silva Xavier (1746–1792), more
popularly known as Tiradentes (tooth-puller), was captured, tried, and bru-
tally executed, while his co-conspirators were sent into exile. The martyrdom of Tiradentes sealed Ouro Preto's claims to the triumph and tragedy
of Brazil's Age of Gold.

By the final decade of the eighteenth century, when the gold boom had
ended and the Crown had reestablished imperial authority, Vila Rica remained a vibrant city where the daily interactions of slaves born in Africa
and the New World, free people of color, poor European immigrants, regular and secular clergy, confraternities, royal officials, a large artisanal class,
and wealthy miners and merchants created a rich and complex social structure. The level of cultural achievement in Vila Rica was especially notable,
marked by some of the finest examples of sacred art and architecture, civil
construction, and musical composition in the Americas. Sadly, though, the
end of the gold cycle put Ouro Preto on a path of economic decline.

With the transfer of the state capital to Belo Horizonte in 1896 and the
shift in economic growth toward the southeastern regions of the state, the
pace of decline increased. Population loss was a symptom of economic dis-
tress, with the municipal population dropping from 51,136 residents in 1920
to 27,890 in 1940.[11] The local agricultural economy was stagnant and the
post–1950 mining and historical tourism booms that would return prosperity to the region were still decades off. Eighteenth-century Ouro Preto
remained an important city in the national civic imaginary. The Inconfidência Mineira and Tiradentes, the "Protomartyr of Independence," afforded
the town a privileged place in the national memory. However, the Ouro
Preto of the twentieth century suffered from a weak economic base, de-
population, crippling social underdevelopment, and extensive infrastructural decay.

Until 1933, Ouro Preto would have been an unlikely candidate for the
term *"monumento."* Under the Second Reign and First Republic, the cen-

16 Panorama of Ouro Preto, Minas Gerais, *c.* 1940. Taken for *A Obra Getuliana,* an unpublished photographic essay on the achievements of the Estado Novo regime, this photo captures the artistic and architectural legacy of the eighteenth-century Age of Gold. Courtesy of CPDOC-GC.

tral government had periodically underwritten the cost of erecting commemorative statues, plaques, and markers to honor leaders of state, military battles, and combat heroes in public squares, border areas, and military zones. The *Monument to Dom Pedro I* (1862), built in Rio's Praça Tiradentes (then known as the Praça da Constituição), perhaps best exemplified the use of commemorative monuments for the greater glory of the Nation. Yet the request to designate Ouro Preto as a national monument stretched the meaning of the monumento well beyond monumental statues to include historic urban centers that had not been built to commemorate anything or anyone. In making his case to Vargas, Minister Pires argued that by designating Ouro Preto as a national monument, the Provisional Government would be defending Brazil's unique national identity, on the one hand, and participating in the larger civilized world, on the other. Citing preservationist legislation passed in France, Germany, and the United States, Pires envisioned Ouro Preto as a center for the study of "our antiquities." [12] Here, one sees how the state combined a language of internationalism with the search for a Brazilian locale in which to invest a national identity with an ancient pedigree stretching back into time immemorial. Vargas accepted this rationale, approving Pires's request by executive decree on 12 July 1933.

The decree was foundational for the imaginary of a national community called Brazil, giving a country of continental proportions and immense regional and ethnic difference its first "national" monument. Even if residents of German immigrant communities in the south and *caboclo* rubber tappers in the Amazon Basin had no knowledge of one another, and even if the historical events, architectural styles, and political values associated with Ouro Preto were specific to eighteenth-century Minas, the new national monument provided all Brazilians with the raw materials to imagine a historical and artistic community greater than the sum of its parts. Federal preservationist policies would soon promote Ouro Preto's secular and sacred art and architecture as the preeminent markers of Brazilianness, to be celebrated by all Brazilians and valued by foreigners.

In the short run, the decree designating Ouro Preto as a national monument was more symbol than substance. The municipal government of Ouro Preto had hoped that the decree would boost tourism, only to discover that inferior accommodations, poor road conditions, and lack of habit made historical tourism into the interior unattractive to all but the most adventurous. Decree 22.298 made no provisions for any special federal subsidies, leaving the municipal and state governments to shoulder the costs of maintaining and restoring the town's decaying churches, bridges, fountains, and civil constructions. Unlike Williamsburg, Virginia, another early American town that underwent significant restoration in the interwar years, Ouro Preto had no Brazilian Rockefellers to underwrite preservation. Apathy was another challenge, as the notion of a national monument resonated weakly outside Minas and the federal capital. But change was afoot. The Provisional Government pushed aside the political culture of federalism that had guided federal lawmaking during the Old Republic to create a national cultural imaginary inflected through historic Minas.

If Decree 22.298 initiated a shift in federal law by authorizing protectionist provisions that would have been nearly unthinkable under the liberal Constitution of 1891, article 148 of the Constitution of 1934 further expanded state powers of preservation, mandating federal, state, and municipal incentives for the "sciences, arts, letters, and culture in general, [as well as] the protection of objects of historical interest and the artistic patrimony of the country." The authoritarian constitution of the Estado Novo, promulgated 10 November 1937, would go much further, stating "historical, artistic, and natural monuments, including open areas and locales especially blessed by Nature, fall under the protection and the special care of the Federal, State, and Municipal governments," adding "any attacks against such monuments will be considered attacks against the national patrimony." Patrimony quickly became an official charge of the state, influencing the scope of federal powers, federal-local relations, and criminal law.[13] The promulgation of Decree-Law 25, on 30 November 1937, further consolidated this intimate relationship between the state, preservationist law, and civil society.

Administrative innovations closely accompanied changes in the law. The call for an institutionalized approach toward historical patrimony began during the Provisional Government, when Rodolfo Garcia, the director of the MHN during Gustavo Barroso's forced absence, proposed to the minister of education that the federal government create a federal agency to "inspect, restore, and inventory the monuments which extend throughout the country and attest to our national evolution and the spread of civilization in Brazil."[14] Upon his return to federal employment, Barroso endorsed Garcia's proposal for the creation of a federal agency to catalog and restore historically significant sites. On 14 July 1934, Vargas authorized the creation of the Inspetoria dos Monumentos Nacionais (National Monuments Inspection Service, IMN), which answered to the Museu Histórico. Once confined to a patchwork of public statuary and history painting, "monuments" assumed a status worthy of routine administration.

Barroso immediately set his sights upon Ouro Preto. There, the MHN director enlisted the technical assistance of Epaminondas Macedo, a graduate of Ouro Preto's well-known School of Mines who had remained in Minas as an engineer for the Post and Telegraph Service, to coordinate restoration activities. Working with a two-year budget of 200 contos (approximately US$17,000),[15] Macedo made contact with the municipal government, ecclesiastic officials, local preservationists, and local artisans to stem the deterioration of the town's religious and civil constructions.[16]

As restoration work progressed, photographic and textual descriptions of Ouro Preto under scaffolds began to appear in the national and regional press, creating the visual iconography of the Golden Age brought back to life. Old, decrepit structures located in remote towns quickly took on the aura of holy sites that all good Brazilians should visit, at least in their imaginations. It may seem ironic that the restorations in Ouro Preto initially failed to attract much interest among the town's residents, yet this is consistent with the idea that Ouro Preto was being saved for the nation, not the locality. The surviving documentation strongly suggests that the locals employed as artisans and manual laborers were some of the few residents who initially expressed a vested interest in preservation. The limited social and ideological impact of early preservation does not diminish the fact that preservation helped link the local to the national and vice versa. Márcia Chuva's recent study of the SPHAN provides an excellent analysis of the way in which restoration created strong social and economic linkages between culture managers in Rio, their regional agents, the local civil and ecclesiastical elite, and a local network of artisans and laborers who carried with them the memory of construction techniques and materials that had fallen into disuse.[17] Implanted on a provisional basis in Ouro Preto, this network would rapidly spread after 1936, when Mário de Andrade laid the discursive and administrative groundwork for nationalizing the politics of preservation and restoration.

Legalizing Patrimony: The SPHAN and Decree-Law 25

Decree-Law 25, promulgated 30 November 1937, legally transformed the "national monuments" managed by the Inspetoria dos Monumentos Na-

17 Chafariz do Passo de Antônio Dias in Ruins, Ouro
Preto, December 1935. Courtesy of CPDOC-GC.

cionais into the "national historical and artistic patrimony." More than sixty
years after its promulgation, the decree remains the central legal text in
what is now commonly called "cultural patrimony," or simply, *patrimônio*.

   The definition of the national historical and artistic patrimony codified in Decree-Law 25 originated in early 1936, just as Ouro Preto's major
churches and fountains were obscured by scaffolding. Gustavo Capanema
sought out Mário de Andrade, then serving as the director of the Department of Culture and Recreation of the city of São Paulo, to draft an *anteprojeto* (preliminary study) for a federal agency responsible for the classification, protection, and administration of Brazil's historical and artistic

18   Restoration of Chafariz do Passo de Antônio Dias, early 1936. The Inspetoria dos Monumentos Nacionais and the Serviço do Patrimônio Histórico e Artístico Nacional popularized images such as these to document the achievements of federal preservation. As figure 18 suggests, federal preservation efforts would be impossible without the collaboration of local artisans. Courtesy of CPDOC-GC.

heritage. Capanema's choice of Andrade is highly suggestive of the minister's close ties to the principals of modernismo, as well as Capanema's deep suspicions of Gustavo Barroso, a vocal preservationist who had assumed a prominent role in the protofascist Integralist movement. By entrusting the anteprojeto to Andrade, Capanema guaranteed that Barroso and other conservative traditionalists would have little influence in the design of a future government agency that would replace the IMN.

Andrade submitted his proposal for the Serviço do Patrimônio Artístico Nacional on 24 March 1936. In the proposal, the national artistic patrimony was defined to be "all works of pure and applied arts; popular or erudite art; art produced by nationals and foreigners; and, art owned by public entities, independent organizations, private individuals, and foreigners residing in Brazil."[18] Asked not merely to define the national patrimony but also to devise the mechanisms through which patrimonial art would be formally recognized and administered, Andrade's proposal stipulated, "The National Artistic Patrimony will include only those objects of art which have been inscribed, by single or group entry, into one of the four *Livros do Tombo.*" These four registries—dedicated to archaeology and ethnography, history, fine arts, and applied arts—were to be the perpetual record of patrimonial art, documenting the physical characteristics and artistic significance of objects of art deemed to be of national importance. Each of the four registries was to correspond, in turn, to four national museums that would display a copy of the *Livro do Tombo* as well as representative samples of the items inscribed into the book.[19] Andrade hoped that the comprehensive study of every artistic object, historic site, and cultural practice in Brazil necessary to fill the *Livros do Tombo* and national museums would take no more than five years, at the cost of 10,000 contos (approximately US$850,000). The project was immensely ambitious.

In April 1936, Capanema secured Vargas's approval for the preliminary organization of a new federal agency called the Serviço do Patrimônio Histórico e Artístico Nacional. Capanema nominated Rodrigo Melo Franco de Andrade, a lawyer from the state of Minas Gerais who had served as chief of staff to the first minister of education, Francisco Campos, to head the service. Capanema and "Dr. Rodrigo" immediately set out to transform Mário de Andrade's anteprojeto into legislation that would guarantee legal recognition for the new service and its preservationist activities. In drafting the revisions, the two mineiros drew upon Brazil's thin legal history of preservation as well as preservationist legislation passed in other countries.

In the bill readied for congressional approval, the SPAN described in Mário de Andrade's anteprojeto had been renamed the SPHAN (Serviço do Patrimônio Histórico e Artístico Nacional). Capanema justified the name change to Vargas, arguing that the SPAN's responsibilities had been too narrowly defined. Stating that the SPHAN would be responsible for "historical patrimony, artistic or otherwise," Capanema argued that historical patrimony and artistic patrimony were inseparable.[20] The federal government would still be responsible for protecting and administering cultural patrimony. However, a more historical understanding of patrimony replaced Mário de Andrade's ethnographic definition of the nation's cultural treasures. The legislation sent before Congress had dropped Andrade's interest in cataloguing popular culture.

Andrade accepted the changes to his original proposal without protest. The poet had previously advised Rodrigo Melo Franco de Andrade, "I already knew that every part of the anteprojeto would not be accepted . . . feel free to make and unmake, modify, and make concessions to circumstances. . . . I am not so stubborn or vain as to believe that the things I create are perfect. Never fear that changes or accommodations to my anteprojeto will offend me." [21] It is still plausible that Mário de Andrade was disappointed to see that the definition of patrimony had shifted decisively away from an ecumenical understanding of cultural expression toward a more refined, technical understanding of cultural production consistent with Capanema's vision of culture. Andrade's ethnographic interests would survive in the nascent folklorist movement. However, the folklorists had little luck gaining state support until the second Vargas regime (1951–1954).[22] It would take another two and a half decades before Aloíso Magalhães and the members of the Centro Nacional de Referência Cultural could successfully convince the SPHAN to embrace Andrade's broad vision for cultural protection.[23] During the first Vargas regime, cultural patrimony would be synonymous with high art.

Vargas forwarded the Capanema-Andrade text to the Chamber of Deputies for consideration in October 1936. Perhaps the greatest difference between the anteprojeto and the bill presented to Congress was the latter's legalisms. *Tombamento* (registration in a *Livro do Tombo*) passed from an act of aesthetic consecration to a technical designation regulated by law. The shift was understandable: historical preservation had many legal ramifications that likely meant little to a modernist poet. However, the shift was also indicative of the way in which patrimony was inserted into the legalist-statist politics of cultural management in the months preceding the declaration of the Estado Novo. The proclamation of the authoritarian regime would provide an added impetus for the close association between state politics and the legalization/regimentation of cultural renewal.

As the revised bill made its way before Congress, the SPHAN operated on a semiprovisional basis. Legal recognition for the agency came during the

January 1937 reorganization of the Ministry of Education, but the service could not proceed with tombamentos without a special act of Congress. Just as final legislative approval seemed assured, the golpe de estado of 10 November 1937 closed the legislature and suspended all pending legislation, leaving the agency without a legal mandate to register and administer patrimonial goods. Capanema intervened, petitioning Vargas to formalize the legal basis of tombamento through executive order. On November 30, twenty days after the coup, Vargas invoked the powers of decree-law authorized by the authoritarian Constitution of 1937 and issued Decree-Law 25 to "organize the protection of the national artistic and historical patrimony."

Decree-Law 25 opened with the statement: "The national historical and artistic patrimony is comprised of the totality of the material goods and real estate [bens móveis e imóveis] existent in the country whose preservation is found to be in the public interest, either by their association with the memorable facts of Brazilian history or by their exceptional archaeological, bibliographic, ethnographic, or artistic value," adding "also subject to tombamento are natural monuments, open spaces, and landscapes made worthy of conservation and preservation by a gift of Nature or human industry." Like Andrade's anteprojeto, Decree-Law 25 stipulated that only those goods inscribed into one of the four Livros do Tombo were to be officially considered part of the national artistic and historical patrimony. But in a departure from Mário de Andrade's anteprojeto, Decree-Law 25 included a lengthy discussion of the legal nature of tombamento, including the distinction between voluntary and compulsory tombamento, the rights and responsibilities of the owner of a tombado (registered) good, and the penalties for attacks on the national artistic and historical patrimony. Decree-Law 25 anticipated that the creation of a patrimonial canon would generate a clash of interests to be proscribed, regulated, and adjudicated by law.

In regard to the question of managing cultural patrimony after the promulgation of Decree-Law 25, a few important dimensions of the law's history help frame the entire discussion at hand. First and foremost, Decree-Law 25, and the entire category of historical and artistic patrimony, must be understood as legal constructs. Heritage may be described in spiritual and patriotic terms, theoretically open to any and all who might celebrate the past, but it is law that turns old structures into patrimony. Controlling the laws of patrimony became tantamount to controlling patrimony itself. Closely tied to the legal aspect of patrimony was the administrative process that canonized patrimonial goods. Mário de Andrade had dedicated a considerable amount of attention to defining patrimony and little to its actual administration. By contrast, Decree-Law 25 devotes just four articles to the actual definition of patrimony, while the administrative procedures of tombamento are detailed in nineteen articles. The Estado Novo's ascendant culture of legalism and statism would be fundamental to the administration of patrimony.

The historical conditions under which Decree-Law 25 came into being indicate why patrimony must be understood in its political context. The law was initially drafted at the request of a young minister of education looking to expand the powers of a federal ministry interested in administering culture. The legislative bill sent before Congress was the brainchild of modernists and their allies eager to stake out institutional territory against challenges from cultural conservatives. The decree actually came into existence by an executive act made possible by the coup of 10 November. While the early proposals to create a federal preservationist agency received some public scrutiny, the actual preservationist law issued by Vargas was a unilateral executive decision made possible by the political powers of decree-law granted to the president by the Constitution of 1937. Decree-Law 25 is a political and cultural by-product of the Estado Novo, and the political culture of patrimony engendered by Decree-Law 25 would be highly reflective of the Estado Novo.

Inventing a Patrimonial Canon

The incipient patrimonial canon made possible by Decree-Law 25 had some distinct taxonomic biases. Religious structures, government buildings, military fortifications, and civil works built in the seventeenth and eighteenth centuries dominated the list of sites considered for tombamento. There was a strong regional bias as well, with 85 percent of the 236 tombamentos made in 1938 located in the Federal District (82), Bahia (55), Pernambuco (37), and Minas Gerais (26). The most significant inscriptions made in 1938 protected the urban centers (*conjunto arquitectônico e urbanístico*) of six historic cities in Minas, including Ouro Preto (1940 *município* population: 27,890), São João del Rey (45,335), and Diamantina (49,540) (see table 4). Measures of this type were unprecedented, turning entire urban centers into federal protectorates. The broader regional bias toward the

Table 4   *Tombamentos* by State, 1938–1945

	1938	1939	1940	1941	1942	1943	1944	1945	TOTAL
Alagoas				1					1
Amazonas									0
Bahia	55	6	1	25	2	25	3		117
Ceará				1					1
Espírito Santo		1				3			4
Goiás				1					1
Maranhão			3						3
Mato Grosso									0
Minas Gerais	26	32	1	3			1	2	65
Pará		1		5	1		1		8
Paraíba	11			2			1		14
Paraná	6		1	2					9
Pernambuco	37	2	1						40
Piauí	2	2	2						6
Rio de Janeiro	82	2	3		3	1	1		92
Rio Grande do Norte									0
Rio Grande do Sul	8		1	2	1				12
Santa Catarina	4	1							5
São Paulo	4	1	4	6		1	1		17
Sergipe				1		17	3		21
TOTAL	235	46	19	49	7	47	11	2	416

Note: Rio de Janeiro includes the Federal District and state of Rio de Janeiro.
Source: *Bens móveis e imóveis nos Livros do Tombo do Instituto do Patrimônio Histórico e Artístico Nacional,* 4th ed. (Rio de Janeiro: Ministério da Cultura, Instituto do Patrimônio Histórico e Artístico Nacional, 1994), 247.

colonial sugar belt, the mining zone of Minas Gerais, and the city of Rio de Janeiro would continue for several decades.

If the geographic scope of patrimony was confined to a few privileged regions, the aesthetics of patrimony were explicitly nationalist. In 1936, when the SPHAN was still operating on an "experimental" basis, Rodrigo Melo Franco de Andrade stated, "In nations with a more developed artistic patrimony, every day one hears more calls for the primitive or exotic art of other peoples. But, above all else, what are most important in every nation are the monuments which characterize that nation's art and history. The poetry of a Brazilian church of the colonial period is, for us, more moving than the Parthenon. And any statue that Aleijadinho carved into soapstone

19 Missão São Miguel, Santo Ângelo, Rio Grande do Sul, *c.* 1940. The eighteenth-century Jesuit-Guaraní mission at São Miguel was one of the first tombado structures to be surveyed and restored by the SPHAN. Modernist architect and SPHAN collaborator Lucio Costa played an instrumental role in setting the initial principles for the stabilization of the main mission structure and the creation of a museum. Courtesy of CPDOC-GC.

for the churchyard of Congonhas [do Campo] speaks to our imagination more loudly than Michealangelo's *Moses*." [24] Distancing himself from both the European fashion for "primitive" art and more conventional tastes in European high art, Andrade indicated that the agency's official aesthetic would be trained to see through the lens of nationalism and national heritage. A baroque church anywhere in the world was not to be as moving as a *Brazilian* baroque church.

Deeply encoded into Andrade's aesthetic nationalism was an ethnic understanding of Brazilianness that tended to exalt the Luso-Catholic above all other cultural traditions. Contemporary discussions about formal recognition of former maroon communities, centers for *candomblé,* and immigrant settlement houses as cultural patrimony would have been unthinkable in the 1930s and 1940s. Even in cases in which tombado sites had been built and largely occupied by non-Europeans, as was the case in the Jesuit mission of São Miguel (São Miguel das Missões [formerly part of the municipality of Santo Ângelo], Rio Grande do Sul) restored in 1938–1939, the SPHAN severely downgraded the significance of non-Europeans in the artistic and cultural foundation of a Brazilian canon.[25] At the Jesuit-Guaraní Mission at São Miguel, restoration efforts concentrated on preventing the total collapse of the main church, an early-eighteenth-century stone structure modeled on the Jesuit mother church in Rome. The spatial and decorative presence of the Guaraní catechumens who resided in long, wood-frame houses constructed in front of the church were left implied rather than restored. The restored mission, set in a broad, open field broken by a few low-lying stone walls in ruins and some stately trees, is truly awe-inspiring. The nearby Museu das Missões, designed by Lucio Costa, impressively integrates sacred art from the mission era into a structure that combines a colonial frame with modernist plate-glass walls. Obscured, though, is the Guaranís' place in the mission's daily rhythms and cultural life. The physical markers of an Amerindian presence are overwhelmed by an aesthetic of patrimony highly informed by the European canon.

To the north, the SPHAN was preoccupied with preserving the architectural and artistic vestiges of Brazil's Age of Gold. The agency devoted considerable resources to the *barroco mineiro.* The absolute number of tombamentos made in Minas between 1938 and 1945 (65, or 15 percent of all tombamentos for the period) is deceptively small, as the historic districts of the mining towns of Ouro Preto, Diamantina, Mariana, São João del Rey, Serro, and Tiradentes were registered as single entries, elevating all structures located within the designated district to the level of patrimony. As this architectural and artistic world of the barroco mineiro was duly consecrated, the social world of gold mining, dominated by poor immigrants from northern Portugal, enslaved Africans, and free people of color, was much harder to find in the official narration of a Brazilian baroque. In its preservationist efforts in Minas, the SPHAN was primarily concerned with protecting the architectural-decorative culture of the church, slave holders, and free artisans, at the expense of the enslaved and free peoples who often played central roles in the construction and maintenance of this very same material and aesthetic culture. Nonelites were never completely written out of the historical narratives provided by the SPHAN, but the priorities of federal preservation efforts separated the interrelated cultural worlds of elites and nonelites.

In the consecration of a national artistic canon, the SPHAN helped bestow on certain artistic genres and individual artists the laurels of genius. Recent analysis of the sequence in which registries were made into the *Livros do Tombo* demonstrates that the majority of tombamentos made during the "heroic phase" can be found in the Registry of Fine Arts.[26] Between 1938 and 1945, 185 entries were made into the registry of fine arts, versus 44 for the registry of history and a paltry 10 in the registry of archaeology, ethnography, and landscape and the registry of applied arts. Joint inscriptions were not unusual, but again, the registry of fine arts dominates, with 200 additional entries shared with another registry.[27] These were not mere designations of convenience, but rather conscious choices made after extended archival, bibliographic, and field research into the qualities of works considered for tombamento. The scholarly and technical rigor under which the SPHAN worked was a well-deserved point of pride for Rodrigo Melo Franco de Andrade and his colleagues. The aesthetic politics of preservation, nevertheless, pushed the SPHAN into exalting artistic beauty, rather than historical significance or ethnographic representativeness, in works deemed eligible for protection. Ouro Preto's Age of Gold was rendered a dazzling gilded age, rather than the grimy, hard-scrabble, and exploitative world of mining that actually characterized the social experience of the province of Minas Gerais in the eighteenth century.

I do not mean to imply that the preservationists at the SPHAN were unwittingly starstruck by the material and artistic opulence of gold. Far from it. The Gold Museum, opened to the public in Sabará in 1945, focused on mining technology rather than gilded church altars. The SPHAN's regional agents surveyed and photographed hundreds of less-than-spectacular sites in the process of identifying works potentially eligible for inscription into the four *Livros do Tombo*. The scholarly work in the history of art and architecture published in the SPHAN's annual *Revista* and occasional papers was typically excellent. Nevertheless, the organizational and ideological logic of tombamento plotted patrimony onto the national cultural imaginary as works of artistic beauty and genius. Alternative readings, especially in a cultural context in which few Brazilians had the erudition to challenge the SPHAN's scholarship, had little chance of survival.

The attention devoted to the works of Aleijadinho perhaps best illus-

20 Aleijadinho, *Jonah*. Courtesy of LC-AHC.

trates the process in which preservation traded upon the notion of artistic genius. The free son of a white architect and a black slave, victim of a
degenerative disease, and one of the most gifted interpreters of the Luso-
Brazilian baroque, Aleijadinho's personal biography is compelling. His artistic production, including the soapstone sculptures of the lesser prophets
located in front of the Santuário do Bom Jesus de Matosinhos in Congonhas
and decorative and architectural elements to be found in various churches
in the mineiro gold zone, is astounding. If for no other reason than preserving the works of Aleijadinho, the SPHAN had sufficient cause to justify state
intervention into historical preservation. The sculptures at Congonhas are

21 Igreja de São Francisco de Assis, Ouro Preto, *c.* 1944. Designed by Aleijadinho in 1765, the Igreja de São Francisco de Assis was completed in 1794. Following tombamento in 1938, members of the church's holy brotherhood actively courted the federal government for funds destined for restoration of the church. Courtesy of CPDOC-GC.

so magnificent that they now form part of UNESCO's World Heritage List. Yet, the process under which Aleijadinho was elevated to the apex of artistic genius in Brazil and the genius of state preservation is a complicated one, interwoven into the political culture of the first Vargas regime.

The SPHAN invested heavily in Aleijadinho. Rodrigo Melo Franco de Andrade and Judith Martins, a secretary and archivist at the SPHAN headquarters in Rio, expended countless hours and pages writing about the life and artistic production of Aleijadinho and his father, the Portuguese *mestre-de-obras* Manoel Francisco Lisboa. The Igreja de São Francisco de Assis in Ouro Preto (1766–1794), designed and decorated by the mulatto sculptor,

22 Plaster Casts of Aleijadinho's Prophets, SPHAN Headquarters, 1940. As the SPHAN embraced Aleijadinho as a symbol of Brazilian artistic genius, the agency commissioned sculptor Eduardo Tecles to execute plaster castings of the Twelve Prophets found in Congonhas do Campo, Minas Gerais. The replicas were put on permanent exhibit in the SPHAN headquarters in Rio de Janeiro. Courtesy of CPDOC-GC.

was one of the first churches in Minas to be tombado in 1938. Dozens more works by Aleijadinho would be registered in the coming years. The SPHAN valued Aleijadinho so greatly that the agency took the unprecedented step of commissioning plaster castings of the prophets at Congonhas for a permanent exhibit installed in the agency's headquarters in Rio.[28] Aleijadinho was the SPHAN's unofficial calling card.

One of the great frustrations for the SPHAN, then, was that traditionalists embraced Aleijadinho and the baroque just as enthusiastically as the modernists who controlled the government's official preservationist agency. In 1937, Vicente Racioppi, director of the Instituto Histórico de Ouro Preto, complained to the Third Order of Franciscans, the governor of Minas, the mayor of Ouro Preto, Capanema, and Rodrigo Melo Franco de Andrade about alternations made to Aleijadinho's Igreja de São Francisco de Assis. Racioppi, the SPHAN's bête noir, was shocked to see his beloved Aleijadinho corrupted by state-sponsored modernization.[29] In Rio, Gustavo Barroso and José Mariano shared Racioppi's interest in the baroque, and particularly Aleijadinho as the carrier of national genius. Mariano wrote extensively on Aleijadinho, sparring with Andrade and others on the sculptor's personal and artistic biography. Barroso also expressed his displeasure over the manner in which the SPHAN operated in the shadow of Aleijadinho's masterpieces. What united all actors was the idea that Aleijadinho was a genius. The question remained, though, as to who would manage this genius.

The latent animosity between traditionalists and modernists regarding who would control the national patrimony boiled over in 1938, when Lucio Costa advised Rodrigo Melo Franco de Andrade and Capanema to reject the proposed design for a new tourist hotel to be built in Ouro Preto. The design in question had been submitted by Carlos de Azevedo Leão, an ENBA-trained architect who sat on the SPHAN's advisory council, after the municipal government of Ouro Preto and the federal government agreed to share the cost of a new hotel in Brazil's sole national monument. Although Leão was generally considered part of the modernist camp, his design for the tourist hotel slated for Ouro Preto used neocolonial adornments to harmonize the hotel's structural and decorative elements into the surrounding eighteenth-century urban landscape. Advocates of neocolonialism, including José Mariano, supported the design. Local authorities in Ouro Preto were noncommittal on aesthetics, expressing more concern for the hotel's capacity and amenities.[30] Costa, one of the leading interpreters of modernist architecture in Brazil who also played a central role in formulating federal preservationist policies, opposed Leão's project, which he criticized as sentimental, unoriginal, and overly reliant upon illusion rather than substance. Costa capitalized on his close ties to Rodrigo Melo Franco de Andrade to convince Capanema to reverse the decision to build Leão's neocolonial design. In a private letter to Andrade, which became one of the most influential texts in federal preservationist policy making, Costa wrote:

> I know from personal experience that the only way that the [traditional] style of the houses in Ouro Preto can be reproduced is through the use of a great amount of inauthentic elements. Even if we admit that the unique environment of such historical cities merits the use of artifice, what we are left with

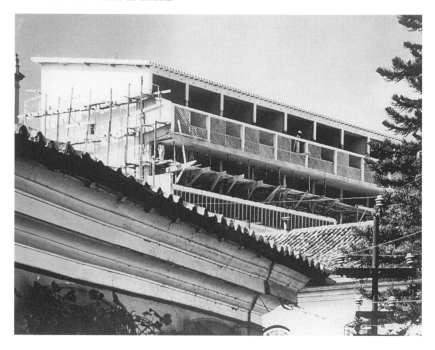

23 Grande Hotel de Ouro Preto, 1942. In the foreground, the photo captures the colonial architecture that modernists and traditionalists were so eager to preserve; in the background, Oscar Niemeyer's Grande Hotel, a symbol of the modernists' ascendancy in the politics of patrimony and a turning point in the discourse of affinities between modernism and the baroque. Courtesy of LC-AHC.

is either a perfect imitation, which the tourist may well mistake for one of the true monuments of the city, or a total failure, in which we will have built a 'neocolonial' fake which has nothing to do with the true spirit of the old constructions.[31]

In the same letter, Costa made the case for a substitute design executed by fellow modernista and collaborator Oscar Niemeyer. The Niemeyer design was characteristic of the modernist principles most closely associated with Le Corbusier, containing such standard elements as a rectangular shape, reinforced concrete, large glass windows, and a minimum of embellishment. Everything about Niemeyer's original design appeared to reject the irregular, curving, and heavy colonial architecture seen throughout Ouro Preto. When Capanema agreed to substitute the Leão project with Niemeyer's, a bitter war of words erupted over the meaning of his-

torical preservation and the politics of federal commissions. Leão's sup-
porters argued that awarding the design to Niemeyer contradicted the
Vargas regime's campaign to rationalize public administration through
merit-based procedures that discouraged nepotism and favoritism. José
Mariano opposed the design on aesthetic and ideological grounds, calling
Niemeyer's project a "watertank encased in slabs of reinforced concrete."
In the invective against the Niemeyer plan, Mariano once again leveled the
charge that modernism was the thin edge of a terrifying Jewish, commu-
nist menace against Brazilian traditions.[32]

In the face of opposition from the defenders of "traditional" architecture, Niemeyer's design went forward. Leão, feeling betrayed by his own
allies, resigned from the SPHAN's advisory council. The nod to Niemeyer
indicated that the official celebration of the barroco mineiro would not
prevent the insertion of an uncompromisingly modernist structure in the
middle of the most tombado of all Brazilian spaces. Costa justified this
measure on the principle that well-designed modernist art complemented
traditional art for the precise reason that the new would never be confused
with the old, whereas a neocolonial design, if well executed, might be mis-
taken for an original. Worse still would be a neocolonial design that fell in
the netherland between a good reproduction and a bad adaptation. Costa
conceded that the contrast between Niemeyer's modernist box and the
surrounding architecture was too harsh, prompting Niemeyer to modify
his design by softening the rectilinear lines originally planned for the hotel
and adding widow treatments reminiscent of latticework seen in period
windows. What remained clear was that Costa saw great compatibility
between the principles of modernist architecture laid out by the International Congress of Modern Architecture and the architectural patrimony
that fell under the protection of Decree-Law 25. Costa would go so far as
to argue that construction materials and techniques of modern architecture—notably reinforced concrete—remained faithful to the pau-a-pique
(daub-and-wattle) used to create the "masterpieces" of eighteenth-century
mineiro architecture.[33] Through this creative, though stretched, theory of
affinities, Costa was able to project the genius associated with baroque architecture onto the principles of architectural renewal espoused by modernists. With Costa and Niemeyer receiving federal commissions to design
buildings in Rio, Ouro Preto, and New York (and later, Brasília), there was
little room to wonder who the modernists were promoting as the Aleija-
dinhos of the twentieth century.

One final quality of SPHAN activities was that the SPHAN had to rely on the collaboration of many local, regional, and ecclesiastic entities to successfully invent a patrimonial canon. Social collaboration in the protection of cultural patrimony was a recurrent theme, bordering on a mantra, in Rodrigo Melo Franco de Andrade's public interviews and speeches. In 1939, for example, Andrade took on the question of social collaboration, arguing, "The SPHAN has been charged with a task of indisputably national dimensions. . . . We act from this premise, given that the very notion of the common interest must be understood by all, and not merely an elite. For the common good, the efforts must be common as well. The spirit of protecting the torchbearers [*testemunhas*] of our history and art must be shared among all classes."[34] Andrade's *deep* investment in an ideal of social collaboration was reflected in technical documentation shared among SPHAN employees as well as the speeches publications, and radio addresses drafted to familiarize the general public with the agency's mission. The marketing of the SPHAN's efforts, imbued with the rhetoric of social collaboration, reached a high point near the end of the Estado Novo, when an eighteen-segment radio program on the service's history, activities, and accomplishments was broadcast on Friday nights on Rádio MES.[35] Several programs were devoted to the question of social collaboration.

By 1945, 416 inscriptions had been made into the *Livros do Tombo,* representing just under half of *all* entries made between 1938 and 1994.[36] Decree-Law 25 had set in motion a patrimonial frenzy that has not been duplicated since. In seven years, the Brazilian government lay claim to four registries, which were treated as the nation's birth certificate, baptismal record, record of military service, proof of residency, title of property, and identity papers all combined.

Contesting Patrimony: The Arco do Teles Case

The SPHAN faced numerous obstacles in creating and protecting a national patrimonial canon, and even more in convincing society that official preservation was in the public's best interests. Uncooperative private collectors were especially troublesome. The SPHAN simply did not have the resources to fulfill its legal obligation to regulate the private art market, where antique dealers and treasure hunters scoured the interior of the country in search of secular and sacred artwork to be sold to the highest bidder.[37] Decaying or abandoned churches, town halls, and residences were especially vulnerable to pillagers, much to the frustration of federal preservation-ists.[38] Private property holders who refused to participate in the politics of canon formation represented an even greater obstacle to the success of federal preservation initiatives. The tension between private property and preservation was one of the most significant and lasting tensions in cultural management.

The state's power to compromise the rights of private property owners for the sake of historical preservation was indeed a radical innovation to a political culture that had protected private property and the rights of the propertied classes since the early empire. Under the Constitution of 1891, private property rights were highly protected, and it would be near unthinkable that historical preservation could infringe on the free use of private property.[39] Under the provisions of the authoritarian Con-stitution of 1937 and Decree-Law 25, however, the federal government en-joyed broadened powers over private property. Compulsory tombamento —the SPHAN's right to summarily register historically significant proper-ties against the owner's wishes—was the strongest of the federal govern-ment's increased powers.[40] Since tombamento placed several restrictions on the use of registered property (for example, the SPHAN had to approve all cosmetic and structural alterations to the tombado structure and its sur-roundings), compulsory tombamento and the classic liberal right to the free use of private property were clearly at odds.

Publicly, the SPHAN did not present tombamento as antithetical to estab-lished property rights.[41] In 1944, SPHAN spokesperson Antônio Leal argued, "The incorporation of any good, real or movable, into the national histori-cal and artistic patrimony does not imply, as you see, the [state's] assump-tion of control: it is merely an act which declares the good's historical and artistic value, and for this reason, places it under special rules [*fica sujeito a um regime especial*]." When conflict arose, the agency stressed the state's role in balancing the rights of the private individual and public welfare, with public welfare defined to include historical preservation. The hope was clearly that compulsory tombamento would not be necessary because private citizens and municipal authorities would see it as their patriotic duty to aid in the protection of the national historical patrimony.

The vast majority of property owners were wholly unaffected by tom-bamento, and thus expressed little interest in the politics and patriotism of preservation. Of the hundreds of thousands of properties, objects, and artwork potentially eligible for tombamento, the SPHAN officially registered less than 500. Most property owners who faced an inscription into one of the four registries freely submitted to the "special rules" applied to protected properties, motivated by the noble ideals of the common social good and more pedestrian hopes of gaining federal assistance in restoring dilapidated properties or making a profit off of the patrimonial designation. In a small number of cases, however, the politics of preservation and the exercise of private property came into direct conflict. These cases severely tested the notion that the state pursued preservation in the interests of public welfare. The resolution of such cases revealed the illiberal undertone of preservation, itself a reflection of a larger authoritarian regime.

The most significant challenge to the state's ability to invent the national cultural patrimony came out of the compulsory tombamento of the Arco do Teles, an eighteenth-century structure located on Rio de Janeiro's Praça XV de Novembro. The case gave definition to the ideological and legal boundaries of preservation implied in Decree-Law 25 and the administrative procedures established by the SPHAN in the earliest stages of its "heroic phase." The case provided the SPHAN and the federal government with the perfect vehicle for articulating the idea of the common social good, protected and administered through the central state. The SPHAN would frequently cite the victory in the Arco do Teles case in its defense of the legal and moral mandate to manage patrimony.

The property in question was a commercial arcade and adjoining residential structures once owned by a wealthy judge, Francisco Teles de Menezes. Set among these structures was an arched passageway that linked the Praça do Carmo (today's Praça XV de Novembro) to the Travessa do Commércio and the Rua da Cruz (today's Rua do Ouvidor). From the mid-eighteenth until the late nineteenth century, the archway and surrounding edifices occupied a privileged place in downtown Rio, making up one side of an urban square that was the political, commercial, and ecclesiastic center of Rio de Janeiro. Many eighteenth- and nineteenth-century visual representations of Rio depict the Arco as a backdrop to major political events, ritual life, commerce, and sociability. Sadly, by 1938, the commercial and political powers of the national capital had migrated to other parts of the city, including the port region near Praça Mauá, the commercial and shopping districts surrounding Avenida Rio Branco, and the upscale neighborhoods of the Zona Sul. What the SPHAN saw as a historical treasure was to many just another old and poorly maintained edifice located in the capi-

24 Leandro Joaquim (attributed), *Revista Militar no Largo do Paço*. Late eighteenth century, oil on canvas, 110 × 130 cm. This late-eighteenth-century painting depicts the Arco do Teles at the epicenter of political, economic, religious,
and ceremonial life of late-colonial Rio de Janeiro. Viewed from the bay, the
Praço do Carmo (today's Praça XV de Novembro) is surrounded by the viceregal place (left), the Convento do Carmo and the main Cathedral (center background), and the Municipal Chamber (right, with the arched passageway to
the Travessa do Commércio clearly visible). In the foreground stands the public
fountain designed by the mulatto architect Mestre Valentim. Courtesy of Museu
Histórico Nacional/Banco Safra.

tal's historic downtown. Both preservationists and reformers saw the Arco
do Teles as a symbol of a Brazil that was no more. The question remained
whether the state had the right to compel private citizens to maintain reminders of a lost past for the good of the nation. The twentieth-century
owners of the Arco do Teles, Jaime Lino and Maria da Conceição Souto
Maior, weighed in as opponents to any conflation of compulsory preservation and the commonweal.

When the Inspetoria dos Monumentos Nacionais was operational
(1934–1936), neither Barroso nor his representative, Epaminondas Macedo,

expressed much concern over the potential for opposition from local property holders. Aside from an occasional complaint from Vicente Racioppi, a local history buff, the IMN encountered little opposition in Ouro Preto. When Mário de Andrade turned to the question of institutionalizing preservation, he too seemed largely unconcerned with the potential for conflict between a state preservationist agency and private property owners.

Minister of Education Capanema and Rodrigo Melo Franco de Andrade, by contrast, were *extremely* anxious about the possibility that private property owners might refuse to submit their historical properties to the regulations of the SPHAN. In 1936, Andrade made reference to the deleterious effects of "inertia of public powers and the ignorance, negligence and greed of private individuals." [42] The following year, Capanema complained, "property owners without scruples and ignorant people have allowed the most precious of goods to waste away or disappear." With patrimony so intimately tied to a rhetoric of a sovereign national identity, it is quite easy to see how Andrade and Capanema understood threats to patrimony as threats to the very existence of the nation. [43] As self-proclaimed nationalists, these culture managers were discursively and administratively prepared to fight private property owners who failed to see the aesthetic or moral reasons why their property rights should be compromised for the sake of preservation. The challenge to the tombamento of the Arco do Teles both confirmed the anxieties expressed by Capanema and Andrade about an unruly and unpatriotic propertied class, as well as provided the SPHAN with the opportunity to aggressively consolidate its power against private property holders unwilling to cooperate with the mandates of Decree-Law 25.

The conflict over the fate of the Arco do Teles began soon after the SPHAN came to identify historical sites suitable for tombamento. The Souto Maiors, who hoped to demolish the archway in order to build a modern office building or hotel, were disappointed to discover that the SPHAN intended to tombar the property. [44] Hoping to block the planned tombamento, the owners exercised their right of protest (*impugnação*) proscribed in Decree-Law 25, automatically triggering a review by the SPHAN's advisory council. On 10 August 1938, the council found that the property did indeed fall under the legal definition of historical and artistic patrimony and declared the tombamento valid. Invoking the provisions of compulsory tombamento, the SPHAN inscribed the property into the history and fine arts registries. [45]

Without additional avenues of appeal with the SPHAN, the property owners filed a lawsuit against the federal government arguing that the property did not possess the qualities of a historical or artistic monument and that compulsory tombamento was unconstitutional under long-established legal protections for the rights of private property holders. The SPHAN disputed both allegations, defending the historical importance of the construction, the constitutionality of compulsory tombamento, and the jurisdiction of the advisory council. Francisco Noronha Santos, director of the municipal archive of Rio de Janeiro and SPHAN consultant, submitted a detailed history of the site, establishing a historical argument why the archway was a central component of the architectural heritage of Praça XV de Novembro worthy of preservation.[46] In a legal brief that drew on the Noronha Santos report, Rodrigo Melo Franco de Andrade defended the wisdom of tombamento and the inviolability of the decisions taken by the advisory council. Writing as a trained lawyer, Andrade reminded the state's attorney that Decree-Law 25 designated the advisory council as the final arbiter of disputed tombamentos. Since the decree did not include provisions for appeal, Andrade argued, the Souto Maiors' suit lacked any legal basis. After hearing court arguments, the presiding judge found in favor of the SPHAN.[47] In his published decision, appearing 19 April 1940 (one of the most important civic holidays of the Estado Novo — Vargas's birthday), the judge accepted the SPHAN's defense without comment.

The judge's decision came to be a pivotal moment in the political culture of the first Vargas regime, consolidating the political and cultural forces assembled in the invention of a patrimonial canon. From a legal perspective, the decision reaffirmed the constitutionality of compulsory tombamento based upon the legitimacy of Decree-Law 25 and the Constitution of 1937. (Ironically, the judge failed to recognize that the constitution had never been sanctioned by the proscribed national plebiscite.) From an administrative perspective, the judge reaffirmed the legitimacy of the advisory council, an entity whose decision-making powers were not subject to any independent oversight. This legitimated the emergence of insular state agencies that managed national resources yet were protected from pressure politics.

The cultural ramifications of the Arco do Teles case were equally deep, as the category of national historical and artistic patrimony took on a charismatic weight that did not exist just three years prior. Cultural patrimony became inviolate, ritualized in tombamento, sacralized in law. If the modernists' interests in the baroque began far from the state in 1924's Caravana

Modernista, by 1940, the modernist vision of preservation invoked the coercive powers of the central state. The intertwining of state power, cultural canon, the law, and modernism was vital to the process of inventing a particular politics of culture that characterizes the Vargas era.

Still dissatisfied with the court decision, the Souto Maiors appealed the case to the Supremo Tribunal Federal (STF), the nation's highest court. In his appeal, Jaime Souto Maior petitioned for monetary compensation for what he argued to be the state's de facto expropriation of his property. Souto Maior based his claims on an 1894 law that restricted the state from seizing private property without compensation, as well as a later case in which the city of Rio de Janeiro had compensated a property holder for land that had been expropriated for preservationist purposes. The demand for formal expropriation and monetary compensation, coupled with the invocation of the rights of the private property holder against the wrongful seizure of personal property, dramatically altered the nature of the Arco do Teles case.

A legal brief, written by Attorney General Gabriel Rezende Passos in response to the STF appeal, disqualified any link between the Souto Maior suit and the compensation paid in earlier cases, arguing that the plaintiffs' position, if accepted, would mean that the state would have to "expropriate hundreds of buildings, churches, out-of-the-way places, artistic and literary works, and even entire cities." Passos specifically mentioned Ouro Preto, a national monument since 1933, and Olinda (Pernambuco) as candidates for costly expropriation should the Souto Maior position be upheld. Passos then shifted his argument to elaborate a social understanding of patrimony that had not been argued earlier in the case. Stating "there is a grave mistake in the call for expropriation, a defective understanding of the meaning of defending our historical and artistic patrimony," Passos argued that "the defense of our historical and artistic monuments is a duty of *everyone*, including private individuals, and as strange as this may seem to the appellants, it is also a duty of the property owners of those monuments." In his concluding remarks refuting the allegation of an illegal attack on private property rights, Passos argued:

> [The SPHAN] does not engage in attacks on property; it justly protects property of historical or artistic value against ignorant or greedy property holders.
> The Service protects with an eye for the common utility, which is mani-

fest in the conservation of monuments that serve as markers of our cultural evolution or testaments to the great events in our history.

The defense of the national historical or artistic patrimony places certain limits on the use of property in that the owner cannot *abuse,* demolish, mutilate, or in any way diminish the qualities which brought the site to be tombado.

These restrictions are done in the public interest, and rest in the precedent of law.

And our laws and administrative practices are not anomalous. Rather, they reveal the preoccupation seen in more advanced countries which have similar laws with the same function as Decree-Law 25 of 1937.[48]

In a report on the SPHAN's accomplishments, submitted to Minister Capanema at the end of 1940, Rodrigo Melo Franco de Andrade made explicit mention of Passos's arguments concerning "bad property owners" who placed personal economic goals above the mandates of the law. Stopping short of unilaterally denying property owners their rights to dispose of their property as they wished, Andrade reiterated a commitment to the constitutional provisions that enabled the state to compromise property rights in the interests of the collective. "The federal constitution is very clear in defining the right to property," wrote Andrade, "such that these rights have been adapted to contemporary social needs and the prevailing notions of modern law."[49]

When the state's case was argued in the Supreme Federal Tribunal in late 1941, the legal basis of the SPHAN's defense remained unchanged. State's Attorney Passos reviewed past arguments concerning compensation, legal precedent, and civic duty. The major distinction between arguments made in the early stages of the Arco do Teles case and the 1941 hearing before the STF concerned an emergent notion of the social meaning of preservation. With the legal rationale for compulsory tombamento secure, Passos turned to the social rationale, asserting:

> An arch often is of no interest to an owner who would rather use that space to plant wheat, corn, potatoes, or beans. But, the arch may be of interest to the community because it stands as a historic symbol; the Arco do Teles does not seem to interest its owner, who is tired of looking at a structure which could easily be replaced by a skyscraper or hotel, transforming the location into a source of profit, rather than maintaining it as it stands, an eyesore. . . .

In this case, the interests of the individual should bow before the common interest, the social interest, the interest which has been transfigured into the historical value of the Arco facing demolition.

It is vital that the court recognize not only the legitimacy of the Service's actions, but also the noblest endeavors pursued by those who defend our historical and artistic patrimony.[50]

In February 1943, the Supremo Tribunal Federal reached a 9-2 decision in the government's favor.[51] The majority opinion stressed the social dimensions of property ownership and the state's right to limit property rights for the sake of the public good, defined in this case as historical preservation. The minority opinion cited a more classical interpretation of absolute protections of private property rights. TSF Minister Orozimbo Nonato, a member of the majority, characterized the case as a fight between the "conservative, individualist principle [of private property] and the socially minded tendency . . . that dominates the panorama of contemporary life." [52] The SPHAN would subsequently use this case in a print and radio campaign to promote the legal foundation of tombamento and the social basis of patrimonial preservation. In late 1944, Antônio Leal summed up the SPHAN's view on the ramifications of the Arco do Teles case by stating, "It is the interests of education and culture which demand the conservation of monuments of historic and artistic value, imposing upon the property holder the duty to collaborate with the State in order to achieve that objective." [53] Tombamento had become a political artifact of Estado Novo rule.

For the SPHAN, the Arco do Teles became emblematic of the legitimation of the state's ability to protect what it defined as a higher social good. The agency may have been staffed by modernistas who demonstrated strong differences with the conservative ideologues who supported the Estado Novo, but in defending the legality of compulsory tombamento, the insularity of the advisory council, and the state's privileged access to the higher social good through cultural management—in the absence of liberal institutions—the SPHAN leadership demonstrated a practical affinity toward the larger goals of state-led authoritarian renewal. Even after the Estado Novo fell in October 1945 and the Constitution of 1937 was suspended, the SPHAN's advisory council continued to defend its powers of tombamento based upon an understanding of the constitutionality of Decree-Law 25 and the idea of a higher social good articulated in the Arco do Teles case.

The Political Culture of Preservation

Although the SPHAN was prepared to invoke the higher powers of Decree-Law 25, it much preferred to stress the need for a collaborative alliance between the state and civil society in the celebration and defense of the national historic and artistic patrimony. Rodrigo Melo Franco de Andrade consistently touched upon the theme of social collaboration when justifying the politics of tombamento. As early as 1936, Andrade identified the Catholic Church, and especially Cardinal D. Sebastião Leme, as a close partner in preservation.[54] By 1939, after the initial wave of tombamentos was complete, Andrade turned to the nation's engineers and architects to work with the government in the coordination of urban renewal and preservation.[55] The Arco do Teles case provided a perfect opportunity to promote even broader parameters for social collaboration among the legal and propertied communities. By the late Estado Novo, the language of collaboration was boilerplate in the service's pronouncements on the importance of preservation.

In its quest for social collaboration, the SPHAN won over certain key sectors of Brazilian society. With few exceptions, the church was one of the service's most reliable allies. Cardinal Leme and Dom Helvécio Gomes de Oliveira, the archbishop of Mariana, played instrumental roles in guaranteeing the state access to a rich and varied ecclesiastical heritage that could be subsumed into the nation's heritage. Archbishop Oliveira was especially generous to Ouro Preto's Museu da Inconfidência, selecting 260 objects from the archdiocesan museum for the new federal museum.[56] The SPHAN, in turn, provided financial assistance toward the restoration of the diocesan cathedral in Mariana. Oliveria's words of thanks for federal aid were widely circulated in the press as a sign of fruitful church-state collaboration.[57] Following the lead of the church hierarchy, several holy brotherhoods also collaborated with the SPHAN in the preservation of church properties maintained by the sodalities. Church leaders and the lay brotherhoods grew increasingly adept at extracting pledges from the SPHAN to finance the restoration of ecclesiastical properties deemed to be of patrimonial quality.[58]

Municipal authorities also assisted preservation. The municipal leaders in Ouro Preto expressed their support for federal assistance soon after the town had been designated a national monument.[59] Once the town's historic core had been tombado en bloc in 1938, the municipal leadership came to treat the federal government as a major defender of the city's precarious economic health and cultural life. That same year, Mayor Washington de Araújo Dias sought out federal assistance for improvements in the town's tourist infrastructure.[60] The mayor's request was subsequently fulfilled with the construction of the Grande Hotel de Ouro Preto. The local notion that federal intervention had rescued the city from oblivion was summed up at the 1944 inauguration of the Museu da Inconfidência, when Mayor Dias said, "Ouro Preto will never forget the benefits and projects that it has received from the Government of the Republic. In its long and glorious existence, this old city, sometimes misunderstood and derided, did not receive the government favors and benefits to which it held an incontestable right. Only under the Government of the great Getúlio Vargas have the sights of our great government leaders been refocused on the old city of the Inconfidentes." [61] These "government favors and rights" included federal and state financing for the Grande Hotel and assurances that the National School of Minas in Ouro Preto would not be allowed to relocate to another city, which provided stimuli to the local civil construction sector and new sources of revenue generated by an emergent tourist industry whose health was directly tied to government propaganda promoting the wonders of Brazil's recovered patrimony.[62]

With the Catholic Church and many municipal leaders on its side, the SPHAN still found it difficult to win over sustained popular support for the preservationist cause. True, the SPHAN received only thirteen formal challenges in more than 500 inquiries into tombamentos opened between 1938 and 1945, upholding all but two disputed inscriptions.[63] Tombado works became integral parts of local and regional constructions of place, memory, and identity. Yet, the service's efforts did not stimulate a great wave of preservationist sentiment in civil society. Requests for tombamento originating outside of the federal government were uncommon, and those requests that did come from outsiders were typically rejected.[64] The Sociedade dos Amigos de Ouro Preto, founded in 1944, was the sole private preservationist league to engage federal preservation policy. The limited records available indicate that the society made little headway until the late 1940s, when private philanthropy and cultural mobilization began to affect state cultural patronage. Here, the Brazilian case differs significantly from preservation movements in the United States and Great Britain where civil society, through local preservationist leagues, museum auxiliaries, and public trusts, have played the most important role in creating a national historical patrimony.[65]

The state's inability to cultivate a broad base of social support for preservation was a product of several factors. Budgetary constraints prevented the SPHAN from directly financing the restoration of most nonmonumental historic structures, undercutting the agency's ability to build a large client base. This problem was especially acute for historic residential structures whose owners were poor. In its negotiations with property owners of means, the SPHAN was often able to build working relationships between the state and elites.[66] The agency had much less success with property owners without means. On the rare occasion when impoverished residents of historic structures managed to petition the state for assistance in saving their properties from ruin, the SPHAN was generally unable to meet their requests. In 1945, Rodrigo Melo Franco de Andrade took up the issue of how the state might take a more proactive stance toward the preservation of nonmonumental properties whose owners did not have the financial ability to maintain, much less restore, historic properties. Recognizing that historic preservation could never provide badly needed social services for the impoverished, Andrade modestly proposed that the state intervene when historic structures were on the verge of total collapse.[67] This stopgap posture undermined the notion that the state and all society shared a common investment in protecting the common good bound up in the national cultural patrimony.

In extreme cases, preservation precipitated violent conflict between the central state and civil society. The archival documentation on popular mobilization against preservation is sketchy, but anecdotal evidence, oral testimonies, and a handful of journalistic reports indicate that preservation did, on occasion, provoke popular ire, especially in locales where preservation became a major obstacle to civil construction, exterior decor, and commercial zoning. Perhaps the most humorous case on record comes from Edgard Jacintho, SPHAN representative in São João del Rey, who recalled that in the early 1940s, local residents commandeered a group of itinerant lepers into a historical residence with the intention of preventing Jacintho from surveying the house for possible restoration. In his 1983 deposition, Jacintho also recalled that angry residents in São João once stoned SPHAN representatives.[68] The case of the lepers was clearly an isolated response, likely instigated by a disgruntled local property owner. A more represen-

25 Historic Quarter of São João del Rey, Minas Gerais, *c.* 1942. The residents of
São João periodically clashed with the SPHAN over the question of property rights
and urban development in the town's historic quarter. Courtesy of LC-AHC.

tative response might be the reaction of those residents who simply left
their town's historic districts to reside in neighborhoods that did not fall
under the restrictive rules of tombamento.[69] In either case, there is evidence
that civil society could develop strategies to resist preservation mandates
emanating from Rio.

Municipal authorities occasionally presented a more organized challenge to the SPHAN, especially when preservation threatened progress.
Again in São João del Rey, local authorities criticized the SPHAN for being
too stringent in its regulation of the construction of new buildings and
urban improvements in historic sections of the municipality. In response,
Rodrigo Melo Franco de Andrade denied that the SPHAN had impeded any
improvement projects, while reiterating that the colonial nature of historic
cities like São João would be maintained.[70] Local residents in Diamantina,

eager to make residential and commercial improvements in the city center, went so far as to appeal directly to Vargas to allow the city to demolish the historic town market to make way for the construction of a new post and telegraph office. With echoes of the Arco do Teles case, residents of Diamantina challenged the SPHAN on several grounds, including the artistic criteria used to judge the town market as historically significant and the legal jurisdiction over a building that had been previously ceded to the federal government with the express purpose of constructing a post office. Countering the 250 residents who signed the petition sent to the president, Andrade, Capanema, and Minister of Justice Campos advised Vargas to uphold the tombamento and allow the SPHAN to proceed with restorations. Vargas listened to his advisors, and restoration plans went forward.[71] In the annual report of 1945, Andrade expressed his frustration that the municipal authorities in Diamantina were scapegoating the SPHAN for the city's housing crunch, going on to reaffirm his commitment to the SPHAN's constitutional right to defend and protect tombado properties, even at the expense of local populations who valued the real estate upon which historic structures stood more than the structures themselves.[72]

The one instance in which the SPHAN failed to prevent a municipality from destroying tombado properties was in Rio de Janeiro, where the municipal government authorized the demolition of several hundred historical structures, some of them tombado, for the construction of the Avenida Presidente Vargas, one of the largest works of urban reform completed since the belle époque.[73] Irreplaceable historical structures that sat along the thoroughfare's path included the churches of São Pedro dos Clérigos (1773), Bom Jesus do Calvário (1719), São Domingos (1791), Nossa Senhora da Conceição (1758), as well as the Town Hall (1876). Rodrigo Melo Franco de Andrade protested the planned demolitions, arguing that Decree-Law 25 unilaterally prohibited the destruction of these protected properties.[74] On 29 November 1941, Vargas issued Decree-Law 3.866, giving the president of the republic the discretionary power to revoke tombamentos. Andrade protested even more vehemently, to no avail, and the disputed buildings were razed. Dr. Rodrigo found himself caught in a political culture in which the patrimonial canon could be unmade by the same authoritarian right of decree-law that had invented the state's right to preserve.

The relationship between the central state and the municipalities of Minas Gerais was the most complex in an already complex cultural landscape created by the politics of preservation. As previously indicated, municipal leaders in Ouro Preto tried to capitalize on the politics of restoration, welcoming federal investment in civil construction and the incipient hospitality industry. Town authorities treated preservation as an antidote to the region's economic problems brought on by the shift in economic productivity toward the more dynamic agro-pastoral and manufacturing economies of the southern and western portions of the state.[75] But even in Ouro Preto, the central state and the municipality occasionally came into conflict over the management of cultural patrimony and the enforcement of certain restrictions on the commercial use of tombado properties. In September 1945, Rodrigo Melo Franco de Andrade felt compelled to remind Mayor Dias of the municipality's obligation to enforce federal restrictions on commercial signage in the town's main square.[76] Town leaders in São João del Rey and Diamantina faced a more recalcitrant federal agency that rejected allegations that preservation compromised the towns' abilities to promote commercial growth in areas containing historical structures. Conflict over zoning restrictions in historical zones became so frequent that state government in Belo Horizonte instructed the mayors of historic towns in Minas to pursue urban improvements that did not subvert the legal protections of historical patrimony.[77]

The patrimonialization of Minas Gerais through tombamento, restoration, and museumification levied a toll on the region's imagination of itself. The modernistas mineiros, many of whom had left Minas to take positions in Rio, were extremely successful in integrating regional patrimony into a project of national imagination. But in the historical towns of Minas, local claims to local patrimony increasingly had to compete with national claims to the national historical and artistic patrimony being invented throughout the old mining regions. Paradoxically, by celebrating the richness of a regional cultural patrimony, the SPHAN undermined the region's ability to call that patrimony uniquely its own. Although this type of sacrifice was made in almost every city that contained objects or sites of interest to the SPHAN, it was especially acute in the historic towns of Minas, where Ouro Preto and Mariana were named national monuments, and São João del Rey, Sabará, and Diamantina faced large numbers of tombamentos. In all of these cities, the federal definition of tombamento grew to be an inescapable, often intrusive part of local property rights, aesthetics, and identity politics.

The trials and tribulations of Vicente Racioppi, the founding director of the Instituto Histórico de Ouro Preto, local history buff, and onetime owner of a poorly managed collection of historical artifacts related to the history of Minas Gerais, exemplify the latent discord between local memory keepers and federal preservationists. In the mid-1930s, this self-designated defender of local rights frequently expressed his displeasure with the restoration work undertaken by the Inspetoria dos Monumentos Nacionais. When the SPHAN assumed preservationist responsibilities in 1937, Racioppi increased the volume of his antifederal invective, writing a series of vitriolic (largely unsubstantiated) attacks on the government's activities.[78] These criticisms generally fell on deaf ears in Rio, but in October 1940, Rodrigo Melo Franco de Andrade countered Racioppi's call for a review of restoration efforts with an editorial that asserted that the SPHAN would not be subjected to outside oversight.[79] Andrade's harsh words for Racioppi reflected a disdain for the local's intrusions into SPHAN affairs and for the power relations between an agency of the central state that could legally isolate itself from challenges posed by private citizens and public regulatory agencies. In a legal context enabled by the authoritarian politics of the Estado Novo, those local preservationists who did not wish to collaborate with the federal state could be marginalized easily.

The repatriation of the remains of the Inconfidentes, completed in 1937, most vividly illustrates how the federal preservation policies placed local and regional authorities at a great disadvantage when local and federal interests clashed over the control of historical artifacts and local memory. During the democratic interregnum of 1934–1937, Augusto de Lima Junior (1889–1970), a well-published mineiro historian, petitioned Vargas to lend federal support for the repatriation of the remains of Inconfidente poet Tomás Antônio Gonzaga (1744–c. 1810) and the other conspirators exiled to Portuguese Africa. At the urging of several prominent mineiro politicians, including Gustavo Capanema and state governor Benedito Valladares, Vargas agreed to the proposal, signing Decree 756 on 21 April 1936. Citing the Inconfidentes' struggle for national independence and the shame of a patriot's burial in non-Brazilian soil, the decree authorized the Ministries of Education and Foreign Relations to pursue repatriation. The decree also authorized the publication of the trial records of the Inconfidência, the *Autos da Devassa*. Finally, the decree stipulated that a mausoleum be built in Ouro Preto to house permanently the Inconfidentes' remains. José de Souza Reis, a SPHAN architect with strong modernista credentials, was later contracted to design a crypt to be built within the Museu da Inconfidência in Ouro Preto. With the assistance of the government of Portugal,

Lima located the remains of those Inconfidentes buried in Mozambique and Angola and personally oversaw their exhumation and transfer to Brazil. When the remains arrived in Rio in late 1936 in porcelain urns draped in the Brazilian flag, they were paraded through the streets of the capital.

In July 1938, the remains were relocated to temporary storage in Ouro Preto's Igreja de Antonio Dias. Vargas used the occasion to praise the sacrifices of the Inconfidentes and to reaffirm certain principles of Estado Novo rule, thanking the population of Minas Gerais for its commitment to "order, a healthy reverence for tradition, and the norms of a hard-working and tranquil life." The dictator went on to praise the Inconfidentes for their exemplary actions in patriotism, duty, and sacrifice.[80] The historical revisionism was thick, with Vargas praising the Inconfidentes for their aversion to regionalism and foreign ideologies when the Inconfidência Mineira was, at its heart, a conspiracy hatched at the regional level that drew on imported ideals about self-determination to challenge central authority. In order to make sense of the repatriated patrimony, Vargas emptied the Inconfidência of its historical truth and created a new history of collective sacrifice in the name of national liberation and the protection of internal order. The locals took the politically expedient position of tolerating the revisionism.

On 21 April 1942, the sesquicentennial of Tiradentes' execution, the Panteão dos Inconfidentes (Pantheon of the Inconfidentes) was inaugurated on the ground floor of the Museu da Inconfidência. Museum records indicate that the Pantheon was intended to be the first gallery visited in the new museum. Souza Reis's severe design made few concessions to conventions in civic iconography deployed with great flourish at civic ceremonies held in Rio de Janeiro. There were no Brazilian flags, green-and-yellow bunting, or smiling images of Vargas. Instead, the repatriated remains of thirteen of the twenty-four conspirators implicated in the Inconfidência lay entombed in crypts set at floor-level within a stark, open room built out of stones taken from local quarries. Similar to the Tombs of the Unknowns which honor martyrs and patriots in other nations, one crypt was left uninscribed to commemorate those conspirators whose remains could not be located in 1936. Tiradentes, whose dismembered body had been left to rot following his execution in 1792, was commemorated in a simple inscription that ended "*O Governo da República, em 1942, aos Inconfidentes de 1789.*" An altarlike table, an eighteenth-century silver chandelier, and the flag of the Inconfidência completed the quasi-religious tableau.

26 Panteão dos Inconfidentes, *c.* 1942. Perhaps the most sacred of all civic spaces created under the authoritarian Estado Novo, the Panteão dos Inconfidentes is also a monument to modernism. Courtesy of LC-AHC.

In a recent reading of the Pantheon, Dora M. S. Alcântara has argued that the Vargas regime used the repatriation of the Inconfidentes' remains and the Pantheon's construction as an opportunity to stage an elaborate drama of civic spectacle to divert attention away from the regime's move toward authoritarian rule.[81] While Alcântara seems correct in describing the Pantheon as a national altar that combines the civic and sacred, the political lessons to be drawn from the creation of the Pantheon were not so hidden. This Pantheon was an artifact of the Estado Novo regime—patriotic, nationalist, baroque, and modernist. Moreover, the Pantheon was also a monument to the modernists. Souza Reis's stark design was possible only in a heritage site managed by the SPHAN, where modernism and preservation went hand-in-hand. Had the Inconfidentes been entombed in the National Historical Museum, Gustavo Barroso would have ensured that their final resting place would be more faithful to the exuberance of the baroque.

Many locals knew that the Pantheon had been built at the expense of competing claims to the Inconfidentes' remains. In the years prior to the transfer of the Inconfidentes' remains to Ouro Preto, Gustavo Capanema had denied the town councils of Taubaté (São Paulo) and São Gonçalo do Sapucaí (Minas Gerais) in their request to acquire the remains of hometown Inconfidentes Luiz Vaz de Toledo Pisa and Inácio José de Alvarenga Peixoto on the grounds that Ouro Preto had been designated by federal decree as the sole repository for the remains.[82] Federal agents would manage officially the memory of the Inconfidência. Municipal leaders in São Gonçalo do Sapucaí surely were disappointed to learn that they would be unable to bury Alvarenga Peixoto alongside his wife and fellow conspirator Bárbara Helidora (a.k.a. Bárbara Elidora Guilhermina da Silveira). Augusto de Lima Junior, the historian who had originally sought out presidential approval for repatriation, was also disappointed to see that it would take nearly twenty years before the remains of Marília de Dirceu, lover and muse to Inconfidente Tomás Antônio Gonzaga, would be included in the Museu da Inconfidência (and even then, outside of the actual Pantheon).[83] Federal law trumped Taubaté and São Gonçalo do Sapucaí in their bids for obtaining the remains of hometown heroes, and federal law trumped various proposals to tell a story of the Inconfidência that departed from the martyrdom of Tiradentes and his male co-conspirators.

The Pantheon, thus, was no diversion. The casual visitor could see clearly that the site was part of the celebratory patriotism of heritage cultivated by the nationalistic Estado Novo. The savvy visitor also would recognize the Pantheon as a war trophy for modernism and centralism. Hindsight also reveals that the Pantheon was a site that reproduced at the regional level the centralist powers of the Estado Novo state and the cult of masculine heroism cultivated in other memory sites such as the National Historical Museum.

Rodrigo Melo Franco de Andrade touched upon the centralizing overtones of federal interest in regional patrimony at the 1944 inauguration of the Museu da Inconfidência. As Andrade praised the regime's push to open museums outside of the Federal District, he spoke of the increasing ease with which local and regional populations could celebrate the national historical and artistic patrimony through the celebration of their own local and regional historical patrimony.[84] In these remarks, Andrade stated, "It is impossible to cultivate an appreciation of national traditions without acknowledging the zeal for regional traditions." What Andrade was less eager

27 Museu da Inconfidência, 1941. Originally built as the town hall and jail for Vila Rica at the end of the eighteenth century, this structure opened as the Museu da Inconfidência in 1944. Courtesy of CPDOC-GC.

to acknowledge, but what was evident from his mere presence as a representative of the federal government at the inauguration of a "regional" museum run by the national government, was that the invention of "the national historical and artistic patrimony" nationalized regional historical patrimony. The directives of a federal agency based in the Federal District progressively undermined regional controls over local art, history, and heroes. The SPHAN may never have been explicitly charged with promoting political centralism. Historical preservation was nonetheless a vehicle for the expansion of the central state's control over historical sites of regional awareness and pride.

Conclusions

After 1930, a national cultural heritage came to resonate in numerous objects, edifices, and locales that stood on precarious ground in the national imaginary in the decades before the federal government raised historical preservation to a national priority. The consecration of an expanding set of historical sites and objects was a marked departure from the type of historical representation practiced before the Revolution of 1930, which tended to rely on a limited number of historical texts produced by historical institutes such as the IHGB and a handful of historical paintings, sculptures, and statues—all to be enjoyed by an extremely small portion of the national population. As part of its post-1930 attack on the political culture of oligarchical liberalism, the Vargas regime made great strides in opening up the field of historical patrimony to a growing slice of Brazil's cultural and social matrix.

The radical innovations in historical protection spawned by the Revolution of 1930 still had their limitations. Given the criteria used to select particular kinds of sites and objects, primarily originating from the social and ecclesiastic elite, federal preservationist activities assured that prevailing regional, class, and racial biases would persist in the way in which the federal government reconstructed, ordered, and displayed national history. The "identity documents of the nation" excluded many as they purported to include everyone. Moreover, the imprinting of these identity documents created new forms of political exclusion that marginalized the input of preservationists who did not adhere to the principles of modernism as well as private property holders and locals unwillingly to play by the SPHAN's rules.

It would be unreasonable to argue that historical preservation was the tool of first choice in the pursuit of authoritarian politics. Tombamento was, nonetheless, an instrument of an authoritarian central state. As regional interests, ecclesiastical authorities, history buffs, locals, and tourists tried to make patrimony for themselves, the state fortified its claim to managing the nation's identity by managing the national heritage. In the grand squares of Rio and Salvador and the small hamlets of Minas, small plaques inscribed with the simple words "Patrimônio Histórico e Artístico Nacional" structured an emotional but asymmetrical bond between state, society, and the past.

5

Museums and Memory

In the First Republic, the combination of urbanization, industrialization, and technological advances in communication radically changed the perception of the passage of time. Older structures were razed at the same time that modern edifices pushed eyes toward the future. The wave of foreign immigration that flooded southern Brazil loosened the personal and generational connections to a distinctly Luso-Brazilian past. The burgeoning city of São Paulo appeared to be given over entirely to a frenetic embrace of the new.[1] With the past fleeting away, some Brazilian elites searched out strategies in which to maintain vestiges of a past that was disappearing before their eyes. President Epitácio Pessoa gave shape to a new landscape of memory in August 1922 with the creation of the first National Historical Museum. Thereafter, the national memory could be collected, managed, and displayed within a public museum dedicated exclusively to the "national" past. Savvy to the power of managing the past, the Vargas regime picked up on President Pessoa's initiative, investing in museums the power to maintain a sacred relationship between the past and present in an era of change.

Museums, of course, had many ideological and historical attributes that made them well suited to managing the past. Museums were, by function, in the business of collecting and preserving historical items. They had equally prominent roles in shaping memory. The well-traveled elite of Brazil's belle époque recognized that museums played a central role in the imagination of national communities throughout the North Atlantic. Gustavo Barroso, Brazil's most vocal museum advocate of the early twentieth century, looked enviously to England, France, Spain, and Portugal, where historical, military, and art museums created national traditions on a mass scale. Brazil's slowness to join these civilized nations in the foundation of national museums stoked Barroso's fears that the Brazilian nation would soon lose touch with its past, and by extension, its claims to nationhood. Barroso, therefore, agitated for a place where the fleeting past could be forever fixed in hallowed galleries. The fruit of these efforts—the National Historical Museum—"saved" the material and spiritual vestiges of that past. It mattered little that the past saved from oblivion was wealthier, nobler, whiter, and more stable than any citizen of Brazil could actually remember. The enticing fiction of a pristine national past, enshrouded in the mantle of *national* memory, would soon attract the reformers who came to power in the Revolution of 1930.

The problem for the new class of politicians and memory keepers that emerged out of the regime change of 1930 was that the past was not nearly as secure in the museum as they would want. Federal museums rarely produced the type of tensions generated in the politics of preservation. The permanent exhibit at the National Historical Museum did not spark embittered history wars. Nearly everyone who visited the Imperial Museum built in Petrópolis left with a positive feeling toward the Brazilian Empire. The National Museum of Fine Arts was a venue for quiet reflections of the history of beauty in Brazil.

Museums could, however, produce anxiety about the Brazilian past. The history of European colonialism, race mixture, slavery, and poverty engendered discomfort among museum professionals and museum-goers about the proper way a modern Brazil should remember its past. These anxieties concerned more than just the dead past. At stake was discomfort with the process in which Brazilian culture formed. The articulation and partial containment of these anxieties rendered the museum a *realm of memory,* where elite, professional, and popular actors tried to fashion the past around the needs of the present.[2] When hegemonic control of the past fell short of this goal, as it did in the summer of 1940 at the National Museum of Fine Arts, the museum could serve as a site of contested, divided, and anxious national memories. However, when museums were able to contain the past, as the Imperial Museum did at the end of the Estado Novo, a self-selecting class of museum professionals and museum-goers reveled in the opportunity to remember a national past that was grand, noble, and heroic. Under Vargas, museums were central to the politics of memory.

Building *A Casa do Brasil*

President Pessoa can be credited as the first federal official to museumify the republic's relationship to the national past. But the idea was not his. It was Gustavo Barroso, a fellow northeasterner and relative of the president, who envisioned the institutional relationship between past and present through a national museum. Born in 1888 into a traditional family in the state of Ceará, by the first decade of the twentieth century, Barroso had moved to Rio de Janeiro where he established himself as an essayist, journalist, and chronicler. Barroso witnessed dramatic changes in the capital's urban and social infrastructure, as tree-lined boulevards, chic cafés, and beaux-arts façades radiated out from the old city center, and *favelas* (shantytowns) sprung up on nearby hillsides. When Barroso witnessed the "civilizing process" at work in the national capital, he commented on the cultural meanings of modernity in Brazil. His first major publication, an ethnographic study of the northeast entitled *Terra do Sol* (1912), reminded his carioca readers that civilized Rio was still part of a larger society that included the drought-afflicted interior, with its resilient inhabitants, popular culture, and agrarian rhythms.

The same year *Terra do Sol* first appeared, Barroso published a short essay entitled *O Culto da Saudade* (The cult of nostalgia), which directly addressed the meaning of memory and modernity in Brazil.[3] The short piece would mark the northeasterner as one of the principal figures of Brazilian memory politics during Brazil's transition from an agrarian, seigniorial monarchy into an urban, industrializing republic. Writing under the pseudonym of João do Norte (likely a wordplay on the pen name of a widely read chronicler of early-twentieth-century Rio, Paulo Barreto, a.k.a. João do Rio), Barroso blasted the republican political culture for its disregard for traditions and fallen heroes. Barroso characterized his fellow Brazilians as spiritually impoverished in comparison to Europeans who, he argued, celebrated their heritage in historical pageants, festivals, and reenactments of long-past military battles. Barroso applauded the Germans, French, and British for their interest in preserving historic sites—an ethos he claimed was wholly unknown to Brazilians. As for Brazil, Barroso lamented that traditions were so undervalued that anyone who should try to put on a historical pageant would be showered with ridicule.[4] In their wanton disregard for historical pageantry and historical artifacts, Barroso found Brazilians incapable of transporting their past into the present. Barroso ended the essay decrying, "*O Culto da Saudade* is still not for us."

Largely ignored when it first appeared in the Rio daily *Jornal do Commercio*, Barroso's lament has become a pivotal text in the history of Brazilian memory. The text established some of the basic parameters for historical preservation in a political culture that had not fully committed to the idea that the national past merited celebration and that historical objects should be systematically preserved as proof that Brazil did indeed have a past worth remembering. The text is equally significant for the manner in which it illustrates how certain members of the educated urban male elite were highly critical of the "Tropical Belle Époque," which refashioned Rio in the image of Paris. Like much of the café society of the turn of the century, *O Culto da Saudade* idealizes Paris, but it is a Paris of picturesque market festivals at Les Halles, not bourgeois outings at the Tulleries. Like João do Rio, Barroso marveled at a transformed Rio, but what he found most stunning was the loss of the old city. For Barroso, boulevards did not create a visually pleasing, hygienic city, but rather destroyed the routes once taken by Christmastime street processions in years gone by. In lamenting the loss of tradition, Barroso criticized the same markers of modernity that the white elite were supposedly embracing as symbols of their transformation into modern citizens. Barroso would cultivate this antimodern, anticosmopolitan romanticism throughout his lengthy career as author, museum director, and ultraconservative political activist.

After the First World War, Barroso continued to call on public leaders to take remedial action against the loss of historical artifacts. Typical of Barroso's prose was the following passage, published in 1921 in the popular Rio magazine *Ilustração Brasileira:*

> There is just one nation in the world that does not possess a historical museum. That nation is Brazil. This nation's disinterest in its past has come to the point where historical objects—remembrances of the lives and deeds of our grandparents—are being grabbed up by foreigners through auction. Worse still, some objects are simply disappearing for all time.
>
> It is nearly impossible to come across locales containing relics dating from the earliest years of our nation's life. One cannot find any objects dating from the Expulsion of the Dutch [1641] or the War of the Mascates [1710–1714]. Objects dating from the more recent past are also being lost. A scant few objects are preserved in the National Archive, the Army's Munitions Depot, and the Naval Museum. Preservation has been left to the actions of private individuals rather than the government.
>
> Yet this policy has achieved very little. On a daily basis the newspapers decry the public sale of furnishings and tableware once used at the Imperial

Palace by our country's most eminent figures. They warn our public officials that works of art and historic objects are at risk of leaving the country. Yet the Government does not hear, see, nor care. Its greatest preoccupation is the deficit.[5]

Barroso's harsh words for government priorities — mediated through an apocalyptic vision of a vanishing national past — went unanswered until 1922, when Pessoa agreed to create a national historical museum to mark the celebration of the centennial of Brazilian independence. In the museum's founding decree, President Pessoa authorized the institution to collect, preserve, classify, and exhibit objects related to national history and to act as a "school of patriotism for the understanding of the History of the Fatherland [*História Pátria*]."[6] Barroso, who had worked with Pessoa at the international peace conference in Versailles, was designated as the museum's director. Barroso immediately began collecting materials for a museum set to be inaugurated at the Centennial Exposition. Fittingly, the museum was part of the Industrial Pavilion, a neocolonial structure that symbolized the compatibility of the new and the old. Perhaps the Culto da Saudade was not a lost cause.

In spite of the lofty ideals evoked in its founding decree, the museum's early days were precarious. The popular press poked fun at the collection of odds-and-ends that Barroso managed to cobble together from public agencies and scouting expeditions in the interior. Some federal legislators grumbled that the museum would be ripe for government waste and clientelism.[7] Public visitation, which topped 20,000 during the Centennial Exposition, plummeted once the fair ended. When a reorganized permanent exhibit opened to the public in 1923, the small number of visitors found the museum's physical accommodations to be cramped and ill-equipped for storing and displaying delicate objects. In its early years, the museum found it extremely difficult to attract visitors without the added lure of commercial emporiums, exotic foreign pavilions, and amusement parks.

Barroso continued to collect historical artifacts and paintings from other federal buildings, while cultivating the goodwill of private philanthropists, including the industrialist-financier Guinle family. In 1924, the museum also published its first catalog, offering a systematic overview of the objects upon which a national memory was being built. Still, federal funding remained anemic during the presidencies of mineiro Artur Bernardes

28 Caricature of Gustavo Barroso Founding Museu Histórico Nacional. Barroso, astride a stately white horse, wears the uniform of the Dragões da Independência, the ceremonial guard of the nation. This caricature by Calixto Cordeiro (a.k.a. Klixto) implies that the collection destined for the new Historical Museum amounted to little more than discarded household utensils. *Fon-Fon*, 1922.

(1922–1926) and paulista Washington Luiz (1926–1930). Brazilian historical memory may have had an official home in the Museu Histórico, but that house was small, shabby, and built on unstable ground.

The museum's future clouded when Getúlio Vargas came to power and summarily dismissed Barroso in retribution for his support of Júlio Prestes in the presidential campaign preceding the Revolution of 1930.[8] Barroso's replacement, historian-linguist Rodolfo Garcia, was a respectable intellectual, but he lacked the technical experience and personal investment in museum management that Barroso had demonstrated since the early 1910s. Aside from the flag which Vargas donated to the museum on Flag Day 1930, Vargas and the Provisional Government initially exhibited little interest in supporting the museum. The uncertainties of the Provisional Government did not deter Garcia and his staff from taking a more proactive stance toward historical display. Innovations included an April 1931 exhibition commemorating the centennial of the abdication of Dom Pedro I, the acquisition of several hundred pieces of artwork and historical objects from the defunct Naval Museum, the transfer of several major history paintings from the Escola Nacional de Belas Artes, and the organization of a post-secondary course in museum curatorship, the first of its kind in Brazil.[9]

The Exposição Comemorativa do Centenário da Abdicação, which opened to the public on 7 April 1931, set a new paradigm for museums and memory.[10] First and foremost, the four-hundred-piece exhibition signaled a definitive change in collection management within an institution that was initially not far from a storeroom of historical bric-a-brac. The temporary exhibit demonstrated that the museum could develop a systematic approach to its collection, tailoring temporary and permanent displays to distinct historical narratives. In this case, the narrative was built around the events leading up to the end of the First Reign, but the precedent had been set for a multitude of narratives drawn from the same collection of national treasures. The exhibit also indicated that size and physical space of the permanent collection had reached a critical mass sufficient to sustain smaller, limited-run exhibitions that could be separated from the permanent displays. The exhibit foreshadowed larger shifts in collection management as the organization and classification of the museum's collection drifted away from ahistorical groupings toward a more selective strategy of object grouping organized around chronological affinities, thematic coherency, and provenance. This organizational change was manifest in the gradual renaming of museum galleries from object-referent galleries (for example, Sala dos Retratos, Sala das Bandeiras, Arcada dos Canhões) to figure/period-referent galleries (for example, Sala Pedro I, Sala Almirante Barroso, Sala do Paraguay). Finally, the Exposição Comemorativa do Centenário da Abdicação formalized new cataloguing procedures, where accession and transfer records were systematized, assigning each object an archival niche in the official repository of the nation's material heritage.

When Barroso resumed the directorship of the MHN in November 1932, he returned to an institution that had assumed a leading role in memory politics by taking a systematic approach to collection management, research in material culture, and display techniques. Barroso continued the changes initiated under Garcia as he pursued further innovations in collection management through the creation and expansion of galleries named after prominent museum patrons, including Armando Guinle, a wealthy financier, Miguel Calmon (du Pin e Almeida), a Bahian statesmen and diplomat active in the republic, and Júlio Ottoni, a descendant of an important nineteenth-century mineiro family. Fallen national heroes, including Dom Pedro I and General José Francisco de Miranda Osório (1800–

1887), earned their place in the museum galleries. Although the ideological underpinnings of this new grouping strategy would not be fully apparent until the late 1930s, as early as 1932 it was evident that the MHN had altered its strategies of collection management in order to consolidate the material and taxonomic foundations for the veneration of patrons and heroes within rationalized gallery spaces. Moreover, the rising profile of state and private donors indicated that the Museu Histórico was moving from the margins of the cultural arena toward a more central place in the symbolic and institutional production of the national historical memory.

The political instability outside the museum contrasted sharply with the calmness reigning inside the museum. On the left, a popular front movement hoped for radical change in the Brazilian social order. On the right, the Integralist movement challenged the viability of the liberal constitutional state. Barroso, meanwhile, redoubled his efforts to build a safe, reverent, well-managed "home" for the national memory in the heart of downtown Rio, just feet from the municipal market. As a leading member of the Integralist movement, Barroso's politics were ruthless.[11] As an intellectual, his politics were confrontational, paranoid, and conspiratorial. As a museum director, however, his politics were wholly domesticated. The moniker *A Casa do Brasil* (Brazil's House), popularized at the museum entrance and in the press, is indicative of Barroso's attempts to portray the National Historical Museum — and national history by extension — as a hallowed hearth safe from the storms that swept through the political world outside of the museum walls.

When Barroso invoked a stable, patriarchal home for the nation, he appealed to the same leitmotivs of reverence and nostalgia originally deployed in lobbying for the creation of a national historical museum. An early proponent for a "museum to store those glorious objects which stoically accompanied our warriors and heroes," Barroso acquired the material relics necessary to venerate the heroes of the Paraguayan War, the imperial state, and the early days of the republic.[12] The museum made the armaments, vestments, and personal effects once used by these figures into totems of nationhood. By 1939, when the MHN reopened after a large expansion and remodeling of gallery space, the organization of the MHN collection had completed the transition from the early object grouping based upon typology to object grouping based upon the veneration of patrons and heroes, where the names of the galleries celebrated patrons for their munificence and national "heroes" for their self-sacrifice. The Culto da Saudade was rendered a viable faith in a museum in which visitors were presented with an increasing number of sacralized objects and the sacralized space necessary to venerate the heroes of the national past.

Scientific collection management was the key distinction between early formulations of the Culto da Saudade and the organization of the MHN during the Estado Novo. In 1935, Barroso rehearsed the idea that the MHN was a "university establishment dedicated to historical studies."[13] In a more detailed mission statement, written for the first anniversary of the Estado Novo in 1938, Barroso expanded upon earlier definitions, characterizing the MHN in: "its conventional responsibilities, that is, the classification, cataloguing, and preservation of traditional historical objects, as well as its innovative responsibilities, including courses, conferences, lectures, commemorative exhibitions timed to special dates, and the defense of the historical and artistic patrimony of the country." Barroso continually stressed the museum's evolving educational and technocratic responsibilities, arguing that the MHN was charged with the double mission of "holding and preserving the relics of our past" and "making these relics into instructive lessons for present and future generations."[14] The memory keepers at the MHN, like their counterparts in other branches of the state, judged themselves against ascendant notions of the educational and technical importance of museum management within a larger framework of state politics.

Several factors justified Barroso's appeal for recognition and support based upon the educational and technical aspects of MHN operations. Between 1933 and 1944, the museology course, organized in 1932, trained ninety-six women and thirty-six men. The graduates formed Brazil's first cadre of museum professionals trained in art history, Brazilian history, and conservation.[15] Major private donations, complemented by a smaller number of publicly funded acquisitions, provided the new cadre of museum professionals opportunities to apply their expertise to the difficult task of classifying, cataloguing, and memorializing hundreds of memory artifacts. The magnificent Miguel Calmon collection, donated to the MHN in 1936, required significant forethought in the creation of classification criteria and display techniques appropriate for a gallery space that could honor donor Alice Calmon, her deceased husband, and the Brazilian state, *while simultaneously* illustrating the most recent innovations in collection management.[16] Although the romantic sentimentalism of the Culto da Saudade could never be abandoned, the museum staff had to demonstrate its technical expertise and professionalism at a crucial moment in which the federal

Table 5 National Historical Museum Permanent Exhibit, 1924–1945

HISTORICAL SECTION		
1924	c. 1930	1945
S. dos Ministérios	S. Pedro I	S. Guilherme Guinle
S. dos Retratos	S. Smith de Vasconcelos	S. Dom Pedro I
S. das Bandeiras	S. do Trono	S. Dom Pedro II
Pátio dos Canhões, das	S. Osório	S. General Osório
Pedras, e das Coches	S. do Paraguai	S. Duque de Caxias
S. do Trono	S. dos Ottoni	S. Smith de Vasconcelos
S. do Septro	S. Mendes Campos	S. dos Ottoni
S. da Constituinte	S. Almirante Barroso	S. Mendes Campos
S. dos Capacetes	S. Otávio Guinle	S. Arnaldo Guinle
S. Osório	S. Arnaldo Guinle	S. Barbosa Rodrigues
S. dos Trofeus	S. da República	S. Carlos Guinle
Escadaria dos Escudos	S. Guilhermina Guinle	S. dos Vice-Reis
Escadaria das Armas	S. da Abolição	S. Barão de Amazonas
Galeria das Nações	S. Carlos Gomes	S. Almirante Tamandaré
S. da Abolição	S. dos Capacetes	S. Conde de Bobadela
S. do Exílio		S. Conde de Porto Alegre
S. da República		S. Almirante Saldanha
		S. Coelho Netto
		S. Miguel Calmon
		S. Deodoro da Fonseca
		S. da República
		S. Tiradentes
		S. João VI
		Pátio Epitácio Pessoa
		S. Getúlio Vargas
		S. Carlos Gomes

NUMISMATICS		
S. Guilherme Guinle	S. Guilherme Guinle	S. Guilhermina Guinle
	S. Zeferino de Oliveira	S. Zeferino de Oliveira
	S. Cândido Sotto Maior	S. Otavio Guinle
		S. Cândido Sotto Maior

S=Sala [Gallery]
Sources: *Catalogo Geral* (1924); MHN-AP DG 1 1 (7) *Relatório Anual de 1930* (1931); Winz, *A Casa do Trem* (1960), 466–76; *Guia do Visitante* (1957)

29 Sala Miguel Calmon, Museu Histórico Nacional, *c.* 1944. Courtesy of Museu Histórico Nacional/Banco Safra.

state apparatus assumed a more systematic and bureaucratized position toward all aspects of public policy.

The dual forces of sentimentalism and professionalization allowed the MHN to assemble a collection of goods and gallery spaces that purported to narrate the full sweep of the Brazilian historical experience, from the colonial period through the declaration of the Estado Novo. Barroso had yearned for a comprehensive view of Brazilian memory since the early 1910s. By the 1940s, journalists praised the MHN for providing opportunities to "see" all of Brazilian history at one place in one visit. One newspaper report published in 1941 stated that a visit to the museum "was easier, faster, more interesting, and more enjoyable than reading a history book [which can never] transmit the emotion of real, everlasting images which fill the silent gallery of museums."[17]

The question remained, though, whether the view of Brazil was truly panoramic, or merely panoptic. As historians and curators, Barroso and his staff had access to a wide variety of sources about the Brazilian past. The bibliographic and archival collection assembled between 1922 and 1945, in conjunction with the material culture on permanent display, offered—and continues to offer—a wealth of information on the national historical formation. The museum staff had at its disposal the raw materials to tell many stories of the Brazilian past. The museum, moreover, was part of a network of cultural and educational institutions that produced historical narratives based upon professional training, primary research, and debate. Barroso circulated within the same universe as many of the most important historians of the Vargas era. Yet unlike some contemporaries, Barroso and his staff chose to avoid questions of class formation, labor relations, and racial mixture. The three most innovative historians of the period, Gilberto Freyre, Caio Prado Junior, and Sérgio Buarque de Holanda would have seen little of their historiographic innovations in the National Historical Museum. What visitors to the MHN saw, instead, was a noble view of the Brazilian past where production and labor were largely absent and the faces were overwhelmingly white. Dom Pedro II reigned not as an abstract monarch known only in likeness, but as a real personage whose material effects were accessible. The *saudades* invoked by the MHN were, at their core, longings for a seigniorial, aristocratic, and bellicose society that lived in the light of God and glory. Upon entering the gallery, the visitor was to be spiritually *moved* by the proximity to small and monumental relics of elite life.

This emotional narrative of the national past was built upon a collection of *durable material objects* that made their way into the museum's collections and galleries. The durable-materialist bias circumscribed the social scope of historical representation to the regions, families, social classes, and corporate institutions that lived in a highly evolved material culture. Hence, the overwhelming presence of the aristocracy, the landed elite, the military, and the high church in the MHN's galleries, because it was these groups that historically had comprised the social strata living within a material culture of durable tableware, metalwork, armaments, jewelry, furniture, and liturgical vessels. These groups developed the built environment and cultural habits to protect semidurable items such as painting, fabrics, and paper from the elements. The galleries at the Museu Histórico were literally bursting at the seams with durable and semidurable objects. Objects were piled into display cases; statues and busts covered tabletops; paintings hung one above another. The effect of this display strategy actually exaggerated the material wealth of the social experience consecrated in the galleries. That was the point of the MHN displays.

Those social strata that lived in a nondurable material culture were effectively pushed to the margins of the representative reconstruction of the national history. When nonelites did appear, they were viewable only through the durable objects of elites. Such was the case of slaves, who were inserted into the museum's narrative in the Sala Mendes Campos, but through the shackles and other instruments of torture and punishment used by the master class. These display strategies not only failed to illuminate the public and private lives of slaves but also obscured the presence of skilled slave artisans in the manufacture of many of the material objects found in adjacent galleries.

Lest one believe that Barroso deliberately eliminated all references to nonelites in collection organization, two points should be kept in mind. First, Barroso could accept the idea of folkloric and popular history, as long as these were separated from the national historical museum. Barroso began his publishing career as an amateur folklorist. In 1942, he proposed that a national ethnographic museum be organized around a collection representing regional diversity and popular life.[18] The National Historical Museum was a museum for elite history, but the national museum system could accommodate nonelites. Second, the collection inherited by the MHN was made up of objects that already distorted the historical agency of the popular well before museum curators intervened. For example, *Allegory of the Law of the Free Womb,* one of a small number of objects in the MHN's permanent exhibit to represent blacks, was in reality a product of white memories, produced to glorify the memory of an enlightened emperor, rather than the slaves and free people of color who actually participated in the destruction of slavery. The same can be said of Vitor Meireles's *Batalha Naval do Riachuelo,* a work of enormous proportions that erased the presence of Afro-Brazilian sailors at the famous 1865 naval battle, and then reinscribed this erasure in the shrine to the nation's memory. The exclusionary memories of nineteenth-century monumental works could be transferred to, not necessarily created by, the memory sites of the Vargas regime. Of course, the MHN did little to dispel the notion that freedom was a magnanimous act of the emperor, rather than a hard-fought victory won by a broad range of historical actors including those Afro-Brazilians in the Brazilian navy at Riachuelo. Historical amnesia was produced in the nineteenth *and* twentieth centuries.

In spite of the silences inscribed onto the objects themselves, the exhibition strategies adopted by the MHN reinforced elitist cultural values inherited from the nineteenth century. The accession criteria and object

30 A. D. Bressae, *Allegory of the Law of the Free Womb, c.* 1880. Plaster, 171 cm. Courtesy of Museu Histórico Nacional/Banco Safra.

placement glorified the achievements of the propertied elite, the nobility, and the officer class as the protagonists of national history. These same criteria wrote nonelites out of the story. In a sense, the display strategies exaggerated social stratification, because the material culture of nonelites were summarily disarticulated from the material culture of elites. The museum visitor would find it impossible to understand how the elite interacted with the poor and their dependents.

Again, many of the monumental works executed for the imperial state were explicitly designed to glorify the national elite as the agents of Brazilianness. The objects in the collection conditioned the memories of Brazilian history on display at the MHN. Nevertheless, textual and pictorial labeling that may have helped to better locate any object within its larger material and social context was limited. Guided tours were available only by special request, and the 1924 catalog provided little more than physical dimensions, medium, and provenance. (The privately published guidebook *Guias do Brasil/Green Guides* offered the most comprehensive overview of the museum galleries.)[19] Photographic reproductions of objects in the museum collection were difficult to come by. Unlike the Museu Nacional, a museum of natural history, the Museu Histórico Nacional did not have an educational services division. The MHN was undoubtedly a realm of memory. However, access to this realm was highly restricted.

Of course, the MHN was a public museum open to most any visitor who took the initiative to enter the imposing entrance. However, only a small group of museology students, historians, and antiquarians had the tools to "read" objects for their historical, artistic, and material significance. The scholarship produced by the museum's curatorial staff, published in the museum's *Anais,* could be highly nuanced in its analysis of the complex, interconnected social and cultural processes in which objects were produced, used, and ultimately museumified. Yet, this information was unavailable to the uninitiated museum-goer. Instead, the uninformed museum-goer was asked to see the museum galleries as sites of enchantment and romantic nostalgia, heightened by the pronounced disconnect between the history embedded in the exhibited objects and the viewer's ability to see that history. There is clear evidence that some visitors did indeed find enchantment in the museum galleries. Others were just as likely to be distracted by overstuffed galleries. The vast majority simply stayed away.

The MHN adapted itself to the Estado Novo regime by strengthening its ties to the ideological underpinnings of authority, domesticity, and patriarchy that legitimated the Vargas dictatorship, while concurrently strengthening its ties to the technocratic and administrative impulses that also legitimated the regime. The MHN of the Estado Novo would continue to imagine itself as Brazil's emotional home, but it built this home around a self-representation of education, scientific management, and civic imperative. Although Barroso would find himself somewhat marginalized from

the modernists who enjoyed direct access to Capanema, the MHN successfully maneuvered itself into a comfortable position within the Estado Novo
state apparatus by appealing to a broad range of regime goals, including
reverence for authority, elitism, and patriotism. The dilemma lay in the
projection of these ideals onto the nation's memory.

Rehabilitating the Memory of Empire: The Museu Imperial

The legal ban on the Braganças, issued soon after the Proclamation of the
Republic, had been a sensitive area in the national memory since the late
nineteenth century.[20] News of Dom Pedro's death in December 1891 generated fond memories of Brazil's long-reigning monarch at a time when
the republic was embattled from within. For certain elites with monarchist
sympathies, the Hotel Bedford, Pedro's Parisian home-in-exile, became a
pilgrimage destination during their European travels. Within Brazil, the
emperor's daughter Isabel continued to command an especially loyal following among the popular classes who credited her, justifiably or not, with
the abolition of slavery. During the First Republic, the Instituto Histórico
e Geográfico Brasileiro pushed to reintegrate Pedro into a national civic
pantheon, requiring that all new members deliver a public speech on the
fallen monarch.[21] Radically inclined republicans, by contrast, saw little to
be gained in resurrecting the image of the emperor. The violent backlash
against sebastianist (a millenarian-monarchist phenomenon common to
the Portuguese-speaking world) elements at Canudos and Contestado was
unquestionably fueled by antimonarchist hatreds. Radical republicanism
notwithstanding, Pedro II and the Brazilian Empire continued to nag at
the memory of the republic. In 1920, even Ruy Barbosa, a Historical Republican par excellence and author of the original prohibition against the
Braganças, questioned the wisdom of denying the nation its emperor. The
celebration of the centennial of Brazilian independence helped accelerate
a process in which the 1889 ban was rescinded and the remains of Pedro
and his wife Tereza Cristina could be repatriated to Brazilian soil. As Lilia
Mortiz Schwarcz has eloquently argued, the reign of Pedro II may have
ended in November 1889, but Pedro remained king well into the twentieth century. Pedro was a ghost who haunted the nation's memory.[22] After
1930, federal museums played a crucial role in giving this ghost flesh and

blood and physical sites in which the nation could enact its affectionate, occasionally ambivalent, relationship with the empire.

The museumification of Dom Pedro II began in 1920, when Edgard Roquette-Pinto assembled several objects once belonging to the monarch for the installation of a new gallery at the Museu Nacional.[23] The following year, Alfredo Ferreira Lage, a wealthy industrialist from Minas Gerais, used his personal collection of vestments, portraits, and furnishings once belonging to the Braganças to create the Museu Mariano Procópio, located in Juiz de Fora, Minas Gerais. By the time President Epitácio Pessoa authorized the organization of the National Historical Museum to commemorate the centennial of Brazilian independence, the imperial family was well on its way to rehabilitation. Gustavo Barroso eagerly collected materials once belonging to the emperor for the new national historical museum, setting the stage for a full embrace of the empire within the museum setting.

The pace of rehabilitation accelerated after the Revolution of 1930. Institutions such as the IHGB and the National Library underwrote historical research on the Braganças.[24] The MHN organized separate galleries for the material and monumental worlds of Pedro I and Pedro II. Encouraged by officialdom's turn toward the imperial past, Alcindo Sodré, town councilman and director of the Historical Museum of the city of Petrópolis, petitioned Vargas to authorize the construction of a mausoleum for Pedro II and Empress Tereza Cristina. Sodré also called for the creation of a public museum in the emperor's former summer palace, located in the historic district of the mountainous town. A frequent visitor to Petrópolis, Vargas accepted Sodré's petition and authorized the construction of a mausoleum for the emperor and empress, while making preparations for the foundation of a federal museum dedicated to the memory of the empire.

Vargas's speech at the mausoleum's dedication praised Dom Pedro II as a heroic leader, great man of letters and science, and patriot who brought stability and dignity to nineteenth-century Brazil. Under Pedro's benevolent rule, Vargas argued, Brazil experienced internal integration, the defense of national territory, the "evolution" from slavery to free labor, and the birth of industrialization. In this highly sympathetic portrait of the monarchy, an aged and sickly D. Pedro II willingly sacrificed the throne to make way for the new republican order. The republicans, according to Vargas, remained respectful of their deposed leader who willingly departed for exile in Europe rather than provoke internal division.[25] Vargas's vision

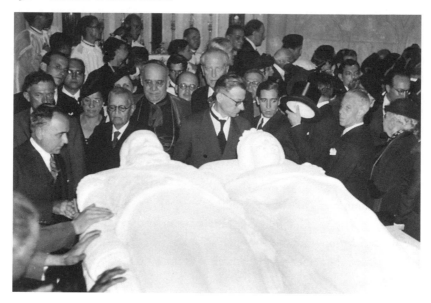

31 Vargas Attends Inauguration of Imperial Mausoleum, 5 December 1939. The inauguration of the Imperial Mausoleum was a highpoint in Vargas's romance with the memory of Dom Pedro II. Courtesy of AN-Fundo Agência Nacional.

of the history of the empire and the events surrounding the Proclamation of the Republic was highly attractive. As memory, it fit perfectly into the Vargas regime's attempts to complete the rehabilitation of the Bragança monarchy. As history, however, there were many flaws in Vargas's version of nineteenth-century Brazilian society. The rehabilitated empire was a fiction written on nostalgia.

With the emperor and empress safely entombed at the intersection of civic and sacred space, Sodré turned toward the creation of a larger monument to the memory of the imperial state. In March 1940, Vargas authorized the Ministry of Education to organize a museum to "collect, classify, and exhibit objects of historical or artistic value related to the Brazilian Monarchy, with special focus on Dom Pedro II."[26] As director of the new museum, Sodré secured a guarantee that the Museu Imperial would also be responsible for the history of Petrópolis. This is one of the best examples in which local history enthusiasts used federal resources to preserve and display local memory.

The patronage networks set in motion by the organization of the Museu

Imperial paralleled many relationships that drove the expansion of the Museu Histórico's collections. Like the early MHN, the Museu Imperial's core collection was built around objects transferred from other federal institutions. Key objects acquired from other federal agencies included the crowns, mantle, and scepters of Pedro I and Pedro II, as well as several important pieces of official portraiture commissioned by the imperial family as monuments to their own memory. In rebuilding a memory of the imperial state, the federal government could easily recycle many of the memory objects it already owned.

Additional objects acquired through purchase, trade, and donation augmented the collection assembled from within the federal government. The federal government purchased at auction a significant collection of nineteenth-century furnishings and decorative arts formerly owned by the noted antiquarian Djalma da Hermes Fonseca. Other acquisitions came from high-level political elites, including Vargas and the interventor of the state of Rio de Janeiro Amaral Peixoto. Guilherme Guinle, the Rio industrialist-financier who had already made several major gifts to the Museu Histórico and Museu da Cidade do Rio de Janeiro, joined state elites in making donations to the Museu Imperial. The most symbolic patronage came from Pedro Gastão de Orleans e Bragança, grandson of Dom Pedro II, who responded to the federal government's favorable policies toward the imperial family by offering to repatriate the archives of the Imperial Household.[27]

Throughout the museum's organizational phase, Sodré tried to depart from what he termed the antiquated "museum-bazaar" where a voluminous number of heterogeneous items were heaped one atop another. Without making mention of the MHN, Sodré imagined an institution that would not mirror Barroso's overstuffed galleries. Instead, Sodré envisioned a specialized museum that could be responsive to the needs of the local visitor and serve as a repository of "spiritual patrimony." In step with international currents in museum management, Sodré also saw the Museu Imperial as a center of scientific research and public education.[28] What Sodré may have failed to see was that the organization of a federal museum outside of the federal capital was part of a general tendency in federal management of cultural patrimony that celebrated regional patrimony while consolidating a direct federal presence in the cultural lives of areas outside the national capital.

Sodré faced numerous obstacles to creating a truly scientific retelling of the imperial past. With the former imperial residences at the Paço Imperial and Palácio São Cristóvão no longer recoverable as imperial residences (the former was a post office and the latter a museum of natural history), the Museu Imperial became more of a collage of the imperial state than a faithful reproduction of the summer palace as the Braganças would have known it. The challenge faced by Sodré was how to make the museum appear as authentic as possible, yet also invoke the aura of grandeur appropriate for the nation's monument to the empire. Sodré confronted the difficult choice between creating a memory through reproduction or metaphor. The balance was clearly tipped toward metaphor: Sodré opted to bring to Petrópolis a full range of symbols of regal authority, including the emperor's Crown, scepter, and mantle, which may not have been part of the ceremonial life of the mountain retreat but served to evoke the splendors of regalism.

Ironically, Sodré sometimes spoke as if the museum was a faithful rendition of the past, telling Rodrigo Melo Franco de Andrade the museum was to be installed in the "most appropriate historic house of the country, where the special rooms, such as the Throne Room, Pedro II's office, Ambassadors' Suite, Empress's Suite, Billiards Room, Chapel, Dining Room, and Bedroom of Brazil's last Imperial couple [could be] reproduced with the same pieces characteristic of the old Palace."[29] In fact, what opened to the public in March 1943 was an interpretation, rather than a reproduction, of the Braganças' life in Petrópolis. The size and orientation of some rooms and passageways had to be altered to accommodate a museum. Many of the objects installed in the galleries were not identical to the material culture of 1889, because the possessions of the imperial family had been dispersed after the republican state seized the Braganças' assets.[30] The majority of the collection assembled for the museum dated from the Second Reign, but many objects had never been used at the summer palace. Many items were typical of aristocratic taste, but never actually owned by Brazilian nobles.[31] The furniture in several rooms was arranged to suggest that the palace was the official seat of government, when in actuality it was not. The permanent exhibit incorporated aspects of the emperor's private life, which would have been unknown to a nineteenth-century visitor, including the imperial couple's sleeping quarters, chamber pots, and private chapel. The twentieth-century visitor was able to see the palace not as a modern-day courtier, but as a member of the Imperial Household, crossing boundaries between public and private spaces more freely than any nineteenth-century visitor. Naturally, these formerly invisible spaces were "staged" with the same care shown in public areas of the palace.

The Museu Imperial was not a fake. The Imperial Palace was indeed the home of a monarchy, with many of the trappings of kingship. The Braganças often stayed in their summer palace for extended periods, making Petrópolis the second capital of the Brazilian Empire. Foreign diplomatic missions even took up residence in Petrópolis, to be close to "Court." Still, the museum traded upon a fantasy of a national past that never actually existed, yet rarely failed to impress.

So, we ask, what did the visitors make of the fact that the Museu Imperial recreated the material world of the Braganças, but in doing so, also invented a world of spatial relationships, aesthetic refinement, and ceremonial events that did not necessarily correspond to any "real" life lived by the imperial family? Established intellectuals, writing in the press, were generally impressed by the museum. Pedro Calmon, the noted historian, spoke favorably of the way in which the "splendor of the tableware, the brilliance of the crystal, the severity of the corridors, the purity of the walls, the richness of the paintings" evoked another time where a king and an entire age resided. Max Fleiuss, secretary of the Instituto Histórico e Geográfico Brasileiro, called the museum a magnificent lesson of the past sure to attract tourists.[32]

If museum visitation can be used as a rough measure of popular reception, the poetic licenses taken by the curatorial staff increased, rather than diminished, public interest in the museum. The museum was an immediate hit and continues to be so. In its first ten months of public exhibitions, more than 22,000 visitors donned the unusual slippers required of all visitors and viewed the collection. The number of annual visitors quadrupled during the following three years. Visitation to the Museu Imperial soon exceeded the *combined* visitation to all other federal historical museums. These figures reflect not only a growth in the habit of museum-going but also the emergence of a new public interest in the life and material world of the empire. In founding the Museu Imperial, the Vargas regime struck a resonant chord in Brazil's collective historical memory.

Scholarship supported the popularization of Pedro II. Preservationist journals including the *Anais do Museu Histórico Nacional* and the *Revista do SPHAN,* the high-brow review *Estudos Brasileiros,* and the popular press all contributed to the renaissance of interest in the imperial state. The Imperial Museum's *Anuário* dedicated considerable scholarship to the Braganças, helping add an academic veneer to the museum's message that the emperor was a magnanimous, moral, erudite leader who led Brazil forward. Director Sodré led the recovery of the emperor, with passages like:

> Dom Pedro II has reached the point where he can be judged for all time. He can be credited for his love of country, the dignified way in which he dispatched his duties, his philanthropy, and his careful selection of human values. He was the wise philosopher-king. Dom Pedro II, liberal monarch whose soul was republican and whose habits were democratic, can be described by the following phrase: he ruled with a dictatorship of public morality.[33]

This type of scholarship did not refute the standard charges of radical republicans that the emperor had failed to modernize the empire's political structure and acquiesced to the maintenance of a slave regime when he himself was reputed to be opposed to slavery. Sodré did not suggest that the overthrow of the empire was wrong. State-sponsored histories sympathetic to the Braganças were not intended to encourage the small monarchist movements active in the 1930s.[34] Nevertheless, this scholarship indicates that the cultural apparatus of the Vargas state built a material and rhetorical world that undermined long-standing strains of antimonarchism in Brazilian republicanism and elevated the emperor to the status of a national hero who transcended the Proclamation of the Republic. Sodré encouraged Brazilians to treat the emperor as a leader "whose soul was republican and whose habits were democratic."

Vargas quickly caught on to the image of the philosopher-king, seeing in Dom Pedro the opportunity to make the empire and post–1930 republic part of the same historical continuum. Thus, Vargas was a regular visitor and patron to the Museu Imperial. The museum returned the favor by placing a bust of the dictator along the entrance to the restored palace. In a conscious re-creation of the material world of the emperor and the Second Reign, the bust was a clear anachronism. When Pedro II looked out of the palace's windows, he certainly did not see a bust of Vargas. But in terms of the cultural politics of the first Vargas regime, the bust made perfect sense as it stood to represent the president's watchful eye over the memory and materiality of Brazil's last emperor. Every visitor who took a few moments to step back into the world of the Second Reign brought Vargas along with them.

A Universal Survey Museum in the Tropics:
The Museu Nacional de Belas Artes

At first glance, the Museu Nacional de Belas Artes (MNBA), founded in 1937, would not appear to be a museum of national memory. Its collection was primarily made up of objects of art, not historical artifacts. Acquisitions privileged the works of contemporary artists who primarily painted non-historical themes. The museum dedicated a considerable amount of gallery space to non-Brazilian artists. Yet, like the Museu Histórico and the Museu Imperial, the MNBA played an important role in the management of memory during the first Vargas regime. The museum was founded at the same moment in which other federal institutions of memory, including the MHN, the Museu Imperial, and the SPHAN, were actively articulating a vision of the national historical self. Like those other agencies, the MNBA's primary function was the collection, cataloguing, and exhibition of a set of cultural goods—painting, sculpture, decorative arts, and numismatics—deemed to be representative of national traditions. Like more conventional history museums, the MNBA used objects produced in heterogeneous chronological and regional circumstances to position the Brazilian present such that it could lay claim to certain important markers of the national and "universal" past. The MNBA used these cultural goods to stage a narrative of the evolution of national culture that was intended to be read through the ritual of public visitation.

The National Museum of Fine Arts was legally created on 13 January 1937. Soon after, the National School of Fine Arts (Escola Nacional de Belas Artes, ENBA) was instructed to transfer a large portion of its permanent collection as well as the upper floors of its beaux-arts headquarters in the heart of downtown Rio to the new national museum. Works transferred from the ENBA included paintings that arrived with the Portuguese Court in 1808 as well as works brought to Brazil by the French Artistic Mission of 1816.[35] Other objects ceded by the ENBA included plaster statues once used as teaching tools at the national art academy, works awarded at the official salons, and works commissioned by the imperial and republican governments, including some monumental history paintings executed by Vitor Meireles and Pedro Américo. Subsequent acquisitions were made through purchase or private donation.

The majority of the collection followed the stylistic and thematic conventions established by the Imperial Academy of Fine Arts. The permanent exhibit at the MNBA showed a strong bias toward the neoclassical, romantic, and naturalist schools that had shaped "academic" painting in Brazil after independence. Artwork dating from the colonial period was scarce. A number of works done by contemporary artists appeared in the museum's collection, but the modernista style introduced at the Modern Art Week in 1922 was conspicuously absent when the galleries opened to the public. The one major exception to the unspoken prohibitions against modernista art was Cândido Portinari's much-acclaimed *Café* (1935), which had been acquired by the federal government after the painting won Second Honorable Mention at the Carnegie Institute International in Pittsburgh, Pennsylvania. Popular art, folk art, and indigenous art were not included in the permanent collection.

Oswaldo Teixeira, a native of Rio de Janeiro of humble origins who received his artistic training at the ENBA in the late 1910s and early 1920s, directed the MNBA. Teixeira's credentials as an academic painter were impeccable. After winning the Prêmio de Viagem à Europa, the coveted prize given to the winner of the annual salon that paid for two-to-five years of artistic study in Europe, Teixeira returned to Brazil to establish himself as a painter of conventional themes (still lifes, nudes, studio portraits, allegories) who experimented with new techniques, such as impressionism, while never abandoning his academic training in nineteenth-century sensibilities. Teixeira actively opposed modernism, reserving special criticism for Portinari, a former classmate at the National School of Fine Arts, and Pablo Picasso.[36] Like many of his predecessors who came out of the academic system, Teixeira exhibited a strong reliance upon state-sponsored artistic institutions for critical success and material sustenance. Teixeira's support for state patronage was manifest in his 1940 sycophantic essay, *Getúlio Vargas and Art in Brazil,* which lionized political leaders who supported the arts, most of all Vargas.

The appointment of such an avowed academic to the new National Museum of Fine Arts was bound to cause polemics within the art world where modernists and academics had been at odds since Lucio Costa's failed reforms of 1931. Artists and art critics were left to wonder how the Museu Nacional de Belas Artes could accurately document the historical evolution of Brazilian art when the director's opposition to modernism was so strong. By 1937, the pioneer modernists, including Lasar Segall, Anita Malfatti, Tarsila do Amaral, and Emiliano di Cavalcanti had earned their place in the history of Brazilian art. A slightly younger generation of modernists, led by Portinari, had brought Brazilian modernism to the attention of national and international critics. Defenders of modernism asked whether Teixeira would treat modernism as an aberration in Brazilian aesthetics that reflected the cultural dislocations of the early twentieth century and degeneracy of European art, or as a valued paradigm shift, as neoclassicism had been in the early nineteenth century. These debates were not just about art; they were about the organizing principles of Brazilian culture.

Under Teixeira's watch, the permanent exhibit at the MNBA managed to contain modernism. However, temporary exhibitions, foreign expositions, and the press proved more fertile ground for the culture war between the moderns and the academics. The 1940 season proved to be particularly important in the struggle to fix the memory of the neoclassic tradition brought to Brazil in 1816.

Before the defenders of academic and modernist art squared off in 1940, the initial challenge faced by the MNBA was remodeling the outmoded galleries ceded by the ENBA. The curatorial staff also set out to reverse the damage to the permanent collection wreaked by decades of severe heat and humidity, inadequate storage facilities, and water infiltration.[37] Early work included improvements in storage and conservation facilities, modernizing lighting and ventilation, reconfiguring the gallery floor plans, and the restoration of works damaged in a major flood.[38] In the meantime, Teixeira and his staff rethought the entire organization of the permanent collection, guided by the principle that the MNBA could be transformed into a scaled-down, Brazilian version of the major museums built in the most important cities of Europe and the United States between the late eighteenth and early twentieth centuries. Teixeira wanted nothing less than to create a *universal survey museum* in the tropics.

The idioms and idiosyncrasies of "universal survey museums" would have been quite familiar to Teixeira and many of his colleagues who had firsthand experience with the grand narratives of civilization ritualized at the Louvre, the British Museum, and the Metropolitan Museum of Art.[39] As a recipient of the Prêmio de Viagem à Europa, Teixeira knew that the grand survey museum would be intelligible to the conservative cultural elite who cultivated the past amidst the acceleration of time. Teixeira could easily understand how large public art museums that divided their collections by nation, time period, and school created ritual spaces that could cre-

32 Interior of Museu Nacional de Belas Artes, *c.* 1938. The transformation of the *Pinacoteca* of the National School of Fine Arts into the National Museum of Fine Arts required significant repairs to the belle époque structure as well as a total reorganization of the cramped permanent galleries. Courtesy of CPDOC-GC.

ate canon, citizen, and nation through a progressive, yet compartmentalized movement through museum space.[40] The commemoration of canon would be important especially to a culture manager so heavily invested in the protection of the academic tradition.

The reorganization of the *pinacoteca* (art collection) of the National School of Fine Arts into a universal survey museum called the National Museum of Fine Arts involved a number of tasks, including the completion of structural improvements to the upper galleries of the belle époque edifice; a complete reinstallation of the permanent collection into regional schools and chronological periods; the transfer of the majority of the collection into storage; the reduction in the amount of wallspace used for exhibition, narrowing the vertical space allotted for wall hangings and increasing the voids between displayed objects; the commissioning of photographic reproductions of the permanent collection; and improvements in gallery illumination through the use of skylights, artificial lighting, and light-colored paint.

The actual collection changed relatively little, but changes to the organizational logic and the scenography created a museum space that could indeed ritualize canon, memory, and nation in new ways.

The academics who controlled the MNBA most surely felt comfortable within a museum space where the air of Europe hung heavily. Even the "Brazilian" masterpieces evoked Europe, many of which were actually painted in Europe. The academics could also take comfort in the scarcity of contemporary painting and sculpture of the modernist strain (in conflict with Teixeira's early pledges to be ecumenical in acquisition and exhibition choices).[41] Defenders of modernism were not so pleased. A short headline in the influential carioca art journal *Bellas-Artes* asked rhetorically, "Would not it have been more logical for the National Museum of Fine Arts to organize its first galleries (greenhouses, dare we say) exhibiting contemporary national painters, rather than drawing upon the collections of French painting, which are by and large of little value?"[42] The battle lines for the spatial and discursive control of the MNBA had been drawn.

When Getúlio Vargas visited the Museu Nacional de Belas Artes in August 1939, he toured the closest approximation to a universal survey museum ever created in Brazil. The permanent exhibit was divided into eight galleries, organized by period and national school, and five collections, organized by donor.[43] The permanent exhibit also included a sculpture hall, dominated by Brazilian and international examples of classical sculpture, as well as a gallery to honor Rodolpho and Henrique Bernadelli, two brothers who had prominent roles in the visual arts during the late empire and First Republic. A final gallery, the Sala da Mulher Brasileira, exhibited an eclectic collection of portraits of Brazilian women.[44]

The thematic progression of galleries and the manner in which objects were distributed throughout the museum closely paralleled the display strategies of universal survey museums. The visitor entered the permanent galleries by ascending a grand staircase set within a soaring atrium. Classical sculpture was placed throughout the vestibule. The galleries intermixed painting, sculpture, and decorative arts steeped in academic conventions, while excluding nonacademic and popular art. The exhibition of national and international schools in distinct, yet adjacent galleries created a narrative of universal aesthetics that was broken down into discrete national specificities. The exhibition of classical sculpture, including a plaster replica of *Victory of Samothrace* (*Winged Victory,* second century B.C.), built bridges between Brazilian culture and the Ancients, as well as between the Brazilian national gallery and the Louvre, the reigning monarch of universal survey museums. Individual artistic genius was stressed in the exhibition of works by European masters, including Caravaggio, Rubens, and Van Dyck, as well as the organization of separate galleries reserved for the works of Brazilian masters Rodolpho Amoedo and the Bernadelli brothers. The genius of philanthropy was celebrated in the exhibition of donated collections.[45] Finally, the MNBA was similar to other universal survey museums in its selective display of only a small portion of the total collection, with the majority of its holdings being held in storage.[46] Maria Barreto, curator at the MNBA, described the choice to place only a portion of the total collection on permanent exhibit as proof that the MNBA was a modern museum that had shed any vestiges of the curiosity cabinet that once characterized the organization of museum display.[47]

The organization of the MNBA fit certain standards established by the universal survey museums of Europe and the United States. The translation of the European ideal to a Brazilian reality was not without problems, though, because the MNBA's collection was not as comprehensive as that of its North Atlantic models. The MNBA simply did not possess the range of objects held by universal survey museums such as the Louvre. More importantly, the history of the Brazilian national collection differed significantly from its counterparts in Europe. Few of the works owned by the Brazilian government had been acquired as trophies in foreign wars or archaeological expeditions. There were no Elgin Marbles or Benin Bronzes to grace the Brazilian collection. The curatorial staff could not make use of a collection of foreign masterpieces, stripped of their original contexts, to demonstrate the conquests of the Brazilian state and spirit. The state's collections did contain many objects of archaeological value, as well as a number of war trophies seized from outsiders during the wars of the colonial era and nineteenth century. But these objects were on exhibit at the National Museum and the National Historical Museum, not the National Museum to Fine Arts.

The number of copies, replicas, and works of mediocre quality further undermined any claims to "universal" status. Although Oswaldo Teixeira pledged to separate copies from originals, replicas of works by Velazquez and Raphael remained part of the permanent galleries. The sculpture gallery contained numerous plaster castings acquired in the nineteenth century.[48] Under the empire, the replicas had worked quite well as instructional devices for students enrolled in an art academy located far from the production centers of European art. But in a national museum trying to insert Brazilian art into the universal history of Western art, copies of universal works suggested that the national tradition might be less than authentic. At a moment in which modernists such as Lucio Costa were offering sharp criticism of neocolonial architecture and other forms of aesthetic mimesis, the preponderance of copies at the MNBA compromised the aura of singular masterpiece and artistic genius that a universal survey museum cultivates. The presence of copies located Brazil in a peripheral, dependent position to the centers of artistic production celebrated in the classical, Renaissance, and baroque galleries in major European collections. The intermixture of copies and originals, coupled with the paucity of national works predating the early nineteenth century, destabilized the MNBA's quest to be a peer of the acclaimed museums of Europe.

Nevertheless, the mere presence of the copies, and their incorporation into galleries highlighting the development of Western art, is emblematic of the MNBA's attempts to provide the Brazilian public with a grand narrative of art that culminated in the national artistic tradition and its masters. Moreover, the state's relationship to the National Museum of Fine Arts was not all that different from major European museums whose collections originated as princely collections, which were made public during an antimonarchist moment, and then augmented by national art academies and state patronage. Although the accent may have been heavy, Brazilians came to speak the lingua franca of the universal survey museum.

1940: French Art and the National Memory

Historical art could be as controversial as contemporary art is today, especially when exhibited at the self-proclaimed guardian of the nation's pictorial sensibilities. I concentrate my comments here on the Exposição da Missão Artística Francesa de 1816, a major retrospective of nineteenth-century Franco-Brazilian art held at the MNBA in December 1940.[49]

The late-year exhibit under consideration was actually one of two exhibitions of French art held at the National Museum of Fine Arts in 1940. The first exhibit, held midyear under the title Exposição da Pintura Francesa, assembled 175 paintings by major nineteenth- and twentieth-century French artists. Drawn from various public and private collections in France, the exhibit came to Brazil on the heels of an enthusiastic reception in Buenos

Aires and Montevideo. The well-received retrospective began with the neo-classical painting of Jacques-Louis David and followed through various schools of nineteenth- and twentieth-century French painting, including the romanticism of Eugène Delacroix, the impressionism of Claude Monet and Paul Cézanne, and the modernism of Henri Matisse, Pablo Picasso, and André Lhote. Most of the artists and nearly all of the works included in the exhibit had never been shown in Brazil.

From its opening night, the exhibit was a phenomenal success, attracting more than 40,000 visitors during its six-week midwinter run.[50] Public interest in the exhibit was undoubtedly stoked by the shocking news of the German occupation of Paris. The exhibit's blockbuster status could also be credited to the MNBA's strenuous efforts to publicize the show through press releases, newsreels, and public advertisements. The museum organized guided tours (*promenades*) of the special exhibit, enhancing the visitors' experience.[51] For the social elite and upwardly mobile middle classes targeted through advertisements posted in Rio's commercial center and upscale residential neighborhoods, the exhibit was the highlight of the 1940 cultural season. The exhibit was equally popular among the artistic community, which viewed up close original works by the French masters. Several art historians have commented that the 1940 show was highly influential among the students enrolled in the National School of Fine Arts, many of whom would become major cultural figures after the fall of the Estado Novo.[52]

An art exhibit of this significance was bound to influence the cultural debates of the day. The modernists were especially interested in the French art as a medium for understanding Brazilian art. In a review of the MNBA exhibit, Quirino Campofiorito, one of the more active artists and critics of the Vargas era, criticized the Brazilian artistic tradition for its failure to express the type of innovation seen in French art. Dismayed that the Brazilian academic tradition was slow in adopting new styles, Campofiorito admonished, "In the vanguard we will achieve noble expression, but if we remain in the situationist rear-guard, we will always be a servile shadow [of Europe], without personality, without our own physiognomy."[53] A critic with similar sensibilities ironically observed, "Those among us who are accustomed to giving opinions on painting will see once they have visited the French exhibit that reputed aesthetic absurdities and extravagances, not to mention those so-called 'degenerate' works attributed to the modernist demon are not creatures of Brazilian artists. One can already find them in the Louvre."[54] Although the exhibit itself made few explicit connections between French art and Brazilian culture, the exhibit occasioned another round of debate over the direction of artistic innovation in Brazil. A second exhibit of French art organized by the MNBA in 1940 brought the debate over art to the complex, contradictory memory of brasilidade.

The Exposição da Missão Artística Francesa de 1816 was made possible when Raimundo Ottoni de Castro Maya, a prominent industrialist-financier and art collector, purchased several hundred original watercolors and sketches executed by Jean-Baptiste Debret, history painter to the French Artistic Mission during a fifteen-year stay in Brazil (1816–1831). Castro Maya's purchase was a minor coup among a select group of wealthy Brazilians who had taken an interest in Brasiliana following the First World War. Largely forgotten for much of the nineteenth century, Debret's visual and textual impressions of Brazil, published in Paris under the title *Voyage Pittoresque et Historique au Brésil* (1834–1839), had reemerged as a coveted collector's item in the early twentieth century. Private collectors sought out the three-volume folio edition as a sign of distinction. A select group of collectors hoped to locate Debret's original watercolors, supposedly lost after the images had been converted into lithographs for the print edition of the *Voyage*. In 1939, Roberto Heymann, a Brazilian book dealer living in Paris, informed Castro Maya that he had discovered an unidentified number of originals in the possession of Debret's great-granddaughter. The Rio industrialist quickly agreed to purchase the works. Castro Maya claimed that the 300,000 francs paid for some 360 watercolors and sketches was the highest sum ever paid for any work of art about Brazil.[55]

With the purchase rights secured, Castro Maya briefly entertained the idea of donating the works to the Museu Nacional de Belas Artes before deciding upon a temporary exhibition at the museum. With the aid of well-placed allies in the federal government, Castro Maya won an exemption of import duties by claiming that the repatriated Debret originals would enrich the national artistic patrimony. In the meantime, the MNBA began to make arrangements for a sweeping retrospective on the French Artistic Mission. The Exposição da Missão Artística Francesa de 1816, inaugurated 23 November 1940, assembled nearly 570 works drawn from public and private collections. The Debret watercolors were the visual centerpiece of the show.

Early reviews of the exhibit were favorable. Oswaldo Teixeira, Gustavo Capanema, and the Rio press celebrated Castro Maya for reintroducing

Debret to Brazilian audiences. Art critics were especially impressed by the opportunity to take an intimate look at the public and private life of the Bragança Court. Debret received special praise for carrying on Lebreton's charge to institutionalize the neoclassical tradition in Portuguese America. For historians, art connoisseurs, antiquarians, and an urban public increasingly drawn to Brazil's imperial past, the exhibit brought together two great treasures of the nineteenth century: the memory of the Imperial State and the genius of the Academy.

Sweeping as it was, the exhibit's narrative of the formative period of the Brazilian nation-state raised ambivalent and at times downright disturbing memories of a historical and aesthetic past. Few questioned the pleasures of getting an up-close look at the pageantry of the Bragança Court and the material culture of early-nineteenth-century domestic life. What proved more difficult to embrace were the social relations of a slave society that had pretensions to being an enlightened empire in the tropics. In an era in which the empire was under rehabilitation, what was to be made of the unsavory aspects of nineteenth-century Brazilian society that were inseparable from the grandeur of the imperial family?

Certain images on display in the 1940 MNBA exhibit had a long history of causing discomfort among the Brazilian elite. One lithograph appearing in Volume II (1835) of Debret's *Voyage,* entitled *Feitors corrigeant des nègres à la roça* (Overseers punishing slaves on the farm) (see plate 2), had been especially troubling for nineteenth-century elites. In the immediate foreground is a master's house, built of stucco and brick. A partially disrobed European man is depicted in the midst of whipping a bound black male who has fallen to the ground. In the background, to the left, stand a cluster of daub-and-wattle huts. To the right, in front of a solitary hut, another slave has been lashed to a tree and is being whipped by a black man, under the watch of two other blacks — at least one of whom is carrying another whip. In the far distance, cultivated fields lead into virgin forest. The accompanying text described Brazil's overseers as prone to habitual cruelty. "When we arrived in Brazil," wrote Debret, "the overseers were generally Portuguese. Irascible and rancorous, it was quite common to see them punish their own slaves. In such circumstances, the victims suffered with resignation, enduring their torture." [56]

Overseers Punishing Slaves was but one of a number of scenes that portrayed the culture of slavery in Portuguese America. As a corpus, Debret's *Voyage* remains one of the most important documents on slavery in

Four Lithographs from Jean-Baptiste Debret's *Voyage Pittoresque et Historique au Brésil* (1834–1838). Not merely concerned with the ceremonial life of the Braganca Court, Debret was fascinated by social relations, labor and commercial practices, material culture, ethnic diversity, and gender relations in Brazilian society. Courtesy of Library of Congress–Rare Books and Special Collections.

33 *Dinner*

34 *Interior of the Gypsies' House*

35 *The War Cry of the Cororados*

36 *Overseers Punishing Slaves on the Farm* (detail)

nineteenth-century Brazil, including the brutality of master-slave relations. However, the *Voyage Pittoresque* was neither a sensationalist nor overly critical text. Debret was neither abolitionist nor sadistic voyeur. The majority of the scenes painted by Debret, including the scenes depicting slaves, capture moments of peace and sociability, not conflict. In comparison to other Europeans who traveled through Latin America in the nineteenth century, not to mention the broader visual culture of abolitionist propaganda which circulated throughout the North Atlantic, Debret was not particularly prone to fantasy or exaggeration. The entire genre of the picturesque journey was more sensitive to curiosity than scandal.[57]

Nevertheless, images such as *Overseers Punishing Slaves* deeply disturbed the nineteenth-century Brazilian elite who wanted so desperately to bring enlightenment to the tropics. In the third volume (1841) of the *Revista do Instituto Histórico e Geográfico Brasileiro,* the most important historical journal of the empire, a short article praised certain aspects of the *Voyage* but cautioned readers that Debret grossly misrepresented Brazilian society. The review specifically singles out *Overseers Punishing Slaves* as an image that offended due to its content and untruthfulness. Describing the Portuguese master class as the most benevolent among Europeans, the reviewer speculated that perhaps Debret had the misfortune to witness a scene of cruelty atypical of Brazil. However, the author would not concede that the Portuguese were cruel masters.[58] Other authors expressed displeasure with the intermixture of popular and elite society that runs throughout the *Voyage*.

With the success of nation building dependent upon a Europeanization of the *image* if not the reality of Brazilian society, Brazilian master class shuddered to see Debret expose the dark underside of Brazilian society, where slavery and brutality were ubiquitous. They bristled at the suggestion that the Portuguese character was unruly. They were repelled by Debret's multiethnic representation of Brazilianness. In a recent analysis of Debret's work as a neoclassical artist, art critic Rodrigo Naves goes further, arguing that Debret's watercolors of a slave society were so disturbing because they drew upon the aesthetic and ideological notion of degradation. Debret's overseers, and most especially his slaves, were debased and unredeemable as objects of noble and sublime neoclassical art. These figures exhibited neither the physical dignity nor the moral virtue of the neoclassical subject.[59]

Overseers Punishing Slaves crystallizes the forces of degradation that constantly destabilized and debased the implantation of enlightenment in Brazil. On the one hand, one observes the forces that degraded the slave: the white *feitor* and the agricultural field that denied the slave his freedom. The ultimate symbol of the slave's degradation is his violated body: thrown to the ground, bound, and bleeding. On the other hand stand the forces that degraded the white master class: callous cruelty and irrational treatment of productive capital. This European is neither a gentleman nor a scholar, but rather a brute whose clothing, staff, and body position differ little from the black figures in the background. Equally degraded are those Afro-Brazilians in the background who stand caught between agricultural work and cruelty. Outside of the scene stand those Brazilian aristocrats who tolerated, or even profited from, the persistence of a slave society. Scenes such as *Overseers Punishing Slaves* tacitly questioned the universal claims to civilization made by the nineteenth-century Brazilian elite.

The discomfort expressed in 1841 toward Debret's *Voyage* helps explain why the work went largely unread throughout the Second Empire. The vivid depiction of the citizenry transforming Afro-Brazilian slaves into objects of barbaric cruelties was simply too raw for Brazilian elites who fancied themselves to be sons of classical liberalism.[60] Rather than own up to the complex truths in Debret's observations, Brazilian intellectuals, including the IHGB historians, steeped in an ideology of liberalism and progress largely acted as if the *Voyage Pittoresque* had never been written. The artistic class, moreover, made a radical turn away from any depiction of slavery in the decades that followed Debret's departure for France in 1830, pushing the subject matter of Debret's *Voyage* to the margins of official art and memory. Aside from critical observations mentioned above, Debret's double monument to the foundation of the Brazilian Empire and the ambiguous implantation of the neoclassical tradition in a slave society went unknown on both sides of the Atlantic until the late nineteenth century. Only when slavery had been relegated to the historical record did Brazilian historians and antiquarians begin to place value on the original imprints. It would take several more decades before Debret would be integrated successfully into the national historical consciousness.

The problem was that the rehabilitation of Debret reopened some of the same distasteful memories of slavery that nineteenth-century liberals and artists had preferred to forget. With its frank representation of a society born out of slavery, images such as *Overseers Punishing Slaves* could be just as off-putting in 1940 as they had been one century earlier. Debret's *Voyage* was a poor candidate for Gustavo Barroso's Culto da Saudade. It was equally ill-suited for the Imperial Museum in Petrópolis. It contributed little to the ideology of Luso-tropicalism. The fact that the *Voyage* was presented to the public in their original colors (the original folios and the first Brazilian translation contained black-and-white lithographs, some hand-colored) heightened the potential for discomfort, as museum-goers could see raw, bloodied flesh in vivid detail. A close comparison of the black-and-white lithographs and the originals indicates that color greatly enhanced the splendor and the horror of Debret's Brazil. In message and media, the Debret watercolors called into question the image of benevolent slavery, imperial grandeur, and social harmony expounded by the sociologist Gilberto Freyre, the organizers of the fiftieth anniversary of the abolition of slavery, and most federal museums.

An equally unsettling problem raised in the rehabilitation of Debret was the disputed interpretation of the French Artistic Mission's contributions to Brazilian culture. Since the late nineteenth century, certain strains of Brazilian art criticism had argued that Lebreton and his compatriots tried to impose aesthetic dictates that were incompatible with a Luso-Catholic cultural context. Critics charged that the Frenchmen were out of step with their Luso-Catholic surroundings. The mission members did more damage than good, creating lesser works in the neoclassical and romantic tradition and short-circuiting Brazil's local artistic evolution.[61] The mission had many apologists in the nineteenth and early twentieth centuries, led by Afonso E. Taunay, descendant of two of the mission members, and Adolfo Morales de los Rios Filho, former director of the National School of Fine Arts. Nevertheless, when Castro Maya lent his collection as the anchor for an exhibition commemorating the French Artistic Mission, he faced the difficult fact that the mission members' artistic production would not generate the unconditional acclaim directed toward the painters featured in the French art retrospective held earlier in the year.

The ambiguous legacy of the French Artistic Mission never diminished the fact that the works exhibited in 1940 were of immeasurable historical and artistic value. Debret's watercolors were the most important of a corpus of visual materials documenting the political transition from colony to co-kingdom to independent empire. The repatriated watercolors offered valuable insights on land use, urban planning, architecture, material culture, decorative arts, and rural landscape at the beginning of the nineteenth century. The works of Debret, the Taunay family, and others captured the

Plate 1 Georgina de Albuquerque, *Primeira Sessão do Conselho do Estado*. 1922, oil on canvas, 260 × 210 cm. Exhibited during the Centennial Exposition of 1922, this state-commissioned painting embodied republican idealism of national history — elitist, heroic, and beautiful. Albuquerque's use of impressionistic effects in history painting is indicative of the domestication of the avant-garde in Brazilian academic painting. Courtesy of Museu Histórico Nacional/Banco Safra.

Plate 2 Jean-Baptiste Debret, *Feitors corrigeant des nègres à la roça*. 1828, watercolor on paper, 15 × 19.8 cms. In vivid color, the official history painter to the Portuguese and Brazilian Crowns depicted a scene of utmost cruelty and degradation. This image would rattle elite sensibilities in the nineteenth century and continue to haunt the memory of Brazil's historical formation in the twentieth century. Courtesy of Museus Castro Maya.

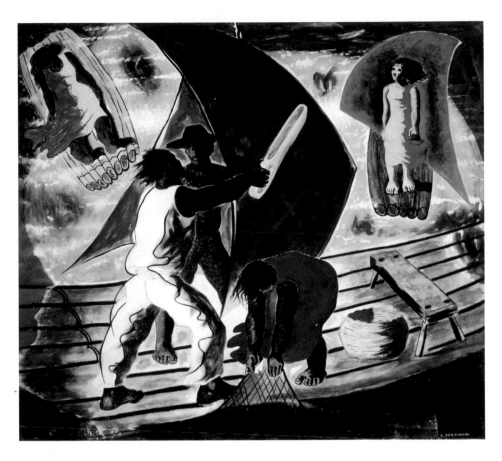

Plate 3 Cândido Portinari, *Jangadas do Nordeste*. 1939, tempera on canvas, 310 × 347 cm. In a radical departure from typical artwork sent abroad, *Jangadas do Nordeste* introduced American audiences to the Afro-Brazilian in bold brushstrokes and bright colors. The murals provoked significant discussion, mostly favorable, among American critics who took an interest in Brazil's multiracial cultural heritage. Courtesy of João Cândido Portinari.

Plate 4 Cândido Portinari, *Morro*. 1933, oil on canvas, 114 × 145.7 cm. Acquired by the Museum of Modern Art in 1939, *Morro* was exhibited in the museum's "Art in Our Time" exhibit, held during the summer of 1939. Although not officially part of the Brazilian mission to the New York World's Fair, *Morro* helped shape American ideas of Brazilian culture as tropical and modern. At the same time, *Morro* challenged Brazilians' notions of self, by undermining long-standing prohibitions on the depiction of blacks, shantytowns, and figures of questionable moral character (as suggested by the malandro in the lower left) in artistic representations sent abroad. Courtesy of Museum of Modern Art, New York. Abby Aldrich Rockefeller Fund.

ceremonial and mundane lives of the Portuguese aristocracy, local elites, slaves, Indians, and the popular classes at a time in which Rio de Janeiro's importance in the Atlantic world system grew immensely. Debret's works were especially valuable for their attention to the ethnic plurality of Portuguese America. The works documented the pervasiveness of slaves and slavery, and the relationship of coerced laborers to freemen. The works illustrated how Brazilian society was organized by gender, age, race, and national origin. Finally, the Debret originals documented the way in which social habits and artistic tastes underwent significant mutations in the first three decades of the nineteenth century, when the temporary transfer of the Portuguese Court permanently secularized and internationalized a society whose cultural life had been dominated by restrictive colonial policies and Iberian Catholicism. In short, the exhibit was a major event in opening a space in which scholarly and popular audiences could come to know more about the history of the mission and the nation's cultural past.

The impact of the 1940 exhibit would be felt throughout Brazilian society in the succeeding years. At the MNBA proper, the gallery dedicated to the French Artistic Mission took on new importance within the museum's grand narrative of universal and Brazilian art. The museum's curatorial staff produced a series of scholarly works on the mission and organized temporary exhibits that drew upon the artistic production of Lebreton and his colleagues.[62] In 1940, the carioca memorialist Luiz Edmundo used Castro Maya's collection to illustrate a popular history of D. João VI's sojourn in Rio.[63] Sérgio Milliet's Portuguese translation of Debret's *Voyage*, appearing that same year, initiated a steady stream of Brazilian publications of traveler's accounts that are now standard reading for popular and academic audiences interested in the Brazilian past.[64] Debret's watercolors have been widely reproduced in Brazilian and international historical scholarship, the popular press, commercial literature, textbooks, postage stamps, and even consumer novelties. Today, Debret's Brazil is nearly inescapable. The 1940 exhibit at the MNBA introduced a visual culture of the Brazilian past that contemporary Brazilian society cannot resist.

More problematic was the way in which the 1940 exhibit opened a space in which various social actors confronted the ambiguities of the nation's artistic and historical past and its relationship to the nation's memory of itself. The comments made by art critics, collectors, journalists, and museum professionals demonstrate that the 1940 exhibit rattled sensibilities about the meanings of cultural development in Brazil. When Castro Maya and the MNBA brought the French Artistic Mission into full public view, the memory of the nation's cultural heritage proved to be highly unsettled.

MNBA director Oswaldo Teixeira argued that the mission was a testament to Brazil's transition from colonial obscurantism to postcolonial enlightenment. In the preface to the exhibition catalog, Teixeira commented that the exhibit should be considered a valuable portrait of colonial Brazil and the moment at which the culture of colonialism would undergo significant transformations with the arrival of the French artists.[65] Likening Debret to a *bandeirante* (the famed trailblazers of the colonial era), Teixeira praised the history painter for an eagerness to depict the unfamiliar tropical landscape, including blacks and Indians. The documentary value of Debret's works received special praise, as Teixeira argued that without Debret, "We would be deprived of such solid, abundant, and truthful documentation about the social milieu and the human landscape of Debret's time. The works capture this land in its picturesque, visual, and sociological immensity. For this, many historians and artists have benefited."[66] Teixeira ultimately suggested that in coming to Portuguese America, Debret and the other mission members were transformed and improved as they themselves transformed and improved culture and the arts in Brazil. Rejecting any notion of debasement, Teixeira used the exhibit to narrate how Europe and Brazil basked in luzes.

Defenders of traditional Luso-Brazilian art were less eager to praise the exhibit as a document of the civilizing process. José Mariano questioned the canonization of a group of artists who had been poorly received by local artisans and whose artistic "mission" to establish a rationalized, academic tradition shunned "traditional" Luso-baroque art. According to Mariano, the mission ruined Brazil's "older artists, mestizos of humble origins whose hard-won talents did not receive the protection afforded the persecuted foreigners seeking asylum."[67] Mariano recognized the valuable cultural innovations brought by the mission, while insisting upon an alternative genealogy of genuine Brazilian art that began well before 1816. In reading Mariano's critique of the French Artistic Mission, one sees a cautionary tale about the influence of foreigners. Always the traditionalist, Mariano concluded his longest published piece on the mission stating, "The experience of the French Artistic Mission is not merely a lesson in history, but also a warning."[68] At a moment in which the modernists looked to foreigners such as Le Corbusier and Picasso for inspiration, Mariano expressed grave reservations about a national culture contaminated by the outsider.

As the MNBA exhibit divided academics from traditionalists (two groups who united in their opposition to modernists), remembering the French Artistic Mission also challenged proponents of modern art to make sense of the history of Brazilian culture. Lebreton, Nicolas Taunay, Grandjean de Montigny, and Debret were undoubtedly central actors in the evolution of the arts in Brazil. Several of the mission members established a direct connection between Brazilian art and the canons of Western cultural production. Recognizing the contributions of the early academics, in 1941, the Modernist Division of the Salão Nacional de Belas Artes paid homage to Lebreton and Taunay. Yet the modernists still had to make sense of the fact that the French Artistic Mission was a foundational moment for the history of academic painting in Brazil. Debret and Grandjean de Montigny played central roles in normalizing the activities of the Academia Imperial de Belas Artes and the official salons of the empire. Without Debret's perseverance, formal art instruction in the national academy of art likely would have foundered. Ever since the fracas surrounding 1931's Salão Revolucionário, the modernistas continually clashed with the academics over the direction of national taste, art education, and patronage for the arts. Remembering the French Artistic Mission was a delicate balancing act. Academics saw in the mission the genesis of the academic tradition. Modernists, by contrast, tried to devise schemes that celebrated Brazil's first academics, without celebrating academicism.

A few final observations on the Exposição da Missão Artística de 1816 and the politics of memory: the repatriation of Debret's *Voyage* revealed a multiethnic Brazil that included European monarchs, white aristocrats, mixed-race free peoples, African slaves, and Indians. The watercolors and engravings revealed not just a pluralistic Brazil, but one in which the races were depicted as sharing the same public and private spaces. This vision of a multiethnic, interdependent society had been largely absent from all Brazilian painting in the nineteenth and early twentieth centuries. Even the modernist renewal of the 1920s and 1930s failed to depict Brazil's multiracial interdependence as forthrightly as Debret. In 1940, at a moment in which Gilberto Freyre continued to incite controversy for his characterization of Brazilian society as racially interdependent, the French Artistic Mission exhibit was destined to receive many contested readings.[69] A select

handful of the Debret watercolors directly challenged the myth of benevolent slavery; the exhibit as a whole undermined an intellectual tradition in
postabolition memory politics that worked hard to forget slavery and the
presence of Africans in the formation of Brazilian civilization.[70]

I raise this last point to argue that the Exposição da Missão Artística
Francesa de 1816 was one of the most important cultural events of the first
Vargas regime. It is strange to observe that the exhibit does not figure in
any cultural history of the period. Part of the silence may be attributed to
the fact that the exhibit went largely unseen by the public. In contrast to
the unparalleled popularity of the Exposição da Pintura Francesa, the exhibit on the French Artistic Mission registered a meager 1,201 visitors. Both
exhibits received support from the highest levels of the Ministry of Education. Both exhibits presented French art never before seen in Brazil. Both
exhibits were well advertised in the capital. The press coverage was generally favorable. However, the French retrospective and the French Artistic
Mission show produced extremely different visitation patterns.

The low attendance for the second exhibit leaves some troubling questions related to the politics of memory during the first Vargas regime. A
certain logic would hold that the collaboration between public and private collectors should have produced impressive attendance figures. Castro
Maya's newly acquired watercolors were joined by works drawn from several of the most important private collections in Brazil. Why did the same
high society in which Castro Maya and his fellow donors circulate stay away
from MNBA in December 1940? The historical significance of the Debret
watercolors alone should have been sufficient to attract a cross-section of
Rio's educated classes, and the extremely broad vision of Brazil's multicultural society held the potential to attract individuals who typically would
never have visited a federal museum. The art community certainly recognized that the works assembled for the late-year show were of some significance. Patriotically inclined critics could also take pride in the exhibit.
Moreover, one early review informed the artistic smart set that the entire
exhibit was a "lesson in brasilidade that will touch the core of the nation's
psyche."[71] So, why did the public fail to show?

As suggested earlier, Debret's watercolors would become an integral
part of Brazil's everyday visual culture within a few decades of Castro
Maya's purchase. Why, then, does one see so little evidence of the Frenchman's appeal in 1940? Why, moreover, did the same people who would soon
flock to Petrópolis to see splendor of the imperial state staged at the Museu

Imperial not make the much easier journey to downtown Rio de Janeiro to catch a glimpse of early-nineteenth-century Brazil? Castro Maya anticipated that the Brazilian public would be most interested in the works documenting the major historical events of the Bragança Court.[72] The exhibit contained dozens of images documenting the splendor of the implantation of a Brazilian Empire, including Debret's *Acclamation of D. João VI*, Simon Pradier's engraving of the grand ceremony welcoming the arrival of Princess Leopoldina in 1817, as well as life-sized history paintings of D. João VI and D. Pedro I in full regalia. With so much regalism, how could the public resist?

In a report to Capanema, Teixeira attributed the low visitation to the daytime heat afflicting the capital at the onset of summer. Teixeira also noted that the December scheduling meant that the holidays prevented schoolchildren from visiting on class excursions (one of the rare mentions of childrens' visitation to the MNBA). At best, the summer heat must be treated as a partial and unsatisfying explanation. Monthly visitation figures to other museums in Rio typically dropped in December, but they did not plunge. The Exposição da Missão Artística Francesa, moreover, was the kind of temporary exhibit that typically drew more visitors than usual. The galleries at the MNBA were empty because the public, apparently, preferred not to look at the wonderful collection of artwork organized around the repatriated Debret watercolors.

I put forth that many of the works produced by the French Artistic Mission remained as unsettling in 1940 as they had been in 1841, when the IHGB criticized Debret's suggestion that Brazilian masters were unmercifully cruel to their slaves. The memories evoked by certain images produced by the French Artistic Mission, the contested history of the mission proper, and the entire enterprise of importing a foreign mission to civilize Brazil were simply too raw in an era in which the state was promoting strong, confident, and unified visions of Brazil's past, present, and future. Cultural critics outside of the state seemed more open to the possibility of expressing doubts, or even disgust, with the way in which Brazilian culture remained servile to international influences. Nevertheless, neither the traditionalists, who tried to anchor Brazilian culture in the Luso-Catholic past, nor the modernists, who spoke of consuming the outsider to strengthen the miscegenated national body, could uncritically embrace Lebreton's civilizing mission. No one denied the historical significance of the mission. Yet few seemed to be interested in giving the mission a privileged place in the national memory. Thus, in December 1940, the National Museum of Fine Arts was a realm of memory that most of Brazilian society chose to avoid. This was a largely unsuccessful project of willful forgetfulness; the museum itself and the objects exhibited therein remained forums for establishing a complex relationship with a complicated past well after the summer heat of 1940 abated.

Museums of Memory and Their Publics

Thus far, I have tried to correlate the institutional history of federal historical museums with the politics of memory. Chief among my concerns has been the way in which museums participate in the construction of historical memories and cultural identities. I now turn to this question from the perspective of the museum patron and the museum visitor — the two groups that made the museum a public institution and the memories therein public memories. Together, patron and visitor provide the social basis for understanding how and why the Vargas regime could insert museums into the politics of memory.

Unlike patrimony and its special relationship to private property, museums had little direct impact upon most projects of economic modernization. Unlike radio listeners and consumers of other forms of mass media, the museum-going audience was highly restricted by geography. Unlike expositions, museums were not paired with amusement parks and other forms of popular leisure capable of attracting a broad cross section of society. Nevertheless, museums had a significant cultural impact, grounding the ideals and policies of modernity in the ideals and accomplishments of the past. Museums organized an impressive *material, visual,* and *ritual* representation of historical success that pointed toward the order and progress so dearly craved by old-style republicans and authoritarian modernizers. The Vargas-era museum was an optimal environment to disseminate a view of modernization that synthesized and glorified the past as a didactic book of lessons, role models, and wonder. This narrative strategy had great appeal for state leaders and private citizens who wanted to insert themselves into this narrative. Thus, museum patronage became a major component of the politics of memory at precisely the same period that the federal government was rapidly expanding the number and quality of federal museums.

Four groups can be identified as patrons of historical museums: (1) the federal elite, led by Vargas; (2) descendants of the nineteenth-century elite; (3) the Catholic Church; and (4) entrepreneurs and industrialists with vested interests in state-sponsored economic modernization. All four groups were regular museum visitors and frequent donors. The museums celebrated these figures as heroes and patriots.

The rituals of patronage performed by high government officials are emblematic of the politicized nature of memory during the first Vargas regime. Vargas ingratiated himself into the MHN, the official repository of Brazil's historical memory, immediately after assuming power. He subsequently used the MHN to legitimate his claim to be a valiant defender of national interests. Invoking his commitment to the protection of the national past, Vargas donated numerous objects to the MHN and Museu Imperial and acted as an intermediary for other donors. Fellow regime members followed Vargas's lead, legitimating their political mandate through museum patronage. Following the precedent set on Flag Day 1930, when Vargas presented the MHN with a flag used in the October coup, official museum patronage became especially useful for sanitizing and nationalizing acts of sectarian violence. Various regime members presented the MHN with artifacts associated with the Revolution of 1930, as well as items connected with the Constitutionalist Rebellion of 1932 and the golpe of 10 November 1937. The most blatantly politicized donation, which "historicized" an act of extreme symbolic violence that still echoes in Brazil's political memory, involved the donation of an urn containing the ashes of the state flags burned in the Queima das Bandeiras of 27 November 1937. The remains of the symbolic end to federalist regionalism (intimately tied to the attack on individual freedoms and democratic rule) and the dawn of the Estado Novo were stripped from their contemporary political setting and placed within the rarefied confines of the Museu Histórico. Within the Casa do Brasil, the material evidence of *estadonovista* authoritarianism sat alongside the museum's reverent memorials to the heroes and patrons of Brazil's past. Partisan politics instantly became inviolate historical patrimony.

The politics of presidential patronage deserve special attention, because Vargas was by far the most visible patron of historical museums during the Estado Novo. Vargas's patronage of the MHN set the tone for a much deeper relationship between Vargas and the national historical memory that would far outlast the Estado Novo dictatorship and even Vargas himself. Aside from an early donation made to the MHN on Flag Day 1930,

Vargas remained relatively distant from federal museums until the proclamation of the Estado Novo. Thereafter, the president directed significant
attention and resources to national museums. Between 1930 and 1945, Vargas donated more than six hundred objects to the Museu Histórico and
dozens more to the Museu Imperial.[73] The president paid repeated visits
to the MHN, Museu Imperial, and Museu Nacional de Belas Artes, as well
as a onetime visit to the Museu da Inconfidência in Ouro Preto. According to Vargas's supporters, presidential patronage embodied the regime's
attention to the proper veneration and celebration of the nation's past.

Vargas's first tour of the MHN was particularly expressive of presidential patronage. On 10 June 1939, Vargas toured the recently reorganized
galleries. News reports of the three-hour visit—which were most likely
scripted by the Departamento Nacional de Propaganda—were particularly
careful to report that the president-dictator took a strong interest in the
personal effects of the Duque de Caxias, a nineteenth-century war hero,
as well as armaments used in the Paraguayan War and selected correspondence of D. Pedro I.[74] Newspaper accounts reported that Gustavo Barroso
carefully informed Vargas about the objects' former owners as well as their
method of acquisition. The fixation on provenance indicates how Barroso
was consciously demonstrating to the chief of state how material objects
spoke not just of the past but of those who actually owned the past. The
stress on accession also showed Vargas how patrons could become peers
of the historical heroes venerated in the galleries. The MHN offered Vargas
a vision of national history that rested upon the material culture of public heroes and private patrons. This was a vision that Vargas could easily
appropriate for his own uses.

Near the conclusion of the presidential tour, two aspects of state and
private patronage were brought into sharp relief. First, Barroso made a personal appeal for money, asking the president to authorize a special credit
for the preservation of the objects that Vargas had just seen. Vargas reportedly replied, "Without a doubt. The budget for the coming year includes
special appropriations for these types of things."[75] Sure enough, in 1940
the MHN received authorization for a modest increase in staff size and a
special credit for the purchase of a valuable collection of Indo-Portuguese
ivories.[76] The wheels of patronage were oiled with money. Second, education minister Capanema personally saw to it that Vargas viewed objects
that the President himself had donated to the museum. The objects were
rather mundane, made up of small ceremonial gifts presented to the presi-

dent by Brazilian and foreign delegations. But the fixation on presidential provenance reminded the dictator that he had been successful in utilizing the MHN to build his persona as eminent statesmen, national hero, and museum patron. On seeing how the objects he had donated were placed alongside objects once used by Caxias or Deodoro da Fonseca, Vargas received confirmation that the museum could be quite good at the manufacture of hero cults. Vargas would repeatedly turn to the MHN to manufacture a controlled version of historical memory for the remainder of his life (and even in death if we consider the most famous museum space in modern Brazil—the site of Vargas's suicide in the Museum of the Republic).

Vargas's patronage of the MHN would soon become an integral part of the museum's institutional memory. The 1940 inaugural issue of the *Anais do Museu Histórico Nacional* concluded an institutional history of the MHN with a chronological listing of all donations made by the president. This would establish a long-standing pattern in the writing of the institutional history of the MHN (and to a large extent, all cultural institutions active during the first Vargas regime), which celebrates the 1930s and 1940s as a period of growth and prosperity. By the late 1960s, when Vargas and Barroso were dead, the Museu Histórico found itself in a profound crisis, reinforcing the institutional memory that associated institutional vitality with Vargas.[77] Of course, a careful examination of the museum's trajectory strongly indicates that the Revolution of 1930 was not the sole catalyst for growth. Alternative periodizations may more accurately reflect the transformations experienced by the institution. Nevertheless, the Museu Histórico hung its memory on Vargas. The president, in turn, provided the MHN with a stream of donations, which eventually comprised the Sala Getúlio Vargas, a separate gallery dedicated exclusively to Vargas that opened in 1945. The MHN ensured that the memory of the diminutive president-dictator would always remain at home within the Casa do Brasil.

The aura of patriotism and perpetuity associated with presidential patronage encouraged wealthy private citizens to also patronize federal historical museums. In patronizing these institutions, private donors claimed their place in the nation's temples of memory. Descendants of nineteenth-century families that may not have adapted to the changes wrought by the end of the empire and the rise of republican rule were especially prominent donors who looked to the MHN, the Museu Imperial, and the Museu Nacional de Belas Artes to assure that their place in the national memory would not be forgotten, regardless of the socioeconomic changes afoot. In an era in which the last of the nineteenth-century titled nobility was dying out — and with them, the firsthand memory of the imperial aristocracy — federal museums assured that a once-titled family would always remain a titled family.[78]

The descendants of the Barão de Cotegipe, Miguel Calmon, Carlos Gomes, Coelho Neto, and Dom Pedro II were the most prominent donors to the Museu Histórico and Museu Imperial. The social and cultural origins of these donors exemplify the yearning for a fixed place in the national memory among the surviving members of the old order. In the case of Cotegipe and Calmon donations, the executors of the estates of imperial nobles explicitly stipulated that the donations were contingent upon the creation of special galleries named after their deceased relative. The donors also demanded that, once installed, the collection had to remain indivisible. In 1936, Barroso assured Alice Calmon, Miguel's widow, that she could take a personal role in guaranteeing that the Calmon family, as heirs to an illustrious political and social lineage, would be commemorated with dignity.[79] Due to Alice Calmon's efforts, the Sala Miguel Calmon became one of the most impressive galleries in the museum. Cotegipe's executors had died before the collection could be fully installed at the MHN. Nevertheless, the museum curators made sure that the collection was installed in a separate gallery — a memory site within a memory site — that honored the Bahian statesman of the empire. As these material goods entered into the grand narrative of Brazilian history, the donors worked to assure that the materials would also be used to narrate familial as well as national history. Barroso could hardly oppose these conditions, which reinforced his long-standing admiration for the historical agency of elites. Alcindo Sodré, director of the Museu Imperial, was equally accommodating to the representatives of the Bragança e Orleans family who expressed an interest in helping "restore" the Imperial Palace in Petrópolis to its former grandeur. After three decades of official antimonarchism, the remnants of the empire looked to the Vargas state to perpetuate its memory. Federal museums answered the call.

A handful of prominent entrepreneurial families that had much to gain from federal economic planning also acted as important donors to the official repository of the national historical patrimony. This was certainly true of the millionaire Guinle family, which controlled a wide array of lucrative economic enterprises, including textile manufacturing, banking, Rio's

posh Palace and Copacabana Palace Hotels, and the government concession to the port of Santos. Guilherme Guinle (1882–1960) exercised strong
influence in shaping federal economic policy, serving as the first president
of the National Steelworks Company as well as the principal financier of the
field explorations that led to the discovery of the Lobato (Bahia) oil fields
in 1939. Guinle's political prominence and strategic investments put him in
an excellent position to become one of the principal entrepreneurs of the
first Vargas regime.[80] As his economic fortunes grew, Guilherme and his
two brothers, Carlos and Otávio, became loyal patrons of several major
museums, including the MHN, MNBA, and the Museu da Cidade do Rio de
Janeiro. The Museu Histórico honored the Guinles' support by naming
several galleries after family members.

Although the elite earned great cultural capital in patronage, it would
be difficult to argue that the old or new economic elite won any direct
financial benefits from museum patronage. Federal law did not offer tax incentives for cultural underwriting. Philanthropy was rarely part of business
culture. Museum patronage may have enhanced political access for some
wealthy patrons such as the Guinles, but the industrial and entrepreneurial
influence held by Guilherme was sufficient to merit direct attention from
the president and the minister of the treasury. Federal museums exalted
museum patrons as patriots and heroes—the same labels heaped on the
historical figures celebrated in the museum galleries proper. The symbolic
value of such associations far outweighed any financial return.

Due to inconclusive documentation, it is difficult to assess the extent
to which the general public should be considered a "patron" of museums.
Small-scale private donations were unusual and auxiliary organizations
equally insignificant. It is, nevertheless, possible to document to some degree the socioeconomic status of museum-goers as well as the experience
of museum-going during the first Vargas regime. In this fashion, we begin
to fathom how the general public participated in the politics of memory. It
is important to underscore that museum patronage was led by elites seeking to participate in brasilidade. Museum patronage, whether in donation
or visitation, operated on the logic of ritualizing nationhood. Those Brazilians outside of the nation were mere shadows in the federal museum
gallery. The internal records at most federal museums provide scant information on the resonance of federal museums outside Rio, suggesting that
there may have been little. Only in a handful of cases did I discover writ-

ten evidence to suggest that antiquarians and journalists from outside Rio were actually disgruntled by the way in which their local histories were (mis)represented at the MHN. [81]

Museum Visitation

In turning to a more focused discussion of visitors and visitation patterns, I forewarn my readers that the source materials on the museum-going public are much less complete than I would wish. The quantitative data on museum visitation must be treated with extreme caution, as most Brazilian museums did not standardize their methods for counting visitors until the 1970s. The qualitative data on museum visitation are equally troublesome. Visitor surveys are a recent phenomenon in Brazilian museum management. There is much to be made of what museum professionals *wanted* museums to be, but it is much more difficult to perceive what museum visitors made of museums. The available data do provide enough information to make some educated guesses about museum visitation during the first Vargas regime. My intention here is to suggest how the museum-going public might be integrated into a discussion about the politics of memory during the first Vargas regime.

Between the Revolution of 1930 and the fall of the Estado Novo, the Ministry of Education recorded a three-fold increase in the total number of museums open to public visitation. In 1930, the ministry recognized twenty museums, of which fourteen were public and six were private. In 1944, the number had increased to sixty-six, of which thirty-six were public and thirty were private. [82] The Federal District had the largest concentration of museums—a strong indication of the concentration of memory in the national capital. A rise in museum visitation accompanied the increase in the number of museums. In 1933, the ministry listed total visitation to all reporting museums at 381,751. The figure had increased to just over one million by 1947. These figures indicate that the museum infrastructure and the habit of museum-going were clearly on the upswing during the first Vargas regime.

Of the museums under discussion, the Museu Histórico maintained the most complete visitation records. There, visitation steadily increased from under 7,000 in 1930 to nearly 25,000 in 1945. Documentation is also good for the Museu Imperial, which experienced the most rapid growth in visitors,

Table 6   Reported Public Visitation to Federal Museums, 1929–1954

	BRAZIL	MHN	CRB	MNBA	MIOP	MI	MM	MO
1929		6,850						
1930		6,778	1,189					
1931		9,250	1,176					
1932		11,069	1,262					
1933	381,751	14,334	2,695					
1934		17,671	2,140					
1935		18,793	2,193					
1936		18,930	3,125					
1937	446,649	9,397	2,124					
1938		0	1,241					
1939		11,838	1,482	36,946				
1940		15,955	2,442	>42,000				
1941		17,317	1,372					
1942		22,276	2,256					
1943		22,307	2,719			22,090		
1944		24,296	3,000		3,901	32,828	4,523	668
1945		24,402			12,281	54,611	2,540	938
1946		30,926			12,442	91,154	3,000	3,095
1947	1,013,006	28,146		9,220	9,741	85,881	2,722	4,972
1948	1,203,109	30,123		8,476	9,503	101,199		5,383
1949		23,807		14,262	10,060	100,780		7,994
1950	1,576,108	20,914		14,785	12,143	111,284		
1951	1,624,039	22,033		46,945	13,095	112,842		
1952	1,226,000	26,447		59,233	14,926	117,284		
1953		24,720		10,507	22,434	132,196		
1954		10,936		32,662	29,018	135,758		

Note: All figures should be treated as estimates due to a lack of standardization in counting and reporting procedures.
Brazil: Total visitation to all public and private museums that submitted reports to the Ministry of Education. Source: *Anuário Estatístico do Brasil*, 1936–1995. Museu Histórico Nacional (MHN): Source: *Relatórios Anuais*. 1937: January through June only; ?/38–6/39: closed for repairs; 6/54–3/55: closed for repairs. Casa Ruy Barbosa (CRB): Source: Brazil, Ministério do Educação e Saúde, *Casa Rui Barbosa* (Rio de Janeiro, 1946). Museu Nacional de Belas Artes (MNBA): Source: *Anuário do Museu Nacional de Belas Artes*. Museu da Inconfidência (MIOP): Source: IPHAN-ATA *Relatórios Anuais* 1944–1949; MIOP-Museologia, Report on museum visitation prepared by João Orisóstomo Ribeiro, 17 May 1983. Museu Imperial (MI): Source: *Anuário do Museu Imperial*. Museu das Missões (MM): Source: IPHAN-ATA *Relatórios Anuais* 1944–1949. Museu do Ouro (MO): Source: IPHAN-ATA *Relatórios Anuais* 1944–1949. 1944: April–December; 1945: May–December.

whose number rose from 22,000 in 1943 to 91,000 in 1946. Year-to-year figures for the MNBA during the first Vargas regime are inconclusive, but the available evidence indicates that visitation to the MNBA was highly sensitive to the popularity of temporary exhibits. The Exposição da Pintura Francesa of 1940 attracted more than 40,000 visitors. The comprehensive exhibit on the French Artistic Mission of 1816, held that same year, attracted a dismal 1,201 visitors.[83] The Museu da Inconfidência in Ouro Preto, which had no temporary exhibits, attracted just over 12,000 in 1945. Visitation to that museum would remain under 20,000 until the mid-1950s when improved road conditions to Ouro Preto and an increase in automobile tourism spurred a dramatic increase in visitors to the region (see table 6.)

In documenting the number of visitors passing through these museums' entrances, it should be noted that there were, ostensibly, few economic barriers to visiting federal museums during the Vargas era. In sharp contrast to the contemporary museum experience throughout the industrialized world, admission to federal museums in Brazil was free of charge until the early 1970s. Moreover, Vargas-era federal museums were extremely under-commercialized. The modern museum's mix of gallery floorspace, public facilities, restaurants, and commercial outlets was alien to museum culture in Brazil prior to the 1960s. Once a potential visitor decided to visit a federal museum, money was simply unnecessary.

The public, at least in Rio, had relatively easy access to federal museums. All museums were open Tuesday through Sunday, making it possible to visit museums on weekends, when commercial and industrial activity dropped.[84] All federal museums were open in the afternoons, and the National Museum of Fine Arts was open until 6:30 P.M., making evening visitation possible. The Museu Histórico and the MNBA were located in central areas of Rio de Janeiro, readily accessible by public transportation. Located outside of the Federal District, the Museu Imperial could still be reached by rail and road. Petrópolis had been a favorite weekend destination for many residents of Rio since the nineteenth century, putting the Imperial Museum within reach of a large urban population. The Museu da Inconfidência was much more isolated, but it too could be reached by rail. The only federal museum situated at great distance from any major population center was the Mission Museum in São Miguel, Rio Grande do Sul. Visitation figures there were unsurprisingly low. On the whole, the museums of memory were accessible to a sizable cross-section of the population, especially those residing in the densely populated Southeast. These are important logistical considerations to keep in mind in assessing the type of public that actually visited museums, especially in comparison with the type of public that *could* visit museums.

Hard data on the gender, race, age, and socioeconomic status of the museum-going public are sketchy. What documentation exists indicates that federal museums in Rio targeted individuals who lived or worked in downtown Rio or the more upscale neighborhoods of the Zona Sul. In 1940, the National Museum of Fine Arts distributed promotional posters around downtown, the well-heeled shopping areas of Flamengo and Botafogo, and the beach neighborhood of Copacabana. The close-in middle-class neighborhood of Tijuca was the only Zona Norte region to receive promotional advertising. This marketing strategy strongly suggests a middle- to upper-middle class bias in museum visitation. Records at the MHN, Museu Imperial, and the MNBA confirm that federal museums received relatively well-off visitors, including political personalities, visiting dignitaries, military cadets, historians and antiquarians, and schoolchildren. Press reports on art museums consistently mention the presence of journalists, artists, and socialites. With a few limited exceptions, there is little evidence to suggest that museums attracted popular followings.

The demographic information available indicates that the overwhelming percentage of visitors was adult. Children made up less than 15 percent of the visitors at the Museu da Inconfidência and less than 10 percent at the successful Museu Imperial. I have found no statistical reference to children visiting the Museu Histórico or the MNBA. Organized school visitation is mentioned sporadically for the MHN and MNBA, but there seemed to be no consistent educational outreach programs. The Museu Nacional—a museum that fits poorly into the category of museums of memory—was the only institution that explicitly targeted children in its educational and visitor services. The lack of childhood visitation at the museums of memory underscores the gap between the rhetoric of museums serving as centers for the education of youth and the reality that adults overwhelmingly visited museum galleries (see tables 7 and 8).

Another group conspicuously missing from museum visitation records are members of auxiliary associations. Curators at the MNBA made mention of their intention to help create a friends club, in order to increase their base of patrons, but this idea would not be implemented before the Estado Novo fell. As far as I have been able to determine, only the Museu Nacional could count on the support of an auxiliary organization during

Tables 7 and 8   Visitation to Museu Imperial and Museu da Inconfidência, by Gender and Age Group, 1943–1946

MUSEU IMPERIAL

	Men	Women	Children	Groups	Total
1943	9,232	10,389	1,232	1,237	22,090
1944	12,808	15,485	2,645	1,890	32,828
1945	22,471	26,443	3,285	2,412	54,611
1946	38,243	44,061	4,620	4,230	91,154

Source: *Anuário do Museu Imperial*, 1943–1947.

MUSEU DA INCONFIDÊNCIA

	Men	Women	Children	Total
1943				3,901
1944	7,085	3,492	1,704	12,281
1945	7,160	3,731	1,551	12,442

Source: IPHAN-ATA *Relatórios do DPHAN*, 1944–1949.

the period under study.[85] The absence of auxiliary societies is a strong indication that civil society did not organize itself around collective museum visitation, even when elite patronage and overall museum visitation were on the increase.

The gender dynamics of museum visitation—intimately tied to the gendering of memory—present some perplexing contradictions. The collections of federal historical museums were dominated by men. Men directed all federal museums with the exception of the Museu Nacional. The permanent exhibitions of these museums aggressively cultivated a cult of masculinity, led by heroic emperors, liberal professionals, generals, and landowners. The permanent collection of the National Museum of Fine Arts contained a large number of works with a feminine subject matter, but this too was a product of male cultural production and curatorial choice. Of the 1,600 paintings owned by the MNBA in 1939, only twenty-two had been painted by women.[86]

The paradox was that while men dominated the national museum space and its privileged access to the national memory, women far outnumbered men in the graduating classes of the MHN's Curso de Museus. Women also outnumbered men in winning permanent career posts as curators (*conservadores*), once the occupational category was formally incorporated into the civil service in 1939.[87] While the social history of museum curatorship in Brazil has yet to be written, these numbers suggest that museum work was a new career path for educated white women, made possible by expanding federal interest in cultural management and shifts in memory politics. The professional opportunities opened by museums offered a select number of women, such as Bertha Lutz (1894–1976), suffragist and Museu Nacional curator, and Regina Leal, art critic and MNBA curator, opportunities to effect change within the museum space and within the larger society. While much work needs to be done in order to determine how gender influenced individual career choices and the professional category of the museum curator, it should be underscored that women remained in the minority at all federal museums, especially at the higher-ranking posts of division chief and general director. Male and female curators jointly built a masculine vision of Brazilian memory, but they did not necessarily do so as equals.

Interestingly, the gender imbalance seen among those who managed memory was not necessarily representative of the gender ratios of museum-goers. Visitation figures for the Museu Imperial indicate a slight numerical advantage of adult females to adult males. These figures may be an anomaly within the overall context of museum-going before the end of the Second World War. Or, they may be indicative of the larger number of family visits to the Museu Imperial. However, this numerical relationship may also suggest that females were discriminating in their museum-going habits. Differing gender ratios in museum visitation suggest that women may have been drawn to museum spaces dedicated to the memory of the Braganças in numbers disproportionate to the number of women drawn to other historical museums like the Museu da Inconfidência, where adult males outnumbered adult females nearly two-to-one. Future research may flesh out the hypothesis that women were carriers of memories of the imperial past, whereas the memory of the Inconfidência Mineira was more masculine.

The demographic information on museum visitation must be compared to the qualitative descriptions of the museum-goer and the museum-going experience. Again, the documentary record is not as complete as one would hope, but museum directors and other culture managers, educators, and journalists all made references to who they believed should be visiting federal museums and why.

As early as 1920, Gustavo Barroso had established the notion that museum-goers should be "true friends of the nation's traditions [*veros amigos das tradições pátrias*]."[88] Throughout his tenure as director of the Museu Histórico, Barroso would continue to play upon the image of the visitor-patriot. Roquette-Pinto, Mário de Andrade, and others interested in the educational potential of museums would never refute Barroso's link between museum-going and civic duty. Instead, these liberals would imagine the ideal museum visitor as a student, eager to use the museum collection and museum staff to gain scientific and artistic knowledge. In 1937, on the eve of the rapid expansion of the federal museum network, Andrade went so far as to propose that students and workers be required to visit museums on a regular basis.[89] The proposal was never adopted, but it indicated how Andrade hoped to expand museum visitation beyond the scholar, dilettante, and humanist imagined by most museum professionals. In all of these various formulations, the museum was located alongside the school and the armed forces as an institution that could shape values, convey knowledge, and strengthen national cultural identity.

On 7 January 1941, the DIP's nightly radio program, the *Hora do Brasil,* included a feature on the Museu Histórico describing a changing museum-going public. Barroso most likely wrote the text. The description serves as a model for analyzing the regime's expanding imaginary of the museum public during the first Vargas regime. Listeners heard:

> Today's typical Brazilian is a museum-goer. He is attracted to the lessons which reverberate through those venerable and hushed houses. This taste for museum-going grows and spreads across class lines. It is no longer just the scholar or impassioned researcher who roams the galleries of art or history. Now, students, schoolchildren, the young academic, and even the worker taking his Sunday leave linger in the galleries, contemplating the pieces and relics which enrich the nation's collections.[90]

The text was a mixture of wishful thinking and fact, as visitation to the MHN was never as egalitarian as the script indicated. Sunday visitation by members of the popular classes was indeed possible, but it would have been episodic rather than typical. MHN regulations excluded visitors who could not "present themselves in a decent manner."[91] This restriction would not necessarily exclude the unionized worker, but it surely meant that members of Rio's vast underclass who lacked access to running water, clean clothes, and footwear would be prevented from visiting the museum even if they were so inclined. The reality of low visitation among the popular classes should not discount the interesting fact that one of the most politically conservative culture managers of the Vargas era could imagine the museum as a space in which memories of heroic deeds and notions of belonging were to be forged across class lines in public spaces open to all. This text is a testament to the potential for the museum to serve as a new forum for cultural citizenship in post–1930 Brazil.

The *Hora do Brasil* script is equally notable for its description of the ideal museum-going experience. Counter to the description of a museum as an interactive classroom, the MHN galleries are described as hushed spaces in which the visitor was to stand in awe of the assembled collection. The hushed silence was a common way in which the MHN was frequently described in the press. Stephen Greenblatt's notion of the *wonder* of museum-going is appropriate for the way in which the institutions of memory imagined the actions and reactions of the museum-goer.[92] The ideal museum experience was one in which the visitor would be stopped dead in awe of the beauty and significance of the objects on display. Adalberto Ribeiro, a journalist for the Departamento Administrativo do Serviço Público, captured the sense of wonder cultivated by the major federal historical museums when he described his experience at the Museu Histórico's Sala Dom Pedro II as an encounter with "a world of objects and episodes from another time which swirl up from the mists of the past, come together and move about, until they gently sweep over us, not unlike certain scenes from the silver screen."[93]

Certain personalities closely tied to the museum movement described the museum-going experience in less mystical, but equally personal, terms. Alcindo Sodré imagined a museum space where the selection of objects and the allocation of gallery space would offer the visitor direct access to the museum's principal collection without the distraction of bric-a-brac. Regina Leal, a curator at the Museu Nacional de Belas Artes, made similar proposals for art museums, stressing the need for improving illumination and ventilation, avoiding clutter on the gallery walls, stripping the galleries of unnecessary decorative elements, and rotating pieces of the permanent collection between the public galleries and storage in order to enhance the visitor's experience.[94] Mário de Andrade, one of the most prolific cultural critics of the era whose anteprojeto on preservation proposed a radical reorganization of all federal museums, where the main object on display would be a registry of cultural patrimony, stressed the need for informed tour guides to make the most of the museum-going experience.[95] In drafting plans for the formation of the Museu das Missões, Lucio Costa advocated an open-air museum that provided enough visual and textual clues that the poorly educated visitor could imagine seeing eighteenth-century Jesuit brothers and Guaraní Indians going through their daily routines of manual labor, creative expression, and prayer.[96] Costa's main interlocutor, Rodrigo Melo Franco de Andrade, argued that the SPHAN's network of regional museums allowed citizens living in the interior to celebrate regional culture in familiar surroundings, heightening the museum-going experience by reconfirming the visitor's personal connection to the display.[97] In this instance, the mineiro intellectual tried to formulate a solution to the anxiety that national museums located in the federal capital stripped nonmetropolitan areas of a regional heritage in the process of inventing a national memory.

At issue here was how the museum was to manage its collection of artifacts and how it was to manage the encounter between the visitor and the artifact of memory. The tendency among museum professionals was clearly to create a museum space that engaged the visitor's imagination. Figures employed outside of federal museums, including Mário de Andrade, Francisco Venâncio Filho, Edgard Roquette-Pinto, and Edgard Süssekind de Mendonça, envisioned public museums that engaged the visitor's intellect, turning the museum into an extension of the classroom.[98] For both camps, tedium, stuffiness, and great temporal distances between object and visitor were seen as threatening to the quality of the museum-going experience.

Sadly, none of the museums under consideration could completely free themselves from these problems. Even as museum visitation grew, most federal museums could never shake the image of being *casas de velharia* (houses of old things). Federal museums exerted diminished influence over popular memory precisely because federal museums were never popular institutions. The contemporary reader should be troubled by the Vargas regime's inability to make better use of the museum as a site for popularizing the kind of sentimental, patriotic memories that were carefully crafted within the museum walls. Nevertheless, the politics of museum display were highly consistent with a program of cultural management that typically underplayed the importance of popular culture, while it simultaneously exalted the memory of national unity and greatness.

Conclusions

The landscape of memory shaped by museums gradually shifted after 1945, as the national museum infrastructure expanded and private philanthropy shifted toward new institutions. When industrialists and media magnates began to devote their considerable financial and cultural capital to museum patronage in the postwar period, the number of memory sites and the possible memory of brasilidade expanded enormously. The underclass remained marginal to postwar museums, but museum visitation became a habit of the urban middle class, especially along the Rio-São Paulo axis where a handful of privately funded art museums, opened in the late 1940s, offered new opportunities for museum visitation, cultural patronage, and class formation. The growing presence of educational outreach activities seen in the postwar period also placed the museum in a more prominent role in everyday memories of Brazilianness.

The more expansive landscape of memory created after 1945 reinforces the interpretation of the museum of the first Vargas regime as an important site for the manufacture of memories that were eminently nationalistic, but closed to most of the nation. This did not necessarily make these memories irrelevant. To the contrary, the memories guarded by the federal museums most active during the first Vargas regime gave the state and its allies privileged access to the historical artifacts upon which the memory of brasilidade could be defined and staged. As the French Artistic Mission episode suggests, not all of these memories were pleasant. Nonetheless, it was the federal museum that remained the memory keeper, drawing upon its storage facilities and public galleries to invent a history of Brazilianness that made the most of the national cultural evolution and even more of those enlightened state officials who dedicated themselves to keeping the past alive against the competing demands for a forward-looking modernization that turned its back on the colonial and imperial pasts.

6

Expositions and "Export Quality" Culture

Expositions offered the Vargas regime the opportunity to construct an idealized vision of cultural renewal. The regime prized expositions, especially those staged abroad, for their potential to imagine a unified national community confident in the recovery of the national cultural vocation. The Brazilian delegations to the New York World's Fair and Golden Gate International Exposition of 1939–1940 and the Exposição do Mundo Português of 1940 painted triumphant portraits of a modern, stable society that had exorcised the demons of colonialism, liberalism, communism, and underdevelopment to be at peace with itself. At these foreign expositions, the Brazilian delegates and their foreign hosts — be they liberal democrats or conservative corporatists — rhapsodized about the impressive renewal of culture underway in Brazil. Overseas, the Estado Novo could celebrate a hegemonic national culture in full possession of its faculties.

Closer examination of the rosy portraits of Brazilian culture painted by the Brazilian delegates and their foreign hosts reveals traces of the same tensions that tore at cultural management back in Brazil. The official delegations sent to New York, San Francisco, and Lisbon took with them the battle cries, strategies, and armaments used in the culture wars fought on the domestic front. The Brazilian pavilions erected in Flushing Meadows, on Treasure Island, and near the banks of the Tagus River became foreign fronts for cultural conflicts originating in Brazil. The Brazilian delegates were naturally reticent to acknowledge discord. It was nonetheless obvious that the Brazilian missions sent abroad drew deeply from domestic conflicts over cultural management and brasilidade. The transposition of domestic culture wars onto foreign shores shaped the representation and reception of Brazilian culture throughout the Atlantic world.

Expositions in Context

The Brazilian state had used national and universal expositions to invent
a more perfect vision of national culture well before Vargas extended his
approval for the Exposição do Estado Novo, held in Rio in December 1938,
and the organization of official delegations to be sent to the international
expositions held in New York, San Francisco, and Lisbon between 1939 and
1940.[1] The Bragança monarchy took an interest in expositions in the early
1860s. Dom Pedro II opened the first National Exposition on 2 December
1861. For Brazil's nineteenth-century exposition organizers, national expositions lent a local dialect to the language of modernity sweeping over the
world after the runaway success of the Great Exposition of 1851, held in
London's Crystal Palace. Brazil's first national exposition, like future expositions organized during the Second Reign, brought together a sampling
of Brazil's most "modern" agricultural and industrial activities at the precise moment in which the monarchy and landholding elite confronted the
end of the transatlantic slave trade and, by extension, the declining viability
of a slave-based political economy. Expositions help sell visions of a new
Brazil to domestic and foreign audiences.[2] Thus, the imperial government,
alongside private commercial interests and representatives of provincial
governments, took national expositions seriously precisely because these
events created the ephemeral spaces in which the slavocratic aristocracy
and national bourgeoisie could test out visions of a cultured, industrious,
white society freed from the scourge of slavery and slaves and truly ready
to join in the concert of civilized nations.[3]

Brazilian interest in international expositions accompanied the increasing prominence of national expositions. Official delegations sent to the
world's fairs held in London (1862), Paris (1867 and 1889), Vienna (1873), and
Philadelphia (1876) all drew from materials and ideas exhibited at earlier
national expositions. National expositions and the organization of Brazilian delegations to international expositions were, therefore, conjoined
together as precious moments in which the Brazilian elite worked to invent a civilized Brazil for Brazilian and international eyes. The standards
of civilization were always European, but civilization itself was exhibited
as a national project.

In practice, the stark differences between Brazil's agrarian, patriarchal, slavocratic society and Europe's rapidly industrializing, imperial metropoles made it difficult for nineteenth-century planners to master the cultural idioms of expositions. The colonial dimensions of European fairs proved to be particularly difficult for nineteenth-century Brazilian elites to assimilate. Financial and logistical problems diminished the success of grand schemes. National organizing committees complained that the materials sent from the provinces differed little from objects typically found in curiosity cabinets and traveling road shows.[4] Visitors to the Brazilian pavilions built abroad were said to express great skepticism toward the viability of material and moral progress south of the equator. If expositions were intended to document the march of progress across space and time, for many, that march seemed slow going for Brazil. Nevertheless, the Brazilian presence at universal expositions became an appendage to a transnational process of bourgeois modernity that characterized the nineteenth century.

The Proclamation of the Republic did not dampen elite interest in national and international fairs. Embattled at home, the young republican government did not hesitate to send official delegations to the universal expositions held in Chicago (1893) and Saint Louis (1904). As the republic matured, national expositions became larger and more extravagant. In 1908, a grand national exhibition celebrated the one-hundredth anniversary of the liberalization of commercial trade between Portuguese America and the Atlantic. Opened at the height of the capital's belle époque, the National Exposition of 1908 set new standards for the imaginary of a civilized republic marching to the accelerated pace of modernity. With attendance exceeding one million visitors to a city in miniature built at the foot of Rio's picturesque Sugarloaf Mountain, the 1908 event marked the dawn of a new era of urban planning, public transport, consumerism, and leisure for the burgeoning capital.[5] Following the success of the 1908 event, Brazilian delegations made appearances at the universal expositions held Brussels (1910) and Turin (1911).

The republic's crowning achievement was the Centennial Exposition of Brazilian Independence, opened in Rio on 7 September 1922. Like its 1908 predecessor, the Centennial Exposition was a city-within-a-city where the marvels of modern life danced in illumination and sound. Within the pavilion grounds, broad streets crisscrossed among stately pavilions housing delegations from all Brazilian states and a number of foreign countries. From the watchtower erected high above the Industrial Pavilion, a visitor could "see" the modern world in a dazzling display of urbanization, electric light, and technology. When the exposition closed in 1923, more than 3.6 million visitors had participated in the republic's triumphant entrance into an elite club founded in the famed Crystal Palace. Of course, just beyond the field of vision of most Brazilian nationals and the foreign delegates who marveled at the exposition grounds, the regional oligarchical parties that dominated national political and economic life were fighting off challenges from alienated regional interests, disgruntled midranking army officers, communists, labor radicals, suffragists, and modernistas. But within the exposition proper, Brazil's century of independence was a cause for celebration.

The Vargas regime initially exhibited limited interest in expositions, which seemed unnecessary extravagances during an international depression. Vargas's personal interest in exhibitions was limited to periodic appearances at the international trade show organized annually by the government of the Federal District.[6] Political instability and lack of funds precluded Brazilian participation in the international fairs held in Chicago (1933–1934) and Brussels (1935). But by late 1935, with the national economy showing signs of early recovery, midlevel civil servants within the Ministry of Labor, Industry, and Commerce began to consider organizing a national exposition to showcase the economic and social reforms brought on by the Revolution of 1930.[7] Early plans for the national exposition envisioned a comprehensive event that brought together samples of the best in the sciences and arts; agro-pastoral and mineral production; industrial activity; the energy sector; transportation networks and civil construction; public works; commerce; and tourism, sports, and leisure.[8] This preliminary classification system differed little from pre–1930 national expositions. It did, however, depart from the focus on technical arts and colonial enterprises that distinguished the universal expositions organized in Chicago (1933) and Paris (1937), and the colonial expositions held in Paris (1931) and Oporto (1934).

In August 1936, Vargas approved a proposal to organize a national exposition to be held in Rio in March 1938. Significantly, the plan contained provisions prohibiting individual state pavilions — an explicit reversal from previous expositions and trade shows. The plans also called for product

37 Entrance to Exposição do Estado Novo, Rio de
Janeiro, December 1938. The towering symbol of the
New Brazil built between 1930 and 1938. Courtesy of
CPDOC-GC.

labeling that indicated the type and grade of commercial products, but
not their provenance. Although subsequent plans might have allowed São
Paulo and Minas Gerais to organize their own pavilions, antiregionalism
was seeping into the regime's cultural imaginary well before the notorious
27 November 1937 Queima das Bandeiras, in which the flags of all states
were publicly burned. By the time the Estado Novo regime threw its weight
behind the organization of a national exposition, the conservative, antifederalist provisions first proposed in 1936 became official policy.

The Exposição do Estado Novo opened on 10 December 1938, on fair-
grounds cleared near Rio's Santos Dumont airport. Organized by the
Ministry of Education and the Departamento Nacional de Propaganda
(precursor to the Department of Press and Propaganda), the exposition

presented the public with a compelling case for national renewal.[9] Trumpeting the overthrow of the so-called inorganic, divisive political culture of liberal republicanism, the exposition was "oriented by a vision of the collectivity which makes no room for state peculiarities and regional differences. The event's principal mission is to outline the broad strokes of the nation's recent transformation."[10] The triumphal column standing over the exposition's entrance set the political tone for the entire event, combining the seal of the Republic and the motto *"O Novo Brasil 1930–1938."* The message was clear: the Brazilian republic had been stripped from its conventional temporal associations with the Proclamation of the Republic (1889) and promulgation of the Constitution (1891) to be redeemed by the Revolution of 1930 and the first year of Estado Novo rule.

Official press releases praised the exposition for laying out a blueprint for national action. Within the pavilions, visitors walked through modules that offered dozens of statistics, graphs, maps, photographs, and models documenting the social and cultural achievements of the Vargas state. National defense, economic reform, labor legislation, educational reform, public works, and health care received special attention. Images and quotes of Vargas were located strategically throughout the exposition. These didactic, patriotic, and self-congratulatory displays fulfilled the exposition's mission statement to "give the common man off the street access to the achievements of the Federal Government realized since 1930."[11] The closely monitored press stressed the moral lessons learned by the event's estimated 100,000 visitors.[12]

The Ministry of Education Pavilion was especially effective at illustrating how cultural management had returned the nation to a path of cultural prosperity and physical security. State patronage for the humanities and sciences was prominently featured in a special module that listed state incentives toward historical preservation, museums, cinema, literature, theater, civic culture, and civic and moral education. The symbolic centerpiece of this display of cultural renewal was a scale model of the new ministerial headquarters, which brought together the daring design originally sketched out by Le Corbusier in 1936, with a decorative scheme that brought together the most important figures in Brazilian contemporary art and sculpture. Exposition visitors were given the impression that the Vargas state had mastered the technical and symbolic idioms of political unity, social progress, and renovação.

From the state's perspective, the Exposição do Estado Novo was a tri-

38 Scale Model of the Ministry of Education and Health Building, 1938. In late 1938, the public was treated to a scale model of the Ministry of Education and Health headquarters under construction in downtown Rio de Janeiro. A daring, controversial structure, the ministerial headquarters was promoted as the symbol of renovação. In the background are studies for Portinari's mural series of Brazilian economic life. Courtesy of CPDOC-GC.

umph, setting the tone for the extremely nationalistic, patriotic, modernizing (and modernist) cultural imagery that defined the Estado Novo. As such, the Exposição do Estado Novo was an excellent rehearsal for the articulation of a positive image of Brazilian society soon to be offered up to foreign audiences.

Brazilian Culture and the World

The Exposição do Estado Novo largely succeeded thanks to the charismatic message of renewal and the repressive state apparatus that exercised broad leeway in refashioning the national political culture after the golpe of 1937. The Vargas state found it more difficult to draw foreign audiences into this celebration of the Estado Novo. The pejorative characterizations of Brazilian culture circulating among elite and popular audiences of the North Atlantic had been longtime irritants to commercial and cultural interests in Brazil. To make matters worse, the worldwide depression, the rise of political isolationism and cultural nationalism in Europe, and a sharp drop in international migration flows alienated Brazil from the West's imaginary, making it doubly hard for the Estado Novo regime to capture the world's attention.

Brazilian culture was not wholly unknown in the North Atlantic during the Great Depression, but no Brazilian wielded the international celebrity once commanded by diplomat-historian Manoel Oliveira Lima, the pioneer aviator Alberto Santos Dumont, or Tarsila do Amaral, the wealthy avant-garde painter who captivated the Parisian art scene in the 1920s. In the early 1930s, Brazilian art and architecture had very little impact on the international stage. Freyre's *Casa-grande e senzala* and Euclides da Cunha's *Os Sertões,* two works of social science that attracted a large international readership once translated into English in the immediate postwar period, had yet to make their impact on the foreign imaginary of Brazil. The totalitarian overtones of the Estado Novo did not sit well with neighboring Argentina, which feared a possible increase of geopolitical tensions, nor the United States, which wanted Brazilian guarantees against the spread of fascism into the South Atlantic. Popular audiences in the United States and Europe were likely to see Brazil as an exotic movie set where Fred Astaire and Ginger Rogers could dance and romance, as they do in the 1933 RKO Radio Pictures release *Flying Down to Rio.*

Facing the disinterest, prejudices, and misplaced romanticizations of foreigners, the Vargas regime formulated plans to improve the nation's profile in international circles. In 1935, trade bureaus opened in New York and several European capitals to promote Brazilian commerce. Meanwhile, the Ministry of Foreign Relations and official propaganda agencies looked for opportunities to cultivate positive images of Brazil, especially among commercial representatives and travel agencies in the United States and Western Europe.

Increasingly, cultural relations joined commercial propaganda as a vehicle for improving Brazil's stature in the international community. Cultural promotion found its warmest reception in the United States, where the government of Franklin Delano Roosevelt proved exceedingly receptive to strengthening cultural relations with the strategically important

Brazil.[13] The Hollywood studio system, in collaboration with the Office of the Coordinator of Interamerican Affairs, looked for Brazilian celebrities who could put a welcoming face on the abstract slogan "good neighbor." Walt Disney Studios literally invented a Brazilian character, Zé (Joe) Carioca, to join its regular rotation of animated characters.[14] Zé Carioca's international popularity, strong as it was, paled in comparison to the runaway success of Carmen Miranda, the Portuguese-born, Brazilian-raised entertainer who become Brazil's best-known cultural ambassador to the United States until Antonio Carlos Jobim and Astrud Gilberto sparked the Bossa Nova craze in the late 1950s. A stage, film, and recording star, Miranda was best known for her over-the-top roles as the fiery Latina in films like *Weekend in Havana* (1941) and *The Gang's All Here* (1943). Miranda proved so popular with U.S. audiences that late in the war it was reported that "the Brazilian Bombshell" was the highest-paid woman to file a U.S. tax return.[15]

Celebrity diplomacy was not without its pitfalls, especially for figures like Miranda who tried to please both Brazilian and American audiences. U.S. actor-director Orson Welles's notorious troubles completing *It's All True* in 1942 have provided rich materials for discussing Welles's megalomania, the Estado Novo police state, and the complex politics of race in Brazil.[16] Miranda never had the misfortune to run afoul of the authorities in large part because she made few public statements that might have been construed as politically compromising. Miranda, nevertheless, encountered choppy waters trying to negotiate Brazilian-American cultural relations after she became a star. Following the release of *Down Argentine Way* (1940), a lighthearted, but insensitive, pastiche of Latin American culture set in Argentina, Brazilian film reviewers criticized Miranda as a caricature of Brazilian culture who pleased Americans at Brazil's expense.[17] Miranda soon became a target for parody north and south of the equator. In the face of her critics, Miranda remained extremely loyal to her interpretation of Brazil's cultural heritage and her signature screen-and-stage personality, the *Bahiana*. Before and after the controversy surrounding *Down Argentine Way,* Miranda's song lyrics continued to make innumerable references to Brazilian cuisine, dance, locales, and humor. Support among popular audiences for *A Pequena Notável* (The Little Notable One) remained high. But after a 1940 benefit ball held in Rio in which the high society audience showed hostility to a performance that included Dorival Caymmi's *Que é que a bahiana tem* (a signature song about the Afro-Bahian woman), Miranda found it difficult to win back the support of the Brazilian elite.[18]

(Ironically, Miranda had been discovered by Broadway mogul Lee Shubert while performing for well-to-do carioca audiences with her exaggerated interpretations of bahianas.)

The Vargas regime, for its part, never censured Miranda or Zé Carioca for their on-screen and off-screen personalities. Neither character threatened the basic tenets of state-sponsored cultural renewal. International expositions, on the other hand, proved much more troubling, as the regime tried to seduce and discipline the foreign imagination of Brazilian culture against significant internal debate over the look and meaning of Brazilianness.

Brazil at "The World of Tomorrow"

The Exposição do Estado Novo demonstrated that the coming of the Estado Novo presented the Vargas regime with multiple opportunities to construct compelling, highly patriotic images of Brazil for Brazilian audiences. Developments in the international community presented the regime with equally attractive opportunities to construct positive images of Brazilian culture for foreigners. When the U.S. government extended an invitation to each American republic to organize a delegation to the New York World's Fair of 1939, a fair dedicated to "The World of Tomorrow," the Vargas regime hesitated little before committing. Brazilian participation at the fair served well many interests. American officials hoped to see Brazil take a prominent role among the Latin American nations represented at the fair. The Vargas regime hoped to strengthen commercial relations with the United States, elevate Brazil's place within the interamerican community, and bring to foreign eyes and ears the news of cultural renewal made possible by Vargas's stewardship. On the eve of the imposition of the Estado Novo, the Vargas regime sent formal acknowledgment of Brazilian participation at the New York World's Fair and the Golden Gate International Exposition, both to be held in the summer of 1939.[19]

In a departure from the organizational scheme of the antifederalist Exposição do Estado Novo, the official steering committee for the U.S. fairs invited representatives of state governments and the Federal District as well as several commercial and professional associations to help plan the overseas missions. (Representatives of the working classes were not invited to participate — a development that calls into question the regime's stated mis-

sion to include the working classes in the process of nation building.) More
than one hundred private exhibitors, led by agro-pastoral enterprises and
mining interests with close ties to the export markct, received an invitation
to provide commercial samples for possible inclusion in the Brazilian pavilions. This proved to be a somewhat hollow concession to private concerns,
as the potential exhibitors were instructed to avoid corporate branding,
"always keeping in mind that our overriding preoccupation is to show the
world a Brazil which is economically united, homogenous, and indivisible
in all of its productive capacities." [20] In a final report on the Brazilian mission to New York, Commissioner General Armando Vidal reaffirmed his
commitment to a national representation which conveyed national unity
sem particularismos (without internal differences).[21]

The proper display of the Brazilian economy was of utmost importance
in the preparatory discussions for the New York and San Francisco fairs.
The original charge given to the Brazilian Commission explicitly authorized the commission to play up Brazil's productive capacities.[22] Stating
"What Brazil desires to show [in New York] is her achievements and her
most exceptionally inviting field for foreign investment," Vidal assembled
an impressive sampling of tropical hardwoods, fibers, industrial-grade oils,
and mineral ore to be sent to North America.[23] Vidal was concerned that
primary products were to be displayed in relation to their industrial application. Thus, the displays of commodities installed in New York and San
Francisco were organized such that the visitor would leave with a clear
sense that Brazil's natural resources had great economic potential in an industrializing, militarizing world economy. The Brazilian Commission was
equally concerned that the commercial displays be simple and severe, in
hopes that austerity would distinguish and dignify Brazil in the minds of
North American fair-goers more accustomed to seeing tropical nations as
carefree, chaotic, or underdeveloped. At the completion of the New York
fair, Vidal assured the minister of labor, industry, and commerce that the
Brazilian pavilion had been organized "avoiding the curiosities of museums." [24] With the ultimate success of the Brazilian mission abroad measured by increased trade orders, Vidal was especially proud to state that
industrial and trade concerns had been duly impressed to discover that Brazil could out-produce Africa, Asia, and the Pacific, as well as satisfy the
growing U.S. demand for strategic minerals.

Of course, popular audiences were so not easily moved by the industrial
applications of oiticica palm oil or the strategic uses for Brazilian nickel.

39 Promotional Literature Distributed at Brazilian Pavilions. Alongside the controversial cultural artifacts assembled for the Brazilian missions to the New York and San Francisco fairs, the Brazilian delegates distributed richly illustrated documentation of Brazil's economic modernization. Ironically, the message of material modernity most effectively conveyed to American audiences fulfilled conventional understandings of Brazil as a primary producer. Courtesy of Sanion Special Collections Library, Henry Madden Library, Larson Collection, California State University, Fresno.

Clearly aware that the vast majority of fair-goers were not industrialists, the Brazilian Commission had to package an equally attractive Brazil based around consumer products available to the mass market. Coffee, then, occupied a privileged position in the Brazilian presence overseas, making the coffee bean into Brazil's calling card abroad.[25] The New York pavilion dedicated more floorspace to coffee-related displays than to any other aspect of Brazilian civilization. Exterior and interior decorations on the San Francisco pavilion depicted the coffee harvest cycle, while interior stands documented the importance of coffee cultivation in a modern Brazil.[26]

40 Interior of Brazilian Pavilion at the Golden Gate International Exposition, San Francisco, 1939. Coffee cultivation was one of the important themes in the Brazilian missions to the New York and San Francisco fairs. Courtesy of CPDOC-VF.

Both pavilions included coffee bars decorated in lush tropical motifs, where young women *de boa aparência* (a codeword for white) served Brazilian coffee, yerba matte tea, and hot chocolate while musicians performed popular Brazilian music.[27] By all accounts, these coffee bars were wildly popular with fair-goers on the East and West Coasts.

This aggressive marketing of Brazil as the world's largest coffee producer illustrates the Brazilian delegations' reticence to disturb some of the conventional images of Brazilian society, especially when the images touched on Brazil's place in the international economic system. At the Exposição do Estado Novo, the Vargas regime treated coffee cultivation as an important, but diminished, aspect of the Brazilian political economy. After all, coffee had been the downfall of the national economy in 1930. However, the New York and San Francisco fairs still served up a gratifying image of Brazil as the world's most modern and attractive coffee producer. Fair-goers would be hard-pressed to identify the economic restructuring that accompanied the arrival of the Vargas regime.

The selling of a modern coffee industry certainly made sound economic sense. All protestations to the contrary, coffee remained vital to the national economy. Moreover, American consumers in New York and San Francisco, like their counterparts at earlier universal expositions, clearly wanted to hear (and taste) more about Brazilian coffee. The Brazilian delegation played off of North America's thirst for coffee, distributing novelties that paired images of sacks of Brazilian coffee with the catchy slogan "America's Favorite Drink." The coffee bar set up in San Francisco was so popular that admission had to be regulated to prevent overcrowding. Brazilian coffee imports to the U.S. West Coast reportedly rose 64 percent in the trimester following the San Francisco fair.[28] Yet, the use of coffee as the symbol of Brazilian culture was highly ironic, as high-ranking Brazilian diplomats and military officers used the Brazilian presence in New York as a springboard for courting U.S. assistance in establishing a national steel industry to help wean the Brazilian economy from its overdependence upon the import-export sector.[29]

Of course, coffee alone would never provide enough capital to pay Brazil's entrance fee into the World of Tomorrow imagined in New York. The organizing committee recognized that Brazilian *modernity* would only make sense if the pavilion could illustrate how noncommercial aspects of Brazilian civilization pointed toward the future. As Armando Vidal observed, the Brazilian delegation had to work hard to overcome U.S. misconceptions that Brazil was yet another impoverished republic living the good, but indolent life in the "South American Way." How, the commissioner asked, would North Americans understand renovação and brasilidade?

The problem for Vidal and his fellow commissioners was that they confronted a narrow range of cultural markers that the Vargas regime would deem acceptable and that American audiences would read as legitimately Brazilian. The minister of labor scrapped early plans to send an exhibit on

41 Coffee Favor Distributed at the Brazilian Pavilion at the Golden Gate International Exposition.
The Brazilian delegates were eager to market Brazilian coffee to American consumers. Courtesy of
Sanion Special Collections Library, Henry Madden
Library, Larson Collection, California State University, Fresno.

social policy and labor reform, on the premise that U.S. audiences wanted
evidence of capitalization and consumerism, not social reform directed at
the underclass.[30] The mission to New York included some educational films
on scientific advances in tropical medicine, but in general, the delegates
feared that overemphasis on local achievements in the sciences and industry would pale in comparison to the impressive industrial and commercial
pavilions built in New York. The celebration of the Brazilian baroque would
likely fall flat with U.S. audiences, who might find it hard to see the sublime in eighteenth-century Ibero-American art. The explicit glorification
of the political or cultural renewal under the Estado Novo dictatorship—
a strategy pursued at the Exposição do Estado Novo and Lisbon's Exposição do Mundo Português—ran the risk of alienating U.S. liberals. (The

New York fair was ostensibly celebrated in honor of the 150th anniversary of George Washington's inauguration of the first president of the United States.) The Brazilian commission wanted to tell the Americans about the renewal of Brazilian culture in the broad sense, but they struggled to find a vocabulary appropriate for U.S. ears.

The regime hit upon modernismo as the carrier of national identity. This seemed an entirely appropriate choice, because the modernistas employed cultural idioms of modernity accessible to international audiences, while maintaining a commitment to Brazilian sensibilities. For the North Atlantic nations represented at the New York fair, Brazilian modernism provided a language that bespoke of tomorrowness *and* otherness. The great dilemma for the Brazilian delegation was how to introduce Brazilian modernity to foreign eyes, without bringing to the United States the culture wars over modernism fought in Brazil. Ultimately unable to contain the domestic culture wars, the fight to define brasilidade traveled northward.

The architectural language used in the Brazilian pavilion built in New York is an excellent example of the simultaneous celebration of the modernist movement and the transposition of domestic culture wars to foreign soil. Early plans for the Brazilian mission to New York described a national pavilion "built and decorated in typical Brazilian style."[31] The design competition called upon Brazilian architects to envision a structure that could favorably represent *Brazilian* culture abroad. The New York hosts immediately absorbed their guests' interest in cultural nationalism. Promotional literature distributed by the New York Fair Commission described the winning design as "distinctly tropical in conception," reconfirming the standard interpretation that a "typical" Brazil was a tropical Brazil.[32]

In truth, the pavilion design could not be described as "typical" of any Brazilian architectural tradition. The pavilion's tropical character would be equally difficult to discern from the winning blueprints. The building made no reference to Ibero-American, colonial, or Amerindian architectural traditions. The pavilion did not evoke the mystery and grandeur of tropical architecture on display at the 1931 Colonial Exposition in Paris, nor contain decorative motivs that might be associated with warm climates. Instead of typical architecture, the design brought to New York the bold, unconventional idioms of the "new architecture" that took hold of Brazil's modernists in the 1930s to the great displeasure of defenders of traditional and eclectic architecture.

42 Entrance to the Brazilian Pavilion, New York World's Fair of 1939. This temporary structure marked the Brazilian modernists' triumphant entrance into the world of international modernism. *Pavilhão do Brasil, Feira Mundial de Nova York de 1939.*

Designed by Brazilian modernist Lucio Costa and his younger disciple, Oscar Niemeyer, the L-shaped, two-story pavilion synthesized many of the essential features of an emergent "international school" associated with the Swiss-French architect Le Corbusier and the International Congress of Modern Architecture. The Le Corbusian imprint was unmistakable in the flat roof, raised support columns, non-load-bearing walls, entrance ramp, *brise-soleil* (sun-breaks designed to regulate heat and light in structures built in hot climates), and surrounding greenery. Of the central elements of modern architecture synthesized in Le Corbusier's 1927's "Five Points for a New Architecture" (*pilotis,* roof garden, free plan, free façade, and ribbon windows), only the roof garden was missing (although there was a garden adjacent to the pavilion).[33] The liberal use of plate glass set within thin metal frames and the dramatic use of artificial lighting created an open, bright, and functional space that was hardly typical of Brazilian architecture. Modernist design and modern construction materials had brought a thoroughly modern, but not recognizably Luso-Brazilian, space to New York. The well-traveled architectural critic was unlikely to think of Brazil when confronted with the same structural and design elements found in prototypes of modern architecture built or idealized for private and public patrons in northern Europe and the United States.

With such solid internationalist credentials, had the Costa-Niemeyer pavilion really met the standard of *typical* Brazilian architecture? Was the pavilion a reflection of the type of cultural nationalism that the Vargas regime so dearly wanted foreign audiences to know and respect? Was this modernismo also brasileiro?

In Costa and Niemeyer's lyrical reading of design and structural principles laid out by the International Congress of Modern Architecture, the response to such unsettling questions was an unequivocal yes. Unmistakably internationalist, the pavilion still managed to deploy structural and decorative elements that spoke to Brazil's unique status as a modern, tropical nation. The gentle curves of the exterior walls, the undulating interior balcony, and the sweeping ramp leading to the pavilion's main entrance made a bold statement about the plasticity of modernist architecture when interpreted by Brazilians. Niemeyer and Costa sent the message that modernity did not necessarily have to be marked by right angles. The coffee bar's furnishings and décor were more warm, sensual, and inviting than anything one might expect from modernists associated with the Bauhaus or De Stijl schools, but they still shared certain design elements that were indeed modern. The exterior brise-soleil told northerners that modern architecture, with its thin exterior walls and ample glass windows, could work in a tropical setting, where the sunlight and heat were intense. The exotic landscaping, set around a small lagoon, and the storks and snakes on display outside of the pavilion, made an unmistakably tropical imprint upon an architectural style most closely associated with the frigid North. The water lilies (*vitória-régias*) growing in the lagoon told visitors that this pavilion came from a nation that could invoke the Amazon. In sum, the Costa-Niemeyer pavilion achieved functionality, drama, beauty, *and* otherness without recourse to deracinated internationalism or the excessive exotica so typical of non-European pavilions built at world's fairs.

This careful negotiation between modernism and tropicalism, the established bearers of modernity and the emergent ones, was an unqualified success among foreign critics. North American and European architectural critics praised the Costa-Niemeyer pavilion in influential architectural reviews including *Architectural Forum, Architectural Record,* and *Architecture d'aujourd'hui*.[34] The innovative nature of Brazilian modernism quickly became a hot topic at architectural symposiums held in Boston, New York, Mexico City, and London.[35] Catapulting Lucio Costa, Oscar Niemeyer, and the Brazilian modernist style into an international architectural canon, the

43 Patio Garden of the Brazilian Pavilion, New York World's Fair of 1939. The internationalist credentials of the Brazilian Pavilion did not inhibit architects Lucio Costa and Oscar Niemeyer from incorporating stylistic and decorative elements that evoked the tropics. *Pavilhão do Brasil, Feira Mundial de Nova York de 1939.*

Brazilian pavilion paved the way for the world's fascination with "tropical modernism." In a review of the highly acclaimed *Brazil Builds* exhibit, organized at the Museum of Modern Art in New York in 1943, one well-placed U.S. critic located Brazilian architecture at the vanguard, arguing that Brazilian modernism represented "a whole new school of modern architecture whose intelligent solutions of special problems, original development of the possibilities of reinforced concrete, and widespread application, put to shame the desultory experience with contemporary International style building in the United States, Mexico, and Argentina."[36] The international attention devoted to Brasília in the late 1950s had been conditioned by nearly two decades of interest in a particular understanding of cultural renewal in Brazil that connected the baroque to Le Corbusier to the Amazon to Flushing Meadows.[37]

Amidst all the international acclaim, the pavilion never fully shed the nagging anxiety about the genealogy of cultural renewal in Brazil. The general layout and decorative elements begged the question whether the pavilion (and, by extension the culture it housed) had been overrun by the international school. Conservatives could rightly ask whether the pavilion conveyed the cultural idioms of Brazilian nationalists or foreign internationalists. The pavilion was built at a critical moment in which the Vargas regime searched for a national architectural language. Could modernism really be more Brazilian than eclecticism or indigenism? Was the brisesoleil really more sensible than the thick adobe walls, shaded patios, and cool floor tiles favored by the neocolonialists? Should an anticommunist state be in the business of commissioning architecture with a socialist pedigree?

Victorious in the design competition for the Ministry of Education headquarters, the modernists needed to assure their multiple audiences that modernismo and brasilidade were synonymous. A powerful alliance of critics, culture managers at the Ministry of Education, and diplomats posted in the United States found resonance in this logic. Proponents of neocolonialism, by contrast, continued to challenge modernism on the grounds that it was not Brazilian. The neocolonial school, led by José Mariano, made emotional appeals to Luso-Brazilian traditions. With public and private interests still drawn to the aesthetic and ideological values of neocolonial and eclectic architecture, the modernists knew that they had to make a concerted attempt to demonstrate the *Brazilian* nature of modernist architecture, especially if they were to continue to associate their project with the official commissions coming from a nationalist state. The conundrum was that the moderns were employing an "international" style to achieve the national.

In describing the pavilion, Costa indicated that he had rejected the temptation to design a "pseudo-modern" edifice lacking the technical and aesthetic supports distinctive to true modern architecture.[38] Costa and Niemeyer were guided by the principle that as representatives of a poor and underdeveloped country, the Brazilian delegation could not be housed in a monumental pavilion that would compete with the nearby British and French pavilions.[39] The team wanted a building that harmonized art and architecture, interior and exterior space. The pavilion had to speak to Brazil's place as an emergent, tropical nation. The spiritual leader of the modernist camp likened the national pavilion to his country's unusual location in human development—at the tropical edge of modernity.

Ironically, U.S. and British critics seemed largely unpreoccupied by the national-international debate. Foreign reviews of the Brazilian pavilion freely commented on the imprint of Le Corbusier in the New York pavilion. (Such comments were certainly influenced by Costa's remarks acknowledging his indebtedness to internationalism.) While some critics praised the Brazilian pavilion qua Brazilian, most treated the pavilion as a transnational solution to design problems in international architecture.

In order to stabilize what were clearly unstable claims to the national, Brazil's moderns found themselves redoubling their efforts to read the Brazilian pavilion as symbolic of a new direction in *Brazilian* culture. Confronting conservative critics who labeled modernist architecture as antinational, not to mention ugly, the modernists stressed the national bases of modernist architecture. The commission that originally awarded the commission to Costa saw in the pavilion a "spirit of brasilidade" that drew upon the principles of modern architecture only when appropriate.[40] More recent analysis of the pavilion updates this interpretation, arguing that Costa and Niemeyer treated the Brazilian pavilion as an opportunity to demonstrate that Brazilian modernism was not a mere "corollary" to an international movement led by Le Corbusier, but a reflection of a genuinely Brazilian project of aesthetic renewal.[41] Thus, the pavilion included a sense of lyricism and tropicalism that would seem wholly out of place in any Radiant City. In echoes of Oswald de Andrade's anthropophagy, the national had overcome the international by consuming it.

It bears repeating that as New Yorkers visited the unusual marriage of modernity and Brazilianity, the Vargas regime continued to face resistance to the imposition of modernism in public commissions. Just as Brazilian modernism made its international debut, Lucio Costa had to convince culture managers and architects that Oscar Niemeyer's modernist design for the Grande Hotel de Ouro Preto bested neocolonialism as a better bridge to Brazil's Age of Gold. Elsewhere, Capanema faced stiff resistance to the plan to separate definitively the National School of Architecture from the National School of Fine Arts, where conservatives feared that the modernists would try to subvert "good" architectural instruction just as they had tried to do with artistic instruction in 1931. When the National Faculty of Architecture finally achieved autonomy in 1945, the academics' fears seemed justified. At the school's inaugural ceremonies, Capanema called upon the faculty and students to create architectural and urban spaces that harmoniously balanced beauty, functionality, and form. The minister cited the architecture of Le Corbusier and the baroque cities of Minas as achieving this balance.[42] This type of genealogy worked well for Brazil's modernists. For traditionalists, the ascendancy of the modernist camp in state commissions was most distressing.

When the Brazilian Pavilion in New York was torn down in the fall of 1940, modernists in Brazil and overseas could point to the structure as a monument to the victory of modernist architecture in the tropics. The structure's success redounded well with the Vargas regime, which gained its ticket into the World of Tomorrow. But in retrospect, it is also possible to read the pavilion as an artifact of an ongoing war about the fundamental bases of Brazilian culture. The modernists undoubtedly made great strides in New York, winning the resources and international acclaim to redefine "typical" Brazilian architecture. But hegemonic control of brasilidade remained more elusive, as the antimodernists continued to resist the modernists' ideological and aesthetic appropriation of nationality, and modernist architecture itself could never be fully contained by the nationalist rhetoric expounded by the Vargas regime and its clients.

The artwork that accompanied the Brazilian missions to New York and San Francisco in 1939–1940 can also be read as artifacts of culture wars waged back in Brazil. Artistic representations organized for foreign expositions had historically brought out the best and the worst of the Brazilian cultural establishment since the mid-nineteenth century. Vitor Meireles's monumental *Batalha Naval do Riachuelo* dazzled U.S. audiences at the Centennial Exposition held in Philadelphia in 1876. Conversely, the Brazilian delegates to the First International Congress of Race, held in London in 1911, brought with them Modesto Brocos's *Redemption of Ham* (1895), a paean to the ideology of whitening. The New York and San Francisco fairs held in 1939 and 1940 were yet another venue for art to play a significant role in the representation of Brazilianness for foreign eyes.

In planning for the 1939 fairs, the selection of artwork appropriate for the U.S. was particularly tricky. In New York, Brazilian art was to appear in several locations, including the Pan-American Art Exhibition to be held at the Riverside Museum, the International Art Exhibition sponsored by the International Business Machines Corporation, local museums with no formal relationship to the fair, and the Brazilian pavilion proper. The general organizing commission and a separate committee charged with the artistic representation to be sent to the 1939 Pan-American exhibit had to negotiate cautiously between the gains made by the modernists in winning state commissions with long-standing prohibitions against artwork that seemed to suggest anything other than conventional understandings of valor, dignity, and beauty south of the equator.

Race and underdevelopment had been a major preoccupation for Brazilians responsible for sending art representations abroad and continued to be in 1939. According to Mário de Andrade, convention treated scenes of poverty, favelas, popular life, and Afro-Brazilians as inappropriate subject matter for official cultural missions sent abroad.[43] It is commonly reported that *Café,* Cândido Portinari's celebrated painting of the Afro-Brazilian rural proletariat, had been rejected for the art collection at the Brazilian Embassy in Washington and the art representation sent to the 1937 World's Fair in Paris due to its Afro-Brazilian subject matter.[44] The question was not official racism per se; *Café* was in the permanent collection at the National Museum of Fine Arts, and Portinari's mural series at the Ministry of Education told the national history through the labors of nonwhite workers. The overriding concern was audience. On domestic soil, Brazilians enjoyed access to official spaces that included, at a minimum, some recognition of Brazil's multiethnic character. On foreign soil, however, the steering committees who organized narrated Brazilianness abroad most often consciously tried to censor blackness and manual labor on the principle that foreign eyes needed to see a white and civilized Brazil.

The criteria used to select the works to be sent to the Pan-American exhibit did not automatically reproduce past conservatism, but much of the Brazilian artwork on display at the Riverside Museum did not differ greatly from previous sensibilities. To meet basic eligibility requirements, works to be considered for selection merely had to be paintings, sculpture, or engravings executed between 1933 and 1938, submitted with an appraised value and the artist's credentials. The selection committee headed by MNBA director Oswaldo Teixeira was more discriminating, favoring only works which followed academic conventions. The committee's conservative bias meant that of the forty works sent to the Pan-American, not a single work had been painted by a participant in the Modern Art Week of 1922. The second and third generations of modernists, many of which were under state contract for the Ministry of Education headquarters, were absent. The Paulista Art Family, a heterogeneous group of Brazilian and foreign-born painters active in São Paulo who charted a middle path between the academic rear-guard and modernist avant-garde, also went unrepresented. The subject matter was equally conservative. Most of the works on display at Riverside could be categorized as romantic or impressionist takes on rural scenes, still-lifes, and interiors. *Fire Dance* (1936?), a symbolist painting executed by the eclectic academic painter Helios Seelinger (1878–1965), was the only work to suggest that Afro-Brazilians could be objects worthy of art. Proponents of the incorporation of the Afro-Brazilian in foreign art exhibits could hardly look to the Seelinger canvas, which depicted what seemed to be an erotic satanic ritual, with hopes that foreign audiences would see more than barbaric obscurantism in Afro-Brazilian life. In sum, the majority of the works sent to New York were conservative works from conservative painters.[45]

The committee in charge of the Brazilian pavilion (as opposed to the art exhibit at the Riverside) was much more open to the possibility of integrating nonacademic subject matter into a synthetic overview of Brazilian society. At the suggestion of Lucio Costa, the commissioners turned to Cândido Portinari and Celso Antonio, two artists who had broken with their academic training to embrace modernism, for the decorative elements of the Brazilian pavilion.[46] Portinari agreed to paint a mural series for the main hall depicting three regional archetypes, the *jangadeiros* (fisherman) of the North, the bahianas of the Northeast, and gaúcho cattlemen of the extreme South. Antonio agreed to sculpt in granite a stylized reclining female nude holding a child. The estimated eight million visitors who passed through the Brazilian pavilion encountered images of a nation not populated just by pretty white faces but also by weathered mestizo fishermen, powerful black washerwomen, and brawny cowboys. These Brazilians were larger-than-life, dominated by oversized extremities that overwhelmed the viewer. These were Brazilians who worked. Typical of Portinari's muralwork, the images combined rough textures and brilliant colors that departed from academic convention. This was a Brazil that was rawer, more human, more vibrant than the one represented at the Riverside Museum (see plate 3).

Across town, at the Museum of Modern Art, hung another piece of Brazilian artwork that spoke of a Brazil not represented at the Riverside Museum. The venue was the *Art in Our Time* exhibit, a comprehensive show of

44 Portinari Murals, Brazilian Pavilion, New York World's Fair of 1939. Portinari's three murals, depicting the regional and ethnic diversity of Brazilian society, were a huge success at the New York World's Fair. Courtesy of Projeto Portinari.

modern art organized for the inauguration of the museum's new home on West Fifty-Third Street.[47] The piece of art in question was an easel painting, *Morro* (literally: hill; figuratively: shantytown) (1933), acquired by MOMA in 1939 when the museum director, Alfred Barr, took a liking to three of Portinari's paintings appearing in a favorable spread in *Fortune* magazine. Portinari's compelling portrait of life in Rio's favelas was the only Brazilian work to be included in MOMA's wide-ranging overview of twentieth-century art. It was also the boldest piece of Brazilian art on display in New York in the summer of 1939.

Morro proclaimed that poverty and blackness were not merely picturesque elements of folkloric peoples residing in the tropics; they were legitimate subjects of modernity and brasilidade. Alongside Degas's dance studios and Rousseau's noctural jungles, *Morro* made the shantytown into a modern space, in direct dialogue with skyscrapers, oceanliners, and airplanes. The *favelados* living within this modern space were not automatons of the industrial marketplace, nor unemployed drunkards. These figures did not suffer from anomie or psychosis. Instead, the Afro-Brazilians inhabiting Portinari's *Morro* are real persons, full of subjectivity and life. The malandro who stands in the lower-left corner of the canvas exudes an air of arrogant sexual power uncontained by poverty and the conventions of academic painting. The figure staring straight out in the lower right projects a self-awareness not easily domesticated by the viewer's gaze. The women making their way up the hill confound all expectations that manual labor degrades. U.S. audiences were denied a heroicized proletariat living in a romanticized poverty. They were denied the image of a people beaten down by blackness and work. Instead, *Morro* gave them a complex and textured visual language to understand the juxtaposed subjectivities of contemporary brasilidade (see plate 4).

If Brazilian conservatives wanted U.S. audiences to see a modern Brazil that was white, sentimental, domesticated, and civilized, *Morro* and the pavilion murals asked Brazil's U.S. hosts to see Brazilian culture turned on its side. The contentious debates surrounding the meaning of Brazilian art sent to New York, held among Brazilian and foreign critics as well as the fair-going public, illuminate the unresolved questions of state cultural management and, more broadly, the shape and meaning of cultural identity in Brazil.

Some of the criticism leveled against the art selection on display in New York was strictly internalist, with little repercussion outside the art community. For example, the president of the Association of Brazilian Artists, F. Guerra Vidal, complained that the selection committee for the Riverside show should have been more discerning.[48] Thomaz de Santa Rosa lamented the long-standing tradition for excluding modernist art from foreign delegations, combined with an even longer-standing tradition of excluding works depicting popular life.[49] Quirinio Campofiorito, artist and art critic, opened up the larger issue of Brazilian modernity. How, Campofiorito asked, could Brazil establish its place in the World of Tomorrow with artwork that was closer to a "pallid shadow."[50] In the United States, Robert C. Smith, assistant director of the Hispanic Foundation at the Library of Congress and one of the most active critics of Latin American art, expressed similar disappointment for the lack of innovation at the Riverside Museum.[51]

Disappointed by the works on view at the Pan-American exhibit, Smith and other critics were drawn to the handful of works that departed from convention. The Portinari murals gracing the Brazilian pavilion were, far and away, the most interesting to foreign observers looking for something fresh. Smith seized the opportunity to promote new directions in Brazilian art, championing Portinari to his U.S. audiences. Smith was enthusiastic about Portinari's technical style, which he compared to those of Pablo Picasso and Diego Rivera. (Portinari himself was clearly impressed by Picasso, but discouraged comparisons to Rivera.)[52] Smith was equally enthusiastic about Portinari's compelling choice of subject matter, which included rural landscapes, family compositions, and religious festivals that captured the lives of everyday people. In his review of the Brazilian paintings on display in New York in 1939, Smith told U.S. readers, "Portinari shows that complex life without sentimentality or undue vulgarity. In *Morro,* as well as in the World's Fair frescoes, he remains the straightforward, understanding painter of the Brazilian lower classes."[53] In Portinari's small and monumental renderings of blacks, mulattos, fishermen, and children at work, ritual, and play, Smith saw the essence of Brazil.

The buzz surrounding Portinari grew rapidly in the second year of the New York fair, when Portinari won over U.S. audiences at the Latin American Fine Arts Exhibition organized at the Riverside Museum, a one-man show organized at the Detroit Institute of Arts and the Museum of Modern Art in New York, and a traveling exhibit that passed through Chicago and the South.[54] The Riverside, Detroit, and MOMA shows received particularly broad and favorable coverage in the U.S. press.[55] Public praise for the painter's work increased once the University of Chicago Press published an impressive catalog of Portinari's work in late 1940.[56] In the meantime, Portinari and his wife Maria came to New York for the MOMA show to be feted by prominent members of the New York art world, including John Hay Whitney and publisher William S. Paley. America's cultural elite treated Portinari as the quintessential Good Neighbor, good painter, and good Brazilian. Popular audiences seemed to be equally impressed with the diminutive Portinari.

In reading Portinari, the popular press invariably recounted an up-by-the-bootstraps narrative of an impoverished son of Italian immigrants who labored in the coffee fields of Brazil to then send their adolescent son off to cosmopolitan Rio to earn an art education. The story grew more compelling as the press told of Portinari's poverty in the capital, where he lived in a bathroom and ate little more than soup. The tale turned optimistic as readers were told that Portinari's innate talents won him a scholarship to refine his talents in Europe. The story ended, naturally, with Portinari's triumphant conquest of Manhattan. In the fall of 1940, U.S. readers in Minneapolis, Boston, Dallas, and Evanston read headlines like "Ragamuffin Becomes Great Artist," "Poor Boy Wins Fame as Artist," "Brazilian Artist Wins Hard Way," and "Brazilian Artist Got Start on Coffee Farm." In describing the painter in New York, the popular press was taken by the news that Portinari was a fan of American cinema and that he was a devoted husband and father to his infant son João Cândido, for whom the painter had set aside several works. This was a story of personal and moral uplift sure to enliven the United States, which found itself in the depths of the Great Depression.

The art press took a more critical, if not necessarily less enthusiastic, take on Portinari's accomplishments. In August 1939, Robert C. Smith told U.S. audiences that Portinari "has demonstrated that Brazilian painting, in spite of its exotic past and constant borrowings from foreign sources, can be both monumental and original." [57] From here sprang a series of comparisons to the established leaders of modern art, including the Mexican muralists, the Catalan surrealist Joan Miró, and, of course, Pablo Picasso. Works by Portinari quickly appeared in several prominent American museums, the Library of Congress, and the private collections of noted American collectors including U.S. diplomat Jeffrey Caffrey and cosmetic manufacturer Helena Rubenstein.

Beyond the enthusiastic praise, it is important to recognize what American critics took from Portinari's work, as the interpretation of Portinari's subject matter reveals how brasilidade was read in the United States. Robert Smith, above all others, was drawn to the paulista's attention to Brazilian popular life. In describing Morro, Smith claimed that Portinari had accurately captured a life that "like that of our Southern cities [is] inextricably bound up with the life of the negro communities within its boundaries. Portinari shows that complex life without sentimentality or vulgarity." [58] In a speech delivered in the summer of 1939, Smith observed how Portinari broke from the standard representation of the Afro-Brazilian in "a kind of subequatorial 'Uncle Tom's Cabin,' " calling the paulista "the foremost interpreter of that great force who is daily growing articulate — the Negro of the Americas." [59]

Florence Horn, art critic for *Fortune* magazine and a personal friend of Cândido and Maria Portinari, speculated that the artist's difficulties with conservative critics might be attributed to the insistence upon painting his fellow Brazilians, especially the Afro-Brazilian agriculturists he once knew in the interior of São Paulo and the Afro-Brazilian city dwellers he encountered in Rio, with complexity and humanity. In describing the one-man show at MOMA, Horn asserted, "Believing that the mulatto and the negro are indeed important elements in Brazil, [Portinari] paints them no matter what the consequences to him might be. . . . His paintings reveal not only his affectionate interest in them but also a gentle humor which can come only from a thorough understanding of their lives." [60]

Not all American art critics were so taken by Portinari's representations of Afro-Brazilians. After seeing the 1940 show at MOMA, Elizabeth MacCausland, a professor of art history at Sarah Lawrence College well known for her interests in the social context of art, charged that Portinari's blacks were not real Afro-Brazilians, but merely figures upon which the artist chose to express his undoubted talent. In a direct response to Smith's favorable review of the Portinari works on view in 1939 and 1940, MacCausland wrote:

> The life of Brazil (where the writer has never been) is not made clearer by these visual images: the place of the Negro and mulatto in Brazilian civilization is not interpreted. What the Portinaris do is to make one aware of the esthetic experience which produced them. . . .
>
> What of the Brazilians — white, Negro, mulatto, Indian, Spanish, or what — who till the coffee plantations which produce 63 percent of the world's supply? These paintings do not give, at least this writer, a new awareness of the immediacy of existence for Brazil's 43,000,000: they speak only for Portinari. What of the burgeoning meat-growing industry? What of the slums, what of malnutrition? In *Morro* the section "across the tracks" is painted, but it is a painting only, not additionally a human and social experience as in [the nineteenth-century French satirist Honoré] Daumier's *Laundress*. Malnutrition there is, it is evident in the swollen bellies of the children in *Dispossessed,* but the observation is static. [61]

American critics clearly lacked unanimity on how successfully Portinari captured the reality of Afro-Brazilians. Did the painter humanize or merely caricaturize the Afro-Brazilian? What united the critics, however, was their express desire to see more of the Brazilian black. In their interest in Portinari, U.S. critics, elite patrons, and the general public expressed the desire to see a multiracial people that flew in the face of the eugenized whites typically offered by official artistic missions. Portinari let Americans see that black faces had an inner force that went beyond the mere picturesque. Favelas, at least for some, could be beautiful. Favelados could be modern. Fascinated by the possibility that Africanness, racial mixture, and impoverishment might not necessarily lead toward degradation and conflict, some U.S. art critics dared to look to the Portinari works sent to the United States as an alternative space filled by the possibilities of progress and racial harmony. Again in 1940, Horn speculated, "Portinari seems to be indicating that there *is* no race issue among the people themselves, or perhaps that the Brazilian is developing out of a mixture of races."[62] One must ask if Horn were not asking whether the same principle could be applied to the United States.

Such speculation resonates deeply when one considers that the New York World's Fair coincided with rising U.S. interest in Afro-Brazilian culture as Brazilian and transamerican. As the Nazis pushed across Europe, carrying with them the ideology of Aryan supremacy, U.S.-based anthropologists Donald Pierson, Ruth Landes, and Melville and Frances Herskovits conducted field research among Afro-Brazilians in Salvador da Bahia. This work formed the foundation for several studies on race relations and Afro-Diasporic culture in the Americas.[63] Stateside, the prominent African-American sociologist E. Franklin Frazier published a handful of scholarly and popular articles on the Afro-Brazilian and more broadly on comparative race relations in Brazil and the United States.[64] Hollywood took a keen interest in Afro-Brazilian life as well. Orson Welles's ill-fated *It's All True* and Carmen Miranda gave U.S. movie-goers an entertaining, although volatile, sampling of sambistas, malandros, and bahianas. By 1946, U.S. audiences had access to an English translation of Gilberto Freyre's *Masters and the Slaves* and to Frank Tennenbaum's highly influential comparative history of slavery and race relations, *Slave and Citizen*. An influential core of U.S. intellectuals, as well as a broader group of African-American readers who subscribed to the black press, seemed interested in the Afro-Brazilian as an African in the Americas, as a counterpoint to U.S. race relations and most frequently as a Brazilian. Portinari's painting offered American audiences unable to travel to Brazil an introduction to the Afro-Brazilian.

There is no direct evidence to suggest that the Vargas regime intended to use the Brazilian delegation to the New York World's Fair, nor Portinari's subsequent exhibits in the United States, to promote explicitly Afro-Brazilian culture abroad. Clearly impressed by Portinari's work, Capanema still gingerly stepped around Afro-Brazilian culture—all popular culture for that matter—when drafting the legal definition of "cultural development" in 1938. An earlier legal definition of "historical and artistic patrimony" that Capanema drafted with Rodrigo Melo Franco de Andrade had stripped Mário de Andrade's anteprojeto of much of its ethnographic tilt. A 1942 proposal submitted by Gilberto Freyre to create a "National Department of Anthropology" within the Ministry of Education came to Capanema as a dead letter.[65] The Ministry of Education would not integrate ethnography into public policy until well after Capanema had stepped down in 1945. As interested as the minister was in the "total formation" of Brazilian culture, Capanema could never bring himself to put popular culture at the forefront of cultural management. The minister seemed especially reluctant to present popular culture to foreigners. Nevertheless, Brazil's popular culture crept into the language of modernism carefully crafted by the Ministry of Education and the Brazilian mission to New York. Sambas, popular marches, and *choros*—not to mention Brazilian classical music—soothed North American ears at the coffee bar built on the first floor of the Brazilian pavilion.[66] Portinari's bahianas and jangadeiros were a success among American critics. The overseas success of Brazilian popular culture, cautiously ensconced in a curvilinear modernist box, strongly suggests that the Brazilian delegation to the World of Tomorrow carried with it a possible reading of Brazil as a multicultural society that communicated directly with the Afro-Atlantic.

When the New York fair closed permanently in 1940, domestic and international audiences could see tangible evidence that renovação meant something in Brazilian culture. The Portinari murals, set within the Costa-Niemeyer pavilion, signaled an ascendant look of brasilidade that the state and the vanguard could celebrate with unmatched enthusiasm. The forward-looking view of renovação, however, was not an unqualified success as the modernists continued to face competition at home and abroad.

In New York, Portinari's erstwhile colleague and critic, academic painter Oswaldo Teixeira, competed with the paulista for the mantle of brasilidade. In sharp contrast to Portinari's surrealist/social realist interpretations of the material and visual worlds of the Brazilian popular classes, Teixeira offered up a more conventional vision of Brazilian landscapes, nudes, and still lifes that may well have been painted in the 1880s rather than the 1930s. His was a romanticized Brazil. His was a white Brazil. Any critic who thought that Portinari painted ugly things in an ugly way would be relieved to find that Teixeira's *Mater*, a sentimental rendering of a young white mother covered by a damask shawl nursing her infant daughter, hung in the International Business Machines Corporation pavilion in New York.[67] Teixeira's light and airy *Men and Boats of My Country*, on exhibit at the Riverside Museum, reminded North American viewers that romantic beauty could exist between the Tropics. Teixeira's works quietly declared that Brazil's tomorrow would continue to follow the lessons of yesterday.

Thus, the vexing problem for the Brazilian commissioners in New York was how to promote an image of modernity for foreign audiences that invoked the works of both Teixeira and Portinari, yet gave no indication that the two painters offered distinct messages about Brazilianity. Who would produce the image of a modern Brazil? The academic or the modernist? Who would reproduce a modern Brazil? The well-proportioned, calm, white mother-and-child of *Mater* or the black mother-and-child, arms and hips akimbo, depicted in *Morro*?

The easiest solution for the Brazilian commissioners was to send a heterogeneous collection of works to the United States and ignore the political and ideological tensions among the works. So, Portinari figured prominently at the Brazilian pavilion and Teixeira at the IBM International Art Exhibit. Portinari won praise from art critics favorable to modernism and social realism, while Teixeira's *Mater* won high marks in visitor surveys conducted at the IBM pavilion.[68] Portinari's success overseas was amply documented back in Brazil, propelling the painter to the forefront of the Brazilian art world. Teixeira leveraged his international exposure to maintain his cultural authority at the National Museum of Fine Arts. The inclusive strategy worked. Smith and Horn were some of the few U.S. critics to say anything about the explicit aesthetic and political tensions found in the artistic representation sent to New York in 1939 and 1940. However, the inclusion of modernist art spelled trouble in Brazil, where Portinari faced intense criticism in response to his success abroad.

Much of the criticism leveled at Portinari targeted the artist as the state's official painter who won the lion's share of stature and resources for ideological rather than artistic reasons. Portinari's defenders retorted that the painter was indeed talented, and that the Vargas regime had neither official painters nor styles.[69] Another strain of criticism questioned how Portinari could produce two radically different forms of art—easel portraits of the political and cultural elite, and large canvases and murals that privileged nonelites at work, play, and in agony. Recent research has demonstrated that Portinari's relationship with his elite patrons was fraught with many of the same social and national questions raised by his murals. This type of negotiation went largely unnoticed in the 1930s and 1940s, making it seem, instead, that Portinari was an opportunist who exploited the rich to portray the poor (or vice versa, if one considers that Portinari's works of social realism and folklore were acquired by U.S. and Brazilian museums before his portraits).[70]

Still others asked whether the modernist Portinari, in spite of his technical skill, had made any original contribution to an artistic movement that originated abroad. For example, critic Samuel da Costa argued, "Portinari suffers from an ailment which afflicts nearly all Brazilians: we are magnificent at receiving every idea, each movement coming from Europe. Our reinterpretation [of European styles] sometimes surpasses the original. Yet we are incapable of precision, argumentation, comparison, refutation, or critique. Those who try are overwhelmed by the details (a fate so fitting for mestizos), or, simply fall into a twilight of imprecision."[71] Subsequent criticism of Portinari would repeatedly turn on the question whether the paulista merely stylized an avant-garde imported from abroad, or whether he actually invented a new pictorial language that marked Brazilian modernity.

The ensuing slippages between U.S. and Brazilian readings of Portinari's success illuminate the contested readings of brasilidade on the eve of the Second World War. When U.S. critics celebrated Portinari the ethnographer, Brazilian critics explored the painter's artistic talents. Discounting Samuel da Costa's charge of mimesis, Portinari's Brazilian detractors most often labeled him a bad artist, making little of the subject matter as such. His proponents, however, exalted the painter's technique, style, draftsmanship, brushstroke, composition, and sensibility. The Trotskyist critic Mário Pedrosa (1900–1981), writing from exile in New York, led the bandwagon for the talents of the personable painter from Brodowski.[72] Ruben Navarra, one of the most active critics in the Rio art scene, was equally impressed by Portinari's artistry (and, interestingly, not so impressed by the recurrent "picturesque" black figures).[73] The highly influential Mário de Andrade commended the artist for taking an honest interest in the popular classes as national subjects, while arguing that the essence of Portinari's work was its artistic originality.[74] Looking well beyond the state favors extended by Minister of Education Capanema, critics favorable to Portinari saw an innate talent that approached pure art. These supporters would not deny the ethnographic vitality of Portinari's subject choices. How could they? The mural series painted at the Ministry of Education is a masterpiece precisely because it represents the highpoint of the artist's lifelong fascination with black, mulatto, Indian, mestizo, and immigrant workers. But these same critics would not reduce this choice of subject matter to an intrinsically commendable attribute. Rather, these critics treated the ethnographic as if it were a vehicle for the release of art itself.

Thus, the question of state-sponsored art and artists turned, in large part, on the question of the beauty (or lack thereof) in his work. Portinari's harshest critics in Brazil found the painter's rendering of the human form repugnant, and therefore unworthy of official sanction for domestic or foreign consumption. In the preparation for the 1940 MOMA show, Florence Horn observed that Portinari suffered the same criticism leveled against other modern painters "in New York, London or anywhere — working in an environment which possesses judgements as: 'he paints gross subjects grossly; he distorts the human figure; the people he chooses to paint are ugly.'"[75] The oversized extremities used so effectively to convey the force of manual labor in *Café* and the Ministry of Education murals earned Portinari the highly unflattering title "painter of big feet."[76] The harshest critics suggested that his distortion of the human body was a sign of psychosis.[77] An infamous caricature appearing in 1943 in the Rio daily *A Notícia* juxtaposed Portinari's cubist *Mãe* (1942), a work which quoted Picasso's *Guernica,* with Teixeira's *Mater* under the caption "*Arte maluca e arte séria* [Deranged art and serious art]." Portinari's detractors would go to great lengths to demonstrate that his vision of modernity was ugly and unbalanced.[78] The caricature rhetorically asked how the state could associate itself with insanity.

Certain criticisms leveled at Portinari and other painters who received acclaim abroad took on a more xenophobic tone. An editorial appearing in the November 1940 edition of the ultranationalist monthly, *Nação Armada,* suggested that Portinari's success in New York was proof that his painting failed to meet the nationalistic standards demanded by the cultural environment of the Estado Novo.[79] Similar ultranationalist sentiments — mixed with antimodernism and anti-Semitism — would be leveled against other

modernists of foreign birth or training, including Lasar Segall, a Lithua-
nian Jewish painter who was one of the first to introduce modernist principles to the Brazilian art world. The xenophobic criticism lodged against
Segall's 1943 one-man show at the National Museum of Fine Arts caused
such a stir among the cultural elite that Capanema felt compelled to make
a public declaration that the Brazilian state, unlike the totalitarian states
in Germany and Russia, did not sanction one official art style. Moreover,
Capanema asserted, the Segall show served as a test of the Brazilian state's
resolve to redouble its commitments to the principles of democratic nationalism under threat by the state of belligerence with the Nazis.[80]

Portinari, like Segall and the majority of the artists receiving state support, was able to outlast his adversaries. Charges of antinationalism may
have resonated within the most politically conservative redoubts of the
Vargas state, but the argument that the jangadeiros, bahianas, and gaú-
chos painted in New York were anything but Brazilian was spurious. Other
modernists, including Tarsila do Amaral, Alberto Viega Guignard, and
Emiliano di Cavalcanti, painted subjects that were explicitly Brazilian, and
they painted them in a modern way. Moreover, many prominent cultural
figures from the modernist and academic camps were foreign-born or had
extensive training abroad, making it impossible to sustain the argument
that individuals with foreign experience were incapable of interpreting a
Brazilian reality. When foreign audiences saw the works of these painters,
they invariably searched for Brazil, making it all the more difficult to deny
their Brazilianness.

Rising to be one of a handful of Latin American artists to earn the international attention of museums, patrons, critics, and scholars, Portinari continued to receive public and private commissions through the end of the Estado Novo. For American audiences, Portinari approached being the next
Diego Rivera, winning praise in a series of collective and one-man shows
held throughout the United States. In the meantime, the Costa-Niemeyer
pavilion became a symbol of Brazilian modernism and state-led modernization. Other projects signed by Portinari, Costa, or Niemeyer, including
the Ministry of Education headquarters and the Igreja de São Francisco de
Assis at Pampulha (Belo Horizonte, Minas), would quickly pass from controversial public commissions to referential works of Brazilian identity reproduced the world over. If the antimodernists would claim that Portinari
and other modernists were insufficiently nationalistic, the state's response
was to inscribe certain modernist works, led by the Ministry of Education

headquarters, into the *Livros do Tombo,* making them *national* historical and artistic patrimony.

The Brazilian mission sent to the World of Tomorrow was an expressive exploration of modern Brazil's cultural identity. Portinari's critical and popular success in the United States demonstrated that international audiences were highly receptive to daring departures from academic conventions and subject matter in Latin American painting, especially when these departures invoked Latin America's multiracial subjectivities. Brazilian audiences, in turn, looked to Portinari's success in New York as an opportunity to elevate the pictorial language of modernism to the national paradigm.[81] The daring design of the Brazilian pavilion erected in Flushing Meadows, and the resounding international acclaim accruing to it, catapulted Brazilian architects Lucio Costa and Oscar Niemeyer into an elite league of polyglot architects who claimed the right to redefine the world's built environment. The acclaim won by Costa and Niemeyer reinforced their professional and moral weight back in Brazil, where they made modernism the vehicle for redefining Brazil's built environment. In sum, the Brazilian delegation to New York put modernism and the modernists at a great advantage in articulating a cultural imaginary of self that reverberates into the twenty-first century. However, the inclusion of academic painting in the official delegation to the New York and San Francisco fairs, compounded by the intransigent defense of academicism and tradition as the most representative of Brazil's cultural vocation, reveals that official cultural representations sent abroad inflamed, not calmed, the ongoing struggle to fix the iconographic, architectural, and decorative markers of brasilidade.

The Exposição do Mundo Português and the Origins of Luso-Tropicalism

The year after U.S. audiences got a good look at the new (and old) directions in Brazilian culture, Portuguese audiences were treated to the most comprehensive portrait of Brazilian culture organized during the first Vargas regime. It was a fitting honor for the Portuguese, who (as the official story went) had given Brazil its racial, linguistic, and cultural stock in the sixteenth century. Portugal had been the only foreign nation invited to participate in Brazil's National Exposition of 1908, so it seemed highly appropriate that Brazil would be the only *independent* foreign nation to receive an invitation to the Exposição do Mundo Português, a grand exposition organized in the summer of 1940 to mark the eight-hundredth anniversary of Portuguese nationhood and the worldwide civilizing mission of the Portuguese race.

Brazil and Portugal had much to share in 1940. If linguistic affinities and a shared heritage were not sufficient to push the two states closer, then the political climate was. The Portuguese, like the Brazilians, lived under an "Estado Novo" that preached a doctrine of political and cultural renewal under a strong state. Portuguese Chief of State António de Oliveira Salazar and Vargas each basked in a cult of personality, unmercifully disseminated throughout their respective nations by state propaganda agencies. Both nations tried to negotiate a position of neutrality in the months preceding the outbreak of the Second World War. Neither Vargas nor Salazar demonstrated much interest in explicitly modeling their respective New State after its counterpart on the other side of the Atlantic, nor on any totalitarian states in western or central Europe. Both recognized, however, that each Estado Novo offered the other certain possibilities for providing historical and cultural justifications for a conservative form of national modernity. Together, the Brazilian and Portuguese Estado Novos sought out the paths to renovação that might prove useful for the entire Portuguese-speaking world.

The conditions under which Vargas consented to sending a delegation to Portugal highlight the transatlantic implications of cultural renewal around 1940. Salazar had announced the celebration of a Duplo Centenário da Fundação e da Restauração de Portugal (Double Centenary of the Foundation and Restoration of Portugal) in a well-publicized *Nota Oficiosa* made public on 27 March 1938.[82] This "double centenary" commemorated the eight-hundredth anniversary of the first military campaigns to expel the Moors from Portugal and the three-hundredth anniversary of the rebellion to end the Spanish Captivity (1580–1640). Salazar's *Nota Oficiosa* outlined a number of public ceremonies to be held at historical sites associated with the Foundation and Restoration of Portuguese nationhood, as well as an ambitious program of public works designed to modernize transportation, communication, and urban life throughout Portugal.[83] The highlight of the centenary year would be four national expositions showcasing Portugal's civilizing mission, Portuguese art, regional culture within continental Portugal, and the accomplishments of the Estado Novo, respectively. The heavily censored press touted the centenary celebrations as an affirmation of Portugal's historic vocation for civilization, as well as the fulfillment of Salazar's vision of a new *Era do Engrandecimento* (Era of Great Things).

The *Centenários* were ostensibly a national celebration, but Salazar still saw to it that the centenary year be used as an opportunity to identify the cultural and political affinities of Portuguese-speaking peoples worldwide. Hoping that Brazil would play a major role in the festivities, Salazar invited Brazil to take part in the celebrations, arguing:

> The peoples of Portugal and Brazil shared a common history until the dawn of the nineteenth century; and even when the two kingdoms separated, they accomplished the unprecedented act of maintaining an attitude of tenderness and solidarity. We Portuguese naturally take pride in our past and in our descendants. . . . We want the world to see Brazil as one of the most extraordinary pages in the History of Portugal. And we want the world to see what Portugal has been to Brazil . . . the lifegiver, *a Pátria da própria Pátria* [the Fatherland of the Fatherland].[84]

Employing the language of family, hearth, and filial love, Salazar invited Brazil "to be not only our guest of honor, but to join us to receive the honors that the World owes Brazil." Salazar's argument for Brazil's special role in the Centenários set the tone for imagining a common Luso-Brazilian cultural and political mission. The affinities between the Brazilian and Portuguese Estado Novos, set against the failures of liberal democracies and the excesses of totalitarian regimes throughout the rest of Europe, would be a recurring message during the summer of 1940.

Ironically, the language of sacred familial bonds among the Portuguese and their extra-European progeny initially received a lukewarm response on the western side of the Atlantic. The Portuguese immigrant community in Brazil quickly reprinted Salazar's *Nota Oficiosa,* highlighting Salazar's comments about Luso-Brazilian fraternity, but the Vargas regime delayed any commitments to sending a Brazilian delegation to the centenary celebrations.[85] Vargas had previously remarked favorably upon the contributions made by the Portuguese to the formation of Brazilian society, but the nationalistic political culture of the Estado Novo seemingly made it difficult to celebrate dates drawn from Portuguese history.[86] Besides, the organization of official delegations to the New York and San Francisco fairs, in addition to the demands of the national expositions held in 1938 and 1940, stretched limited resources.

Facing Brazilian reluctance, the titular president of Portugal, General Antonio Oscar de Fragoso Carmona, extended a personal invitation to Vargas, asking that Portugal's "sister-nation stand beside us as a member of the family." [87] Vargas deferred making any firm commitments until the Portuguese government sent an official envoy to coordinate formally the terms of Brazilian participation. The mission proved successful, happily coinciding with the passage of a resolution to lift restrictions on Portuguese immigration to Brazil.[88] With Brazilian participation assured, the Foreign Ministry received authorization to organize a commission to be headed by Joint Chief of Staff General Francisco José Pinto. The commission would receive 7,000 contos (U.S.$350,000 in 1940 dollars) during a two-year period.[89]

The Brazilian commission almost immediately expressed concerns about the manner in which Brazilian culture would be represented in Lisbon. The Portuguese invitation to Brazil stipulated that Brazil be represented in two distinct pavilions. The first pavilion, the Pavilhão dos Portugueses no Mundo (Pavilion of the Portuguese in the World), would document Portugal's civilizing presence throughout the world. Portuguese officials would organize and finance the pavilion. The second pavilion, the Pavilhão do Brasil Independente (Pavilion of Independent Brazil), would display a survey of Brazilian society after the end of Portuguese domination. The pavilion was to be organized by the Brazilian delegation.[90] The Portuguese government offered financial assistance for the construction of the second pavilion. The problem with these arrangements was that these plans reinscribed the history of Portuguese colonialism and Brazilian independence onto the exposition's architectural configuration. Objects referring to colonial Brazil, as well as the narration of the meaning of those objects, would be housed in a pavilion managed by Portuguese officials whose task it was to demonstrate the breadth of Portuguese colonial feats from the fifteenth century onward. Objects referring to Brazil after independence would be located in a pavilion managed by Brazilians charged with representing Brazil as a sovereign nation-state.

Nationalism was a highly plastic construction among Brazilian culture managers, but this organizational model rattled nationalistic sensibilities. Could a modern, independent Brazil really exist without controlling the memory of the colonial period? The battles fought between the modernists and neocolonialists over Ouro Preto would suggest not.

The Brazilian response to this dilemma was to negotiate the right to organize and manage an autonomous historical exhibit, located within the

Pavilhão dos Portugueses no Mundo. The entrance to the exhibit would be separate from the main entrance to the pavilion.[91] The Brazilian delegation also secured control of an autonomous Brazilian pavilion dedicated to contemporary Brazil, organized and decorated by Brazilians. The planning stages of Brazilian participation certainly indicated that the Brazilian delegation, while seeking to consolidate a cultural bond with Portugal, had no intention of allowing Portuguese officials to revisit the power dynamics of colonialism—at least where Brazil was involved. Within the exposition's cultural universe, Brazil would speak for itself from Cabral forward. More troublesome would be speaking with one voice.

A scarcity of funds and construction materials, exacerbated by the outbreak of the Second World War, forced the Salazar regime to scale back the four national expositions proposed in 1938 into a single, grand exposition to be held in Lisbon on a site located between the Jeronomite monastery and the Tagus River in the capital's historic Belém district. The new exposition would be known as the Exposição Histórica do Mundo Português, or simply, the Exposição do Mundo Português. The combined exposition, inaugurated 23 June 1940, covered 450,000 square meters divided into the Historical Section, which documented the historical evolution of the Portuguese Empire after 1139, the Colonial Section, representing the modern Portuguese overseas dominions, the Regional Center, which re-created the folkloric life of various regions of mainland Portugal and the Atlantic Islands, and an amusement park.[92] Some 2.8 million admission tickets would be sold by the time the exposition closed on December 2.[93]

In Rio, the national commission readied a representative sampling of Brazilian culture to be sent to Lisbon. This was not necessarily easy, given the ongoing debates about the meaning of Brazilian culture. Ideological and aesthetic differences among culture managers were further compounded by the way in which different audiences reacted to the Brazilian pavilion in New York. The organization of yet another exposition pavilion instigated a new round of self-examination about the content of Brazilian culture and the narrative strategies in which the cultural content of brasilidade would be conveyed to outsiders. The Portuguese exhibit proved especially complicated because the conventional exposition language of commerce, scientific progress, and industrial development would be ill-placed in an event that the Portuguese planners insisted be exclusively cultural.[94] As in New York and San Francisco, the National Department of Coffee sent a delegation to Lisbon, but coffee could not be the carrier of culture. Nor could industrial development. Euvaldo Lodi, president of the Conselho Nacional das Indústrias, was unsuccessful in his efforts to send a representative sampling of Brazilian industry to Lisbon.

In the absence of representatives of major commercial, industrial, and agricultural interests, the Brazilian delegation was composed of military officers, civil servants, educators, and artists with little experience in foreign expositions. Several delegates were better known for their conservative politics, including the Commissioner General Francisco José Pinto, an army officer who had helped foment the red scares surrounding the Intentona Comunista and the *Plano Cohen*.[95] The commissioner in charge of the historical exhibit, Gustavo Barroso, was a well-known reactionary who had played a major role in the Integralist movement before the failed putsch of May 1938. The Portuguese executive committee, dominated by conservative nationalists allied with Salazar, expressed few reservations over the conservative credentials of the Brazilian delegates. To the contrary, the commissioners' conservative politics helped harmonize the Brazilian and Portuguese representations in Lisbon by doing away with the possibility that liberalism or leftism would sully the celebration of Portuguese culture.

Salazar reportedly insisted that the Brazilian pavilions be located in prominent areas in the exposition grounds, as proof that Brazilian and Portuguese civilization were tightly woven together, one into the other.[96] So, the independent pavilion stood near the exposition entrance, and the historical exhibit fronted the Praça do Império (Imperial Plaza) a large square cleared out between the Jeronomite Monastery and the Tagus. The Portuguese hosts went to great pains to remind their Brazilian guests that the Portuguese navigators set sail for the Atlantic just a few hundred yards from the Brazilian pavilions, near the landmark Padrão dos Descobrimentos (Monument to the Discoveries) designed by Portuguese architect Cotinelli Telmo. They wanted to make clear to the Brazilians that the Praça do Império anchored one end of the umbilical cord linking Portugal to Brazil.[97]

While an army of over six thousand architects, engineers, artisans, and manual laborers readied the exposition grounds, the Portuguese hosts assigned great significance to Brazilian participation in the Centenários. Commissioner General Augusto de Castro stated, "Brazil comes to us as a family member returning to his ancestral home, that is to say, to the birthplace of the fifty million citizens who hold on to the race, the language, and the religion bequeathed by Portugal. These Americans will forever carry on the greatness of Portugal. May the Cross of Christ planted by Pedro Álvares Cabral stand as the eternal symbol of our civilization and as the powerful link which binds us to our forefathers whose feats cast forth the Christian Faith and the Portuguese Empire."[98] The Portuguese organizers saw in Brazil an epiphany of Portuguese civilization, Christianity, and overseas expansion.

The constraints of cultural nationalism meant that the Brazilian mission had to be cautious in its embrace of Portuguese civilization. Brazil was, after all, a sovereign nation with a sovereign national culture. An uncritical embrace of the idea that Brazilian culture remained an extension of Portuguese culture would undermine the value of independence and decolonization. But the mission also worked hard to build a history of Brazilian culture upon the grand narrative of Luso-Brazilian civilization cultivated by the Portuguese. At the inaugural ceremonies, Edmundo Luiz Pinto, a member of the Brazilian delegation, informed the Portuguese National Assembly that the Portuguese exceeded all other colonial powers in creating a world empire graced by racial, cultural, and religious harmony.[99]

The historical exhibit organized by Lusophile Gustavo Barroso spelled out these transatlantic civilizational connections in greater detail. Visitors to the exhibit entered a vestibule containing three bronze allegorical sculptures, executed by Eduardo de Sá, depicting the territorial and spiritual conquest of Brazil by Portuguese explorers and friars.[100] On the vestibule wall, an inscription rhetorically asked whether all Portuguese speakers descended from the same stock. The surrounding galleries contained more than six hundred pieces drawn from the MHN's collection documenting Brazilian history from Portuguese occupation in 1500 through the fall of the Old Republic in 1930. Portraits and personal effects of prominent figures of the empire and republic accompanied armaments, maps, cannons, and pictorial representations of Portuguese territorial expansion in Brazil.[101] At the center of the historical exhibit, in a rotunda whose walls listed the names of the governor-generals and viceroys who ruled colonial Brazil, stood a wall-sized mural of a tree. From the Portuguese coat of arms located at the tree's base, sprung forth a trunk and branches representing the triumvirate of Portuguese expansion—Law (A Ley), Kings (Os Reis), and People (A Grey)—as well as the discoverers, missionaries, colonial officials, and bandeirantes that colonized Portuguese America. At the top of the tree sat an illuminated flower, formed in the shaped of the arms of the Republic, labeled "Brasil."[102] Leaving little doubt about Brazil's cul-

45 Brazilian Historical Exhibit, Pavilion of the Portuguese in the World, Exposição do Mundo Português, Lisbon. The Brazilian republic as a radiant flower rooted in Portuguese soil. *Pavilhão do Brasil na Exposição Histórica do Mundo Português, 1941.*

tural heritage, Barroso described the mural as the genealogical tree of the Brazilian race.[103]

The second pavilion dedicated to contemporary Brazil captured a culture less root-bound to the colonial past, but still in step with the fundamental precepts of Portuguese civilization. An inscription appearing above the pavilion's entrance quoted Vargas's statement that Brazil's destiny was to build its own civilization, while never losing sight of the obligation to protect the gifts willed by Portugal. Across the pavilion's interior hung a huge photographic mural that reproduced many of the images of a modern, eugenic, cultured Brazil previewed for domestic eyes at the Exposição do Estado Novo. A special reading room, lined with five thousand volumes of Brazilian arts, letters, and science, stood just off from the entrance. Both sides of the pavilion were lined with booths offering printed, graphic, and pictorial information about the state of urban reform, health and public assistance, the press, literature, tourism, education, and transportation in Portuguese America. Visitors were treated to a large illuminated diorama of the city of Rio de Janeiro, a common feature for Brazilian foreign missions, as well as an art gallery, a photography exhibit of historical patrimony, and an ethnographic exhibit. With the exception of a restaurant and patio bar whose speciality was Brazilian coffee, the Brazilian pavilion organized in Lisbon looked very different from the modernist commercial emporium sent to New York.

By all indicators, the Brazilian delegation was well received by the Portuguese, especially due to the fact that the Salazar regime worked hard to be an accommodating host. The ultimate success of the Brazilian delegation must be explained by certain political and cultural factors that drew the Salazar and Vargas dictatorships close. With Estado Novos in place in Brazil and Portugal, the exposition provided a cultural rationale for a repressive political system that remained ideologically ill-defined, but still powerful, in both countries. The independent rise of *estadonovismo* in the world's two sovereign Portuguese-speaking nations helped conservatives on both sides of the Atlantic claim that the phenomenon fell outside of conventional political ideologies such as liberalism, fascism, or communism and expressed a uniquely Portuguese solution to the crisis of Western civilization. Predicated on metaphors of political authority, social harmony, and cultural renewal, estadonovismo gave the Brazilian and Portuguese governments the opportunity to boast about internal order at a historical moment in which the sectarian violence of nationalism, racism, and imperialism swept across the globe. The geopolitical insecurities raised by the spread of the Second World War provided ample opportunities for conservative ideologues from both sides of the Portuguese-speaking Atlantic to expound upon the cultural and moral virtues of a strong state that could protect their national populations from the failures of liberalism and totalitarianism. Moreover, the celebration of estadonovismo facilitated diplomatic relations between two dictatorial regimes careful not to run afoul of Allied pressures to remain neutral in the expanding war.[104] Thus there were clear ideological and geopolitical reasons why the Brazilian mission to Lisbon was a success.

The culture of colonialism helped along the amicable relationship between the Brazilian and Portuguese governments. The Salazar regime, eager to maintain its colonial possessions in Africa and Asia, looked to the Brazilians to reaffirm an emergent national mythology that the Portuguese had a special cultural aptitude for bringing Christianity and Western civilization to tropical regions without resorting to racialized violence.[105] President Carmona argued that the success of Portuguese colonialism in Brazil proved that Portuguese overseas expansion was conducted "in a humane manner in which we seek to cohabitate with other civilizations, never raising barriers of difference between the colonized and ourselves."[106]

The Brazilian mission, eager to drive Brazil's roots deep into the Portuguese past, dearly wanted to hear that the Portuguese were good colonizers. The Brazilian delegates celebrated the cultural gifts brought by Portuguese explorers to the Americas, working hard to dispel the negative portraits of the Portuguese colonizer found in the nationalistic popular literature of the early republic and the identity tracts of the late 1920s and 1930s.[107] At pains to discount the episodic bouts of popular and elite Lusophobia that ran throughout Brazilian intellectual and social history, the Brazilian mission argued that the Portuguese had given Brazil the invaluable gifts of European racial stock, a common language, and the Catholic religion.[108]

The memory of independence presented unique challenges to the grand narrative of Luso-Brazilian unity. The historical exhibit organized by Gustavo Barroso included the sword used by D. Pedro I in the Grito de Ipiranga, showing the Portuguese a material relic of the failure of recolonization efforts in 1822. The main Brazilian pavilion was named the *Independent* Brazilian Pavilion. If the Portuguese were indeed such good colonizers, why would the Brazilians split from the mother country? In response to this dilemma, various delegates argued that Brazilian independence may have ended a political relationship of subordination, but it never severed the cultural bonds between Portugal, Brazil, and the rest of the Portuguese-speaking world formerly united under the Portuguese Crown. Barroso, the most tireless advocate of the Portuguese civilizing presence, toured throughout Portugal, to then make a risky trip to Nazi Germany, praising the civilizing work accomplished by the Portuguese in Brazil and elsewhere. At the historical congress coinciding with the Exposição do Mundo Português, Barroso summarized his views on Brazil's debt to Portuguese civilization, stating:

> Heirs to a language which stretches from the shores of the Atlantic to the Indian Ocean onto the Pacific; heirs to a Christian civilization eight centuries old; heirs to a culture whose thoughts and expressions are rooted in a

Latin heritage [*latinidade*]; heirs, above all else, to a model of national unity established by the Portuguese, Brazil presents itself at the solemn meeting of the Portuguese World. Our claim to this Portuguese World is founded upon blood, language, and a soul which transcends the ages. . . . By taking part in this great assembly, Brazil completes the historical and spiritual destiny of the Portuguese World. This is not merely some conclave of colonies linked to the metropole by economic and political ties. Rather, this is a gathering for the offspring of the same civilization, the same culture, united in a Christian affirmation of our common purpose and fraternal sentiment.[109]

Barroso's Portuguese hosts were, quite understandably, extremely receptive to these words and images of Lusophone fraternity articulated from outside Portugal. Commissioner General Augusto de Castro summed up his enthusiasm for the Brazilian mission, telling his Brazilian guests and the Portuguese dignitaries and fairgoers who attended the inauguration of the Brazilian pavilion that "We are the same." [110]

The Brazilian delegates were undeniably successful at endearing themselves to their Portuguese hosts. The Portuguese wholeheartedly embraced the idea of renovação. However, both sides proved reticent to acknowledge how the Brazilian mission to Lisbon played into the tensions of the first Vargas regime. By celebrating the Portuguese civilizing presence in Brazil, the Brazilian mission found it impossible to avoid the unsettling questions of cultural genealogy raised at the Exposição da Missão Artística Francesa de 1816 and the New York World's Fair. In spite of their best efforts to the contrary, the Brazilian delegates to Portugal transferred the struggle for the official reading and managing of Brazilian cultural identity to the eastern shores of the Atlantic.

The question of "national" art sent to Portugal illustrates the unstable nature of cultural politicking sweeping across the Lusophone Atlantic circa 1940. Recent scholarship has revealed that the exposition in Lisbon marked a defining moment in the history of art in Portugal, giving Portugal's modernists, led by Minister of Propaganda António Ferro, the upper hand against conservative academics. In language that evoked the polemics of Brazil's neocolonialist José Mariano, the president of Portugal's National Society of Fine Arts, Arnoldo Ressano Garcia, labeled the Portuguese modernists as paranoid "charlatans" bent on using foreign artistic ideas to pervert established morals and standards.[111] The Brazilian delegates may have been unfamiliar with the personalities engaged in controversies surrounding the ascendance of modernism in Portuguese art, but the aesthetic and political terms of Portugal's culture wars could be readily understood. On both sides of the Atlantic, state commissions for the arts were forums for intense politicking over resources and status, as well as the ideological meaning of national cultural identity. By 1940, the modernists in Portugal and Brazil had been quite successful at winning state commissions, although academics like Garcia and Oswaldo Teixeira were not to be counted out from the artistic establishment of either nation.

The art exhibit that accompanied the Brazilian delegation to Lisbon appeared to provide Brazil's academics with the perfect opportunity to tip the scales back in their favor. Heading the commission that selected the paintings to be sent to Portugal, Teixeira turned to the MNBA collection, selecting two dozen works from the permanent exhibition.[112] Late-nineteenth- and early-twentieth-century academic artworks were clearly favored in the selection process. More than half of the artists selected, including Lucílio de Albuquerque, Artur Timóteo da Costa, and Oscar Pereira da Silva, had won the coveted Prêmio de Viagem à Europa, sine qua non for academicism. The selection contained just one painting that fell into the modernist camp — Cândido Portinari's much-acclaimed *Café*. Alongside Portinari's homage to the monumental heroism of the agricultural laborer went twenty-four paintings of refined nudes, elite portraits, quiet interiors, pretty landscapes, and allegorical subjects executed in styles ranging from romanticism to naturalism to neoimpressionism. A viewer with only cursory knowledge of the history of Brazilian art would be hard-pressed to perceive the impact of the Modern Art Week of 1922, the Salão Revolucionário of 1931, or the controversies surrounding Portinari's success in New York.

Had the one modernist work sent to Portugal been of minor importance, it would have been easy for the Brazilian delegation to unequivocably reiterate an ideological position critical of modernism. The modernist style and subject matter could have been easily dismissed as un-Brazilian. But, the inclusion of such a celebrated painting done by such a well-known modernist, alongside a series of lesser paintings representative of such patently conservative sensibilities, tipped off critics and fairgoers that modernism was making inroads even into the most staid museum spaces in Brazil.[113] Looking on the brute faces and oversized hands and feet of the mulatto and immigrant coffee pickers in *Café*, fair-goers and art critics could see that modernism allowed artists to portray Brazilian culture with verve. Seeing up close how manual labor, sweat, and blackness could be legiti-

46 Brazilian Art Exhibit, Exposição do Mundo Português. The selection of art-work sent to the Exposição do Mundo Português was emblematic of the tensions in official cultural policy at the height of the Estado Novo. Academic works such as Lucílio de Albuquerque's *O Despertar do Ícaro* (right) hung side by side with Cândido Portinari's *Café* (left). *Pavilhão do Brasil na Exposição Histórica do Mundo Português,* 1941.

mate subjects for serious painting, fair-goers were left to ponder the unsettling, yet dynamic, changes taking place within Brazilian arts and the larger society. At the Exposição do Mundo Português, Portinari's mulattos confounded any attempts to imagine Brazilians as the all-white, Catholic, and enlightened descendants of Portuguese settlers so eloquently described by Augusto de Castro and Gustavo Barroso.

Even though *Café* received no special attention within the Brazilian exhibit, the painting emerged as a point of reference for modern Brazilian art, and more broadly modern Brazilian culture, in Portugal. Portuguese critics, like their Brazilian and American counterparts, were never quite comfortable with the way Portinari divided his energies between conventional elite portraiture and social realism. Some questioned his talent relative to the standard-bearers of modernism, including Picasso. Nonetheless, Portuguese art critics were clearly impressed by *Café* and its ability to capture an unknown Brazil in an unknown, exciting way. In 1943, one Portuguese critic looking back at the 1940 exhibition argued that *Café* was a symbol of Brazil's multicultural, tropical ethos, captured by an Italian-Brazilian painter indebted to Italian classicism, Mexican muralism, and School of

Paris modernism.[114] Reproductions of *Café,* along with several other works of social realism executed by Portinari in the 1930s and 40s, would soon become part of Portugal's visual vocabulary of Brazilianness and a transnational aesthetic of neorealism.[115]

The lessons to be drawn from the Brazilian art exhibit sent to Portugal were multilayered and contradictory.[116] Conservative audiences could see in the artwork selected to represent Brazil the white faces, sentimental subject matter, and beauty that the Brazilian academics wanted the world to see as a window onto Brazilian reality. Here, Brazil remained safely within the boundaries of the civilizational vocation expounded by the fair organizers in Portugal. Audiences with a more critical eye could see a Brazil that was neither wholly domesticated within its Luso-Catholic heritage nor wholly in keeping with the academic tradition solidified in the nineteenth century on both sides of the Atlantic. *Café* declared that the ruptures of modernism had made their mark in Brazilian art and more broadly in Brazilian culture. From the rupture emerged the Brazilian people who did not participate in the cultural feats immortalized by Camões. In sending *Café* to Portugal, the conservatives at the MNBA inadvertently opened up a possible reading of Brazilian culture that could not be wholly contained by the gifts brought to Brazil by Cabral in 1500.

The antimodernists on both sides of the Atlantic surely took comfort in the overall architectural design of the Brazilian pavilion. The tremors of tropical modernism, as felt in New York, did not reach Lisbon. Raul Lino (1879–1971), a conservative Portuguese architect who might be considered an ideological soul mate of tradicionalista Ricardo Severo, was responsible for the overall design of the independent Brazilian pavilion, while Roberto Lacombe, a Brazilian, designed the interiors. Falling far short of the standard for innovation, functionality, and beauty set by Lucio Costa and Oscar Niemeyer in New York, the Lino-Lacombe pavilion presented a more attenuated narration of brasilidade. Some of the pavilion's most interesting elements included the exterior atrium, where a latticework roof was supported by columns stylized after the imperial palm trees common to nineteenth-century Brazilian landscape design, and the spacious main hall, where the visitor could take in an unobstructed view of ten display stands dedicated to health reform, the press, and transportation, among other themes. A large photomontage mounted inside the main hall documented the achievements of Brazilian civilization under Vargas. In its construction materials and design elements, the Brazilian pavilion set a tone

47 Fonte Marajoara, Brazilian Pavilion, Exposição do Mundo Português. The entrance to the Brazilian pavilion suggested that Brazil's cultural roots predated the arrival of Cabral. This marajoara foundational myth competed with the Luso-tropical narratives promoted by the Brazilian delegates and their Portuguese hosts. *Pavilhão do Brasil na Exposição Histórica do Mundo Português*, 1941.

distinct from the other pavilions built for the fair, but not out of place in comparison to the Portuguese pavilions erected in the vicinity of the Praça do Império. Brazilians, in effect, occupied the same cultural space as the Portuguese.

This image of architectural and cultural unity had one major disruption: the unusual decorative motifs found on the large water fountain located at the pavilion's entrance and a coffee bar located just off the main hall. These unobtrusive decorative elements, designed by Lacombe, had been inspired by ceramics once produced by an indigenous civilization that lived on the Ilha do Marajó before the arrival of Europeans. At first glance, these *marajoara* motifs were merely touches of exoticism, similar to other indigenous and "jungle" motifs employed in the decorative arts and graphic design during the 1920s, 30s, and 40s.[117] The marajoara functioned, perhaps, as a local variation of the indigenista decorative arts so popular in postrevolutionary Mexican state culture and certain Federal Arts Project commissions executed in the U.S. Southwest. Finally, one might read the indigenous motifs as a stylized form of cubism, dominated by interconnecting geometric solids and voids.

The long-standing relationship between *arte marajoara* and nation building strongly indicates that Lacombe touched upon something deeper than mere exoticism. In the nineteenth century, archaeologists and naturalists were drawn to marajoara artifacts uncovered in various field excavations funded by private interests and the imperial state in hopes of finding evidence that the Indians of Marajó may have descended from Andean, Mesoamerican, or, possibly, Asiatic civilizations. Ladislau Netto, a highly influential ethnographer from the northeastern state of Alagoas who directed the Museu Nacional during the late empire and early republic, devoted considerable attention to the study of the marajoara ceramics, publishing several accounts that tried to link Marajó civilization to the American ancients.[118] Pedro II also took an interest in the ceramic shards uncovered at the mouth of the Amazon. Foreigners conducted several archaeological surveys in the late nineteenth and early twentieth centuries, sending specimens of marajoara pottery to a number of anthropological and ethnographic museums located in Europe and the United States.[119] Situated at the crossroads of nineteenth-century science and romanticism, the Museu Nacional in Rio and Museu Emilio Goeldi in Belém do Pará prominently displayed marajoara artifacts in their permanent exhibitions.

Changes afoot in the twentieth century in the field of archaeological research called into question the search for a "lost" civilization in marajoara pottery. Brazilian and foreign archaeologists continued to take an active interest in marajoara ceramics, but the connections between the Marajó Indians and better-known Amerindian empires of Mesoamerica and the Andean highlands grew more tenuous. Heloisa Alberto Torres, director of the Museu Nacional, argued in 1940 that the archaeological evidence collected from excavations on the Ilha do Marajó suggested that the island's former indigenous inhabitants had limited artistic and technological talents, insufficient to sustain a theory that arte marajoara was a vestige of a great pre-Contact civilization.[120] Where scientists and scientific research once played a vital role in imagining the marajoara as Brazilian ancients, by the Vargas era, the scientific community advanced the demystification and de-mythification of Marajó civilization.

Many Brazilian modernists openly questioned the romantic notion that the marajoara were Brazil's lost autochthonous civilization. When a sampling of contemporary marajoara ceramics accompanied the Brazilian delegation to the 1937 International Exposition in Paris, an unsigned editorial appearing in *Bellas-Artes* argued that indigenous society could never be integrated into the Brazilian arts.[121] In 1939, the promodernist U.S. art critic Robert Smith wrote of the marajoara, "The pottery found on the Island of Marajó . . . has not even the quality of primitive patterns found in the crude aboriginal jars of Santiago del Estero in western Argentina."[122] The modernists in control of the SPHAN seemed to share this sentiment. Between 1938 and 1946, only eight of 416 tombamentos were entered into the *Livro do Tombo* dedicated to archaeology, ethnography, and landscape. None of these tombamentos included marajoara art.[123] In their search for the artistic genius of the Brazilian past, the modernists affiliated with the SPHAN exhibited little interest in equating unknown indigenous artists with Aleijadinho.

Although science and modernism had apparently defeated the notion that arte marajoara could be treated as a semaphore in the search for a national cultural identity, marajoara art retained a certain ideological utility for imagining the nation. In 1941, art critic Carlos Rubens argued that marajoara art could be considered "the dawn of Brazilian art," which exhibited pictorial elements similar to the art of ancient Egypt, Mexico, or China.[124] Arquimedes Memória opted to use marajoara motifs to embellish his ill-fated design for the Ministry of Education headquarters. And in a rebuttal to earlier statements in *Bellas-Artes,* Manoel Pestana, the best-known artist to adapt indigenous motifs to ceramics and the decorative arts, documented the vitality of marajoara motifs in things as diverse as municipal bonds, domestic wares, and art exhibits sent abroad.[125] These authors clearly saw the marajoara as Brazilian and as art.

Thus, the marajoara motifs deployed in Lisbon revisited major questions in Brazilian culture that preoccupied the Brazilian cultural elite of the nineteenth and twentieth centuries. In an immediate sense, the marajoara motifs begged the question whether modernism had won the battle to be the official language of cultural renewal. Lucio Costa had inveighed against "false" national styles since the early 1930s. Arquimedes Memória's winning plan for the Ministry of Education headquarters had been scuttled in part because of its marajoara motifs, which Costa and Capanema saw as inappropriate for the structural symbol of cultural renewal. With Costa and other modernists winning the lion's share of state commissions, how could the marajoara continue to creep into the official delegation sent to Portugal, feeding national and international fantasies about Brazil's Indian past? Why did the state perpetuate the image that Brazilian culture may have been born from a mythic indigenous civilization?

At stake here was whether modern Brazil could continue to invoke a "foundational fiction" based on Indians.[126] Noble Indians had been the protagonists of the nineteenth-century novelist José de Alencar, poet Gonçalves Dias, and composer Carlos Gomes. Indians appear—at the margins, but within the frame—in numerous works of monumental history paintings commissioned during the empire, including Meireles's monumental *A Primeira Missa no Brasil* (1861). The royal patronage extended by D. Pedro II toward such foundational narratives made indigenismo a semiofficial style during the Brazilian Empire. Could the Vargas regime go back to the future, invoking the Indian as the telluric bedrock of Brazilian nationhood? Could the marajoara be compared to the Portuguese in the grand narrative of national origins revealed in Lisbon? Around 1940, official state policy tested the possibility that the contemporary Indian could be enlisted as an agent of modernity, particularly in the development of the central-western hinterland.[127] The Brazilian pavilion sent to Lisbon quietly asked whether the Indian past could also carry a modern Brazil. Indeed, Barroso's genealogical tree may have missed part of the story.

The most important foundational fiction written during the first Vargas regime, Gilberto Freyre's *Casa-grande e senzala* (1933), had already rehearsed the narrative that the Indian was indeed present at the foundational moment of Brazilian civilization. Freyre made no mention of the marajoara, but he did situate the invention of Brazilian civilization at the moment at which Portuguese navigators stepped out of their caravels and into the feminized, Indianized water-bodies of coastal Brazil.[128] In a sense, the indigenous motifs integrated into the Brazilian pavilion followed Freyre's logic, putting Brazilian Indians within an exhibitionary space that glorified the Portuguese colonizing spirit. The marajoara suggested that Amerindians were the original Brazilians, present even before the Portuguese sailors sighted Monte Pascoal in April 1500, and it was they who first helped the Portuguese establish a foothold in America. But in an exposition built upon the notion that it was the Portuguese who single-handedly brought civilization to Brazil, these were unstable messages about national origins.

This question of origins was made all the more challenging by the nagging ambivalence about Portuguese colonialism. The Brazilian delegation, led by Barroso, made much of Portugal's civilizing gifts—language, blood, and religion—brought to Portuguese America in the early sixteenth century. This logic of colonialism as a gift extended across the Atlantic was the bedrock of the Brazilian and Portuguese delegates' mutual admiration. This logic was ritualized in the Brazilian mission's presentation of a replica of Henrique Bernardelli's *Monumento ao Cabral* (1900) to the Portuguese government in recognition of the Portuguese civilizing presence in Brazil. Placed in Lisbon's Jardim da Estrela, the Bernadelli statue joined the original, located in Rio's Largo da Glória, in a transatlantic homage to the genius of the colonial exchange, where Cabral, his scribe Pero Vaz de Caminha, and the Franciscan friar Henrique de Coimbra "discover" Brazil without any help from the Tupi.

What the Brazilian delegates could not face, much less celebrate, was the reality that the Portuguese remained a colonial power in Africa, Asia, and Oceania, supposedly offering the same "gift" of civilization to subject peoples who occupied a cultural position in the mid-twentieth century not that different from the Tupi at the beginning of the sixteenth century. The ongoing, as opposed to historical, temporality of Portuguese colonialism put the Brazilians dangerously close to the African and Asian colonial subjects whom the Salazar government invited to the exposition not as close cousins afforded all of the honors of the house, but as dependents, housed outside of the main exposition grounds in a colonial exhibition.

The Colonial Section contained some of the most interesting pavilions in the Lisbon fair. Once visitors took a gondola ride from the main exposition grounds to the entrance to the section (making the metaphorical journey overseas), they encountered lush landscaping that evoked the tropics. Visitors could make a grand tour of the Portuguese Empire, visiting Angola, Mozambique, India, and Timor without losing sight of the Torre de Belém and the Tagus. On this journey, visitors would see the most fantastic and interesting sights, where plaster and concrete elephants, crocodiles, and natives stood guard at the entrances of the colonial pavilions. In the African pavilions, the visitors could take in the ethnographic and commercial variety of the subequatorial Portuguese colonies. A short distance away, the visitor would walk down a bustling street built to look like Macau. Special pavilions highlighted commercial, missionary, and gaming activities throughout the Portuguese Empire. High above the Colonial Section stood the Monumento à Obra Portuguesa de Colonização (Monument to Portugal's Colonial Mission), a triumphal column dedicated to the sublime beauty of Portuguese imperialism. The exposition guide told the Portuguese visitor that a two-hour visit to the Colonial Section would be equivalent to a long journey through a world of diverse climates and mysterious religions where the Portuguese flag flew proudly.[129]

The Brazilian delegates in Lisbon were uniformly silent about the Colonial Section and the modern-day colonialism it staged. The Brazilian delegates participated in various congresses and ceremonial events on the Lusophone world, but they could never bring themselves to identify with the colonized peoples of Portuguese Africa and beyond. Gustavo Barroso could only discuss Portuguese colonialism as a historical artifact of a lost age, to be treated as if in a museum. The Portuguese hosts, by contrast, were *constantly* discussing the Colonial Section. The fair literature produced by the Portuguese consistently mentioned the Colonial Section as a pretext to discussing the wisdom of Salazar's decision to step up Portugal's colonial activities. This literature invariably included a parallel discourse about Portugal's felicitous colonial vocation, which all began with Cabral.

Take, for instance, this excerpt printed in the colonial supplement to the special edition of the Portuguese journal *O Século:*

> As one travels through the Empire from the Mother Country to Timor, one will find it easy to recognize the Portuguese ethos in the hearts of all: whites, blacks, Indians, and Chinese. Everyone who is Portuguese thinks lovingly of Portugal. Skin color, race, distance cannot weaken the notion of shared rights and patriotic duties. In fact, the greater the physical distance from Portugal, the greater the pride in one's Portuguese heritage. . . . Our heroes, our saints, our great names will always be venerated and celebrated by the Portuguese throughout the Empire. Portugal maintains, as we all know, a special place in the hearts of each and every inhabitant of the Empire.[130]

Although this passage was clearly written for peninsular Portuguese living abroad, it traded upon a notion that the Portuguese were good colonizers who were able to assimilate the colonial Other, dissolving the barriers between colonizer and colonized to create a singular Portuguese subjectivity.

The Brazilian mission was eager to celebrate the cultural gifts brought by the Portuguese colonizers, but they remained unable to accept modern Portuguese colonialism, with its openness—at least theoretically—to cultural miscegenation among Portuguese speakers worldwide. The Brazilian mission wanted nothing of the tropical subjects represented in the

Colonial Section. So the Brazilian literature said nothing about the Colonial Section or contemporary Portuguese colonialism. Given the proximity of the Colonial Section to the Brazilian pavilion, the section and its message were not so much unknown as unacknowledged. This defining silence about the world's other Portuguese speakers and the historical processes which linked together the Lusophone world strongly suggests the limits to which the Brazilian culture managers could validate Brazilian culture through the Portuguese Estado Novo. In the summer of 1940, the Salazar regime fell short of providing a model of civilization that could be adopted tout court in large part because an embrace of Portugal hinged on the embrace of Portuguese colonialism past and present.

It would be the *pernambucano* sociologist Gilberto Freyre who would articulate a more palatable synthesis of Portuguese civilization, which briefly allowed the Vargas state to seek value in Brazil's Luso-colonial heritage. Freyre never fully signed on as an official cultural manager of the Vargas regime, but he had helped bridge cultural ties between Brazil and Lisbon in the years before the Centenários. In 1937, for example, Freyre accepted federal sponsorship to travel to Lisbon to participate in the Congress of Portuguese Expansion. The contacts made while in Portugal, in combination with the growing popularity of *Casa-grande e senzala* among Portuguese readers, put the Pernambucan in a good position to articulate a new sense of Luso-Brazilianness that came to be known as Luso-tropicalism.

On 2 June 1940, Freyre accepted an invitation made by the Portuguese consul in Recife to mark the Centenários with a keynote address at the city's Gabinete Português de Leitura. Freyre's speech, *Uma cultura ameaçada: a luso-brasileira* (A threatened culture: The Luso-Brazilian), outlined various threats to Lusophone civilization, including the scourge of Aryan nationalism that had overcome Nazi Germany.[131] Advancing some of the theories of cultural, rather than racial, determinism expressed in *Casa-grande*, Freyre negated the theory of racial purities and immutable hierarchies. The speech described the Portuguese as a mixed-race people who themselves denied any ideology of racial purity equaling racial power. "The Portuguese have perpetuated themselves, always dissolving themselves into other peoples to the point where the foreign blood and culture is lost." Later that year, Freyre published a collection of speeches, appropriately entitled *O mundo que o português criou* (*The world created by the Portuguese*), which gave further substance to the theory that the Portuguese had an innate talent at amicable colonization.[132] Some 3,600 miles from Lisbon, Freyre helped lay out the vision of Portuguese colonialism that fit perfectly with the ideological and cultural climate set by the Exposição do Mundo Português.

It bears repeating that Freyre's speech was not to form a part of the Brazilian delegation to Lisbon. Freyre did not speak as a formal representative of the Vargas regime. The speech was, nonetheless, the germ of a theory of transatlantic civilization that the Vargas regime could embrace for a brief time. In November 1940, Almir de Andrade, the conservative editor of the regime's high-brow political review, *Cultura Política*, pronounced that Freyre got it right. Brazil's Lusitanian heritage, wrote Andrade, was under siege. What was necessary was an embrace of the Portuguese as the bedrock of a cohesive Portuguese-speaking civilization that was at peace with itself.[133]

Still embryonic in 1940, Freyre's developing notion of the *cultura luso-brasileira* searched out the cultural and historical affinities that transcended conventional historical, chronological, racial, and national boundaries to include simultaneously the entirety of cultural interchange between Portugal and the tropical world. In its early stages, Freyre's interests in Luso-Brazilian culture was defensive, positioning the Portuguese-speaking world against the threats of Aryan nationalism and Hispanism. In later years, Freyre's emergent notion of "Luso-tropicalism" offered an "Atlantic" exegesis of race, climate, history, and culture painted with the broad strokes of the Age of Discoveries, the Bahian *engenho* (sugar plantation complex), the port cities of twentieth-century Portuguese Africa, and the Estado Novo states in Brazil and Portugal.[134] When fully developed by the 1950s, Freyre defined the Luso-tropical as a "particular form of behavior and a particular form of accomplishment of the Portuguese in the world: [especially] his tendency to prefer the tropics for his extra-European expansion and his ability to remain successfully in the tropics — successfully from a cultural as well as from an ecological point of view — an intermediary between European culture and such tropical cultures as one found by him in Africa, India, Malaya, and the part of America which became Brazil."[135]

As Freyre grew older, Luso-tropicalist studies made their greatest inroads into the colonial administration of Portugal's overseas possessions in Africa and Asia where the Luso-tropicalist ideal became a legitimating principle for Portugal's "civilizing" presence in Asia and especially in Africa.[136] Freyre's Luso-tropicalist theories became particularly popular among Portuguese colonial officials once the sociologist completed a well-publicized tour of Portuguese Africa and Asia in 1951–1952.[137] In the years following this government-sponsored tour, the rationalization of a theory of Luso-tropical civilization became so deeply embedded in Portuguese colonial policy that Luso-tropicalism became an ideological support for the continuation of Portuguese colonial domination in the face of a full-scale European retreat from colonial enterprises. Not surprisingly, as Portuguese colonial officials defended colonialism by using Luso-tropical ideals, anticolonial movements in Portuguese Africa attacked Portuguese colonialism by attacking the Luso-tropical model. In events unforeseen by Freyre, Portugal's dogged defense of colonial rule transformed the culturalist origins of Luso-tropicalism into a contested terrain of colonial and anticolonial politics, fulfilling, in a perverse way, Freyre's original idea of a common cultural syntax among Portuguese-speaking peoples.

The origin of this syntax was the Exposição do Mundo Português, an event that set up the cultural imaginary necessary for Freyre to declare that the Atlantic was unified by a Luso-tropical civilization. In the afterglow of the exposition, the Vargas and Salazar regimes searched for vehicles with which to strengthen cultural ties between Brazil and Portugal. A Portuguese delegation traveled to Brazil in early September 1941 to receive a warm reception by the Vargas state and the local elite of Portuguese descent resident in Rio de Janeiro. The high point of the visit was the signing of a bilateral agreement of cultural cooperation and exchange. Under the terms of the agreement, the Portuguese and Brazilian propaganda agencies quickly set up subsections dedicated to arts and letters coming from opposite sides of the Atlantic. And with the encouragement of the two Estado Novos, the Brazilian and Portuguese Academies of Letters began to negotiate the terms for a standardization of Portuguese orthography, with the hope that the language gap between Brazilian and peninsular Portuguese could be closed.

The most fruitful outcome of these bilateral negotiations was the publication of *Atlântico,* a semiannual journal subtitled "A Luso-Brazilian Review." Coedited by Portugal's Secretariat of National Propaganda and Brazil's Department of Press and Propaganda, the binational journal solicited literary and artistic contributions from some of the most influential literary and intellectual figures on both sides of the Atlantic (a cultural-geographic space affectionately nicknamed the "Lusitanian Lake" in the journal's 1942 inaugural issue). The Brazilian entries to *Atlântico* were especially noteworthy, coming from a wide range of intellectuals and culture managers including DIP Director Lourival Fontes, poets Mário de Andrade, Carlos

Drummond de Andrade, and Vinicius de Moraes, and novelist Graciliano Ramos. The short-lived journal also included reproductions of the artwork of Cândido Portinari, Tarsila do Amaral, and the Pernambucan Cicero Dias.

The early success of *Atlântico* suggests that the idea of Luso-Brazilian fraternity was initially quite attractive to a broad spectrum of cultural actors in Brazil. Mário de Andrade dubbed another DIP publication, *Cultura Política,* as fascistic. But in the inaugural issue of *Atlântico,* the modernist poet contributed an essay on Aleijadinho. This essay appeared alongside an essay by DIP Director and fascist-sympathizer Lourival Fontes on the "Spiritual Unity" among Brazilians and Portuguese. In both essays, the authors searched for a language of ethnogenesis that sought value in the cultural mixtures made possible by Portuguese colonialism in the tropics. Andrade and Fontes, naturally, stressed the westward transfer of the Portuguese language and the Catholic religion. In both essays, which appeared in a literary outlet made possible by the success of the Brazilian mission to Lisbon, the Luso-tropical ideal was tested.

The Brazilian government would soon drop its active support of the Luso-tropical imaginary, as the Vargas regime's diplomatic priorities were reordered in 1942, when Brazil joined the Allied cause in the Second World War. Brazilian interest in the bilateral agreement signed in 1941 had waned considerably by the final year of the war, because the Department of Press and Propaganda was dismantled. By the time Vargas was forced from office in 1945, Portugal could no longer match the cultural and political capital offered by the United States, which won the lion's share of Brazil's overseas cultural attentions after the war. The close connection between Luso-tropicalism and colonialism became increasingly unpalatable to all but the most conservative Brazilian cultural nationalists. In Portugal, Luso-tropicalism flourished, coming close to being a national foundational myth. Although *Atlântico* went out of print in 1946, Portugal's Agência Geral das Colônias continued to publish *Mundo Português.* Subtitled "a journal of culture, propaganda, art, and literature from the Colonies," the editorial policy of *Mundo Português* was highly consistent with the Luso-tropical ideal, searching out the cultural affinities among Portuguese-speaking peoples. This editorial policy was similar to the power relations established at the 1940 exposition in Lisbon: metropolitan Portugal directly managed the cultural identities of its African and Asian colonies. Freyre, in the meantime, maintained close ties with the Portuguese state, actively promoting

Luso-tropical studies throughout the Atlantic. These efforts went largely ignored by the Brazilian state. In sum, the Exposição do Mundo Português set in motion a transatlantic dialogue over Brazil's cultural formation that initially served the interests of the Vargas regime, but later precipitated troublesome questions about the nature of Brazilian civilization.

Conclusions

The history of the Vargas regime's participation in international expositions illustrates how and why modernism and Lusophilia became pillars of the cultural renewal shepherded by the Vargas regime. Audiences in New York saw a society at the vanguard of modernism. Residents in Lisbon saw a Brazil enamored with its Portuguese roots. But these two pillars were at variance with one another, supporting different ideological, iconographic, and fictive notions of brasilidade. The Brazilianness exhibited in New York was different from the Brazilianness exhibited in Lisbon. Each vision of Brazilianness was, moreover, subject to contestation. The tensions inherent in the Brazilian missions abroad reveal that the content of exposition pavilions, not to mention the pavilions themselves, could never meet the standards of unmitigated cultural triumph touted at the 1938 Exposição do Estado Novo. They show that cultural representation was in a constant state of uncertainty. The Brazilian missions tried to serve up a triumphant vision of Brazilian culture managed by the Vargas state. Many members of the foreign audience accepted the triumphant picture. Others recognized the ongoing anxieties provoked by the organization of an "export quality" portrait of Brazilian culture.

Conclusion

Summarily deposed from office in a bloodless coup, Getúlio Vargas and his cabinet beat a hasty retreat to their home states in the final three days of October 1945. In a preview of things to come, the army high command remained in Rio, coordinating the regime change. Liberals rejoiced at the end of the dictatorship. The press, smarting from years of censorship and government intervention, compared the Estado Novo to the totalitarian regimes recently defeated in Europe. Busts of Vargas adorning Rio's public squares were torn down from their pedestals, completing a cycle of symbolic violence that began on 27 November 1937 when the flags of each state were ceremonially burned to symbolize the dawn of a New State and a New Brazil. Vargas brooded at his ranch in São Borja, Rio Grande do Sul, receiving word that he might be stripped of his political rights.[1] The Vargas regime of renovação had, apparently, been defeated. Or had it?

As the December 2 presidential elections approached, the União Democrática Nacional (National Democratic Union, UDN) threw its support behind Brigadier Eduardo Gomes, in hopes that the high-ranking Air Force officer would reverse fifteen years of authoritarian rule. UDN supporters savored the prospect that Gomes would coordinate a return to liberal constitutionalism, the restitution of individual rights, and the devolution of regional and corporate rights that the federal government had amassed since the Revolution of 1930. The Partido Social Democrático (Social Democratic Party, PSD), founded by regional elites once allied with the Estado Novo regime, held more limited hopes for its candidate, former Minister of War General Eurico Dutra. The PSD also embraced the return to constitutional rule, although the party appeared more willing to maintain a strong state presence in national life. Dutra's longtime association with the Estado Novo and lack of personal charisma were liabilities in a new era

48 Busts of Vargas Being Removed, Rio de Janeiro, 1945. Cultural artifacts, old and new, helped build Vargas's personal and institutional personae as patron, manager, and defender of Brazilian culture. When Vargas was ousted from office in October 1945, the cultural artifacts most closely associated with his rule, including these busts, were removed in a largely unsuccessful attempt to expunge public memory of the president-dictator. Courtesy of CPDOC-GV.

of electoral politics that would be strongly affected by Vargas's masterful use of political ceremony and populist demagoguery. The PSD was further handicapped by the deposed dictator's initial reluctance to endorse Dutra, denying the former minister of war the support of the Partido Trabalhista Brasileiro (Brazilian Labor Party, PTB), the Labor party created in the image of *trabalhismo*, a doctrine of state-labor collaboration that developed during the first Vargas regime.

Dutra managed to overcome his early handicaps and defeated Gomes by nearly twenty percentage points. The military high command may have intervened to oust Vargas from office, but it still could tolerate an election that delivered the presidency to one of Vargas's closest allies. In a somewhat ironic turn of events, the center-right UDN lamented the victory of an antileftist general, while the PTB offered its guarded support for an officer who helped rout left-wing political organizations. Indeed, the post–Estado Novo political landscape was strange and unfamiliar. Vargas remained characteristically enigmatic, supporting Dutra's victory while continuing to cultivate his own political power base as the senator-elect from Rio Grande do Sul and titular head of the PTB. Five years later, Vargas was headed back to the presidential palace. His second term at Catete would be tumultuous, beginning in the euphoria of a multiclass populist alliance and ending in the *tiro no coração* (shot to the heart) on 24 August 1954.

The cultural politics of the Estado Novo were as resilient and contradictory as Vargas himself. The Department of Press and Propaganda may have been dismantled in mid-1945, but the state maintained an active role in regulating mass media, popular culture, and the promotion of Brazil's image abroad well into the 1950s. All of the cultural institutions answering to the Ministry of Education remained intact after the golpe of October 1945. The civil servants who worked at these institutions went about their daily charges, largely unaffected by the regime change. Federal museums in Rio, Petrópolis, Ouro Preto, São Miguel, and Sabará retained their privileged positions as the nation's premier memory sites, soon to be joined by new federal museums in São João del Rey, Joinville, and Recife. The Museu Histórico cultivated a close relationship with the memory of Vargas, maintaining a special gallery dedicated to him. In 1958, the museum reconstructed the bedroom suite in which Vargas committed suicide. Leaving life to enter History, Vargas was given an unofficial masoleum in a national historical museum.

Ouro Preto's privileged place in the national imaginary was enhanced by improvements in roadways and annual commemorations of the Inconfidência Mineira. With the rise of cultural tourism, the city once described by Vargas as the "Mecca of Tradition" became a pilgrimage site for Brazilians in search of a national past.[2] Few seemed to notice, or care, that this national past had just as much to say about the first Vargas regime as it did about the eighteenth-century Age of Gold. Back in Rio, the Ministry of Education headquarters, a double monument to the cultural politics of the first Vargas regime and the modernists' vision of renewal, became an international landmark of brasilidade. In 1947, the building was registered in the SPHAN's *Livros do Tombo,* making modernism a formal and perpetual part of Brazil's national historical and artistic patrimony.

As suggested, much of the cultural elite of the Estado Novo remained close to the orbit of federal power after 1945. This was especially true of the modernist camp: Capanema served as a federal legislator; Rodrigo Melo Franco de Andrade, Augusto Meyer, and Edgar Roquette-Pinto continued to direct the state's most important cultural agencies; and Carlos Drummond de Andrade and Lucio Costa played instrumental roles in the consolidation of the SPHAN's "heroic phase." In 1957, Costa, Oscar Niemeyer, and several other modernist architects who received their first major commissions from the Vargas state would again offer their services to the federal government in the commission of the century — Brasília.

The antimodernists faced diminished influence in national cultural life, but they could not be wholly counted out. Traditionalists and academics continued to occupy some important positions within the cultural establishment maintained by federal funds. Gustavo Barroso remained the unquestioned *dono* (owner) of the Casa do Brasil until his death in 1959. Oswaldo Teixeira continued at the helm of the Museu Nacional de Belas Artes until the early 1960s. The National School of Fine Arts and National Faculty of Architecture remained redoubts for cultural conservatives. Luso-tropicalism wound its way through the Atlantic, transforming itself from an ideology of unity into a justification for the continuation of colonial oppression.

If many of the combatants of the culture wars survived the regime change, so too did the issues. The defeat of authoritarian nationalism, the deaths of Mário de Andrade, José Mariano, Arquimedes Memória, and the consolidation of the modernist canon did not put a stop to cultural conflict. Many of the same issues that sparked cultural tensions during the first Vargas regime continued to resonate after the fall of the Estado Novo. The culture wars were, after all, about more than the Estado Novo. At stake was the power to define and control Brazilianness.

In mid-1946, the Rio daily *A Notícia* took up the question of official cultural management in a postauthoritarian era, asking what type of cultural policies would be pursued by the new minister of education, the paulista Ernesto de Souza Campos. The following unsigned editorial, published in June 1946, is an excellent window onto the lasting memories of the Estado Novo and the reverberating echoes of the culture wars fought throughout the dictatorship:

> For the proponents of classic art, or should we say, sensible art — where the sky is blue, the leaves are green, the clouds white, and the humans anatomically correct — Mr. Gustavo Capanema could once be considered Public Enemy Number One. His excellency favored creators of monstrosities to the point that he decorated his Ministry with the ultimate excess *Prometeu* [a sculpture by the Lithuanian-born modernist sculptor Jacques Lipchitz installed at the

Ministry of Education headquarters], which is nothing less than a frightful vision from a nightmare. . . .

Brazilian artists went unaided as long as Gustavo Capanema wielded the power to veto the reasonable initiatives of Oswaldo Teixeira. . . . Taking advantage of the Minister, the "futurists" lived well at the expense of the National Treasury. Under the protections of the patron of Dada, they were not to be deprived.

Now, under the tutelage of Mr. Souza Campos, it would seem that the fine arts are going to return to what they had once been here in Brazil. Our great masters will not find themselves short-changed by ill-advised policies emanating from the bosom of the government. The new rules governing the National Salons indicate a quick return to good sense. And not a moment too soon. We are overwhelmed by monstrosities. We yearn for works which will help us forget the dictatorship and turn our eyes away from those hellacious images worthy of Dante which captivated the psychology of the leaders of the Estado Novo.[3]

Advocates of a new type of cultural management, which shunned any state support for the avant-garde, were not to be vindicated by changes in government policy. Unlike Capanema, Souza Campos and his successor, bahiano Clemente Mariani, basically left the cultural arena to its own devices. In his 1948 report on ministerial activities and priorities, Mariani made only passing mention of the key institutions of cultural management so dear to Capanema.[4] The lack of ministerial interest would not diminish the acrimony between modernists and academics — Teixeira canceled the National Salon of 1946 over a dispute with the moderns — but it helped push certain aspects of cultural conflict out of the purview of state politics.

As the echoes of earlier culture wars continued to reverberate in the art world, in some areas, the wars continued unabated. Less than one year after the coup of 1945, the SPHAN confronted, yet again, a private property holder who made every effort to subvert the politics of preservation consolidated during the Estado Novo. The battlefield was a three-story residence, built in 1859, located within the historic district of São João del Rey, Minas Gerais. José Wasth Rodrigues (1891–1958), a paulista painter commissioned by the SPHAN to complete several surveys of historical architecture, noted that the structure was one of the rare examples of a building style common to nineteenth-century coffee *fazendas* (plantations) to be found outside of the historic coffee belt of the Paraíba River Valley. According to

Rodrigues, this building "of exceptional artistic value" was likely the model for several important works of civil architecture built in São João.[5]

The residents in São João received such language with mixed emotions, as the "exceptional" nature of local architecture had already hindered private property holders and municipal authorities from modernizing the town's historic quarter, which had been tombado en bloc in 1938. Municipal authorities had previously expressed their frustration with federal preservation, described as a hindrance to local zoning rules and a blatant example of federal intervention into local affairs. Town residents periodically tried to subvert policies that altered the nature of property rights and urban development in a city trying to make a transition from a decayed mining center into an industrial and commercial regional hub. The residents of São João actively participated in many national causes, including the Força Expedicionária Brasileira, the Brazilian contingent sent to the warfront in Europe. The town's "Tiradentes Regiment" suffered 129 casualities in the Battle of Montese, Italy (1944–1945), giving the sãojoanenses bragging rights to patriotic self-sacrifice. But back on the home front, historical preservation was not so easily connected with patriotic duty.

Hoping to make better use of a valuable piece of urban real estate, in 1943 a town local had attempted to circumvent legal restrictions on structural changes in the historic district in hopes of tearing down the 1859 structure fronting the town's Praça Severiano Resende. Once the initial plan to completely demolish the building proved unfeasible, the owner considered remodeling the structure into a hotel. Looking to circumvent official regulations against any structural or cosmetic changes to buildings in the historic quarter, the owner also challenged the SPHAN's opposition to any structural changes to the building on the argument that the structure did not meet the standard for cultural patrimony. The agency rejected this allegation outright. By 1944, the owner went as far as soliciting Vargas to exercise presidential powers to cancel the tombamento. Vargas declined to intervene.[6]

In March 1945, Rodrigo Melo Franco de Andrade received word that the property owner had contracted a construction firm to begin demolition work, in violation of Decree-Law 25 and the federal penal code. Andrade demanded that municipal authorities take action. The mayor apparently chose to ignore the demand, claiming ignorance. The SPHAN retaliated on two fronts, seeking assistance from the attorney general and opening up an inquiry into an individual tombamento. The demolition work halted while the legal machinations continued. The company charged with the demolition used the local press to attack the SPHAN, whipping up popular opposition to the agency. In the interim, the Nazis surrendered, the Estado Novo fell, and the Tiradentes Regiment returned to São João. By August 1946, the SPHAN had successfully blocked any further demolition work, and the building was double-inscribed into the registries of fine arts and history. Preservation had won the day. The structure would later be acquired by the federal government for the installation of the Museu Regional, a regional museum run by the SPHAN to showcase the secular and sacred cultural patrimony of São João and surrounding areas. Patrimony, memory, the modernists, and the State remained victors.

The Arco do Teles case set a precedent that Decree-Law 25 was a legitimate legal document that codified the process in which cultural patrimony was created and protected. The SPHAN clearly had the legal right to prevent private property owners from demolishing works that had been protected. The distinction to be drawn for the disputed structure in São João del Rey is that the legality of Decree-Law 25 was highly suspect after the fall of the Estado Novo. How could a law legitimated by the authoritarian Constitution of 1937 remain valid after the coup of 1945, which suspended the Estado Novo constitution and initiated the transition to democratic rule? How could a cultural process intimately associated with a fallen dictatorship be carried over into a democracy? Given the antiliberal provisions in Decree-Law 25, including compulsory tombamento and the inability to lodge appeals to tombamento beyond the agency that was in charge of tombamento, were the politics of preservation consistent with a restored liberal political culture? Did the notion of a common social good articulated under a dictatorship still hold once that dictatorship had been overthrown?

Confronted with a legal and ethical dilemma of origins, the SPHAN found itself formulating a nuanced justification for preservation that drew upon its victory in the culture wars of the first Vargas regime, while paying homage to the return to democracy. Afonso Arinos Melo Franco (1905–1990), a mineiro jurist, historian, and future politician who sat on the SPHAN's advisory council was charged with articulating the agency's position on the contested tombamento. The end of the Second World War loomed large in Melo Franco's findings. His brief on the contested tombamento in São João made references to a war-ravaged Europe, Nazism, and displaced Jews. Melo Franco could not deny that the laws that justified compulsory tombamento were artifacts of an authoritarian regime. Compulsory tombamento, he acknowledged, compromised the liberal order fundamental to the republican system. Nevertheless, Melo Franco still up-held the necessity and legality of compulsory tombamento, invoking the rationale of the common social good formulated by the SPHAN in the Arco do Teles case and reified in historical and artistic patrimony.[7]

Melo Franco's logic was extended to state-municipal relations in 1947, when Orlando do Carvalho, director of the Department of Municipal Rela-tions for the state of Minas, issued a legal brief reiterating the interpretation that Decree-Law 25 was a legally binding document at the federal, state, and municipal levels. The powers of municipal autonomy granted under Article 28 of the Constitution of 1946 did not invalidate the federal preserva-tionist code. Carefully working his way through a history of federal legisla-tion related to preservation and property rights, Carvalho asserted that the new constitution had not reinstated the status quo ante of the Constitution of 1891 in which private property rights and municipal autonomy reigned supreme. Carvalho reaffirmed, instead, that the SPHAN retained the right to oversee alterations and modifications of tombado properties, even if this meant that the agency's actions compromised municipal autonomy.[8]

Tellingly, both Afonso Arinos Melo Franco and Orlando do Carvalho invoked the SPHAN's victory against the owners of the Arco do Teles in making their case for the continued validity of Decree-Law 25. Through federal and state law, the cultural policies of the Estado Novo burst past the coup of 1945 and shaped the political culture of the post–Estado Novo order. In the process, the victories of the culture wars of the Estado Novo became institutionalized within the political and cultural histories of the Republic.

As the debate continues over the "revolutionary" nature of the Revolution of 1930, it is clear that the Vargas era, and most especially the Estado Novo, stood for a time and place in which the federal government established itself as a center of cultural authority.[9] During the first Vargas regime, the state turned toward the cultural field to shape a regenerated national politi-cal culture. The cultural field, in turn, turned to the state to try to resolve intense differences over the aesthetics of renewal, Brazil's place in interna-tional culture, and the meaning of Brazilianness.

The post-1945 cultural marketplace was undoubtedly more complex than the one managed by the Vargas regime. Professionalization among the cultural establishment, a changing politics of aesthetics, and market forces created ample space for cultural producers to distance themselves

from the state. Within a decade of the fall of the Estado Novo, Brazil's avant-
garde was making a definite turn toward the abstract, an aesthetic that
the state found nearly impossible to harness. The intense capitalization of
mass media, tourism, and sports created new employment opportunities
for cultural figures. Urbanization, rising literary rates, and the increased
access to mass media created new cultural consumers, producers, and critics over which the state had limited control. Private philanthropy, notori-
ously anemic among the twentieth-century elite in Latin America, grew
immensely after the Second World War. Industrialists Francisco Matarazzo
Sobrinho and Raimundo Castro Maya and media magnate Assis Chateaubriand spent a portion of their sizable economic and cultural capital on the
organization of major art museums along the Rio-São Paulo axis. Universities, private publishing enterprises, and international exhibition opportunities and criticism created entirely new outlets for canonization, scholarship,
and debate. The field of cultural production (and its numerous subfields)
manifested the autonomizing characteristics described by Bourdieu.

Nevertheless, monuments to the Vargas regime's culture wars dotted
the cultural field. The national cultural canon and the institutions that managed it continued to blur the line between cultural and political power.
Aleijadinho's Prophets, the Missão São Miguel, Debret's *Viagem Pitoresca,*
and Portinari's *Café* were eternal testaments to Brazilian artistic genius *and*
testaments to the cultural powers wielded by the state between 1930 and
1945. The Museu Histórico Nacional wrapped itself in the title Casa do
Brasil, managing the national memory for several decades. The Museu Imperial gave Brazilians a glimpse into the splendor of the imperial age. The
state-commissioned works of Portinari, Lucio Costa, Heitor Villa-Lobos,
and Oscar Niemeyer enjoyed national and international fame. Celebrated
as monuments to Brazilian culture, any excavation around these works,
sites, and figures would uncover the physical and rhetorical traces of bitter
conflicts over art, nation, and state that invented the art, nation, and state
of the first Vargas regime and, more broadly, of modern Brazil.

Cultural warfare seems to be an inescapable facet of rationalized cultural management, be it in Brazil or elsewhere. Even if the Vargas regime
had wanted to encourage all forms of cultural production (which it most
certainly did not), the regime would still have found itself pulled into the
vortex of conflict precisely because a state's entrance into the cultural market is predicated upon the aggrandizement of political power. Sufficient
political power gives culture managers the ability to consecrate the good

and the authentically national and to censor the bad and unnational. Since political power is constantly under dispute, the good and the bad, national and the unnational become highly subjective, politicized labels.

The contested nature of cultural politicking does not diminish the power of cultural management to be a vehicle for state building *and* nation building. In managing national culture, the Vargas state could be heavy handed, interventionist, and self-interested. The same could be said for culture managers who used the state for their own purposes. The nation could be victimized by the very culture the state promoted and protected. Nevertheless, the heat produced by cultural management guaranteed that the "national culture" envisioned by Vargas had a visual, geographic, and administrative specificity with which all society could identify. The national identities formed under Vargas were not necessarily of the nation's making. They were, nevertheless, national and state mediated, fulfilling the goals of the Revolution of 1930.

Biographical Appendix

The following biographical sketches provide background information on people, groups, and organizations discussed in the book. The information contained in each entry has been culled from a number of sources, including encyclopedias, biographical dictionaries, bibliographic databases, and institutional histories.

Albuquerque, Georgina Moura Andrade de (Taubaté, SP 1885–Rio de Janeiro, GB 1962) and **Lucílio** (Barras, PI 1877–Rio de Janeiro, DF 1939), painters. The Albuquerques met at the Escola Nacional de Belas Artes in 1904. Married two years later, the couple spent several years in Europe, where both practiced a number of styles including impressionism, symbolism, and art nouveau. In Brazil, Georgina was best known for her impressionistic style and her interests in female subjects. Professors at the National School of Fine Arts, both Lucílio and Georgina held the position of director of the Museu Nacional de Belas Artes between 1937–1938 and 1952–1954, respectively.

Aleijadinho. See Lisboa, Antônio Francisco

Amaral, Tarsila do (Capivari, SP 1886–São Paulo, SP 1973), painter. Daughter to wealthy landowners, Amaral left an unhappy marriage and the conservative morays of the interior of São Paulo to study art. In 1920, she traveled to Paris, where she familiarized herself with new fashions in European painting while circulating among the Parisian smart set. After the Modern Art Week, Tarsila returned to Brazil to join forces with Anita Malfatti, Mário de Andrade, Menotti del Picchia, and husband Oswald de Andrade in defining a multiplicity of Brazilian modernisms. Her most productive period was 1922–1935, marked by the Pau-Brasil phase of the mid-1920s, the Antropofagia phase of the late 1920s, and social realism in the early 1930s.

Andrade, Carlos Drummond de (Itabira, MG 1902–Rio de Janeiro, RJ 1987), poet and culture manager. Son of mineiro landowners, Drummond graduated with a degree in pharmacology in 1925. In the late 1920s, Drummond was the editor of the *Diário de Minas,* an important vehicle for modernist literature in Minas. Befriending fellow mineiro Gustavo Capanema in the mid-1910s, Drummond served as the minister of education's chief of staff from 1934 through 1945. With the fall of the Estado Novo, Drummond continued as a public servant and poet.

Andrade, Mário Raul de Morais (São Paulo, SP 1893–São Paulo, 1945), writer, ethnographer, and musicologist. Andrade taught musicology before assuming a leading role in the aesthetic avant-garde that erupted in São Paulo in the 1920s. Author to several works of literature and criticism, including *Hallucinated City* (1922), *A escrava que não é Isaura* (1925), and most importantly, *Macunaíma* (1928), Andrade's contributions to the modernist movement were so great that he earned the nickname of "Pope of Modernism." During the first Vargas regime, Andrade held several influential posts in cultural management, including director of the Department of Culture in São Paulo (1934–1937) and coordinator of the Encyclopedia Division of the Instituto Nacional do Livro. Andrade corresponded with nearly all major figures in Brazilian modernism, including Minister of Education Gustavo Capanema, whom Andrade advised on a number of programmatic and intellectual matters, including the organization of the SPHAN.

Andrade, José **Oswald** de Sousa (São Paulo, SP 1890–São Paulo, SP 1954), writer and critic. One of the most important figures of Brazilian letters, Andrade was author to two of the modernist movement's most important manifestos—the *Manifesto Pau-Brasil* (1925) and the *Manifesto Antropófago* (1928). Unlike many of his fellow modernists, the cosmopolitan Andrade maintained a distance from the Vargas state.

Andrade, Rodrigo Melo Franco de (Belo Horizonte, MG 1898–Rio de Janeiro, GB 1969), preservationist and culture manager. Born into a well-to-do mineiro family, Andrade attended secondary school in France, where he met several notable Brazilian cultural figures including Graça Aranha and Alceu Amoroso Lima. After obtaining a degree in law in 1919, Andrade acted as a journalist and cultural critic before receiving an invitation from Minister of Education and Public Health Francisco Campos to serve as the minister's chief of staff. This began a long career as a civil servant, marked by a long tenure as founder-director of the Serviço do Patrimônio Histórico e Artístico Nacional (1936–1967).

Barroso, Gustavo Dodt (Fortaleza, CE 1888–Rio de Janeiro, DF 1959), author, political activist, and culture manager. Early in life, Barroso was an amateur ethnographer, journalist, and federal deputy. In the 1920s, he became a prominent member of Rio's literary scene, joining the Academia Brasileira de Letras and directing the magazine *Fon-Fon*. An ultraconservative nationalist, Barroso joined the Ação Integralista Brasileira in 1933, holding a high leadership position until the fascistic movement was outlawed in 1938. The most important figure in the professionalization of museum management, Barroso directed the National Historical Museum from 1922–1930 and again from 1932–1959. Barroso was a prolific author, penning works of ethnography, biography, history, and museum management, and an equally prolific ideologue, publishing works highly influenced by nationalism, anticommunism, and anti-Semitism.

Brazilian Commission to Exposição do Mundo Português. Joint Chief of Staff Francisco José Pinto, president; Gustavo Barroso, historical exhibit; Osvaldo Orico, cultural exhibits; Ernesto Jorge Street, booths; Armando Navarro da Costa, artistic representation; Geysa Boscoli, National Department of Coffee stand; José Maria de Almeida, tourism; Flavio Guimarães and Roberto Lacombe, interior design. Portuguese architect Raul Lino designed the pavilion.

Brazilian Commission to New York World's Fair of 1939. Armando Vidal, chief commissioner; Alpheu Diniz Gonsalves and Franklin de Almeida, adjunct commissioners; Décio de Moura, secretary; Alpheu Domingues, treasurer; Leonidio Ribeiro, medical delegation; Oscar Saravia, labor and social legislation representative; Walter Burle Marx, musical director; Lucio Costa and Oscar Niemeyer, architects; Thomas Pierce, landscape design; Paul Lester Wiener, interior design.

Campofiorito, Quirino (Belém, PA 1902–Niterói, RJ 1993), painter and art critic. A graduate of the Escola Nacional de Belas Artes, Campofiorito won the Prêmio de Viagem à Europa in 1929. During the first Vargas regime, Campofiorito was an active painter and caricaturist, professor at the National School of Fine Arts, and founding editor of the influential art review *Bellas-Artes* (1935–1940).

Campos, Francisco Luis da Silva (Dores do Inayá, MG 1891–Belo Horizonte, MG 1968), jurist and politician. A 1914 graduate of the Law School of Minas Gerais, Campos served as a state and federal legislator before assuming the post of state secretary of the interior in 1926. Following the Revolution of 1930, Campos became an important figure in national politics, serving as minister of education (1930–1932) and justice (1932 and 1937–1942). One of the principal ideologues of the authoritarian state in twentieth-century Brazil, Campos authored the Constitutions of 1937 and 1967.

Capanema Filho, **Gustavo** (Pitangui, MG 1900–Rio de Janeiro, RJ 1986), politician. Born into a traditional mineiro family, Capanema was educated in law. In the 1920s and early 30s, the future federal minister worked as a lawyer, educator, municipal councilman, and interventor (governor) in Minas. As minister of education and public health (1934–1945), Capanema demonstrated great political savvy and administrative skills. His personal connections were equally impressive—linking the Ministry of Education to the modernists, Catholic revivalists, and conservative authoritarians. After the fall of the Estado Novo, Capanema became a federal legislator affiliated with the Partido Social Democrático and ARENA.

Carmona, Oscar de Fragoso (Lisbon, Portugal 1869–Lisbon, Portugal 1951), president of Portugal (1928–1951). Rising to power in a military coup in 1926, Carmona was titular president throughout Portugal's Estado Novo. Although Carmona was officially president from 1928 until his death, Prime Minister António de Oliveira Salazar was the effective chief of state.

Castro Maya, Raimundo Ottoni de (Paris, France 1894–Rio de Janeiro, RJ 1968), industrialist and philanthropist. Son to Brazil's nineteenth-century aristocracy, Castro Maya arrived in Brazil at the age of eight. A graduate of law, Castro Maya built his inheritance into the Companhia Carioca Industrial, a diversified manufacturing and retail conglomerate. From the early 1930s until his death, Castro Maya was one of Brazil's most prominent cultural patrons, spearheading diverse philanthropic initiatives including the restoration of the Floresta da Tijuca, the publication of luxury editions of Brazilian literature, the purchase of the Debret originals, and the organization of the Museu de Arte Moderna do Rio de Janeiro.

Costa, Lucio (Toulon, France 1902–Rio de Janeiro, RJ 1998), architect and urbanist. Costa studied architecture in England before entering the Escola Nacional de Belas Artes, which he later directed from 1930–1931. Costa's major accomplishments include the internationally acclaimed designs for the Ministry of Education and Health (1936), the Museu das Missões (1938), the Brazilian pavilion at the New York World's Fair (1939), and, most importantly, the Pilot Plan for Brasília (1957). Undoubtedly one of the world's most influential practitioners and theorists of modern architecture and urban planning, Costa was equally invested in the politics and poetics of historical preservation.

Debret, Jean-Baptiste (Paris, France 1768–Paris, France 1848), painter. Cousin and disciple of the celebrated French neoclassical painter Jacques-Louis David (1748–1825), Debret joined the French Artistic Mission of 1816 as a history painter. During a fifteen-year residence in Brazil (1816–1831), the Frenchman executed a number of works commemorating key moments in the history of the Bragança Court. He also tried, with limited success, to institutionalize neoclassical painting at the Imperial Academy of Arts. After returning to France in 1831, Debret published *Voyage Pittoresque et Historique au Brésil* (1834–1839), an illustrated commentary on his residency in Portuguese America.

Di Cavalcanti, Emiliano (Rio de Janeiro, DF 1897–Rio de Janeiro, RJ 1976), painter. After an early start as a caricaturist, Di Cavalcanti was thrust to the forefront of the Brazilian art scene when he helped organize the Modern Art Week, held in São Paulo in February 1922. Di Cavalcanti was one of the few cariocas to participate in this foundational moment of paulista modernism. The years from 1923–1924 and 1935–1940 were spent in Europe, placing Di Cavalcanti at a marked distance from the Vargas regime. Di Cavalcanti is best known for a lifelong interest in female subjects, painting countless female nudes, prostitutes, mulattas, and gypsies, as well as the colorful denizens of Rio's demimonde.

French Artistic Mission of 1816, artistic mission invited to Brazil to establish a royal art academy modeled upon the French neoclassical tradition. The original members of the French Artistic Mission were: Joachin Lebreton (1760–1819), chief; Nicolas-Antoine Taunay (1755–1830), landscape painting; Jean-Baptiste Debret (1768–1848), history painting; Auguste Marie Victor Grandjean de Montigny (1776–1850), architecture; Auguste Marie Taunay (1768–1824), sculpture; Charles Simon Pradier (1786–1848), engraving; Marc Ferrez (1788–1850), sculpture; and Zepherino Ferrez (1797–1851), engraving. Lebreton's secretary Pierre Dillon, engineer François Ovide, Austrian-born composer Sigismund Neukom (1778–1858), and several artisans accompanied the Frenchmen. Although King D. João VI authorized the organization of the Royal School of Sciences, Arts, and Trades almost immediately after the Frenchmen arrived in Rio, the mission members confronted stiff resistance to the implantation of French neoclassical conventions.

Freyre, Gilberto de Melo (Recife, PE 1900–Recife, PE 1987), sociologist. Born into a traditional family of the once-prosperous sugar-growing region of northeastern Brazil, Freyre came to be one of the most influential social scientists of the twentieth century, earning international recognition (and contempt) for his theories of race relations and sociability among Portuguese-speaking peoples. Educated in the United States, Freyre became a cause célèbre in the 1930s with the publication of *Casa-grande e senzala* (1933, Engl. trans.: *The Masters and the Slaves,* 1946) and *Sobrados e Mocambos* (1936, Engl. trans.: *The Mansions and the Shanties,* 1963), and the organization of the First Afro-Brazilian Congress (Recife, 1934). A prolific writer, commentator, chronicler, and memorialist, Freyre is closely associated with the ideology of racial democracy, Luso-tropicalism, and Afro-Brazilian studies.

Garcia, Rodolfo Augusto de Amorim (Ceará-Mirim, RN 1873–Rio de Janeiro, DF 1949), linguist and culture manager. Garcia graduated from the Law Faculty in Recife, Pernambuco before moving to Rio in 1912, where he was employed by the Instituto Histórico e Geográfico Brasileiro. After 1930, Garcia served as director of the Museu Histórico Nacional (1930–1932) and the Biblioteca Nacional (1932–1945).

Jeanneret, Charles Édouard. See Le Corbusier

Latin American Exhibition of Fine Arts. See Pan-American Art Exhibition

Lebreton, Joachin (Brittany, France 1760–Rio de Janeiro 1819), art critic and chief of the French Artistic Mission of 1816. Lebreton was a prominent figure in the French arts during the revolutionary era, serving as Chief of Museums, Conservatory, and Libraries for the Ministry of the Interior, Director of the Louvre, and Perpetual Secretary of the Institut de France. In 1816, Lebreton accepted the invitation of the Portuguese Crown to organize an artistic mission to be sent to Brazil. See also French Artistic Mission of 1816.

Le Corbusier (La Chaux-de-Fonds, Switzerland 1887–Cap Martin, France 1965), architect, urbanist, and theorist whose given name was Charles Édouard Jean-neret. A titan in twentieth-century architecture and urbanism, Le Corbusier was a founding member and propagandist of the International Congress of Modern Architecture (CIAM, 1929–1959), author of numerous works on modern architec-ture and urban planning, and mentor to an entire generation of modernists. Le Corbusier's precepts on architecture, design, and urban planning, expressed in works including *A Contemporary City for Three Million Inhabitants* (1922), *Towards a New Architecture* (1923), *Plan Voisin* (1925), *The Radiant City* (1933), and various CIAM publications, had an immeasurable impact on urban life, especially in the developing world, where Le Corbusier's plans were implemented on a broad scale. A naturalized French citizen, Le Corbusier visited Brazil on three occa-sions: 1929, when he first impressed Lucio Costa; 1936, when he came at Gustavo Capanema's invitation to help sketch out the Ministry of Education and Health building; and 1962.

Lisboa, Antônio Francisco, a.k.a. Aleijadinho (little cripple) in reference to a degenerative disease that afflicted him (Ouro Preto, MG *c.* 1730–Ouro Preto, MG 1814), sculptor and architect. Aleijadinho was a free mulatto sculptor who carved numerous freestanding and architectural works during the high point of the barroco mineiro. The Igreja de São Francisco de Assis in Ouro Preto and the soapstone sculptures of the Twelve Prophets (1800–1805) located in front of the Santuário do Senhor Bom Jesus de Matosinhos in Congonhas do Campo are generally acknowledged as Aleijadinho's finest works.

Malfatti, Anita (São Paulo, SP 1896–São Paulo, SP 1964), painter. Pioneer and protomartyr of modernist painting in Brazil, Malfatti was strongly influenced by the German and American avant-garde of the 1910s. In 1917, Malfatti agreed to a one-woman show in São Paulo. The fifty-three works on exhibit, many dem-onstrating strong traces of German expressionism, provoked a firestorm of con-troversy over the aesthetic and psychological value of modern painting.

Mariano Carneiro de Cunha Filho, **José** (Igarassú[?], PE 1881–Rio de Janeiro, DF 1946), art critic and philanthropist. Educated as a physician, Mariano was better known as an art critic and cultural patron. In the 1920s, Mariano took up the cause of neocolonial architecture and the defense of "traditional" Brazilian art. Mariano briefly directed the National School of Fine Arts in the mid-1920s. Throughout the first Vargas regime, Mariano was a vociferous opponent of mod-ernism.

Meireles de Lima, **Vitor** (Desterro [Florianópolis], SC 1832–Rio de Janeiro, DF 1903), painter. After five years of study at the Imperial Academy of Fine Arts

(1847–1852), Meireles spent nearly a decade in Europe, with the financial support of Emperor Dom Pedro II. On returning to Brazil in 1861, Meireles became a celebrated history painter of the Second Empire, winning state commissions for *Primeira Missa no Brasil* (1861) *Batalha Naval de Riachuelo* (1872; second version 1882–1883), and *Batalha de Guararapes* (1879).

Memória, Arquimedes (Ipú, CE 1893–Rio de Janeiro, DF 1960), architect. Although Memória was one of the most successful architects of the 1920s and 1930s, his winning design for the Ministry of Education and Health (1936) was scuttled when the modernists convinced Minister of Education Capanema that the structural and decorative aspects of the project were ill-suited for a project of such symbolic and administrative importance. The eclectic Memória was director of the National School of Fine Arts (1931–1937) and a leading Integralist.

Mestre Valentim. See Valentim da Fonseca e Silva

Miranda, Carmen (Marco de Canavezes, Portugal 1909–Beverly Hills, CA, USA 1955), screen and stage entertainer. Miranda immigrated to Brazil at the age of two and was raised in a working-class neighborhood of Rio de Janeiro, where she was strongly influenced by the growing popularity of Afro-Brazilian musical forms, including samba. In the 1930s, Miranda and her sister Aurora became popular stage and screen performers, excelling at musical reviews. Miranda's rise to international stardom came in 1939–1940, in a Lee Shubert Broadway production of *The Streets of Paris* and the 20th Century-Fox musical *Down Argentine Way*. Dubbed "the Brazilian Bombshell," Miranda was a regular in U.S. film and television comedies until her death.

Modernist Movement, a movement in letters, arts, architecture, and music that sought the renewal of Brazilian culture. The Modern Art Week (São Paulo, February 1922) is typically read as the starting point for Brazilian modernism, although some would argue that Anita Malfatti's ill-fated 1917 show was the first major modernist event in Brazil. The most important subcurrents in the first decade of Brazilian modernism include Klaxon (Mário de Andrade, Oswald de Andrade, Manuel Bandeira, and Sergio Milliet), Pau-Brasil (Oswald de Andrade and Tarsila do Amaral), Antropofagia (Oswald de Andrade and Tarsila do Amaral), Verde-Amarelo/Anta (Menotti del Picchia, Cassiano Ricardo, and Plínio Salgado), the northeastern regionalists (Gilberto Freyre, José Lins do Rego, Graciliano Ramos, and Jorge Amado), and the modernistas mineiros (Carlos Drummond de Andrade and Tristão de Ataíde, among others). In the 1930s, modernism abandoned some of its aesthetic iconoclasm to become more closely associated with cultural nationalism. In 1941, Mário de Andrade presented a public lecture entitled *"O movimento modernista,"* giving the heterogeneous phenomena of modernism a discursive and aesthetic cohesiveness that in fact never really existed, but nevertheless came to signify a recognizable historical, artistic, and sociological movement.

Niemeyer Soares Filho, **Oscar** (Rio de Janeiro, DF 1907–), architect. A graduate of the National School of Fine Arts, the young Niemeyer joined ranks with Le Corbusier, Lucio Costa, and a team of Brazilian modernists in the audacious, controversial design of the Ministry of Education and Health building. In the early 1940s, Niemeyer began his fruitful relationship with mineiro politician and patron Juscelino Kubitschek de Oliveira (1902–1976). Niemeyer's Brazilian projects range from single residential structures to major commercial and government buildings. His designs for the government buildings in Brasília exemplify the objective to adapt lyrically the rigid principles of modernist architecture and modern construction materials to a Brazilian sensibility of spectacle, sensuality, and monumentalism.

Pan-American Art Exhibition (1939) and **The Latin American Exhibition of Fine Arts** (1940). The New York World's Fair Commission and the United States Department of Agriculture sponsored the 1939 Riverside Museum show of 350 works of Latin American painting, sculpture, and handicrafts. Brazilian artists included Manoel Constantino, Demetrio Ismalovitch, Maria Margarida, Jordão de Oliveira, José Pancetti, Helios Seelinger, Eugenio Siguard, and Oswaldo Teixeira. A second Latin American art show was held the following year at the Riverside Museum. Painter Cândido Portinari and sculptor Maria Martins were the only Brazilians to be exhibited.

Pedro II (Pedro de Alcântara, House of Bragança) (Rio de Janeiro 1825–Paris, France 1891), emperor of Brazil, 1831–1889. Son to the first emperor of Brazil Pedro I (1798–1834), Pedro assumed full royal powers in 1840 at the age of fourteen. The young monarch confronted a series of regional and slave revolts, put down by imperial troops. Other major events of Pedro's reign included the end of the transatlantic slave trade (1850), the Paraguayan War (1865–1870), the organization of the first Republican Party (1870), Brazil's rapid integration into world commodity markets, and the final abolition of slavery (1888). Pedro was deposed in a bloodless coup announced 15 November 1889. A learned and judicious ruler, Pedro's political acumen was sometimes questionable, especially in the years immediately preceding the Proclamation of the Republic when poor health and rising political partisanship undermined the legitimacy of the sole American monarchy.

Pires, Washington Ferreira (Formiga, MG 1892–Belo Horizonte, MG 1970), politician. Pires was educated as a physician before serving in the state legislature in Minas Gerais (1923–1930). After the Revolution of 1930, Pires served as minister of education and health (1932–1934) and a federal deputy representing the Partido Progressista Mineiro.

Portinari, Cândido Torquato (Brodósqui, SP 1903–Rio de Janeiro, GB 1962), painter. Portinari's artistic career was strongly influenced by his childhood in the coffee-growing zone of north-central São Paulo. Scenes of agrarian life, manual work, folklife, and rural poverty run throughout his artistic production. In 1918, Portinari initiated formal art training at the Escola Nacional de Belas Artes in Rio. Winner of the Prêmio de Viagem à Europa in 1928, Portinari studied in Europe for two years. The painter's career took off in the mid-1930s, when *Café* (1935) was awarded an honorable mention at the Carnegie International. In later years, Portinari won commissions for mural series at the Ministry of Education Headquarters, the New York World's Fair of 1939, the Library of Congress, and countless portraits of Brazil's intellectual and political elite. Portinari's association with the first Vargas regime became a point of great controversy among the painter's proponents and detractors.

Roquette-Pinto, Edgard (Rio de Janeiro 1884–Rio de Janeiro, DF 1954), anthropologist and culture manager. A pioneer of Brazilian anthropology and ethnography, Roquette-Pinto participated in the Rondon Commission (1907–1908), published several well-known works on Brazilian Indians, and served as director of the Museu Nacional (1926–1935). A central figure in educational film and radio, Roquette-Pinto was the founding director of the Instituto Nacional do Cinema Educativo.

Salazar, António de Oliveira (Vimiero, Portugal 1889–Lisbon, Portugal 1970), economist and prime minister of Portugal (1932–1968). Trained as an economist at the University of Coimbra, Salazar accepted the post of finance minister in 1928, becoming prime minister in 1932. The following year, Salazar assumed dictatorial powers during the proclamation of an Estado Novo. He remained in power for the next four decades, defending a vision of Portugal as a Catholic, corporatist, imperialist nation-state of worldwide dimensions.

Severo, Ricardo da Fonseca Costa (Oporto, Portugal 1869–São Paulo, SP 1940), architect and architectural theorist. Before fleeing his native Portugal during the republican revolt of 1912, Severo was a well-known engineer and architect. His residence in Oporto (1904) attempted to define the key elements of Portuguese architecture. Once resettled in Brazil, Severo established a successful practice that catered to clients interested in designs inspired by "traditional" Luso-Brazilian architecture as well as the eclectic styles popular in the 1920s and 1930s.

Smith, Robert Chester (Cranfort, NJ, USA 1912–Glen More, PA, USA 1975), art historian and critic. Educated at Haverford College and Harvard University, Smith became a prolific propagandist of Luso-Brazilian culture at a time when Ibero-American art and architecture were largely unknown in the United States. As assistant director of the Hispanic Division and head of the Archive of Hispanic Culture (1939–1947) Smith coordinated numerous studies of Ibero-American art and architecture. Smith maintained an active correspondence with the SPHAN, closely paralleling the Brazilian modernists' interests in Luso-Brazilian colonial architecture and modernism. After leaving the Library of Congress, Smith taught art history at the University of Pennsylvania until his death.

Sociedade dos Amigos de Ouro Preto do Rio de Janeiro was founded in 1944 by a group of upper-middle-class professional males who resided in Rio de Janeiro. The executive committee was composed of Paulo José Pires Brandão, João Batista Ferreira Velloso, João Velloso Filho, Cônego Assis Memória, Oswaldo Teixeira, Oldemar Oliveira, Lourenzo Cuesta, and Pedro Calmon. Gustavo Capanema was the honorary president. Documentation on the society is extremely scarce, but it appears that affiliated associations were founded in Belo Horizonte and Ouro Preto sometime after 1945. For a brief period, beginning in June 1945, the Society published a newspaper, *Tribuna de Ouro Preto*. In September 1949, the Society became more active as the wives of several important politicians and public figures began to organize charity auctions and fund-raising events to benefit preservation in Ouro Preto. These efforts coincided with a push by mineiro legislator Afonso Arinos de Melo Franco to increase the SPHAN's annual budget.

Souto Maior, Jaime Lino and **Maria da Conceição,** litigants in the Arco do Teles suit against the SPHAN (1939–1943). Biographical information on the Souto Maiors is sketchy, but it appears that the couple was related to a well-established family that dated back to colonial aristocracy.

Teixeira, Oswaldo (Rio de Janeiro, DF 1905–Rio de Janeiro, GB 1974), painter and culture manager. Born into a humble family of Rio's Morro do Castelo, Teixeira studied at the Escola Nacional de Belas Artes, winning the Prêmio de Viagem à Europa in 1924. Strongly influenced by the European canon and the academic tradition in Brazil, Teixeira was a vocal defender and practitioner of academic art. His subject matter and style varied over time, but sentimentality was a common theme in his still-lifes, portraits, nudes, and landscapes. Teixeira was founding director of the Museu Nacional de Belas Artes (1937–1961), making the museum a bastion of academic art even after modernismo had supplanted academismo as Brazil's hegemonic style.

Valentim da Fonseca e Silva (Serro Frio, MG 1750–Rio de Janeiro 1813), sculptor and architect. The mulatto son of a Portuguese diamond contractor and a Brazilian-born female slave, Valentim was educated in Portugal. On returning to Brazil, "Mestre" Valentim executed some of the most significant works of civil and ecclesiastic sculpture and statuary in late-colonial Portuguese America, including the fountain at Praça do Carmo (today's Praça XV de Novembro) and the high altar of the Igreja de São Francisco de Paula, both located in Rio de Janeiro.

Vargas, Getúlio Dornelles (São Borja, RS 1883–Rio de Janeiro, DF 1954), politician. A dominant figure in modern Brazilian politics, Vargas served as minister of the treasury (1926-1928), governor of Rio Grande do Sul (1928-1930), chief of the provisional government (1930-1934), president (1934-1937), president-dictator (1937-1945), senator (1946-1950), and again president (1951-1954). Vargas's suicide in the presidential palace is perhaps the most dramatic event in twentieth-century Brazilian history. See the Introduction for more biographical information.

Notes

Preface

1 Fernando de Azevedo, *Brazilian Culture: An Introduction to the Study of Culture in Brazil* (New York: Macmillan Company, [1943] 1950).

2 Ernesto de Souza Campos, *Instituições culturais e de educação superior no Brasil: resumo histórico* (Rio de Janeiro: Ministério da Educação e Saúde, 1941); and Adalberto Mário Ribeiro, *Instituições brasileiras de cultura,* 2 vols. (Rio de Janeiro: Ministério da Educação e Saúde; Serviço de Documentação, 1945–1948).

Introduction: The Brazilian Republic, Getúlio Vargas, and Metaphors of War

1 The spelling and accentuation of Brazilian Portuguese have undergone numerous changes over the past century. Unfortunately, adherence to official orthographic changes has not been uniform. I have followed the standard practice of using modern spelling and accentuation in all instances, with the exception of proper names and original book titles.

2 José Murilo de Carvalho, *Os bestializados: o Rio de Janeiro e a República que não foi* (São Paulo: Companhia da Letras, 1987).

3 Museu Histórico Nacional–Setor do Controle do Patrimônio (hereafter MHN–SCP) 19/30 Doc. 4, 15 October 1930.

4 MHN–SCP 26/30 Doc. 1, 13 December 1930.

5 *Monumentos da Cidade: reportagens publicadas pelo Diário de Notícias* (Rio de Janeiro: Diário de Notícias, 1946).

6 For more information on Vargas's final days, see Stanley Hilton, "The Overthrow of Getúlio Vargas in 1945: Diplomatic Intervention, Defense of Democracy, or Political Retribution?" *Hispanic American Historical Review* 67, no. 1 (February 1987): 1–38; and John D. French, "The Populist Gamble of Getúlio Vargas in 1945: Political and Ideological Transitions in Brazil," in *Latin America in the 1940s: War and Postwar Transitions,* ed. David Rock (Berkeley: University of California Press, 1994), 141–65.

7 Two distinct versions of Vargas's suicide note have been reprinted in *As instituições da Era Vargas*, org. Maria Celina D'Araújo (Rio de Janeiro: EDUERJ; Editora FGV, 1999), 159 61.

8 For a fuller portrait of Vargas and his political legacy, see Robert M. Levine, *Father of the Poor?: Vargas and His Era* (New York: Cambridge University Press, 1998).

9 Levine, *Father of the Poor?*, 13–15.

10 Getúlio Vargas, *Diário* (Rio de Janeiro: Siciliano; Fundação Getúlio Vargas, 1995), 1:3–21.

1 The Vargas Era and Culture Wars

1 Oswaldo Teixeira, *Getúlio Vargas e a arte no Brasil: a influência direta dos Chefes do Estado na formação artística das pátrias* (Rio de Janeiro: Departamento de Imprensa e Propaganda, 1940), 50. All translations, unless otherwise noted, are my own.

2 Column reprinted in *O pensamento político do Presidente* (Rio de Janeiro: Departamento de Imprensa e Propaganda, 1943), 364–65.

3 Arquivo Gustavo Capanema, Centro de Pesquisa e Documentação da História Contemporânea do Brasil/Fundação Getúlio Vargas (hereafter CPDOC-GC), pi GC/Capanema 43.03.16. Text of speech delivered by Gustavo Capanema at inauguration of the Museu Imperial, 16 March 1943.

4 Projeto Portinari, interview with Carlos Drummond de Andrade (hereafter PP-CDA) 21 November 1983, 25.

5 Samuel Putnam, "Brazilian Culture under Vargas," *Science and Society* VI, no. 1 (1942): 34–57.

6 Pioneering works in Brazilian political history authored by the first-generation of Brazilianists include: Thomas E. Skidmore, *Politics in Brazil, 1930–1964: An Experiment in Democracy* (New York: Oxford University Press, 1967); Robert M. Levine, *The Vargas Regime, 1934–1938: The Critical Years* (New York: Columbia University Press, 1970); John D. Wirth, *The Politics of Brazilian Development* (Stanford: Stanford University Press, 1970); Alfred Stepan, *The Military in Politics: Changing Patterns in Brazil* (Princeton: Princeton University Press, 1971); and Frank McCann, *The Brazilian-American Alliance, 1937–1945* (Princeton: Princeton University Press, 1973).

7 E. Bradford Burns, *Nationalism in Brazil: A Historical Survey* (New York: Preager, 1968), esp. 51–89; Thomas E. Skidmore, *Black into White: Race and Nationality in Brazilian Thought* (New York: Oxford University Press, 1974); Ludwig Lauerhauss Jr., *Getúlio Vargas e o triunfo do nacionalismo brasileiro* (Belo Horizonte: Editora Itatiaia, 1986).

8 For Morse's cultural histories of Latin America, see *New World Soundings:*

Culture and Ideology in the Americas. (Baltimore: Johns Hopkins University Press, 1989); "The Multiverse of Latin American Identity, c. 1920–1970," in *The Cambridge History of Latin America,* ed. Leslie Bethell (New York: Cambridge University Press, 1995), 10:1–129, esp. 15–24; and the infamous essay *Prospero's Mirror* (unpublished in English; Brazilian edition: *O espelho de Próspero* [São Paulo: Companhia das Letras, 1988]).

9 Jean Franco, *The Modern Culture of Latin America: Society and the Artist* (New York: Praeger, 1967).

10 John Nist, *The Modernist Movement in Brazil: A Literary Study* (Austin: University of Texas Press, 1967), esp. 102–12.

11 Randal Johnson, "The Institutionalization of Brazilian Modernism," *Brasil/Brazil* 3, no. 4 (1990): 5–23.

12 Wilson Martins, *The Modernist Idea: A Critical Survey of Brazilian Writing in the Twentieth Century* (New York: New York University Press, [1969] 1971).

13 João Luiz Lafetá, *1930: a crítica e o modernismo* (São Paulo: Duas Cidades, 1974), 11–27.

14 Sérgio Miceli, org., *Estado e cultura no Brasil* (São Paulo: DIFEL, 1984).

15 Antônio Cândido, "A Revolução de 1930 e a cultura," in *Educação pela noite e outros ensaios* (São Paulo: Ática, [1984] 1987), 181–99.

16 Maria Cecília Londres Fonseca, *O patrimônio em processo: trajetória da política federal de preservação no Brasil* (Rio de Janeiro: Editora da UFRJ/MinC/IPHAN, 1997), 147–204.

17 Simon Schwartzman, "O intelectual e o poder: a carreira política de Gustavo Capanema," in *A Revolução de 1930: Seminário internacional* (Brasília: Editora da Universidade de Brasília, 1980), 365–97.

18 Simon Schwartzman, Helena Maria Bousquet Bomeny, and Vanda Maria Ribeiro Costa, *Tempos de Capanema* (Rio de Janeiro: Paz e Terra, 1984).

19 Sérgio Miceli, *Intelectuais e classe dirigente no Brasil, 1920–1945* (São Paulo: DIFEL, 1979).

20 Johnson, "The Institutionalization of Brazilian Modernism," 15–17.

21 The most important works on intellectuals and the state published in the 1980s are: Lúcia Lippi Oliveira, ed., *Elite intelectual e debate político nos anos 30* (Rio de Janeiro: Editora da Fundação Getúlio Vargas, 1980); Lúcia Lippi Oliveira, Mônica Pimenta Velloso, and Angela Maria Castro Gomes, *Estado Novo: ideologia e poder* (Rio de Janeiro: Zahar Editores, 1982); Mônica Pimenta Velloso, *Os intelectuais e a política cultural do Estado Novo* (Rio de Janeiro: Fundação Getúlio Vargas/CPDOC, 1987); Daniel Pécaut, *Os intelectuais e a política no Brasil: entre o povo e a nação,* trans. Maria Júlia Goldwasser (São Paulo: Ática, [1989] 1990).

22 Johnson, "The Institutionalization of Brazilian Modernism," 6–7.

23 Randal Johnson, "The Dynamics of the Brazilian Literary Field: 1930–1945," *Luso-Brazilian Review* 31, no. 2 (1994): 5–7.

24 Benedict Anderson, *Imagined Communities: Reflections on the Origin and Spread of Nationalism,* rev. ed. (New York: Verso, 1991).

25 On the original events that brought culture wars into the halls of Congress, see Richard Bolton, ed., *Culture Wars: Documents from the Recent Controversies in the Arts* (New York: New Press, 1992). For a broader treatment of culture warfare in America, see James Davidson Hunter, *Culture Wars: The Struggle to Define America* (New York: Basic Books, 1991); and James Nolan Jr., ed., *The American Culture Wars: Current Contests and Future Prospects* (Charlottesville: University of Virginia Press, 1996).

26 See Bolton, *Culture Wars;* and Edward T. Linenthal and Tom Engelhardt, eds., *History Wars: The Enola Gay and Other Battles for the American Past* (New York: Metropolitan Books, 1996).

2 Cultural Management before 1930

1 The term "cultural management" is my invention. The closest Portuguese translation would be *administração cultural* (literally: cultural administration). Terms used by the Vargas regime to describe what I call "management" included *desenvolvimento* (development), *apoio* (help), *estímulo* (stimulus), *incentivo* (incentive), *proteção* (protection), and *valorização* (validation). I believe that management/*administração*—with its rationalized, administrative, and bureaucratic connotations—best captures the Vargas regime's relationship to the cultural field.

2 Maria Margaret Lopes, *O Brasil descobre a pesquisa científica: os museus e as ciências naturais no século XIX* (São Paulo: HUCITEC, 1997), 25–29.

3 Azevedo, *Brazilian Culture,* 236.

4 It was once thought that officials in the court of João VI actively sought out Lebreton to come to Brazil. Recent scholarship indicates that it was Lebreton who sought the protection of the Portuguese Court after the fall of Napoleon Bonaparte. See the biographical appendix for a complete list of mission members.

5 Mário Pedrosa, "Os obstáculos políticos à Missão Artística Francesa," in *Acadêmicos e modernistas* (São Paulo: Editora da Universidade de São Paulo, [1955] 1998), 41–113.

6 Jeffrey Needell, "The Domestic Civilizing Mission: The Cultural Role of the State in Brazil, 1808–1930," *Luso-Brazilian Review* 36, no. 1 (1999): 3–6.

7 José Carlos Durand, *Arte, privilégio, e distinção: artes plásticas, arquitetura e classe dirigente no Brasil, 1855/1985* (São Paulo: Perspectiva, 1989), 24–31.

8 Lilia Mortiz Schwarcz, *As barbas do imperador: D. Pedro II, monarca nos trópicos* (São Paulo: Companhia das Letras, 1998), esp. 125–57.

9 Schwarcz, *As barbas do imperador,* 155–57.

10 José Roberto Teixeira Leite, *Dicionário crítico da pintura no Brasil* (Rio de Janeiro: Artlivre, 1987), 330–31.

11 Jeffrey Needell, *A Tropical Belle Époque: Elite Culture in Turn-of-the-Century Rio de Janeiro* (Cambridge: Cambridge University Press, 1987).

12 Velloso, *Os intelectuais e a política cultural do Estado Novo*, 7–13.

13 Sérgio Miceli, *Poder, sexo e letras na República Velha (Estudo clínico dos anatolianos)* (São Paulo: Perspectiva, 1977).

14 Carlos Zillio, "A modernidade efêmera: anos 80 na Academia," in *180 anos de Escola de Belas Artes. Anais do Seminário EBA 180* (Rio de Janeiro: Universidade Federal do Rio de Janeiro, 1996), 237–42.

15 *Reflexos do impressionismo no Museu Nacional de Belas Artes* (Rio de Janeiro: O Museu, 1974), Introduction.

16 Nicolau Sevcenko, *Literatura como missão: tensões sociais e criação cultural na Primeira República* (São Paulo: Brasilense, 1983), esp. 119–98.

17 Monteiro Lobato's famous article appears in Mário de Silva Brito, *A história do modernismo: antecedentes da Semana de Arte Moderna*, 5th ed. (Rio de Janeiro: Civilização Brasileira, 1978), 52–56.

18 Margarida de Souza Neves, *Vitrines do Progresso*, Ph.D. dissertation, Pontífica Universidade Católica do Rio de Janeiro, 1986, 71.

19 On the *tenentes* and *tenentismo*, see John D. Wirth, "*Tenentismo* in the Brazilian Revolution of 1930," *Hispanic American Historical Review* 44, no. 2 (May 1964): 161–79; José Murilo de Carvalho, "Forças armadas e política, 1930–1945," in *A Revolução de 30: Seminário internacional* (Brasília: Editora da Universidade de Brasília, 1980), 109–50.

20 Aracy A. Amaral, *As artes plásticas na semana de 22: subsídios para uma história da renovaçao das artes no Brasil*, 5th ed. (São Paulo: Editora 34, 1998), 123–29.

21 Graça Aranha, "A emoção estética na Arte Moderna," reprinted in A. Amaral, *As artes plásticas na semana de 22*, 268–73.

22 A. Amaral, *As artes plásticas na semana de 22*, 197–218.

23 Andrade's speech, entitled "A escrava que não é Isaura" (The slave that is not Isaura), a wordplay on the Bernando Guimarães novel *A escrava Isaura* (1875), was a preliminary draft of an essay of the same name published in 1925. Quotes taken from Mário de Andrade, "A escrava que não é Isaura," reprinted in Jorge Schwartz, *Vanguardas Latino-Americanas: Polêmicas, manifestos e textos críticos* (São Paulo: Editora da Universidade de São Paulo: Iluminuras: FAPESP, 1995), 126–34.

24 A. Amaral, *As artes plásticas*, 205.

25 Modernismo carioca has recently received the scholarly attention it deserves. See Angela Castro Gomes, *Essa gente do Rio: Modernismo e modernidade* (Rio de Janeiro: Editora Fundação Getúlio Vargas, 1999); and Mônica Pimenta Velloso, *Modernismo no Rio de Janeiro: Turunas e Quixotes* (Rio de Janeiro: Editora Fundação Getúlio Vargas, 1996).

26 Morse, "The Multiverse of Latin American Identity," 19.

27 Although I believe that Randal Johnson underestimates how competition constrained modernism's political institutionalization, I fully endorse his argument that "modernism became institutionalized during and *within* the Estado Novo, thus serving to reproduce the literary/intellectual field's position within the broader field of power and to reinforce the state's role as an agent of intellectual and cultural legitimation" (emphasis in original). Johnson, "The Institutionalization of Brazilian Modernism," 15.

28 Augusto da Silva Telles, "Neocolonial: la polémica de José Mariano," in *Arquitectura Neocolonial: América Latina, Caribe, Estados Unidos,* ed. Aracy Amaral (São Paulo: Memorial da América Latina/Fundo de Cultura Económica, 1994), 237–43.

29 CPDOC-GCg 36.03.24/2 Doc. IV-27, Draft Proposal for "Inspetoria de Monumentos Públicos de Arte," mid-1920s.

30 On the prehistory of the MHN, see Noah Charles Elkin, "1922: o encontro do efêmero com a permanência," *Anais do Museu Histórico Nacional* (hereafter *AMHN*) 29 (1997): 121–40.

31 Ricardo Murues de Azevedo, "Las ideas de Ricardo Severo y la relación con el academismo," in Amaral, *Arquitectura neocolonial,* 249–58.

32 For an illuminating discussion of Le Corbusian modernism that ties in nicely with the history of Brazilian modernism, see James Holston, *The Modernist City: An Anthropological Critique of Brasília* (Chicago: University of Chicago Press, 1989), 31–58.

33 Oswald de Andrade, "Manifesto Pau-Brasil," in Schwartz, *Vanguardas Latino-Americanas,* 135–38.

34 Oswald de Andrade, *Pau-Brasil* (Paris: Sans Pareil, 1925), 99.

35 Aracy Amaral, *Blaise Cendrars no Brasil e os modernistas,* 2d ed. (São Paulo: Editora 34, 1997), 66–70.

36 Oswald de Andrade, "Manifesto Antropófago," in Schwartz, *Vanguardas Latino-Americanas,* 142–47.

37 A. Amaral, *Blaise Cendrars no Brasil,* 74.

38 See, for example, João do Norte (pseudonym for Gustavo Barroso), "Arquitetura Nacional," *O Jornal* (Rio), 26 May 1921, reprinted in *AMHN* 3 (1942): 455–65.

39 On antiurban tendencies within conservative thought in the 1910s and 1920s, see Marly Silva da Motta, *A nação faz 100 anos: a questão nacional no Centenário da Independência* (Rio de Janeiro: Editora da Fundação Getúlio Vargas/CPDOC, 1992), 34–35.

40 Located at Rua Itápolis, 961, in the Pacembú neighborhood of São Paulo, Warchavchik's Casa Modernista combined the functionalist lines of modernist architecture with avant-garde interior decor and landscaping. The

house represented the collaborative works of many of the principals of paulista modernism. See Geraldo Ferraz, *Warchavchik e a introdução da nova arquitetura no Brasil: 1925 a 1940* (São Paulo: Museu de Arte de São Paulo, 1965), 82–99.

41   Vargas, "Discurso de posse na Academia Brasileira de Letras," *Cultura Política* 4, no. 37 (February 1944): 9. See also Velloso, *Os intelectuais e a política cultural*, 7–13.

42   Miceli, *Intelectuais e classe dirigente no Brasil*, 131.

3   Cultural Management, 1930–1945

1   The standard English-language monograph on state building under the Vargas regime remains Thomas E. Skidmore's *Politics in Brazil, 1930-1964.* More recent studies of the Vargas state include Ronald Schneider, *Order and Progress: A Political History of Brazil* (Boulder: Westview Press, 1991); René Gertz, "Estado Novo: um inventário historiográfico," in *O Feixe: o autoritarismo como questão teórica e historiográfica* (Rio de Janeiro: Jorge Zahar, 1991), 111–31; and Dulce Pandolfi, org., *Repensando o Estado Novo* (Rio de Janeiro: Editora da Fundação Getúlio Vargas, 1999). For two contemporaneous assessments of the Vargas state, see Simon Schwartzman, org., *Estado Novo, um auto-retrato* (Brasília: Editora Universidade de Brasília, [1945] 1982); and Karl Lowenstein, *Brazil under Vargas* (New York: Macmillan, 1942).

2   *Dicionário Histórico e Biográfico Brasileiro* (hereafter DHBB), ed. Israel Beloch and Alzira de Abreu (Rio de Janeiro: Forense Universitária/FGV/CPDOC; FINEP, 1984), 1766–69.

3   Francisco Campos, *Educação e Cultura* (Rio de Janeiro: José Olympio Editora, 1940), 117–19.

4   On racial theories and social policy in late-nineteenth- and twentieth-century Brazil, see Thomas E. Skidmore, *Black into White;* Jeffrey Lesser, "Immigration and Shifting Concepts of National Identity in Brazil during the Vargas Era," *Luso-Brazilian Review* 31, no. 2 (1994): 27–48; and Nancy Leys Stepan, *The Hour of Eugenics: Race, Gender, and Nation in Latin America* (Ithaca: Cornell University Press, 1991).

5   Jerry Dávila, *Perfecting the Brazilian Race,* Ph.D. dissertation, Brown University, 1999.

6   Decree 19.560, Art. 96, January 1931.

7   Otaíza de Oliveira Romanelli, *História da educação no Brasil (1930–1973)* (Petrópolis: Editora Vozes, 1978), 131–41; and Schwartzman et al., *Tempos de Capanema,* 44–47.

8   "Dois artistas modernistas na Escola de Belas Artes," *Diário da Noite* (São

Paulo), 25 April 1931, reprinted in Lucia Gouvêa Vieira, *Salão de 1931: marco da revelação da arte moderna em nível nacional* (Rio de Janeiro: FUNARTE, 1984), 83–86.

9   Ferraz, *Warchavchik,* 37.

10 Silva Telles, "Neocolonial," 241.

11 On Mariano's anticommunism and anti-Semitism, see Carlos Kessel, "Estilo, discurso, poder: arquitetura neocolonial no Brasil," *Revista Brasileira da História Social* 6 (1999), 65–94. On totalitarian critiques of modern architecture, see William Curtis, *Modern Architecture since 1900,* 3d ed. (London: Phoidon Press, 1996), 351–69.

12 Lucio Costa, "Uma escola viva de Belas Artes," *O Jornal* (Rio), 31 July 1931, reprinted in Vieira, *Salão de 1931,* 87–91; Yves Braund, *Arquitetura contemporânea no Brasil,* 3d ed. (São Paulo: Perspectiva, 1997), 73.

13 Manuel Bandeira, "O Brasil que insiste pintar," *A Província* (São Paulo), 13 September 1928, reprinted in Vieira, *Salão de 1931,* 79–81.

14 Lucio Costa, *Lucio Costa: registro de uma vivência* (São Paulo: Empresa das Artes, 1995), 71.

15 I borrow the term "The Critical Years" from Robert Levine's 1970 study of the Vargas regime.

16 On Capanema's rise to the ministry, see Schwartzman et al., *Tempos de Capanema,* 23–51.

17 CPDOC-GCpi 35.00.00 GC/Capanema (?), "Programa e planos de ação do Ministério," 1935(?).

18 CPDOC-GCf 34.06.21A, Draft for ministerial reform, 1936.

19 For a more lengthy discussion of the intricacies of the *Brasil legal-Brasil real* dichotomy, as well as the reconstitution of the meaning of the term *democracia,* see Ângela Maria de Castro Gomes, "O redescobrimento do Brasil," in Oliveira et al., *Estado Novo: ideologia e poder,* 109–50.

20 CPDOC-GCg 38.06.06 Doc. 1, Letter from Capanema to Vargas, 6 July 1938.

21 Decree-Law 526, 1 July 1938.

22 *Anuário Estatístico do Brasil* (1937), 751 and (1941/1945), 457.

23 "Cultura e Serviço Social," *Revista do Serviço Público* 1/3, no. 1 (July 1938): 3–5.

24 CPDOC-GCg 35.00.00/2.

25 Arquivo Nacional, Arquivos Pessoais, Arquivo Jonathas Serrano (hereafter AN-AP 55) Caixa 21, Pasta 1, "O cinema na educação de adultos," speech delivered by Celso Kelly to the Associação Brasileira de Educação, 1938.

26 AN-AP 55 Caixa 21, Pasta 1. The Secretariado de Cinema da Ação Católica Brasileira was founded 18 October 1938. Serrano had published earlier works on film and education, including *Cinema e educação* (São Paulo: Melhoramentos, 1930).

27 CPDOC-GCf 34.08.14/2 and CPDOC-GCg 35.00.00/3 Doc. I-8, "Relatório do In-

stituto Nacional do Cinema Educativo ao Ministro de Educação," 24 February 1937.

28   CPDOC-GCg 35.00.00/2 Doc. I-2.

29   CPDOC-GCg 35.00.00/2 Doc. I-1, "Exposição dos Motivos," 24 February 1936.

30   For the complete catalogue of INCE releases for the period 1936–1945, see Carlos Roberto de Souza, *Catálogo: Filmes produzidos pelo INCE* (Rio de Janeiro: Fundação do Cinema Brasileiro, 1990), 138–42.

31   Long-term budgeting for the INCE is nearly impossible to determine. What is certain is that the agency received less than 60 percent of its original request for 680 contos in start-up funding. Underfunding would remain a constant challenge for the agency's director.

32   CPDOC-GCi 34.06.00 Doc. II-10, "Plano de reorganização da administração federal," written by Gustavo Capanema at the request of José Américo de Almeida, July 1937.

33   CPDOC-GCg 38.06.06 Doc. 1, Memo from Capanema to Vargas, 6 June 1938. First mentioned in the 1937 reform of the MES, the Conselho Nacional de Cultura [CNC] was created in July 1938 and convened in October of that year. Capanema modeled the CNC after the National Educational Council. Although the CNC was given broad legal powers to set the ministry's cultural agenda, the council's accomplishments never lived up to its legal potential.

34   CPDOC-GCg 38.06.06 Doc. 9, Unsigned proposal to create Conselho Nacional de Cultura/DIP, 1940. The DIP never received authorization to create its own cultural council.

35   In September 1936, the defunct Radio Sociedade do Rio de Janeiro, a semi-professional radio club broadcasting under the call letters PRA-2, donated its studio and transmission facilities to the Ministry of Education. Capanema and Edgard Roquette-Pinto identified PRA-2 as a perfect vehicle for the federal government to make educational radio a companion to educational film. The Instituto Nacional do Cinema Educativo exercised oversight of educational radio while the Serviço de Radiodifusão Educativa (SRE) awaited administrative autonomy. Despite efforts by Pinto and Capanema to get executive approval of the SRE's internal regulations, ongoing tensions between the Ministry of Education and the Ministry of Justice and the Department of Press and Propaganda prevented the SRE from exercising autonomy until 1943.

36   CPDOC-GCg 36.12.00A Doc. I-6, Letter from Capanema to Vargas, 21 December 1937.

37   CPDOC-GCg 36.12.00 Doc. I-8, Letter from Capanema to Vargas, 28 February 1938.

38   CPDOC-GCg 36.2.00 Doc. I-9, Letter from Luiz Simões Lopes, 10 May 1938.

39   CPDOC-GCg 34.09.22 Doc. 5, Letter from Lourival Fontes to Vargas, 5 July 1942.

40 Schwartzman et al., *Tempos de Capanema,* 83–84.

41 Daryle Williams, "Gustavo Capanema, Ministro de Cultura," in *Capanema, o ministro e o ministério.,* ed. Angela Castro Gomes (Rio de Janeiro: Fundação Getúlio Vargas: São Francisco, 2000), 251–69.

42 CPDOC-GCg 35.04.30 Doc. VI-4, Letter from Capanema to Vargas in response to an earlier letter from Procópio Ferreira, 24 February 1938.

43 Helena Bomeny, *Guardiães da razão: modernistas mineiros* (Rio de Janeiro: Editora UFRJ, 1994), 117–40, esp. 121–27.

44 Miceli, *Intelectuais e classe dirigente,* 159.

45 *Dom Casmurro,* 2 August 1939, as quoted in Paulo Mendes de Almeida, *De Anita ao museu* (São Paulo: Perspectiva, 1976), 145–46.

46 Like many before me, I unsuccessfully tried to locate the DIP files. On the methodological challenge of reconstructing a history of the DIP without the agency's central archive, see Heloísa Helena de Jesus Paulo, "O DIP e a juventude—ideologia e propaganda estatal (1939/1945)," *Revista Brasileira da História* 7, no. 14 (1987): 99–113.

47 Decree-Law 1.915, 27 December 1939.

48 The organization of DEIPs (Departamentos *Estaduais* de Imprensa e Propaganda) were authorized under Decree-Law 2.557, issued on 4 September 1940. The decree also provided for federal assistance in the establishment of municipal DIPs. In practice, municipal DIPs were never organized, while several states were unable to organize a functioning DEIP. For a comparison between the origins and activities of the federal DIP and the DEIP of the state of São Paulo, see Silvana Goulart, *Sob a verdade oficial: ideologia, propaganda e censura no Estado Novo* (São Paulo: Marco Zero, 1990), 121–62.

49 The *Cine Jornal'*s cinematic style was typical of newsreels of the period, with the combination of strategic editing, fast-paced narration, and upbeat orchestration working to imbue conventional film journalism with an overall optimistic and nationalistic tone. Recurrent subject matter included the inauguration of public works, sporting events, visits of foreign dignitaries, celebrity news, news from the European war front, and civic ceremonies.

50 José Ignácio de Melo, *Ação e imaginário de uma ditadura: controle, coerção, e propaganda política nos meios de comunicação durante o Estado Novo,* master's thesis, Universidade de São Paulo, 1990, 330–40.

51 Randal Johnson, *The Film Industry in Brazil: Culture and the State* (Pittsburgh: University of Pittsburgh Press, 1987), 45, 61.

52 Melo argues that distribution outside the major cities of the Southeast was difficult, especially after 1942. Anecdotal evidence indicates that audiences in Rio and São Paulo purposely arrived late, in order to miss the *Cine Jornal,* while others talked during the screening. A full study of the politics of viewership remains one of the greatest gaps in historiography of the Vargas era.

53 *Cine Jornal Brasileiro: Departamento de Imprensa e Propaganda, 1938–1946* (São Paulo: Cinemateca Brasileira, 1982).

54 Martins Castelo, "Radio VI," *Cultura Política* 1, no. 6 (August 1941): 329–31.

55 Álvaro Salgado, "Radiodifusão, fator social," *Cultura Política* 1, no. 6 (August 1941): 79–93.

56 Allison Raphael, *Samba and Social Control: Popular Culture and Racial Democracy in Rio de Janeiro*, Ph.D. dissertation, Columbia University, 1980; Jairo Severiano, *Getúlio Vargas e a música popular* (Rio de Janeiro: Editora da Fundação Getúlio Vargas, 1983); Antonio Pedro Tota, *Samba da legitimidade*, master's thesis, Universidade de São Paulo, 1980, 67–104; and Salgado, "Radiodifusão, fator social."

57 Severiano has collected a number of popular tunes commissioned by the Estado Novo regime, including the Sebastião Lima-Henrique de Alameida samba *Brasil Brasileiro* (1942) and the Benedito Lacerda-Darci de Oliveira samba *Salve 19 de abril!* (1943). One of the most popular DIP-sponsored ufanist songs was the João de Barro-Alcir Pires Vermelho-Alberto Ribeiro samba *Onde o céu azul é mais azul* (1940). Sambas promoting moral uplift included the Ataulfo Alves-Felisberto Martins composition *É negócio casar* (1941). An English translation of the latter appears in Levine, *Father of the Poor?*, 159–60.

58 Bryan McCann, *Thin Air and the Solid State: Radio, Culture and Politics in Brazil's Vargas Era*, Ph.D. dissertation, Yale University, 1999, chap. 3.

59 Arquivo Nacional, Secretaria da Presidência (hereafter AN-SPE 025) Série 13, Lata 510, Departamento de Imprensa e Propaganda, *Relatório*, 1941. In 1941, the DIP classified its daily press releases according to the following formula: sixteen about the presidency, twenty-two about Rio events, forty three about national events, and thirty-three about international events.

60 According to Nelson Jahr Garcia, the number of *registered* radio receivers jumped from 357,921 to 659,762 during the 1939–1942 period. In 1940, University of Wisconsin professor Walter Sharp visited Brazil and estimated that there were one million receivers in operation in Brazil. Sharp also noted the importance of loudspeakers installed in public squares. See Nelson Jahr Garcia, *Estado Novo e propaganda política* (São Paulo: Edições Loyola, 1982), 102–4; and Walter R. Sharp, "Methods of Opinion Control in Present-Day Brazil," *Public Opinion Quarterly* 5 (March 1941): 3–17.

61 McCann, *Thin Air and the Solid State,* chap. 1.

62 CPDOC-GCg 36.12.00 Doc. III-4, "Relatório do Serviço de Radiodifusão Educativa 1945," reprinted in *Anais do Ministério da Educação e Saúde* (April 1945): 353–85.

63 Decree 21.240, issued 4 April 1932, reorganized film censorship, replacing local censorship with a centralized system to be run out of the Ministry of Education. Brazilian filmmakers had lobbied for the reform in hopes of pro-

tecting and regulating the national film industry. Johnson, *The Film Industry in Brazil*, 46–48.

64   CPDOC-GCg 36.12.00 Doc. III-4.

65   Decree-Law 7.582, issued 28 May 1945; Goulart, *Sob a verdade oficial*, 75–76.

4   "The Identity Documents of the Brazilian Nation":
The National Historical and Artistic Patrimony

1   In the English language, the term *heritage* appears more frequently than the Latin-derived *patrimony*. I prefer the latter term for its resonance within the Luso-Brazilian concept of patrimony as a collection of material and spiritual capital, passed on from one generation to the next, much like an inheritance. Formalized in Brazilian federal law in 1937, the term *patrimônio histó-rico e artístico nacional* is closely associated with the modernists' readings of cultural heritage and renewal. Conservatives also used the term *patrimônio* although they were just as likely to use alternative terms such as *monumentos* and *arte tradicional*. Today, the terms *patrimônio histórico, patrimônio cultural*, or simply, *patrimônio*, are frequently used interchangeably. The term *patrimônio da humanidade* (English equivalent: World Heritage), entered into Brazil's preservationist lexicon in the late 1970s, when UNESCO began to maintain a list of sites and structures of international historical, archaeological, and ecological significance.

2   The term *tombamento* (verb: *tombar*) is deeply rooted in Luso-Brazilian history. Originating in the Latin word for archive or repository *tumulum*, the term tombamento was historically associated with official registries of property and wealth. The Portuguese National Archives continue to be called the Torre do Tombo, in reference to the tower that once housed official property registries. When the term tombamento was integrated into Brazilian preservationist law in the mid-1930s, its meaning was fixed in an administrative process of *formally* inscribing important historical sites and works of art in official registries, known as *Livros do Tombo*.

3   Rodrigo Melo Franco de Andrade (hereafter RMFA), *Rodrigo e o SPHAN: coletânea de textos sobre patrimônio cultural* (Rio de Janeiro: Ministério da Cultura, Secretaria do Patrimônio Histórico e Artístico Nacional; Fundação Pró-Memória, 1987), 21.

4   As a descriptor of SPHAN activities under the directorship of Rodrigo Melo Franco de Andrade, the term *fase heróica* appears in *Projeto de vitalização do patrimônio cultural no Brasil: uma trajetória* (Brasília: Ministério da Educação e Cultura: SPHAN: Fundação Pró-Memória, 1980), 27–33.

5   See, for example, Ítalo Campofiorito, "Muda o mundo do patrimônio: Notas para um balanço crítico," *Revista do Brasil* 2, no. 4 (1985): 32–43; and Dalton

Sala Jr., "O Serviço do Patrimônio Histórico e Artístico Nacional: história oficial e Estado Novo," master's thesis, Universidade de São Paulo, 1988.

6 No stranger to the complicated political and aesthetic environment in which the IPHAN operates, Ítalo Campofiorito still chooses to reinforce the conventional wisdom that the figures most closely associated with the SPHAN were "of a humanist strain, progressive, of a democratic or leftist inclination" who wanted little to do with the authoritarian aspects of the regime. Ítalo Campofiorito, "Introdução—as Primeiras Árvores," *Revista do Patrimônio* 26 (1997): 10–18.

7 On the relationship between patrimony and national rituals, see Néstor García Canclini, *Hybrid Cultures: Strategies for Entering and Leaving Modernity* (Minneapolis: University of Minnesota Press, 1995), 107–44.

8 The most important conservation projects accomplished during the Old Republic, all financed by regional governments, were conducted at the Forte de São Tiago (a.k.a. Forte São João da Bertioga, São Paulo), the Forte do Monte Serrat (Bahia), and the Mission at São Miguel (Rio Grande do Sul). For the "pre-history" (that is, pre-SPHAN) of preservation, see RMFA, *Brasil: monumentos históricos e arqueológicos* (Mexico City: Instituto Panamericano de Geografia e História, 1952), 11–60.

9 Main Archive of the Instituto Histórico Geográfico Brasileiro, Rio de Janeiro (hereafter IHGB) Lata 341, Pasta 146, Letter from Conde de Affonso Celso, president of IHGB, to Epitácio Pessoa, 22 December 1921. On 31 March 1922, Minister of Justice Joaquim Ferreira Chaves informed the IHGB that Casa de Marília would be spared and that the Casa dos Inconfidentes would be purchased with the financial assistance of the state of Minas Gerais.

10 For the best English-language study of the Inconfidência Mineira, see Kenneth Maxwell, *Conflicts and Conspiracies: Brazil and Portugal, 1750–1808* (Cambridge: Cambridge University Press, 1973).

11 Brazil, Ministério da Agricultura, Indústria, e Commercio. Diretoria Geral da Estatística, *Recenseamento do Brazil* (1920), vol. IV, part II (Rio de Janeiro: n.p., 1928), 97; Brazil, Instituto Brasileiro Geográfico e Estatístico, *Recenseamento Geral do Brasil (1940),* Série Regional, parte XII—Minas Gerais (Rio de Janeiro: n.p., 1950), 372.

12 IHGB Lata 575, Pasta 64, Memo from Washington Pires to Vargas, "Exposição de Motivos," early July 1933.

13 For more discussion of the legal impact of Decree-Law 25, see Sonia Rabello Castro, *O estado na preservação de bens culturais* (Rio de Janeiro: Renovar, 1991); and Antonio A. Queiroz Telles, *Tombamento e seu regime jurídico* (São Paulo: Revista dos Tribunais, 1992).

14 Museu Histórico Nacional-Arquivo Permanente (hereafter MHN-AP) DG I-I (8), *Relatório Anual de 1931.*

15 Until 1942, the basic unit of Brazilian currency was the *milréis,* written as

1$000. One thousand milréis (1:000$000) equaled one *conto*. In 1942, the *cruzeiro* (Cr$) replaced the milréis as the basic unit of currency. In the currency conversion, milréis were converted to cruzeiros at a 1:1 ratio. One conto equaled one thousand cruzeiros. In a few instances, I have included equivalents amount in U.S. dollars, based on the annual exchange rates cited in Robert Levine, *The Vargas Regime: The Critical Years, 1934–1938.* (New York: Columbia University Press, 1970), Appendix D.

16 Written documentation on IMN's activities in Ouro Preto is limited. Volume V (1944) of the *Anais do Museu Histórico Nacional* reprints correspondence between Macedo and Barroso concerning IMN activities in Ouro Preto, but the two wrote of little besides the technical and financial aspects of restoration.

17 Márcia Regina Romero Chuva, *Os arquitetos da memória: a construção do patrimônio histórico e artístico nacional no Brasil (anos 30 e 40)*, Ph.D. dissertation, Universidade Federal Fluminense, 1998, 51–52, 281–89.

18 The anteprojeto has been reprinted in numerous places including Mário de Andrade, *Mário de Andrade, cartas do trabalho: correspondência com Rodrigo Melo Franco de Andrade (1936–1945)* (Brasília: Secretaria do Patrimônio Histórico e Artístico Nacional, Fundação Pró-Memória, 1981), 39–54. An abbreviated English-language version is available at: http://www.inform.umd.edu/ LAS/projects/neh/papers/MAndrade.html

19 The four *Livros do Tombo* and their corresponding museums were: (1) the Archaeological and Ethnographic Registry and the Museum of Archaeology and Ethnography, responsible for archaeological, Amerindian, and popular art; (2) the Historical Registry and the Historical Museum, responsible for historical art; (3) the Fine Arts Registry and the National Gallery of Fine Arts, responsible for high national and foreign art; and (4) the Applied Arts Registry and the Museum of Applied Arts and Industrial Techniques, responsible for national and foreign applied arts.

20 CPDOC-GCg 36.03.24/2 Doc. I-3, Exposição dos Capanema to Vargas, Exposição dos Motivos.

21 Andrade, *Mário de Andrade, cartas do trabalho,* 60.

22 Luís Rodolfo Vilhena, *Projeto e missão: o movimento folclórico brasileiro, 1947–1964* (Rio de Janeiro: Fundação Getúlio Vargas/MinC, FUNARTE, 1997), 75–124.

23 Fonseca, *O patrimônio em processo,* 159–80.

24 *O Jornal* (Rio de Janeiro), 30 October 1936, reprinted in *Rodrigo e o SPHAN,* 48–49.

25 Dalton Sala Jr., "O Serviço do Patrimônio Histórico e Artístico Nacional e a questão das reduções jesuíticas da Bacia do Prata: um capítulo da historiografia artística brasileira durante o Estado Novo (1937–1945)," *Estudos Ibero-Americanos* 15, no. 1 (1989): 245–57.

26 Fonseca, *O patrimônio em processo,* 125–27.

27 Chuva, *Os arquitetos da memória,* appendix 6.

28 Instituto do Patrimônio Histórico e Artístico Nacional, Arquivo e Biblioteca Noronha Santos, Arquivo Técnico e Administrativo (hereafter IPHAN-ATA), Moldagens, Letter from Eduardo Bejarano Tecles to RMFA, 8 August 1938.

29 *Jornal do Brasil* (Rio), 24 March 1937.

30 Arquivo Municipal da Prefeitura de Ouro Preto (hereafter AMPOP) Caixa 1890/1948, Letter from Washington Dias to RMFA, 5 December 1938.

31 The full text of Costa's wonderful letter to Capanema appears in Lia Motta, "O SPHAN e Ouro Preto: uma história de conceitos e critérios," in *Revista do Patrimônio Histórico e Artístico Nacional* 22 (1987): 108–22, esp. 109–10.

32 José Mariano (Filho), "Le Chaperon Rouge," *Meio-Dia* (Rio), 28 April 1939. For additional texts, see the *pernambucano*'s self-published *À margem do problema arquitetônico nacional* (Rio de Janeiro, 1943).

33 For additional discussion of the debate surrounding the Grande Hotel de Ouro Preto, see Lauro Cavalcanti, *As preocupações do belo: arquitetura moderna brasileira dos anos 30/40* (Rio de Janeiro: Taurus Editora, 1995), 151–70.

34 *Correio da Manhã* (Rio), 12 January 1939.

35 CPDOC-CGg 36.03.24/2-A Doc. III-24. The ten-minute feature program, hosted by Antônio Leal, was broadcast weekly 10 November 1944 through 30 March 1945.

36 *Bens móveis e imóveis inscritos nos Livros do Tombo do Instituto do Patrimônio Histórico e Artístico Nacional,* 4th ed. (Rio de Janeiro: Ministério da Cultura, Instituto do Patrimônio Histórico e Artístico Nacional, 1994), 247.

37 José Carlos Durand makes a variation on the import substitution model, arguing that the drop in the availability of European fine and decorative art brought on by the Great Depression stimulated domestic demand for Brazilian artwork. Although the evidence to support such an argument is mainly anecdotal, Durand's thesis is consistent with his better-substantiated argument that a domestic antique market grew in the 1930s. See Durand, *Arte, privilégio, e distinção,* 92–98; See also *Rodrigo e o SPHAN,* 25–27.

38 Hernan Lima, "Museus regionais," *Cultura Política* 5, no. 49 (February 1945): 98–112.

39 Article 72, Subsection 17 of the Constitution of 1891 stated, "Property rights are fully respected, except in cases in which expropriation is necessary for public utility, subject to indemnification."

40 Decree-Law 25, Chapter II, Article 8 stated, "Compulsory tombamento arises when the property owner refuses inscription [into the *Livro do Tombo*]."

41 CPDOC-CGg 36.03.24/2-A Doc. III-24, Second *Palestra,* 17 November 1944.

42 *O Jornal* (Rio), 30 October 1936, reprinted in *Rodrigo e o SPHAN,* 48–49.

43 José Reginaldo Santos Gonçalves, *A retórica da perda: os discursos do patri-mônio cultural no Brasil* (Rio de Janeiro: Editora UFRJ/MinC/IPHAN, 1996), 32–33.

44 IPHAN-ATA Casos Juridicas: Arco do Teles, "Conciliando o progresso com as relíquias do passado," *Gazeta Judiciário* (Rio), 30 June 1961.

45 IPHAN-ATA Processo de Tombamento 99-T-38: Arco do Teles, 1938.

46 IPHAN-ATA Casos Jurídicos: Arco do Teles, Noronha Santos, "O incêndio do Senado da Câmara e o Arco do Teles," 31 January 1940.

47 *Diário da Justiça* (Rio), 19 April 1940.

48 IPHAN-ATA Casos Jurídicos: Arco do Teles, Brief to Case 7.377, 27 September 1940. Emphasis in original.

49 CPDOC-GCg 36.03.24/2 Doc. II-19, Summary of SPHAN activities, 1936–1940.

50 IPHAN-ATA Casos Jurídicos: Arco do Teles, Brief to Case 7.377 submitted by Gabriel de Rezende Passos to Supremo Tribunal Federal, 24 November 1941.

51 *Diário da Justiça* (Rio de Janeiro), 11 February 1943, 855.

52 CPDOC-CGg 36.03.24/2-A Doc. III-24, Third *Palestra,* 24 November 1944.

53 CPDOC-CGg 36.03.24/2-A Doc. III-24, Fourth *Palestra,* 1 December 1944.

54 IPHAN-ATA Representante: Gustavo Capanema, Pasta I, Letter from RMFA to Capanema, 18 May 1936.

55 Speech delivered to Escola Nacional de Engenharia, 27 September 1939, re-printed in *Rodrigo e o SPHAN,* 49–55.

56 Museu da Inconfidência—Museologia, "Relação das peças do Museu Ar-quidocesano de Mariana oferecidas pelo Sr. Arcebispo ao Museu dos Incon-fidentes [*sic*]," 30 August 1940.

57 See Paulo Duarte, *Contra o vandalismo e o extermínio* (São Paulo n.p., 1938), 217–25, and IPHAN-ATA Representante: Helvécio Gomes de Oliveira.

58 Chuva, *Os arquitetos da memória,* 260–63.

59 AN-SPE 025 (Fundo 25) Lata 21, Governos Estaduais: Minas Gerais, *Memorial* from João Baptista Ferreira Velloso, Mayor of Ouro Preto, May 1934. This petition was likely sent to the interventor of Minas Gerais before being for-warded to Vargas on 23 May 1934. It makes a request for 2,300 contos for public works and infrastructural improvements, which, the municipality ar-gued, were necessary to stimulate regional tourism. There is no record of the federal response, if any.

60 IPHAN-ATA Processo de Tombamento 70-T-38, Letter from Washington de Araújo Dias to RMFA, 29 March 1938; and AMPOP Caixa 1890/1948, Letter from Washington Dias to RMFA, 5 December 1938.

61 CPDOC-GCg 34.12.11g Doc. IV-10, Speech delivered at inauguration of Museu da Inconfidência, 11 August 1944.

62 Two of the most important federally underwritten texts describing Ouro Preto as a tourist destination were *Travel in Brazil* (Rio de Janeiro: Brazilian Representation to New York's World Fair, 1940); and Manuel Bandeira, *Guia*

de Ouro Preto (Rio de Janeiro: Serviço do Patrimônio Histórico e Artístico Nacional, 1939). Another important text, by Germaine Krull, *Uma cidade antiga do Brasil: Ouro Preto* (Lisbon: Edições Atlântico, 1943) was published by the Brazilian Section of the Portuguese Secretariado Nacional de Propaganda. Together, these three texts received wide distribution in Brazil, the United States, and Portugal.

63 Chuva, *Os arquitetos da memória,* 193.

64 Chuva cites only three instances in which a tombamento process was initiated from outside of the SPHAN. My research indicates that this figure is too low. Numerous requests for tombamento were made directly to Vargas. Such requests are scattered throughout the Secretaria da Presidência archives held at the Arquivo Nacional (AN-SPE 025). The annexed documentation indicates that the Office of the President typically forwarded the request to the Ministry of Education, where the matter was considered by the SPHAN. When the correspondence is complete, the documents generally indicate that the requests were denied due to a lack of historical importance. It is interesting to note that these requests typically came from small towns seeking financial assistance for the repair of local churches.

65 For U.S. and British cases, see Diane Barthel, *Historic Preservation: Collective Memory and Historical Identity* (New Brunswick, N.J.: Rutgers University Press, 1996).

66 Motta, "O SPHAN em Ouro Preto."

67 IPHAN-ATA Representante: Eduardo Tecles, Pasta I, Correspondence between Tecles and RMFA, March 1945. Tecles warned Andrade that impoverished property owners in Ouro Preto lacked the means to maintain decaying properties. Well aware of the reality that the SPHAN "was not created for philanthropic purposes," Tecles still warned that should the agency fail to address the question of popular housing located in historical zones, the overarching rationale of preservation would be subverted. Andrade replied that it would be impossible to dedicate the SPHAN's limited budget to residential restorations. Citing the unique case of Ouro Preto and the federal government's special obligations there, Andrade suggested that the service develop a plan to stabilize residential structures on the verge of collapse.

68 Edgard Jacintho, *Memória Oral* (Rio de Janeiro: Fundação Pró-Memória, 1983), 3–7.

69 Arlindo Vieira, "A Cidade dos Sinos," *Correio da Manhã* (Rio de Janeiro), 3 July 1948. Vieira comments, "the residents of the venerated historic zone [of São João del Rey], in fear of the SPHAN's zeal, have sought out the town's modern quarters and abandoned the old city that in the future might become a mound of ruins."

70 CPDOC-GCg 36.03.24/2 Doc. III-13.

71 CPDOC-CGg 36.03.24/2-A Doc. III-24, Twelfth *Palestra,* 2 February 1945.

72   IPHAN-ATA A23 002 05, *Relatório de 1945.*

73   At an estimated cost of 263,897 contos, the municipal government of Rio de Janeiro gained the right-of-way to complete an easterly extension of the Avenida Canal do Mangue 4 kilometers in length and 96 meters in width. The new thoroughfare cut a wide swath directly through an area of downtown Rio containing low-lying commercial-residential structures constructed since the late-colonial era. For a detailed study of the construction/destruction of Avenida Presidente Vargas, see Evelyn Furkim Werneck Lima, *Avenida Presidente Vargas: uma drástica cirurgia* (Rio de Janeiro: Biblioteca Carioca, 1990).

74   CPDOC-GCg 36.03.24/2 Doc. III-9, Letter from RMFA to Capanema, 16 November 1942.

75   See John D. Wirth, *Minas Gerais in the Brazilian Federation, 1889–1937* (Stanford: Stanford University Press, 1977), 20–64, for a synopsis of the regional economies of the state of Minas Gerais during the first fifty years of republican rule.

76   SPHAN-ATA Representante: Eduardo Tecles, Pasta IV, Letter from RMFA to Washington Araújo Dias, 28 September 1945.

77   IPHAN-ATA Correspondência: Estado de Minas, Letter from Ovisio de Abreu, Secretário do Interior, to Mineiro Mayors, 24 February 1943.

78   Numerous letters of protest from Racioppi to Vargas and Capanema are scattered throughout AN-SPE 025 Série 17.3. Racioppi specifically criticized the restorations of the Igreja São Francisco de Assis and Capela Padre Faria and the construction of the modernist Grande Hotel.

79   *Diário de Notícias* (Rio), 12 October 1940.

80   Getúlio Vargas, "Perante as Cinzas dos Inconfidentes," *A nova política do Brasil* (hereafter *NPB*) (Rio de Janeiro: José Olympio, 1938–1947), 5:255–61.

81   See Alcântara's introduction to *O Museu da Inconfidência* (São Paulo: Banco Safra, 1995), 14–15.

82   On São Paulo's attempt to have Toledo Pisa's remains buried in Taubaté, see CPDOC-GC 35.09.26g Doc. II-3, and AN-SPE 025 Série 17.3, Lata 106. On the Peixoto case, see AN-SPE 025 Série 17.3, Lata 22.

83   Augusto de Lima (Junior) *Vila Rica do Ouro Preto: síntese histórica e descritiva* (Belo Horizonte n.p., 1957), 225–28.

84   CPDOC-GCg 34.12.11 Doc. IV-9. At the inaugural ceremonies, Andrade spoke, "The creation of the Museu da Inconfidência in Ouro Preto marks the beginning of a new and significant direction adopted by the federal government with respect to national museums. No longer limiting itself to the organization and development of these institutions in the Capital of the Republic, the government has resolved to create and maintain them in the interior of the country. Thus, the invaluable cultural reach which these institutions attain will not be confined to the Federal District."

5   Museums and Memory

1   Nicolau Sevcenko, *Orfeu extático na metróple: São Paulo sociedade e cultura nos frementes anos 20* (São Paulo: Companhia das Letras, 1992).

2   Pierre Nora's project on "memory sites" has been highly influential in Brazilian cultural history for more than a decade. With the recent English-language translation of Nora's monumental edited collection *Lieux de memóire,* the concept of "realms of memory" resonates in North American scholarship on the cultural history of nationalism. See, for starters, Nora's introduction to *Realms of Memory* (New York: Columbia University Press, 1996), 1: 1–21; and John Gillis, "Memory and Identity: The History of a Relationship," in *Commemorations: The Politics of National Identity,* ed. John Gillis (Princeton: Princeton University Press, 1994), 3–24.

3   Often translated as "nostalgia" or "longing," *saudade* does not have a precise equivalent in English. On the anthropological meanings of saudade, see Roberto da Matta, "Antropologia da saudade," in *Conta de mentiroso: sete ensaios de antropologia brasileira* (Rio de Janeiro: Rocco, 1993), 17–34.

4   "I challenge anyone to try to reverse this lamentable state of things. . . . Put on a historical pageant or organize a traditional mounted procession to remind us of the founding of the city by Mem de Sá, replete with Indians with crowns-of-feathers and helmeted soldiers. Try to reenact the procession that took Tiradentes to the gallows of Lampadosa. You will quickly see that everyone will laugh at your charade." For a full-text English translation, see http://www.inform.umd.edu/LAS/projects/neh/weekIV.html.

5   Text quoted in Adolpho Dumans, "A idéia da criação do Museu Histórico Nacional," *AMHN* 29 (1997): 13–23.

6   Decree 15.596, issued 2 August 1922.

7   On debates surrounding the creation of the Museu Histórico, see Elkin, "1922: o encontro do efêmero com a permanência," 126–131.

8   There is conflicting evidence on the circumstances surrounding Barroso's dismissal from the MHN in late 1930. Winz (1960) ascribes the dismissal to Barroso's support of Prestes, while Barroso claimed in a letter to Vargas that his dismissal was a result of the capricious personal politics of Francisco Campos. See MHN-AP Gustavo Barroso Dodt Personnel File, handwritten draft of letter from Barroso to Vargas, *c.* 1935.

9   MHN-AP *Relatórios* of 1931 and 1932; MHN-SCP 18/32; The Curso de Museus was authorized by Decree-Law 21.129, issued 7 March 1932.

10   *Catálogo da Exposição Comemorativa do Centenário da Abdicação 1831–1931* (Rio de Janeiro: Museu Histórico Nacional, 1931).

11 Somewhat contrary to conventional wisdom, there is little evidence to suggest that Baroso mixed his political and professional lives. In my extensive research in a wide variety of museum documents, I have encountered only two references that make any direct link between Barroso's museum responsibilities and integralism. The first was a letter written to Barroso in which Barroso's correspondent makes a passing reference to Barroso's *integralisando*. The second was Barroso's previously cited letter to Vargas in which the museum director falsely declared that he had not engaged in *any* political activity for more than a decade. There is a possibility that Barroso withheld or destroyed compromising evidence. However, the available documentation suggests what appears to be Barroso's personal decision to maintain a certain distance between integralism and the museum.

12 Dumans, "A idéia da criação do Museu Histórico Nacional."

13 MHN-AP 1935 *Relatório.*

14 CPDOC-GCg 34.12.11 Doc. V-3, "O Museu Histórico de 1930–1938," 1 December 1938.

15 Adolpho Dumans, *A idéia da criação do Museu Histórico Nacional* (Rio de Janeiro: Gráfica Olímpica, 1947), 39–50.

16 For an excellent analysis of the cultural politics of the Calmon Collection, see Regina Abreu, *A fabricação do imortal: memória, história, e estratégias de consagração no Brasil* (Rio de Janeiro: LAPA/Rocco, 1996). See also Barroso's collection catalog, *Catálogo descritivo e comentado da Coleção Miguel Calmon* (Rio de Janeiro: Museu Histórico Nacional, 1944).

17 *O Imparcial* (Supplement) (Rio), 21 September 1941.

18 Regina Abreu, "Síndrome de museus?" *Série encontros e estudos* 2 (1996): 57–58.

19 *Rio de Janeiro e arredores: Guia do viájante* (Rio de Janeiro: Guias do Brasil, Ltda. Companhia Carioca de Artes Gráficas, 1939). An English-language version was published in 1940 under the title *Rio de Janeiro and Environs.*

20 Decree 78-A, issued 21 December 1889, banned the imperial family from Brazil and made provisions for the liquidation of all assets seized from the Braganças after the coup of 15 November 1889. On 3 September 1920, President Epitácio Pessoa signed Decree 4.120, revoking the ban and allowing any surviving Bragança descendant to return from exile. Decree 4.120 also made provisions for the construction of a mausoleum to house the remains of the Emperor Dom Pedro II and Empress Dona Tereza Cristina. The remains were repatriated in 1922.

21 Schwarcz, *As barbas do Imperador,* 496.

22 Schwarcz, *As barbas do Imperador,* 495–515.

23 F. dos Santos Trigueiros, *Museu e educação* (Rio de Janeiro: Irmãos Pongetti, 1958), 81.

24 *Anuário do Museu Imperial* (hereafter AMI), 1 (1940): 326–31.

25 Vargas, "O Imperador D. Pedro II e os seus grandes serviços ao Brasil," *NPB*, 7:147–51.

26 Decree-Law 2.096, issued 29 March 1940.

27 AMI 2 (1941), 297–98. Dom Pedro Gastão de Orleans e Bragança wrote to Vargas on 14 February 1941, offering, "The historical patrimony of a precious archive of documents from our past that the National Dynasty saved from dispersion and guarded for the Pátria." Vargas accepted the offer the following month.

28 IPHAN-ATA Processo de Obras: Transferência, Pasta 3, Letter from Alcindo Sodré to RFMA, 23 August 1940. Reprinted in Alcindo de Azevedo Sodré, *Museu Imperial* (Rio de Janeiro: Imprensa Nacional, 1950), 18–24.

29 Sodré, *Museu Imperial*, 22.

30 Lourenço Lacombe, "O Museu Imperial," *Vozes de Petrópolis* (Petrópolis), July–August 1943.

31 Cecilia Meirelles, "The Imperial Museum of Petrópolis," *Travel in Brazil* 1, no. 4 (1941): 20–32.

32 Quoted in Sodré, *Museu Imperial*, 174.

33 Alcindo Sodré, "Dom Pedro II, Chefe do Estado," *AMI* 3 (1942): 211–18.

34 On the monarchist Pátria Nova movement, see Sandra McGee Deutsch, Las derechas: *The Extreme Right in Argentina, Brazil, and Chile, 1890–1939* (Stanford: Stanford University Press, 1999), 250, 290.

35 Regina Real, "A origem da Pinacoteca do Museu Nacional de Belas Artes," *Anuário do Museu Nacional de Belas Artes* (hereafter AMNBA) 7 (1945): 85–127.

36 According to Teixeira, the tensions with former ENBA classmate Cândido Portinari began about the time that Portinari was awarded the Prêmio de Viagem à Europa in 1928. Teixeira's ill-will toward modernists and modernism intensified after Portinari returned to Brazil in 1930. H. Pereira da Silva, *Oswaldo Teixeira em 3ª dimensão: vida, obra e época* (Rio de Janeiro: Museu de Armas Ferreira da Cunha, 1975), 78–80, 105.

37 "O Novo Museu Nacional de Belas Artes," *Illustração Brasileira* (Rio), 5 April 1938.

38 "O Museu de Belas Artes," *Jornal do Brasil* (Rio), 30 June 1937.

39 Carol Duncan and Alan Wallach, "The Universal Survey Museum," *Art History* 3, no. 4 (December 1980): 448–69.

40 Carol Duncan, *Civilizing Rituals: Inside Public Art Museums* (London: Routledge, 1995).

41 *Bellas-Artes* III, nos. 26–27 (August 1937): 2.

42 *Bellas-Artes* V, nos. 45–46 (January–February 1939): 3.

43 The galleries were organized as follows: French Artistic Mission; Nineteenth- and Early-Twentieth-Century Brazilian Painting; Rodolpho

Amoedo; Late-Nineteenth- and Twentieth-Century Brazilian Painting; the French School; Universal Schools of Painting (Old Masters); South American Artists; and Twentieth-Century Brazilian Artists. The Collections were named for Barão de São Joaquim, Luiz de Resende, Luiz Fernandes, Cyro Azevedo, and Diana Dampt. AMNBA I (1938–1939): 7.

44 CPDOC-GCg 34.12.11 Doc. VII-6, "Relatório das atividades do Museu de sua fundação até a presente data (1938–1940)," 25 November 1940.

45 *Guia do Museu Nacional de Belas Artes* (Rio de Janeiro: Museu Nacional de Belas Artes, 1945).

46 During the period under discussion, approximately 70 percent of a permanent collection was held in storage. *O Imparcial* (Rio), 1 June 1941; *Relatório sucinto das atividades do Museu Nacional de Belas Artes, 1937–1946* (Rio de Janeiro: Museu Nacional de Belas Artes, 1948).

47 Maria Barreto, "Inauguração da nova apresentação do Museu," AMNBA 5 (1943): 19–23.

48 IPHAN Inventário: MNBA Pasta V, A. Galvão, "Rápido histórico das moldagens da estatuária antiga da Escola de Belas Artes," 18 June 1975.

49 Other temporary exhibits mounted by the MNBA during the Estado Novo included sixteenth- and seventeenth-century Italian and Dutch painting (1941), late Renaissance painting (1942), and individual shows featuring the works of João Zeferino da Costa, Pedro Américo, and Vitor Meireles. The Ministry of Education sponsored temporary exhibitions of the works of modernists Cândido Portinari (1939), Lasar Segall (1943), and Noêmia Cavalcanti (1944). In 1942, the DIP used the MNBA galleries for a national exhibit commemorating the fifth anniversary of the Estado Novo. Finally, the museum hosted several traveling exhibits of contemporary European, American, and Canadian art.

50 AMNBA 2 (1940), 32–40.

51 Museu Nacional de Belas Artes-Arquivo Histórico (hereafter MNBA-AH) Exposição de Arte Francesa, Pasta 6, *Relatório,* 1940.

52 Frederico Morais, *Cronologia das Artes no Rio de Janeiro, 1816–1994* (Rio de Janeiro: Topbook, 1995), 164–65, 169.

53 Quirino Campofiorito, "A pintura francesa no Museu Nacional," *Bellas-Artes* VI, nos. 59–60 (June–July 1940): 1–3.

54 O. B., *Jornal do Commercio* (Rio), 13 June 1940.

55 Museus Castro Maya-Museu do Chácara do Céu, Acervo (hereafter MCM). Correspondence exchanged between Raimundo Castro Maya and Roberto Heymann, 1939–1940. The precise value of the purchase is difficult to determine due to the rapidly declining exchange rate between the milréis and franc. Nevertheless, Heymann was eager to close a deal at potentially elevated prices, warning Castro Maya that should he hesitate, the dealer might

be forced to turn to another Brazilian collector. Cursory evidence suggests that paulista media magnate Assis Chateaubriand was also trying to acquire the Debret watercolors.

56 Jean-Baptiste Debret, *Viagem pitoresca e histórica ao Brasil,* vol. I, trans. Sérgio Milliet (São Paulo: Livraria Martins, 1940), 195.

57 For an extended discussion of the visual culture of slavery, including the transatlantic circulation of images depicting slave punishment and martyrology, see Marcus Wood, *Blind Memory: Visual Representations of Slavery in England and America, 1780–1865* (London: Routledge, 2000), 215–91; On Debret, see Dawn Ades, *The Art of Latin America: The Modern Era, 1820–1980* (New Haven: Yale University Press, 1989), 70–73.

58 The linguistic slippage in the 1841 IHGB review is illuminating. The original title of *Feitors corrigeant des nègres* and Debret's commentary directly address the cruel behavior of Portuguese overseers (*feitores*) rather than slave masters (*senhores de escravo*). It would be plausible to argue that Debret was not characterizing *all* Portuguese as cruel, merely Portuguese overseers. Many images in the *Voyage* depict European masters and slaves peacefully cohabitating without any outward signs of violence. However, the IHGB reviewers would not accept a literal interpretation of the lithograph's title. The IHGB critique, in fact, turned on the premise that *Feitors corrigeant des nègres* must be read as an observation on direct master-slave relations.

After comparing Debret's characterization of the grim reality of Rio's slave market to another description authored by Maria Calcott Graham (1785–1842)—a British subject who lived in Brazil between 1821 and 1823—the review turned to *Feitors corrigeant des nègres* and asserted, "*A atitude do paciente é tal que causa horror. Pode ser que M. Debret presenciasse semelhante castigo, porque em todas as partes há senhores bárbaros; mas isto não é senão um abuso. É confessado por escritores de nota que entre todos os senhores de escravo, os Portugueses eram os mais humanos* [Many authors of note confess that the Portuguese are the most humane among all slave masters]; *ao menos não se lhes attribuiam as crueldades praticadas por outras nações com estes infelizes.*" Insisting that Debret wanted to say something about slave masters, not overseers, the reviewer chided the Frenchman for misrepresenting the moral character and comportment of the Luso-Brazilian master class. The reviewer's use of the term *senhores de escravo,* rather than the more accurate *feitor,* brings to the fore the intense ideological anxieties that haunted elite memories of slavery in nineteenth-century Brazil.

Even if Debret had intended to describe the relationship between overseers and slaves in *Feitors corrigeant des nègres,* the *Voyage* included other images of white masters punishing their slaves. These images of cruel Portuguese masters were at variance with elite aspirations to project the idea of a civilized society in the tropics. Hence, the IHGB used its critique of Debret's *Voyage* to advocate a positive reading of the Portuguese civilizing mission in America. The problem was that images of Portuguese cruelty toward slaves continued to circulate with the printed edition of the *Voyage*, making it all but impossible for the imperial elite to assimilate Debret into their visual and ideological vocabularies of Brazilianness.

See "Parecer sobre o 1° e 2° volumes da obra intitulada *Voyage Pittoresque et Historique au Brésil*," *Revista Trimestral de História e Geografia* (later *Revista do Instituto Histórico e Geográfico Brasileiro*), vol. 3 (1841), 98–99.

59   Rodrigo Naves, "Debret, o neoclassicismo, e a escravidão," in *A forma difícil: ensaios sobre arte brasileira*, 2d ed. (São Paulo: Ática, 1998), 102–5.

60   For the classic reading of the contradictions of nineteenth-century Brazilian liberalism, see Emília Viotti da Costa, "Liberalism, Theory and Practice," in *The Brazilian Empire: Myths and Realities* (Chicago: University of Chicago Press, 1985), 53–77.

61   Naves, "Debret, o neoclassicismo, e a escravidão," 47 n9.

62   *Quadros trazidos por Le Breton* (Rio de Janeiro: Museu Nacional de Belas Artes, 1948); and *Le Breton e a Missão Artística Francesa de 1816* (Rio de Janeiro: Museu Nacional de Belas Artes, 1960).

63   Luiz Edmundo, *A Côrte de D. João VI no Rio de Janeiro*, 3 vols. (Rio de Janeiro: Impresa Nacional, 1939–1940).

64   The 1940 Milliet translation inaugurated the series *Biblioteca Histórica Brasileira*, organized by the São Paulo publishing house Livraria Martins. Other *viajantes* included in the series were Johann Mortiz Rugendas (1802–1858), Auguste de Saint-Hilaire (1779–1853), and Daniel Kidder (1815–1891). In 1954, a volume of previously unpublished works by Debret was included in the reedition of the *Viagem pitoresca e histórica ao Brasil*.

65   CPDOC-GCg 38.11.01/1 Doc. 6, Teixeira to Capanema, "Relatório da Exposição Missão Artística Francesa de 1816," January 1941.

66   *Exposição da Missão Artística Francesa de 1816* (Rio de Janeiro: Museu Nacional de Belas Artes), 6.

67   José Mariano (Filho), "Uma linda adventura," *Jornal do Commercio* (Rio), late 1939–early 1940, reprinted in his self-published *Estudos de arte brasileira* (Rio de Janeiro, 1942).

68   Mariano (Filho), "Uma linda adventura."

69   On the reception of *Casa-grande e senzala*, see Ricardo Benzaquem de Araújo, *Guerra e Paz: casa-grande e senzala e a obra de Gilberto Freyre nos anos 30* (Rio de Janeiro: Editora 34, 1994).

70   Dain Borges, "Intellectuals and the Forgetting of Slavery," *Annals of Scholarship* 11, nos. 1–2 (1996): 37–60.

71   "Exposição da missão artística franceza de 1816," *Correio da Manhã* (Rio), 24 November 1940.

72 MCM Correspondence between Raimundo Castro Maya and Roberto Heymann, 1–8 March 1940.

73 MHN-SCP 1/44 contains a full inventory of all donations made by Vargas for the period 19 November 1930–19 November 1945.

74 "É preciso que a alma do futuro entenda a do passado," *A Noite* (Rio), 11 June 1939.

75 "O Presidente da República visitou o Museu Histórico Nacional," *O Jornal* (Rio), 11 June 1939.

76 MHN-SCP 12/39, The Coleção Souza Lima was a collection of 570 objects of Indo-Portuguese ivories formerly owned by José Luiz de Souza Lima and acquired by the Caixa Econômica do Rio de Janeiro.

77 See Daryle Williams, "Sobre patronos, heróis, e visitantes: O Museu Histórico Nacional, 1930–1960," *AMHN* 29 (1997): 141–86.

78 José Bittencourt, "A parede da memória: objetos, memória e perenidade no Museu Histórico Nacional," unpublished ms., 1992, 16.

79 MHN-SCP 15/36 Doc. 1, Letter from Barroso to Alice Calmon, 18 May 1936.

80 DHHB, 1576–77; for additional information on Guilherme Guinle's role in federal economic policies during the first Vargas era, see Geraldo Mendes Barros, *Guilherme Guinle, 1882–1960: ensaio biográfico* (São Paulo: Livraria Agir Editora, 1982).

81 Regional critics included Vicente Racioppi, the local preservationist from Ouro Preto and bête noir to the SPHAN discussed in chap. 4, and paulista journalist A. S. Oliveira Junior, who criticized the MHN for its distorted and incomplete narration of the Constitutionalist Rebellion of 1932. *A Época* (São Paulo), 24 July 1948.

82 *Anuário do Ministério da Educação e Saúde Pública* 1 (1931): 315; *Anuário Estatístico do Brasil* VI (1941/1945).

83 CPDOC-GCg 34.12.11 Doc. VII-21, Relatório do Museu Nacional de Belas Artes, 1937–1945, 1 September 1945; CPDOC-GCg 38.11.01/1 Doc. 6.

84 Opening hours during the Vargas era were: Museu Histórico, 12–4 P.M.; Museu Imperial: 12–5 P.M.; MNBA, 1:30–6:30 P.M.; Casa Ruy Barbosa, 10 A.M.–5 P.M.; Museu Nacional, 9 A.M.–4 P.M. All federal museums were closed to public visitation on Mondays.

85 RMFA, *Brasil: Monumentos Históricos e Arqueológicos*, 167.

86 Brazil, Instituto Brasileiro Geográfico e Estatístico, *Repertório Estatístico do Brasil. Situação Cultural* (Rio de Janeiro, 1941), 1: 384.

87 In the 1939–1941 *concursos* for the post of entry-level *conservador*, fourteen posts were offered to women and nine to men. Mario Barata, "Proteção do nosso patrimônio histórico e artístico no quinquênio 1937–1942," *Cultura Política* II, no. 21 (November 1942): 327–53.

88 MHN-AP AS/DG I-1 (1), "Relatório ao Exmo. Sr. Dr. João Luiz Alves," 1922.

89 Duarte, *Contra o vandalismo e o extermínio*, 217–22.

90 MHN–AP Recortes 1:67–70, later appearing in MHN–AP DG I-I (7).

91 Regulamento do Museu Histórico Nacional, *Diário Oficial*, 25 July 1934, 15235–39.

92 Stephen Greenblatt, "Resonance and Wonder," in *Exhibiting Cultures: The Poetics and Politics of Museum Display*, ed. Ivan Karp and Steven D. Lavine (Washington, D.C.: Smithsonian Institution, 1991), 42–56.

93 Adalberto Ribeiro, "O Museu Histórico Nacional," in *Instituições Brasileiras de Cultura*, 1:90–160.

94 Regina M. Leal, "Que é a técnica de Museu," *Estudos Brasileiros* III, no. 6 (March–April 1941): 109–32.

95 Duarte, *Contra o vandalismo*, 217–22.

96 IPHAN Inventário: São Miguel das Missões, Pasta I, Lucio Costa to RMFA, 20 December 1937.

97 On RMFA and museums, see *Rodrigo e o SPHAN*, 159–62; and Lygia Martins da Costa, "O pensamento de Rodrigo na criação dos museus do PHAN," in *Ideólogos do patrimônio cultural* (Rio de Janeiro: Instituto Brasileiro de Patrimônio Cultural, 1991), 113–29.

98 For debates on the educational value of museums, see Edgard Süssekind de Mendonça, *Extensão cultural dos museus* (Rio de Janeiro: Museu Nacional, 1946); and Francisco Venânio Filho, "A função educadora dos museus," *Estudos Brasileiros* I, no. 6 (May–June 1939): 50–61. On Mário de Andrade and museums, see Mário Chagas, "A ótica museológica de Mário de Andrade," in *Ideólogos do patrimônio cultural*, 99–113.

6 Expositions and "Export Quality" Culture

1 For a more extended discussion of expositions and the national imagination, see Noah Charles Elkin, *Promoting a New Brazil: National Expositions and Images of Modernity, 1861–1922*, Ph.D. dissertation, Rutgers University, 1999; Francisco Foot Hardman, *Trem fantasma: a modernidade na selva* (São Paulo: Companhia das Letras, 1988), chap. 3, esp. 88–91; and Sandra Jatahy Pessavento, *Exposições universais: espetáculos da modernidade do século XIX* (São Paulo: HUCITEC, 1997).

2 Skidmore, *Black into White*, 125–28.

3 Elkin, *Promoting a New Brazil*, 90–129.

4 Hardman, *Trem fantasma*, 74–76.

5 Elkin, *Promoting a New Brazil*, 297–333.

6 The history of Rio's Feira Internacional de Amostras, one of the capital's most-visited public venues in the early 1930s, remains to be studied.

7 AN-SDA 025 Lata 124, Directive from Antonio Luis de Sousa Mello, Conselho Federal do Comercio Exterior, 30 December 1935.

8   AN-SDA 025 Lata 124, Report from Sebastião Sampaio, executive director of the Conselho Federal do Comercio Exterior, to Vargas, 4 August 1936.

9   CPDOC-CGf 35.00.00 Doc. II-21, Capanema's draft for *Propaganda do Estado Novo* Stand, 1938.

10 *Exposição Nacional do Estado Novo* (Rio de Janeiro: Departamento Nacional de Propaganda, 1939), 1.

11 *Exposição Nacional do Estado Novo*, 1.

12 Visitation figure cited in *Correio da Manhã* (Rio), 24 January 1939.

13 Gerson Moura, *O Tio Sam chega ao Brasil: a penetração cultural americana* (São Paulo: Brasilense, 1984).

14 Representing a cleaned-up version of the malandro celebrated in samba lyrics, Zé Carioca was created during Walt Disney's 1941 goodwill tour of South America. In *Saludos Amigos* (1943), Zé Carioca (*viz.* Brazil) introduces Donald Duck (*viz.* the United States) to the pleasures of samba, cachaça, and Rio de Janeiro, set to the enchanting music of Ary Barroso's *Aquarela do Brasil*. Zé Carioca and Donald Duck are joined by a third Disney Good Neighbor, the Mexican rooster Panchito, in *The Three Caballeros* (1945).

15 *Carmen Miranda: Bananas Is My Business*, Helena Solbeg, director, International Cinema and Corporation for Public Broadcasting, 1994.

16 Robert Stam, "Pan-American Interlude: Orson Welles in Brazil, 1942," in *Tropical Multiculturalism: A Comparative History of Race in Brazilian Cinema and Culture* (Durham, N.C.: Duke University Press, 1997), 107–32.

17 Ana Rita Mendonça, *Carmen Miranda foi a Washington* (Rio de Janeiro: Record, 1999), esp. chap. 5.

18 Mendonça, *Carmen Miranda*, 117–29. The chilly reception to Miranda's performance at the Cassino da Urca prompted the performer to sing her famous refrain, "*Disseram que eu voltei americanizada* [They say that I came back Americanized]."

19 New York Public Library, Manuscripts Division, New York World's Fair of 1939 Collection (hereafter NYPL-NYWF) PO.3 Container 96, English translation of letter from Valetim Bouças to Vargas, 19[?] September 1937.

20 Centro de Pesquisa e Documentação da História Contemporânea do Brasil/Fundação Getúlio Vargas, Arquivo Valdemar Falcão (hereafter CPDOC-VF) c 37.11.12 Doc. II-41, Internal regulations to Decree-Law 655, Article 6, late 1938.

21 Brazil, Comissariado Geral na Feira Mundial de Nova York, 1939–1940, *O Brasil na Feira Mundial de Nova York Relatório Geral de Armando Vidal* (Rio de Janeiro: n.p., 1941), 24.

22 CPDOC-VF 37.11.12c Doc. I-1, Decree authorizing Brazilian Commission, 12 November 1937.

23 NYPL-NYWF PO.3 Container 96, Mission statement signed by Armando Vidal, 13 January 1939.

24   *O Brasil na Feria Mundial*, 25.

25   On this point, my research differs from the argument recently put forth by Steven Topik that coffee has played a minor role in Brazilian identity politics. My research unequivocally demonstrates that coffee played a major role in the official iconography of Brazilianness in the late 1930s and 1940s, when the National Department of Coffee took the lead role in organizing the Brazilian missions to the New York and San Francisco fairs and Portinari's *Café* was touted as a work of national artistic genius. See Steven Topik, "Where is the Coffee? Coffee and Brazilian Identity," *Luso-Brazilian Review* 36, no. 2 (1999): 87–92.

26   *Pavilhão Brasileiro na Golden Gate International Exposition* (San Francisco: Departamento Nacional do Café, 1940). The Brazilian pavilion was designed by American architect Gardner Dailey. The murals were designed by Jane Berlandina and Robert Howard.

27   Eurico Pentado, *O Pavilhão do Brasil na Golden Gate International Exhibition: Relatório do Comissário Geral* (1940), 78–79.

28   Penteado, *O Pavilhão do Brasil*, 78–82; Centro de Pesquisa e Documentação da História Contemporânea do Brasil/Fundação Getúlio Vargas, Arquivo Oswaldo Aranha Série cp 39.01.18.

29   During the summer of 1939, Brazilian Foreign Minister Oswaldo Aranha, Army Chief of Staff Góes Monteiro, and other top Brazilian officials met with Cordell Hull, Sumner Wells, and President Roosevelt to secure U.S. financial assistance for domestic industrialization. On 30 June 1939, the Aranha commission held a special reception at the Brazilian pavilion in New York.

30   CPDOC-VF C 37.11.12 Docs. I-26 and I-36, Correspondence from Oswaldo Soares documenting abortive attempts to send information on *economia social* to the New York fair.

31   NYPL-NYWF PO.3 Container 96, João M. de Lacerda, "Preliminary Outline Concerning Brazil's Participation in the New York World's Fair 1939," 19 January 1938. Emphasis added.

32   NYPL-NYWF P4.0 Container 221, Press release on Brazilian participation, 31 May 1938.

33   Curtis, *Modern Architecture since 1900*, 176.

34   Reviews of the Brazilian pavilion appeared in *Architectural Forum* 70, no. 6 (June 1939): 448–49; *Architectural Record* 95 (March 1944): 58–84; and, *Architecture d'aujourd'hui* 13–14 (September 1947): 20–21.

35   Robert C. Smith, "Brazil Art: General Statement," *Handbook of Latin American Studies* (on-line version) 9 (1946).

36   Robert C. Smith, "Brazil Builds on Tradition and Today," *Art News* 41, no. 18 (February 1943): 14–19.

37   The MOMA *Brazil Builds* exhibit merits a study onto itself. See Museum of

Modern Art Archives, New York: Public Information Scrapbooks/Archives of American Art (hereafter MOMA/AAA), Roll 5069:719-821; and Philip L. Goodwin's *Brazil Builds: Architecture New and Old, 1652-1942* (New York: Museum of Modern Art, 1943).

38 *Pavilhão do Brasil, Feira Mundial de Nova York de 1939* (n.p.: Comissariado Geral na Feira Mundial de Nova York, 1939), 3.

39 "In an industrial and culturally developed nation such as the United States and in an event in which richer and more experienced countries will take part, it would be unwise to devise a pavilion which would stand out for its adornment, monumentality, or technical features" (Lucio Costa, *Sobre Arquitetura* [Porto Alegre: Centro de Estudantes Universitários de Arquitetura, 1962], 95).

40 "Termo de julgamento do concurso de ante-projetos para o Pavilhão Brasileiro em New York," reprinted in *Arquitetura e urbanismo* III, no. 2 (March–April 1938): 98-99.

41 Carlos Eduardo Comas, "Modern Architecture, Brazilian Corollary," *AA Files* (summer 1998): 3-13.

42 CPDOC-GC g 35.11.04 Doc. II-3, Speech delivered by Capanema at inauguration of Faculdade Nacional de Arquitetura, 6 September 1945.

43 Mário de Andrade expressed similar complaints. See A. Amaral, *Arte para que?*, 103.

44 PP-CDA, 22-23; *Bellas-Artes* V, nos. 49-50 (June–July 1939): 3.

45 *Bulletin of the Pan American Union* 74, no. 1 (January 1940): 19-30.

46 Projeto Portinari, Interview with Lucio Costa, 22 December 1982, 15-16.

47 *Art in Our Time* inaugurated the Museum of Modern Art's new headquarters and helped consolidate MoMA and its wealthy patrons as the world's most important arbiter of modern art. The European works included paintings by Auguste Renoir, Pablo Picasso, Henri Matisse, and Henri Rousseau, and sculptures by Constantin Brancusci, Jacques Lipchitz, and Henry Moore, as well as five works of German art deemed "degenerate" by the Nazis. American artists included Winslow Homer, Mary Cassatt, and Georgia O'Keffe. Latin American art was represented by Diego Rivera, José Clemente Orozco, and Portinari. MoMA/AAA, Roll 5062: 281 and Roll 5064:3-192; see also *Time,* 22 May 1939.

48 *Bellas-Artes* V, nos. 47-48 (April–May 1939): 1.

49 *Bellas-Artes* V, nos. 49-50 (June–July 1939): 3.

50 *Bellas-Artes* V, nos. 49-50 (June–July 1939): 4.

51 Robert C. Smith, "Brazilian Painting in New York," *Bulletin of the Pan-American Union* 73, no. 9 (1939): 500-6.

52 In an interview given in early 1941, just after returning from the United States where comparisons between Portinari and Rivera were common, the Brazilian stated, "Only a person who knows little of art could compare me

to Rivera [who] has dedicated himself to what has been called social art, putting art at the service of his political convictions. I do not do this. . . . He is prisoner to his ideological convictions, while I have given myself to pictorial adventure" (reprinted in *O Imparcial* [São Luiz de Maranhão], 2 January 1941); on Portinari and Picasso, see Carlos Zillio, *A quarela do Brasil: a questão da identidade da arte brasileira*, 2d ed. (Rio de Janeiro: Relume-Dumará, 1997), 100.

53   Smith, "Brazilian Painting in New York."

54   At the forefront in promoting Latin American art in the United States, the Detroit Art Institute and MOMA played important roles in enriching the artistic component to the Good Neighbor Policy. These two institutions also contributed greatly to the careers of Cândido Portinari and his erstwhile Mexican counterpart, Diego Rivera.

55   MoMA/AAA Roll 5066:516.

56   *Portinari, His Life and Art* (Chicago: The University of Chicago Press, 1940).

57   Robert C. Smith, "Brazilian Art," in *Concerning Latin American Culture,* ed. Charles C. Griffin (New York: Russell and Russell, 1940), 181–97.

58   Smith, "Brazilian Painting in New York," 505.

59   Smith, "Brazilian Art," 194, 196.

60   Florence Horn, "Portinari of Brazil," *Bulletin of the Museum of Modern Art* 7, no. 6 (October 1940): 8–9.

61   MoMA/AAA, Roll 5066:523 Elizabeth MacCausland, "Cândido Portinari at Museum of Modern Art," *Sunday Union and Republican* (Springfield, MA), 13 October 1940. NOTE: If the handwritten notations in the Museum of Modern Art's clippings file are accurate, Portinari expressed great displeasure with MacCausland's criticism.

62   Horn, "Portinari of Brazil," 9, emphasis in original.

63   The results of this field research include: Ruth Landes, *The City of Women* (New York: Macmillan, 1947); and Donald Pierson. *Negroes in Brazil: A Study of Race Contact at Bahia* (Chicago: University of Chicago Press, 1942).

64   See Frazier excerpts in *African-American Reflections on Brazil's Racial Paradise,* ed. David J. Hellwig (Philadelphia: Temple University Press, 1992), 121–36.

65   CPDOC-GCb GC/Freire, G. Doc. 25, "Departamento Nacional de Antropologia (ou Cultura)," signed by Gilberto Freyre, 10 April 1942. Freyre's unrealized project envisioned an agency responsible for the "organization and coordination of services, activities, and research directly related to the study, interpretation, and improvement (eugenics, hygiene, and so on) of the Brazilian man and his culture." Freyre's proposal was largely concerned with instituting mechanisms to distinguish Brazilian culture from Spanish America (*América indoispánica*).

66   *O Brasil na Feira mundial de Nova York de 1939*, 71–92. Popular compositions performed by the Orquestra Romeo Silva included the music of Lamartine

Babo, Ary Barroso, Dorival Caymmi, Donga, Pixanguinha, Noel Rosa, and Vadico—a who's who among popular composers of the era. Classical music performed live or recorded for the Brazilian mission included compositions by Carlos Gomes, Mozart Carmargo Guarnieri, Francisco Mignone, and Heitor Villa-Lobos. At the New York Philharmonic, soprano Bidú Sayó and pianists Noêmia Bittencourt and Bernardo Seigal gave two concerts under the baton of Brazilian composer Walter Burle-Marx.

67 *Contemporary Art of 79 Countries* (International Business Machines Corporation, 1939).

68 *New York Times,* 30 October 1939.

69 Almeida, *De Anita ao museu,* 141–60.

70 Sérgio Miceli, *Imagens negociadas: retratos da elite brasileira (1920-1940)* (São Paulo: Companhia das Letras, 1996).

71 Reproduced in Mauricio Lissovsky and Paulo Sergio Moraes de Sá, orgs., *Colunas da Educação: a construção do Ministério da Educação e Saúde* (Rio de Janeiro: MinC/IPHAN: Fundação Getúlio Vargas/CPDOC, 1996), 247-48.

72 Mário Pedrosa, "Portinari: From Brodowski to the Library of Congress," *Bulletin of the Pan-American Union* 76, nos. 4–5 (1942): 199–211, 258–66; see also A. Amaral, *Arte para quê?,* 101–4.

73 Piedade Epstein Grinberg, *Ruben Navarra e a crítica de arte na década de 40 no Rio de Janeiro,* master's thesis, Universidade Federal do Rio de Janeiro, 1996, Section 4.2.

74 Mário de Andrade, "Cândido Portinari," in *Baile das Quatro Artes* (São Paulo: Martins, [1940] 1963), 121–34.

75 Horn, "Portinari of Brazil," 8.

76 *Cronobiografia de Portinari* (Rio de Janeiro: Projeto Portinari, n.d.), 16.

77 Annateresa Fabris, *Cândido Portinari* (São Paulo: Editora da Universidade de São Paulo, 1996), 89–101.

78 *A Notícia* (Rio) November 1943.

79 "Sadly, we cannot recognize the weight of universalism in the work of our sojourners in that that great city of skyscrapers, internationalist tendencies which do not complement, in any way, the task of nationalism in which Brazil is presently engaged" (*Nação Armada,* November 1940, reprinted in Lissovsky and Moraes de Sá, *Colunas da Educação,* 249–50); Fabris, *Cândido Portinari,* 89–91.

80 CPDOC-GCg 38.11.01/1A Doc. 11, "Arte e Política," May 1943.

81 I have tried to suggest how Portinari can be located within broad cultural debates of the 1930s and 1940s. For a more in-depth discussion of Portinari, see A. Amaral, *Arte para quê?,* chaps. 2 and 3; Annateresa Fabris, *Portinari, pintor social* (São Paulo: Perspectiva, 1990); and Zillio, *A quarela do Brasil,* 90–113.

82 Arquivos Nacionais—Torre do Tombo, Arquivo Oliveira Salazar, Corre-

spondência Oficial, Presidência do Conselho, Centenários (1938–1941) (hereafter ANTT-AOS/CO/PC-22) Pasta I, "Relatório sobre as Projetadas Comemorações de 1939–1940," 24 February 1938; Arquivo Histórico do Itamaraty (hereafter AHI) Lata 788, Maço 10.972.

83　ANTT-AOS/CO/PC-22 Pasta I, "Relatório sobre as Projetadas Comemorações de 1939–1940."

84　"Nota Oficiosa," *Diário de Notícias* (Lisbon), 27 March 1938.

85　ANTT-AOS/CO/PC-22A Pasta I, Ia Subdivisão, *VIII Centenário da Fundação de Portugal e Terceira da Restauração da Independência,* printed by Comissão Executiva da Colônia [Portuguesa] do Rio de Janeiro.

86　Pizarro Loureiro, *Getúlio Vargas e a política luso-brasileira* (Rio de Janeiro: Zélio Valverde, 1941), 137–45.

87　Centro de Pesquisa e Documentação da História Contemporânea do Brasil, Fundação Getúlio Vargas, Arquivo Getúlio Vargas (hereafter CPDOC-GV) 40.06.22/2, Letter from Antonio Oscar de Fragoso Carmona to Vargas, 22 June 1938.

88　Conselho de Imigração e Colonização Resolution 34, 22 April 1939, reprinted in Loureiro, *Getúlio Vargas e a política luso-brasileira,* 134–35. The resolution cites several motives for the exemption granted to Portuguese immigrants, including the statement, "The Portuguese have acted as peaceful collaborators for more than four centuries, and throughout the national territory one will find vestiges of the creative genius of the Portuguese race [*vestígios do gênio criador da raça*], attesting to the fact that their civilization, culture, and feelings are in harmony with ours." Loureiro notes that as a native speaker of the Portuguese language, the Portuguese immigrant was a natural ally in Vargas regime's campaign to nationalize (read: Luso-Brazilianize) immigrant communities, especially in the south of Brazil.

89　Decree-Law 1.410; AHI Lata 788, Maço 10.970, Letter from Francisco José Pinto to Aranha, 1 March 1940.

90　"Programa de representação brasileira nas comemorações centenárias, aprovado pelo Sr. Dr. Getúlio Vargas," *Revista dos Centenários* I, no. 7 (July 1939): 29–30.

91　Gustavo Barroso catalogued, transported, and installed a collection of 632 pieces, drawn from the permanent collection of the Museu Histórico, for the historical exhibition located in the Pavilhão dos Portugueses no Mundo. See Barroso, "A Exposição Histórica do Brasil em Portugal e seu catálogo," *AMHN* I (1940): 235–46.

92　Prompted by the organization of the last world's fair of the twentieth century in Lisbon, several studies on the Exposição do Mundo Português have appeared over the past five years. Two of the best studies are Margarida Acciaiuoli, *Exposições do Estado Novo* (Lisbon: Livros Horizonte, 1998); and Oscar Ribeiro Thomaz and Waldenir Bernini Lichtenthäler, "O Mundo que o Português criou," in *Entre o mito e a história: O V Centenário do Descobrimento da América* ed. Paula Montero. (Petrópolis: Vozes, 1996), 291–336.

93   Acciaiuoli, *Exposições do Estado Novo*, 193.

94   Arquivo Nacional, Fundo Conselho Nacional de Economia, Lata 195, Processo 1046/40.

95   *DHBB*, vol. 4, 2752–53.

96   AHI Lata 788, Maço 10.972, Dispatch from A. G. de Araújo Jorge to Aranha, 15 February 1939.

97   Take, for example, Augusto de Castro's speech of 23 June 1940: "Brazilians! The Tagus is also your river. Over the past four and a half centuries, it has linked two halves of the same Portuguese soul [*da mesma alma lusíada*]. Whenever one of you wants to imagine Portugal from afar, the River of Camões will illuminate your eyes . . . ." Portugal, Secretariado Nacional da Informação, *Mundo português, imagens de uma exposição histórica, 1940* (Lisbon: Edições SNI, 1956), n.p.

98   *Diário da Manhã* (Lisbon), 17 December 1939.

99   *O Século: Número Extraordinário Comemorativo do Duplo Centenário*, 52.

100   These were copies of the life-sized sculptures executed by Eduardo de Sá for the base of Rio's Monument to Floriano Peixoto (1901–1910).

101   *Catálogo descritivo e comentado*, Comissão Brasileira dos Centenários de Portugal, Pavilhão do Mundo Português e Pavilhão do Brasil Independente, org. Gustavo Barroso (Rio de Janeiro: Museu Histórico Nacional, 1940).

102   MHN-AP *Relatório Anual 1941.* See also Gustavo Barroso, "A Exposição Imperial," in *Portugal, semente de Impérios* (Rio de Janeiro: Getúlio Costa, 1941), 24–31.

103   *O Brasil de hoje, ontem, e amanhã* 1, no. 4 (April 1940): 27–29.

104   In a gesture to preserve Portuguese neutrality, the duke of Kent, brother to King George VI, presented Salazar with the Grand Cross of the Most Distinguished Order of St. Michael and St. George, an honor customarily reserved for British subjects. Dwight Homer, "Exposição do Mundo Português," in *Historical Dictionary of World's Fairs and Expositions, 1851–1988,* ed. John Findling (New York: Greenwood Press, 1990), 306–7.

105   Omar Ribeiro Thomaz, "Do saber colonial ao luso-tropicalismo: 'raça' e 'nação'; nas primeiras décadas do salazarismo," in *Raça, ciência, e sociedade,* ed. Marcos Chor Maio and Ricardo Ventura Santos (Rio de Janeiro: Editora Fiocruz/Centro Cultural Banco do Brasil, 1996), 94–98.

106   "Palavras do Chefe do Estado, na Câmara Municipal de Lisboa," reprinted in *Comemorações Centenárias: Programa Oficial* (Lisbon, 1940).

107   Important essays on Brazil's cultural formation published around the Revolution of 1930 include: Paulo Prado, *Retrato de Brasil* (1928); Sérgio Buarque de Holanda, *Raízes do Brasil* (1936); and, Caio Prado Junior, *Formação do Brasil Contemporâneo* (1942). All three attribute many of Brazil's cultural

problems to the defective character of the Portuguese immigrant or the exploitative nature of Portuguese colonization. Gilberto Freyre's *Casa-grande e senzala* (1933) describes the Portuguese colonist in more favorable terms. However, Freyre's notion of the Portuguese male as a mongrelized satyromaniac did not receive universal acceptance.

108   On anti-Portuguese sentiment and ethnic tensions between Brazilians and Portuguese immigrants in the republican period, see Sidney Chalhoub, *Trabalho, lar, e botequim: o cotidiano dos trabalhadores no Rio de Janeiro da Belle Époque* (São Paulo: Brasiliense, 1986), 35–110; and Motta, *A nação faz 100 anos,* 19–20.

109   Gustavo Barroso, "A presença do Brasil," in *Portugal: semente de Impérios,* 203–5.

110   Augusto de Castro, *A Exposição do Mundo Português,* 157–63.

111   José-Augusto França, *A arte em Portugal no século XX, 1911–1961,* 2d ed. (Venda Nova: Bertrand, 1985), 218–25; and Acciaiuoli, *Exposições do Estado Novo,* 120–26.

112   *AMNBA* 2 (1940): 61–62.

113   Acciaiuoli, *Exposições do Estado Novo,* 188.

114   "E Portinari?" *Atlântico* III, no. 3 (1943): 205–6.

115   According to França, Portinari was especially influential among proponents of *neo-realismo* in Portugal. See França, *A arte em Portugal* 356–59.

116   For an outline of a doctoral dissertation that promises to explore these contradictions in much more detail, see Luciene Lehmkuhl, "Brasil: uma imagem em exposição," *Esboços,* Universidade Federal de Santa Catarina, 2000.

117   Paulo Herkenhoff, "The Jungle in Brazilian Modern Design," *Journal of Decorative and Propaganda Arts* 21 (1995): 238–59.

118   José Neves Bittencourt, "Fenícios, sambaquis e Marajó: os primórdios da Arqueologia no Brasil e a formação do imaginário nacional," unpublished ms, 1999.

119   Helen Palmatary, "The Pottery of Marajó Island," *Transactions of the American Philosophical Society,* New Series 39, no. 3 (1949): 270–84.

120   Heloisa Alberto Torres, *Arte indígena da Amazônia* (Rio de Janeiro: SPHAN, 1940).

121   "Arte marajouara," *Bellas-Artes* III, nos. 26–27 (August 1937): 3.

122   Smith, "Brazilian Art," 181–82.

123   Chuva, *Os arquitetos da memória,* 87–88.

124   Carlos Rubens, *As artes plásticas no Brasil e o Estado Novo* (Rio de Janeiro: Departamento de Imprensa e Propaganda, 1941), 6–8.

125   Manoel Pestana, "Arte marajouara," *Bellas-Artes* IV, nos. 31–32 (January 1938): 3.

126 Doris Sommer, *Foundational Fictions: The National Romances of Latin America* (Berkeley: University of California Press, 1991).

127 Seth Garfield, " 'The Roots of a Plant that Today is Brazil': Indians and the Nation-State under the Brazilian Estado Novo," *Journal of Latin American Studies* 29 (1997): 747–68.

128 Gilberto Freyre, *The Masters and the Slaves: A Study in the Development Brazilian Civilization* (Berkeley: University of California Press, [1946] 1986), 81–183.

129 *O Século: Número Extraordinário* (1940), 382; and Carlos Galvão Simões, *Exposição do Mundo Português: Secção Colonial* (Lisbon: Neogravura, 1940), 271–99.

130 *O Século: Número Extraordinário.* Suplemento Colonial (1940), 61.

131 Gilberto Freyre, "Uma cultura ameaçada: a luso-brasileira," in *Uma cultura ameaçada: a luso-brasileira,* 3d ed. (Recife: Gabinete Português de Leitura de Pernambuco, [1940] 1980), 23–55.

132 Gilberto Freyre, *O mundo que o português criou* (Rio de Janeiro: José Olympio, 1940).

133 Almir de Andrade, "Uma cultura ameaçada," *Revista Acadêmica* 52 (November 1940).

134 Claudia Castelo, *"O modo português de estar no Mundo": O luso-tropicalismo e a ideologia colonial portuguesa (1933-1961)* (Oporto: Edições Afrontamento, 1998), 17–43.

135 Gilberto Freyre, *New World in the Tropics: The Culture of Modern Brazil* (New York: Alfred A. Knopf, 1959).

136 For an analysis of Portuguese colonial policy that examines the ideology of lusotropicalism in Portuguese Angola, see Gerald Bender, *Angola under the Portuguese: The Myth and the Reality* (Berkeley: University of California Press, 1978); and Castelo, O *"Modo português de estar no mundo,"* 69–107.

137 Freyre left two accounts of this trip through the Portuguese-speaking world: *Aventura e rotina* (Rio de Janeiro: José Olympio, 1952); and *Um brasileiro em Terras Portuguesas* (Rio de Janeiro: José Olympio, 1953).

Conclusion

1 CPDOC-GV 45.11.05, Letter from Manuel Vargas Neto to Vargas, 11 November 1945; CPDOC-GV 45.12.13, Letter from José Soares Maciel Filho to Vargas, 12 November 1945.

2 Vargas, "Ouro Preto—a méca da tradição nacional," *NPB* vol. 5 (Rio de Janeiro: José Olympio, 1938–1947), 249–54.

3 "Volta ao bom senso," *A Notícia* (Rio), 25 June 1946, in *Colunas,* 246.

4 Centro de Pesquisa e Documentação da História Contemporânea do Bra-

sil/Fundação Getúlio Vargas, Arquivo Clemente Mariani, Série pi 48.01.00 CMa/Mariani, C., January 1948.

5 *Guia dos bens tombados Brasil,* ed. Maria Elisa Carrazzoni, 2d ed. (Rio de Janeiro: Expressão Cultura, 1987), 231, 270.

6 IPHAN-ATA Processo 361-T, "Resolução do Conselho Consultivo do Patri-mônio Histórico e Artístico Nacional," 31 July 1946.

7 IPHAN-ATA Brief accompanying Processo 361-T, signed by Afonso Arinos Melo Franco, 26 July 1946.

8 IPHAN-ATA Legal brief written by Orlando do Carvalho, reprinted in *Minas Gerais* 108, 15 May 1947.

9 On the debate about the "revolutionary" nature of the Revolution of 1930, see Vavy Pacheco Borges, "Anos trinta e política: conceitos, imagens, e temas," *Luso-Brazilian Review* 36, no. 2 (1999): 109–26.

Bibliography

Archives, Libraries, Museums

Archives of American Art, Smithsonian Institution, Washington, D.C.

Arquivo Geral da Cidade do Rio de Janeiro

Arquivo Histórico do Itamaratí, Ministério das Relações Exteriores, Rio de Janeiro

Arquivo Municipal da Prefeitura de Ouro Preto

Arquivo Nacional, Rio de Janeiro

Arquivos Nacionais–Torre do Tombo, Lisbon

Biblioteca Nacional, Rio de Janeiro

Biblioteca Nacional de Lisboa, Lisbon

Centro de Pesquisa e Documentação da História Contemporânea do Brasil, Fundação Getúlio Vargas, Rio de Janeiro

Fundação Cinemateca Brasileira, São Paulo

Gabinete de Estudos Olisiponenses, Lisbon

Henry Madden Library, Larson Collection, California State University, Fresno

Instituto Histórico e Geográfico Brasileiro, Rio de Janeiro

Instituto do Patrimônio Histórico e Artístico Nacional, Arquivo e Biblioteca Noronha Santos, Rio de Janeiro

Library of Congress, Washington, D.C.

Museu Histórico Nacional, Rio de Janeiro

Museu da Inconfidência, Ouro Preto

Museu das Missões, São Miguel

Museu Imperial, Petrópolis

Museu Nacional, Rio de Janeiro

Museu Nacional de Belas Artes, Rio de Janeiro

Museu da Cidade, Lisbon

Museum of Modern Art, New York

Museus Castro Maya, Chácara do Céu, Rio de Janeiro

New York Public Library
Oliveira Lima Library, The Catholic University of America, Washington, D.C.
Prefeitura Municipal de Santo Ângelo, Arquivo Municipal, Santo Ângelo
Princeton University Libraries
Projeto Portinari, Rio de Janeiro
Real Gabinete Português de Leitura, Rio de Janeiro
Stanford University Libraries
University of California Libraries
University of Maryland Libraries

Periodicals

Anais do Ministério da Educação e Saúde
Anais do Museu Histórico Nacional
Anuário Brasileiro de Literatura
Anuário do Ministério da Educação e Saúde Pública
Anuário do Museu Imperial
Anuário do Museu Nacional de Belas Artes
Anuário Estatístico do Brasil
Arquitectura e Urbanismo
Art News
Atlântico
Balanço Geral da União
Bellas-Artes
O Brasil de ontem, hoje, e amanhã
Brasil Novo
Bulletin of the Pan-American Union
Correio da Manhã (Rio de Janeiro)
Cultura Política
Diário de Notícias (Lisbon)
Diário Oficial
Dom Casmurro
Estudos Brasileiros
Estudos e Conferências
Estudos Históricos
Handbook of Latin American Studies
Ilustração Brasileira

O Imparcial

Jornal do Brasil

Luso-Brazilian Review

A Manhã (Rio de Janeiro)

New York Times

Revista Acadêmica

Revista Brasileira de História

Revista do Brasil

Revista do Instituto Histórico e Geográfico Brasileiro

Revista do Serviço do Patrimônio Histórico e Artístico Nacional

Revista do Serviço Público

Revista dos Centenários

O Século

General Reference

Almanaque Abril. São Paulo: Editora Abril, 1991.

Bibliografia histórica, 1930–1945. Org. Ana Lígia Medeiros and Mônica Hirst. Brasília: Editora da Universidade de Brasília, 1982.

Brasil A/Z. São Paulo: Editora Universo, 1988.

Brazil. Presidência da República. Serviço de Documentação do Gabinete Civil. *Governos da República.* Brasília, 1984.

Brazil. Senado Federal. Subsecretaria de Edições Técnicas. *Constituições do Brasil.* 2 vols. Brasília, 1986.

Coleção das Leis da República dos Estados Unidos do Brasil. Rio de Janeiro: Imprensa Nacional, 1889–.

Dicionário da arquitetura brasileira. Org. Carlos A. C. Lemos. São Paulo: Edart, 1972.

Dicionário Histórico-Biográfico Brasileiro, 1930–1983. 4 vols. Ed. Israel Beloch and Alzira de Abreu. Rio de Janeiro: Forense Universitária; FGV/CPDOC/FINEP, 1984.

Encyclopedia of Latin American History and Culture. 4 vols. Ed. Barbara Tenenbaum. New York: Charles Scribner's and Sons, 1996.

Findling, John E., ed. *Historical Dictionary of World's Fairs and Expositions, 1851–1988.* New York: Greenwood Press, 1990.

Leite, José Roberto Teixeira. *Dicionário crítico da pintura no Brasil.* Ed. Raúl Mendes Silva. Rio de Janeiro: Artlivre, 1987.

Levine, Robert M., ed. *Historical Dictionary of Brazil.* Metuchen, N.J.: Scarecrow Press, 1979.

Ludwig, Armin K. *Brazil: A Handbook of Historical Statistics*. Boston: G. K. Hall & Co., 1985.

Novo Dicionário de História do Brasil. São Paulo: Melhoramentos, 1970.

Minas Gerais, Brazil. Departamento Estadual de Estatística. *Sinopse estatística de Minas Gerais*. Belo Horizonte: Oficinas Gráficas da Estatística, 1949.

Smith, Robert C., and Elizabeth Wilder, eds. *A Guide to the Art of Latin America*. Washington, D.C.: Library of Congress, 1948.

Valladares, José. *Estudos de arte brasileira*. Salvador: Museu do Estado da Bahia, 1960.

Exposition and Museum Catalogs

Ades, Dawn. *The Art of Latin America: The Modern Era, 1820-1980*. New Haven, CT: Yale University Press, 1989.

Batista, Marta Rossetti, and Yone Soares de Lima, eds. *Coleção Mário de Andrade: artes plásticas*. 2d ed. São Paulo: Instituto de Estudos Brasileiros, 1998.

Brazil Builds: Architecture New and Old, 1652-1942. New York: Museum of Modern Art, 1943.

Catálogo da Exposição de Arte Contemporânea e da Exposição de Arte Retrospectiva. Rio de Janeiro: Revista dos Tribunais, 1922.

Catálogo da Exposição Comemorativa do Centenário da Abdicação 1831-1931. Rio de Janeiro: Museu Histórico Nacional, 1931.

Catálogo descritivo e comentado. Comissão Brasileira dos Centenários de Portugal. Pavilhão do Mundo Português e Pavilhão do Brasil Independente. Org. Gustavo Barroso. Rio de Janeiro: Museu Histórico Nacional, 1940.

Catálogo descritivo e comentado da Coleção Miguel Calmon. Rio de Janeiro: Museu Histórico Nacional, 1944.

Comemorações Centenárias: Programa Oficial, 1940. Lisbon: Secretariado da Propaganda Nacional, 1940.

Contemporary Art of 79 Countries: The International Business Machines Corporation Collection Exhibited in its Gallery of Science and Art in the Business Systems and Insurance Building at the New York World's Fair, 1939. New York: International Business Machines Corporation, 1939.

Estado Novo: A construção de uma imagem. Rio de Janeiro: Centro de Pesquisa e Documentação da História Contemporânea do Brasil, 1997.

Exposição da Missão Artística Francesa de 1816. Rio de Janeiro: Museu Nacional de Belas Artes, 1940.

Exposição Le Breton e a Missão Artística Francesa de 1816. Rio de Janeiro: Museu Nacional de Belas Artes, 1960.

Exposição Nacional do Estado Novo. Rio de Janeiro: Departamento Nacional de Propaganda, 1939.

Ferraz, Geraldo. *Warchavchik e a introdução da nova arquitetura no Brasil: 1925 a 1940.* São Paulo: Museu de Arte de São Paulo, 1965.

Galvão Simões, Carlos. *Exposição do Mundo Português: Secção Colonial.* Lisbon: Neogravura, 1940.

Guia do Museu Nacional de Belas Artes. Rio de Janeiro: Museu Nacional de Belas Artes, 1945.

Kirstein, Lincoln. *The Latin-American Collection of the Museum of Modern Art.* New York: The Museum of Modern Art, 1943.

Livro de Ouro Comemorativo do Centenário da Independência do Brasil e a Exposição Internacional do Rio de Janeiro. Rio de Janeiro: Annuário do Brasil, 1923.

Murals by Cândido Portinari in the Hispanic Foundation of the Library of Congress. Washington, D.C.: United States Government Printing Office, 1943.

O Museu da Inconfidência. São Paulo: Banco Safra, 1995.

O Museu Histórico Nacional. São Paulo: Banco Safra, 1989.

O Museu Imperial. São Paulo: Banco Safra, 1992.

O Museu Nacional na Exposição Comemorativa dos Centenários de Portugal. Rio de Janeiro, 1940.

Museus Castro Maya. São Paulo: Banco Safra, 1996.

Ouro Preto: Sesquicentenário da elevação de Vila Rica à categoria de Imperial Cidade de Ouro Preto, 1823-1973. Rio de Janeiro: Biblioteca Nacional, 1973.

Pavilhão Brasileiro na Golden Gate International Exposition. San Francisco: Departamento Nacional do Café, 1940.

Pavilhao do Brasil, Feira Mundial de Nova York de 1939. N.p.: Comissariado Geral na Feira Mundial de Nova York, 1939.

Pavilhão do Brasil na Exposição Histórica do Mundo Português. Lisbon: Neogravura, 1941.

Portinari. Rio de Janeiro: Museu Nacional de Belas Artes, 1939.

Portinari of Brazil. New York: The Museum of Modern Art, 1940.

Portinari: Retrospetiva. São Paulo: Projeto Portinari; Museu de Arte de São Paulo Assis Chateaubriand, 1997.

Reflexos do impressionismo no Museu Nacional de Belas Artes. Rio de Janeiro: O Museu, 1974.

Rio de Janeiro. Escola Nacional de Belas Artes. *Catálogo geral das galerias de pintura e escultura.* Rio de Janeiro: O Norte, 1923.

Sodré, Alcindo. *Museu Imperial.* Rio de Janeiro: Imprensa Nacional, 1950.

United States. New York World's Fair Commission. *Latin American Exhibition of Fine Arts.* New York: Riverside Museum, 1940.

Viera, Lucia Gouvêa. *Salão de 1931: marco da revelação da arte moderna em nível nacional*. Rio de Janeiro: FUNARTE, 1984.

Films

Carmen Miranda: Bananas Is My Business. Helen Solberg, director. International Cinema and Corporation for Public Broadcasting, 1994.

Cine Jornal Brasileiro. Departamento de Imprensa e Propaganda. 1938–1946.

O Descobrimento do Brasil. Humberto Mauro, Director. Instituto Nacional do Cinema Educativo, 1937.

The Gang's All Here. Busby Berkley, Director. Twentieth Century Fox, 1943.

Os Inconfidentes: chegada a Capital da República das cinzas dos Inconfidêntes Mineiros. Instituto Nacional do Cinema Educativo, 1936.

Saludos Amigos. Norman Ferguson, Director. Walt Disney Studios, 1943.

The Three Caballeros. Norman Ferguson, Director. Walt Disney Studios, 1945.

Vargas-Era Sources

Achilles, Aristheu. *Aspectos da ação do DIP*. Rio de Janeiro: Departamento da Imprensa e Propaganda, 1941.

"All Aboard! American Republics at the New York World's Fair." *Bulletin of the Pan-American Union* 73, no. 7 (July 1939): 387–412.

Amaral, Azevedo. *O Brasil na crise atual*. São Paulo: Companhia Editora Nacional, 1934.

———. "Departamento de Imprensa e Propaganda." *Revista do Serviço Público* 3/1, no. 22 (February 1940): 11–13.

———. *O Estado autoritário e a realidade nacional*. Rio de Janeiro: José Olympio, 1938.

———. *Renovação Nacional*. Rio de Janeiro: Departamento Nacional de Propaganda, 1936.

Andrade, Almir de. *Aspetos da cultura brasileira*. Rio de Janeiro: Schmidt, 1939.

———. "Uma cultura ameaçada." *Revista Acadêmica* 52 (September 1940).

———. *Força, cultura e liberdade: Origens históricas e tendências atuais da evolução política do Brasil*. Rio de Janeiro: José Olympio, 1940.

Andrade, Mário de. *Aspectos das artes plásticas no Brasil*. São Paulo: Livraria Martins Editora, 1965.

———. *O baile das Quatro Artes*. São Paulo: Martins, 1963.

———. *Mário de Andrade, cartas do trabalho: correspondência com Rodrigo Melo Franco de Andrade (1936–1945)*. Brasília: Ministério da Educação e Cultura,

Secretaria do Patrimônio Histórico e Artístico Nacional, Fundação Pró-Memória, 1981.

——. *O movimento modernista*. Rio de Janeiro: Casa do Estudante do Brasil, 1942.

Andrade, Oswald de. *Pau-Brasil*. Paris: Sans Pareil, 1925.

Arciniegas, German. "Latin America at the San Francisco Exposition." *Bulletin of the Pan-American Union* 73, no. 10 (October 1939): 548–61.

Azevedo, Fernando de. *Brazilian Culture: An Introduction to the Study of Culture in Brazil*. New York: Macmillan Company, [1943] 1950.

Bandeira, Manuel. *Guia de Ouro Preto*. 3d ed. Rio de Janeiro: Casa do Estudante do Brasil, [1940] 1957.

Barata, Mario. "Proteção do nosso patrimônio histórico e artístico no quinqüênio 1937–1942." *Cultura Política* 2, no. 21 (November 1942): 327–62.

Barreto, Maria. "Inauguração da nova apresentação do Museu." *Anais do Museu Nacional de Belas Artes* 5 (1943): 19–23.

Barroso, Gustavo. "A defesa do nosso passado." *Anais do Museu Histórico Nacional* 4 (1943): 579–85.

——. "A Exposição Histórica do Brasil em Portugal e seu catalogo." *Anais do Museu Histórico Nacional* 1 (1940): 235–46.

——. *Introdução à técnica de museus*. 2 vols. 2d ed. Rio de Janeiro: Gráfica Olímpica, 1951–1953.

——. "O Museu Ergológico Brasileiro: o desenvolvimento dos estudos folclóricos em nosso país." *Anais do Museu Histórico Nacional* 3 (1942): 433–48.

——. *Portugal: semente de Impérios*. Rio de Janeiro: Getúlio Costa, 1941[?]

Barroso, Gustavo [João do Norte]. "Culto da Saudade." *Anais do Museu Histórico Nacional* 29 (1997): 32–34.

Brazil. Agência Nacional. *This Is Rio: The First Modern Photographic Book of Rio de Janeiro*. Ed. H. D. Oliveira. Rio de Janeiro, 1938.

Brazil. Comissariado Geral na Feira Mundial de Nova York, 1939–1940. *O Brasil na Feira Mundial de Nova York: Relatório Geral de Armando Vidal*. Rio de Janeiro, 1941.

Brazil. Departamento Nacional do Café. *Travel in Brazil*. Rio de Janeiro, 1940.

Brazil. Departamento Nacional de Propaganda. *Problemas e realizações do Estado Novo*. Rio de Janeiro, 1938.

Brazil. Instituto Brasileiro Geográfico e Estatístico. *Recenseamento Geral do Brasil* [1940]. Série Regional. Parte XII—Minas Gerais. Rio de Janeiro, 1950.

——. *Repertório Estatístico do Brasil. Situação Cultural*. Rio de Janeiro, 1941.

Brazil. Instituto Nacional do Livro. *Guias das bibliotecas brasileiras*. Rio de Janeiro, 1941.

——. *Guias das livrarias brasileiras*. Rio de Janeiro, 1942.

Brazil. Ministério da Agricultura, Indústria, e Commercio. Diretoria Geral da Estatística. *Recenseamento do Brazil* [1920]. Rio de Janeiro, 1928.

Brazil. Ministério da Educação e Saúde. *Casa Rui Barbosa.* Rio de Janeiro, 1946.

Brown, Milton. "Portinari of Brazil." *Parnassus* 12 (November 1940): 37–39.

Campofiorito, Quirino. "A pintura francesa no Museu Nacional." *Bellas-Artes* 6, nos. 59–60 (June–July 1940): 1–3.

Campos, Francisco. *Educação e Cultura.* Rio de Janeiro: José Olympio, 1940.

————. *O Estado Nacional: sua estrutura, seu conteúdo ideológico.* São Paulo: José Olympio, 1941.

Castelo, Martins. "Radio VI." *Cultura Política* 1, no. 6 (August 1941): 329–31.

Castro, Augusto de. *A exposição do mundo português e sua finalidade nacional.* Lisbon: Empresa Nacional de Publicidade, 1940.

"Cultura e Serviço Social." *Revista do Serviço Público* 1/3, no. 1 (July 1938): 3–5.

Debret, Jean-Baptiste. *Viagem pitoresca e histórica ao Brasil.* Trans. Sérgio Milliet. 2 vols. São Paulo: Livraria Martins, 1940.

————. *Voyage pittoresque et historique au Brésil, ou Séjour d'un artiste français au Brésil, depuis 1816 jusqu'en 1831 inclusivement.* 3 vols. Paris: Firmin Didot Frères, 1834–1839.

Delmare, Alcibiades. *Villa-Rica.* São Paulo: Companhia Editora Nacional, 1935.

Duarte, Paulo. *Contra o vandalismo e o extermínio.* São Paulo: n.p., 1938.

Dumans, Adolpho. *A idéia da criação do Museu Histórico Nacional.* Rio de Janeiro: Museu Histórico Nacional, 1947.

————. "O Museu Histórico Nacional através dos seus 19 anos de existência." *Anais do Museu Histórico Nacional* 1 (1940): 211–30.

Edmundo, Luiz. *A Côrte de D. João VI no Rio de Janeiro.* 2 vols. Rio de Janeiro: Impresa Nacional, 1939–1940.

Estado Novo, um auto-retrato (Arquivo Gustavo Capanema). Org. Simon Schwartzman. Brasília: Editora Universidade de Brasília, [1945] 1982.

"É preciso que a alma do futuro entenda a do passado." *A Noite* (Rio), 11 June 1939.

"Exposição da missão artística franceza de 1816." *Correio da Manhã* (Rio), 24 November 1940.

Freyre, Gilberto. *Aventura e rotina.* Rio de Janeiro: José Olympio, 1952.

————. *Um brasileiro em Terras Portuguesas.* Rio de Janeiro: José Olympio, 1953.

————. *Uma cultura ameaçada: a luso-brasileira.* 3d ed. Recife: Gabinete Português de Leitura de Pernambuco, [1940] 1980.

————. *The Masters and the Slaves: A Study in the Development of Brazilian Civilization.* Berkeley: University of California Press, [1946] 1986.

————. *O mundo que o português criou.* Rio de Janeiro: José Olympio, 1940.

————. *New World in the Tropics: The Culture of Modern Brazil.* New York: Alfred A. Knopf, 1959.

————. *The Portuguese and the Tropics.* Lisbon: Executive Committee for the Commemoration of the Vth Centenary of the Death of Prince Henry the Navigator, 1961.

Gastini, Raúl, ed. *Ideário político de Getúlio Vargas.* São Paulo: Empresa Gráfica da "Revista dos Tribunais" Ltda., 1943.

Horn, Florence. "Portinari of Brazil." *Bulletin of the Museum of Modern Art* 7, no. 6 (October 1940): 8–9.

Krull, Germaine. *Uma cidade antiga do Brasil: Ouro Preto.* Lisbon: Edições Atlântico, 1943.

Lacombe, Lourenço. "O Museu Imperial." *Vozes de Petrópolis* (Petrópolis), July–August 1943.

Lamengo, Alberto. "Os Sete Povos das Missões." *Revista do Serviço do Patrimônio Histórico e Artístico Nacional* 4 (1944): 55–70.

"Latin American Exhibition of Fine and Applied Art." *Bulletin of the Pan-American Union,* 74 no. 1 (January 1940): 18–31.

Leal, Regina M. "Que é a técnica de Museu." *Estudos Brasileiros* 3, no. 6 (March–April 1941): 109–32.

Levy, Hanna. "Valor artístico e valor histórico: importante problemas da história da arte." *Revista do Serviço do Patrimônio Histórico e Artístico Nacional* 4 (1940): 181–92.

Lima, Hernan. "Museus regionais." *Cultura Política* 5, no. 49 (February 1945): 98–112.

Lima (Junior), Augusto de. *Vila Rica do Ouro Preto: síntese histórica e descritiva.* Belo Horizonte: n.p., 1957.

Louriero, Pizarro. *Getúlio Vargas e a política luso-brasileira.* Rio de Janeiro: Zélio Valverde. 1941.

Mariano (Filho), José. "Le Chaperon Rouge." *Meio-Dia,* 28 April 1939.

————. "Considerações acerca do templo de Nossa Senhora do Rosário e S. Francisco de Assis de Ouro Preto." *Estudos Brasileiros* 2/4, no. 10 (January–February 1940): 384–401.

————. *Debates sobre estética e urbanismo.* Rio de Janeiro: C. Mendes Júnior, 1943.

————. *Estudos da arte brasileira.* Rio de Janeiro: C. Mendes Júnior, 1942[?].

————. *À margem do problema arquitetônico nacional.* Rio de Janeiro: n.p., 1943.

————. "O pseudo estylo barroco-Jesuítico e suas relações com arquitectura tradicional brasileira," *Estudos Brasileiros* 2/3, no. 9 (November–December 1939): 259–91.

Mattos, Anibal. *Monumentos históricos, artísticos, e religiosos de Minas Gerais.* Belo Horizonte: Biblioteca Mineira de Cultura, 1935.

Meirelles, Cecilia. "The Imperial Museum of Petrópolis." *Travel in Brazil* 1, no. 4 (1941): 20–32.

Mendonça, Edgard Süssekind de. *Extensão cultural dos museus.* Rio de Janeiro: Museu Nacional, 1946.

Monumentos da Cidade: reportagens publicadas pelo Diário de Notícias. Rio de Janeiro: Diário de Notícias, 1946.

"O Museu de Belas Artes." *Jornal do Brasil* (Rio), 30 June 1937.

"O Novo Museu Nacional de Belas Artes." *Ilustração Brasileira* (Rio), 5 April 1938.

"Parecer sobre o 1° e 2° volumes da obra intitulada *Voyage Pittoresque et Historique au Brésil.*" *Revista Trimestral de História e Geografia* [later *Revista do Instituto Histórico e Geográfico Brasileiro*] 3 (1841): 98–99.

Pedrosa, Mario. "Portinari: From Brodowski to the Library of Congress." *Bulletin of the Pan-American Union* 76, nos. 4–5 (1942): 199–211, 258–66.

O pensamento político do Presidente. Rio de Janeiro: Departamento de Imprensa e Propaganda, 1943.

Pentado, Eurico. *O Pavilhão do Brasil na Golden Gate International Exhibition: Relatório do Comissário Geral,* 1940.

Pestana, Manoel. "Arte marajouara." *Bellas-Artes* 4, nos. 31–32 (January 1938).

Portinari: His Life and Art. Chicago: The University of Chicago Press, 1940.

Portugal. Secretariado Nacional da Informação. *Mundo português, imagens de uma exposição histórica, 1940.* Lisbon: Edições SNI, 1956.

"O Presidente da República visitou o Museu Histórico Nacional." *O Jornal* (Rio), 11 June 1939.

Putnam, Samuel. "Brazilian Culture under Vargas." *Science and Society* VI, no. 1 (1942): 34–57.

"Que é o Departamento Nacional de Propaganda." *Revista Acadêmica* 47 (November 1939).

Real, Regina Monteiro. *Casa Rui Barbosa: resumo histórico de suas atividades.* Rio de Janeiro: Ministério da Educação e Saúde: Casa Rui Barbosa, 1957.

———. "A origem da Pinacoteca do Museu Nacional de Belas Artes." *Anuário do Museu Nacional de Belas Artes* 7 (1945): 85–127.

———. "Que é a técnica de Museu." *Estudos Brasileiros* 3, no. 6 (March–April 1941): 109–32.

Relatório sucinto das atividades do Museu Nacional de Belas Artes, 1937–1946. Rio de Janeiro: Museu Nacional de Belas Artes, 1948.

Ribeiro, Adalberto Mário. "A Exposição de Edifícios Públicos." *Revista do Serviço Público* 7/3, no. 3 (September 1944): 90–113.

———. *Instituições Brasileiras de Cultura.* 2 vols. Rio de Janeiro: Ministério da Educação e Saúde/Serviço de Documentação, 1945–1948.

Ricardo, Cassiano. *Marcha para Oeste (a influência da "bandeira" na formação social e política do Brasil)*. Rio de Janeiro: José Olympio, 1940.

Rio de Janeiro e arredores: Guia do viájante. Rio de Janeiro: Guias do Brasil, Ltda. Companhia Carioca de Artes Gráficas, 1939.

Rubens, Carlos. *As artes plásticas no Brasil e o Estado Novo*. Rio de Janeiro: Departamento de Imprensa e Propaganda, 1941.

———. *Pequena história das artes plásticas no Brasil*. São Paulo: Companhia Editora Nacional, 1941.

Salgado, Álvaro. "Radiodifusão, fator social." *Cultura Política* I, no. 6 (August 1941): 79–93.

Serrano, Jonathas. *Cinema e educação*. São Paulo: Melhoramentos, 1930.

Sharp, Walter R. "Methods of Opinion Control in Present-Day Brazil." *Public Opinion Quarterly* 5 (March 1941): 3–17.

Smith, Robert C. "Brazil Art: General Statement." *Handbook of Latin American Studies*. vols. 3-12, 1938–1949.

———. "Brazil Builds on Tradition and Today." *Art News* 41, no. 18 (February 1943): 14–19.

———. "Brazilian Art." In *Concerning Latin American Culture*, ed. Charles C. Griffin, 181–97. New York: Russell and Russell, 1940.

———. "Brazilian Painting in New York." *Bulletin of the Pan-American Union* 73, no. 9 (1939): 500–6.

———. "Latin American Painting Comes into its Own." *Inter-American Quarterly* 2, no. 3 (July 1940): 24–35.

———. *The Portinari Murals in the Hispanic Foundation of the Library of Congress*. Washington, D.C.: Library of Congress, 1942.

Sodré, Alcindo de Azevedo. "Dom Pedro II, Chefe do Estado." *Anuário do Museu Imperial* 3 (1942): 211–18.

Souza Campos, Ernesto de. *Instituições culturais e de educação superior no Brasil: resumo histórico*. Rio de Janeiro: Ministério da Educação e Saúde, 1941.

Teixeira, Oswaldo. *Getúlio Vargas e a arte no Brasil: a influência direta dos Chefes do Estado na formação artística das pátrias*. Rio de Janeiro: Departamento da Imprensa e Propaganda, 1940.

Torres, Alberto. *O Problema Nacional: introdução a um programa de organização nacional*. São Paulo: Companhia Editora Nacional, 1933.

Torres, Heloisa Alberto. *Arte indígena da Amazônia*. Rio de Janeiro: Imprensa Nacional, 1940.

Travel in Brazil. Rio de Janeiro: Brazilian Representation to New York World's Fair, 1940.

Trigueiros, F. dos Santos. *Museu e educação*. 2d ed. Rio de Janeiro: Irmões Pongetti, 1958.

Vargas, Getúlio. *Diário.* 2 vols. Rio de Janeiro: Siciliano; Fundação Getúlio Vargas, [1930–1943] 1995.

————. "Discurso de posse na Academia Brasileira de Letras." *Cultura Política* 4, no. 37 (February 1944) 7–19.

————. *As diretrizes da nova política do Brasil.* Rio de Janeiro: José Olympio, 1942.

————. *A nova política do Brasil.* 11 vols. Rio de Janeiro: José Olympio, 1938–1947.

Venâncio Filho, Francisco. "A função educadora dos museus." *Estudos Brasileiros* I, no. 6 (May–June 1939): 50–61.

Vieira, Arlindo. "A Cidade dos Sinos." *Correio da Manhã* (Rio de Janeiro), 3 July 1948.

Modern Sources

Abreu, Regina. *A fabricação do imortal: memória, história e estratégias de consagração no Brasil.* Rio de Janeiro: LAPA; Rocco, 1996.

————. "Síndrome de museus?" *Série encontros e estudos* 2 (1996): 51–68.

Acciaiuoli, Margarida. *Exposições do Estado Novo, 1934–1940.* Lisbon: Livros Horizonte, 1998.

Ades, Dawn. *The Art of Latin America: The Modern Era, 1820–1980.* (New Haven, NJ: Yale University Press, 1989), 70–73.

Almeida, Paulo Mendes de. *De Anita ao museu.* São Paulo: Perspectiva, 1976.

Amaral, Aracy A. *Arte para quê? A preocupação social na arte brasileira, 1930–1970.* 2d ed. São Paulo: Nobel, 1987.

————. *As artes plásticas na semana de 22: subsídios para uma história da renovação das artes no Brasil.* 5th ed. São Paulo: Editora 34, 1998.

————. *Blaise Cendrars no Brasil e os modernistas.* 2d ed. São Paulo: Editora 34, 1997.

Amaral, Aracy, ed. *Arquitectura Neocolonial: América Latina, Caribe, Estados Unidos.* São Paulo: Memorial; Fundo de Cultura Económica, 1994.

Anderson, Benedict. *Imagined Communities: Reflections on the Origin and Spread of Nationalism.* Rev. ed. New York: Verso, 1991.

Andrade, Rodrigo Melo Franco de. *Brasil: Monumentos Históricos e Arqueológicos.* Mexico City: Instituto Panamericano de Geografia e Historia, 1952.

————. *Rodrigo e o SPHAN: coletânea de textos sobre patrimônio cultural.* Rio de Janeiro: Ministério da Cultura, Secretaria do Patrimônio Histórico e Artístico Nacional, Fundação Pró-Memória, 1987.

————. *Rodrigo e seus tempos: coletânea de textos sobre artes e letras.* Rio de Janeiro: Ministério da Cultura, Secretaria do Patrimônio Histórico e Artístico Nacional, Fundação Pró-Memória, 1987.

D'Araújo, Maria Celina, org. *As instituições da Era Vargas*. Rio de Janeiro: EDUERJ; Editora FGV, 1999.

Araújo, Ricardo Benzaquem de. *Guerra e Paz: casa-grande e senzala e a obra de Gilberto Freyre nos anos 30*. Rio de Janeiro: Editora 34, 1994.

Barreiros, Eduardo Canabrava. *Atlas da evolução urbana da Cidade do Rio de Janeiro—ensaio—1565-1965*. Rio de Janeiro: Instituto Histórico e Geográfico Brasileiro, 1965.

Barros, Geraldo Mendes. *Guilherme Guinle, 1882-1960: ensaio biográfico*. São Paulo: Livraria Agir Editora, 1982.

Barthel, Diane. *Historic Preservation: Collective Memory and Historical Identity*. New Brunswick, NJ: Rutgers University Press, 1996.

Béhague, Gerard. *Heitor Villa-Lobos: The Search for Brazil's Musical Soul*. Austin: University of Texas Press, 1994.

Bello, José Maria. *A History of Modern Brazil, 1889-1964*. Stanford, CA: Stanford University Press, 1966.

Bender, Gerald. *Angola under the Portuguese: The Myth and the Reality*. Berkeley: University of California Press, 1978.

Bennett, Tony. *The Birth of the Museum: History, Theory, Politics*. London: Routledge, 1995.

Bens móveis e imóveis inscritos nos Livros do Tombo do Instituto do Patrimônio Histórico e Artístico Nacional. 4th ed. Rio de Janeiro: Ministério da Cultura/Instituto do Patrimônio Histórico e Artístico Nacional, 1994.

Bittencourt, José. "Fenícios, sambaquis e Marajó: os primórdios da Arqueologia no Brasil e a formação do imaginário nacional." Unpublished ms, 1999.

———. "Observações sobre um museu de história do século XIX: o Museu Militar do Arsenal de Guerra." *Anais do Museu Histórico Nacional* 29 (1997): 211-45.

———. "A parede da memória: objetos, memória e perenidade no Museu Histórico Nacional." Unpublished ms, 1992.

Bolton, Richard, ed. *Culture Wars: Documents from the Recent Controversies in the Arts*. New York: New Press, 1992.

Bomeny, Maria. *Guardiões da razão: modernistas mineiros*. Rio de Janeiro: Editora UFRJ; Edições Tempo Brasileiro, 1994.

———. "Patrimônios da memória nacional." In *Ideológos do patrimônio cultural*. Rio de Janeiro: Instituto Brasileiro do Patrimônio Cultural, 1991.

Borges, Dain. "Intellectuals and the Forgetting of Slavery." *Annals of Scholarship* 11, nos. 1-2 (1996): 37-60.

———. "Puffy, Ugly, Slothful, and Inert: Degeneration in Brazilian Social Thought, 1880-1940." *Journal of Latin American Studies* 25, no. 2 (1993): 235-56.

———. "The Recognition of Afro-Brazilian Symbols and Ideas, 1890-1949." *Luso-Brazilian Review* 32, no. 2 (1995): 59-78.

————. "Review Essay: Brazilian Social Thought of the 1930s." *Luso-Brazilian Review* 31, no. 2 (1994): 137–49.

Borges, Vavy Pacheco. "Anos trinta e política: conceitos, imagens, e temas." *Luso-Brazilian Review* 36, no. 2 (1999): 109–26.

Bourdieu, Pierre. *The Field of Cultural Production: Essays on Art and Literature.* New York: Columbia University Press, 1993.

Bourdieu, Pierre, and Alain Darbel. *The Love of Art: European Art Museums and Their Public.* Stanford, CA: Stanford University Press, 1990.

Braund, Yves. *Arquitetura contemporânea no Brasil.* 3d ed. São Paulo: Perspectiva, 1997.

Brito, Mário de Silva. *A história do modernismo: antecedentes da Semana de Arte Moderna.* 5th ed. Rio de Janeiro: Civilização Brasileira, 1978.

Burman, Alasdair G., and Laura Burman. *São João del Rey: pesquisa, montagem, e opiniões.* São Paulo: Editora Rios, 1989.

Burns, E. Bradford. *A History of Brazil.* 3d ed. New York: Columbia University Press, 1993.

————. *Nationalism in Brazil: A Historical Survey.* New York: Preager, 1968.

Campofiorito, Ítalo. "Introdução—as Primeiras Árvores." *Revista do Patrimônio* 26 (1997): 10–18.

————. "Muda o mundo do patrimônio: Notas para um balanço crítico." *Revista do Brasil* 2, no. 4 (1985): 32–43.

Campos, Reynaldo Pompeu de. *Repressão judicial no Estado Novo: esquerda e direita no banco dos réus.* Rio de Janeiro: Achiamé, 1982.

Cancelli, Elizabeth. *O mundo da violência: a polícia da era de Vargas.* Brasília: Editora da Universidade de Brasília, 1993.

Cândido, Antônio. "A Revolução de 1930 e a cultura." In *Educação pela noite e outros ensaios,* 181–98. São Paulo: Ática, 1987.

Capelato, Maria Helena Rolim. "Estado Novo: novas histórias." In *Historiografia brasileira em perspectiva,* ed. Marcos Cezar de Freitas, 183–213. São Paulo: Contexto, 1998.

Carone, Edgard, ed. *A Velha República: Evolução Política.* São Paulo: Difusão Européia do Livro, 1971.

————. *O Estado Novo.* São Paulo: DIFEL, 1976.

————. *A Terceira República.* São Paulo: DIFEL/Difusão, 1976.

Carrazzoni, Maria Elisa, ed. *Guia dos bens tombados Brasil.* 2d ed. Rio de Janeiro: Expressão e Cultura, 1987.

Carvalho, José Murilo de. *Os bestializados: o Rio de Janeiro e a República que não foi.* São Paulo: Companhia da Letras, 1987.

————. "Forças armadas e política, 1930–1945." In *A Revolução de 30: Seminário internacional,* 107–50. Brasília: Editora Universidade de Brasília, 1982.

————. *A formação das almas: o imaginário da república no Brasil*. São Paulo: Companhia das Letras, 1990.

Castelo, Claudia. *"O modo português de estar no Mundo": O luso-tropicalismo e a ideologia colonial portuguesa (1933-1961)*. Oporto: Edições Afrontamento, 1998.

Castro, Sonia Rabello. *O estado na preservação de bens culturais: o tombamento*. Rio de Janeiro: Renovar, 1991.

Cavalcanti, Lauro. *As preocupações do belo: arquitetura moderna brasileira dos anos 30/40*. Rio de Janeiro: Taurus Editora, 1995.

————, ed. *Modernistas na repartição*. Rio de Janeiro: Editora UFRJ; Paço Imperial/Tempo Brasileiro, 1993.

180 anos da Escola de Belas Artes. Anais do Seminário EBA 180. Rio de Janeiro: Universidade Federal do Rio de Janeiro, 1996.

Chagas, Mário. "A ótica museológica de Mário de Andrade." In *Ideólogos do patrimônio cultural*, 99–113. Rio de Janeiro: Instituto Brasileiro do Patrimônio Cultural, 1991.

Chalhoub, Sidney. *Trabalho, lar, e botequim: o cotidiano dos trabalhadores no Rio de Janeiro da Belle Époque*. São Paulo: Brasilense, 1986.

Chuva, Márcia Regina Romero. *Os arquitetos da memória: a construção do patrimônio histórico e artístico nacional no Brasil (anos 30 e 40)*. Ph.D. dissertation. Universidade Federal Fluminense, 1998.

Chuva, Márcia, org. *A invenção do patrimônio: continuidade e ruptura na constituição de uma política oficial de preservação no Brasil*. Rio de Janeiro: Ministério da Cultura, Instituto do Patrimônio Histórico e Artístico Nacional, 1995.

Cine Jornal Brasileiro: Departamento de Imprensa e Propaganda, 1938-1946. São Paulo: Fundação Cinemateca Brasileira, 1982.

Coelho, Olinio Gomes P. *Do patrimônio cultural*. Rio de Janeiro, 1992.

Comas, Carlos Eduardo. "Modern Architecture, Brazilian Corollary." *AA Files* (summer 1998): 3–13.

Conniff, Michael. *Urban Politics in Brazil: The Rise of Populism, 1925-1945*. Pittsburgh: University of Pittsburgh Press, 1981.

Correia, Marcos Sá. *Oscar Niemeyer*. Rio de Janeiro: Relume-Dumará, 1996.

Costa, Emília Viotti da. *The Brazilian Empire: Myths and Realities*. Chicago: University of Chicago Press, 1985.

Costa, Lucio. *Lucio Costa: registro de uma vivência*. São Paulo: Empresa das Artes, 1995.

————. *Sobre arquitetura*. Porto Alegre: Centro dos Estudantes Universitários de Arquitetura, 1962.

Costa, Lygia Martins da. "O pensamento de Rodrigo na criação dos museus do PHAN," In *Ideólogos do patrimônio cultural*. Rio de Janeiro: Instituto Brasileiro do Patrimonio Cultural, 1991: 113-29.

Cronobiografia de Portinari. Rio de Janeiro: Projeto Portinari, n.d.

Curtis, William. *Modern Architecture since 1900*. 3d ed. London: Phoidon Press, 1996.

Dávila, Jerry. *Perfecting the Brazilian Race*. Ph.D. dissertation. Brown University, 1999.

Deutsch, Sandra McGee. *Las derechas: The Extreme Right in Argentina, Brazil, and Chile, 1890–1939*. Stanford, CA: Stanford University Press, 1999.

Dulles, John W. F. *Vargas of Brazil: A Political Biography*. Austin: University of Texas Press, 1967.

Duncan, Carol. *Civilizing Rituals: Inside Public Art Museums*. London: Routledge, 1995.

Duncan, Carol, and Alan Wallach. "The Universal Survey Museum." *Art History* 3, no. 4 (December 1980): 448–69.

Durand, José Carlos. *Arte, privilégio, e distinção: artes plásticas, arquitetura e classe dirigente no Brasil, 1855/1985*. São Paulo: Perspectiva, 1989.

Elkin, Noah Charles. "1922: o encontro do efêmero com a permanência." *Anais do Museu Histórico Nacional* 29 (1997): 121–40.

———. *Promoting a New Brazil: National Expositions and Images of Modernity, 1861–1922*. Ph.D. dissertation. Rutgers University, 1999.

Enciclopédia do Integralismo. 8 vols. Rio de Janeiro: Edições GRD, 1958.

Fabris, Annateresa. *Cândido Portinari*. São Paulo: EduSP, 1996.

———. *Cândido Portinari: Pintor Social*. 2d ed. São Paulo: Perspectiva, 1990.

Falcão, Joaquim Arruda. "Política cultural e democracia: a preservação do patrimônio histórico e artístico nacional." In *Estado e cultura no Brasil*, org. Sérgio Miceli, 21–39. São Paulo: Difel, 1984.

Fausto, Boris. *A Revolução de 30: historiografia e história*. 8th ed. São Paulo: Brasilense, 1982.

Figueiredo, Paulo Nunes de Augusto de. *Aspectos ideológicos do Estado Novo*. Brasília: Senado Federal, 1984.

Fonseca, Maria Cecília Londres. *O patrimônio em processo: trajetória da política federal de preservação no Brasil*. Rio de Janeiro: Editora da UFRJ/MinC/IPHAN, 1997.

França, José-Augusto. *A arte em Portugal no século XX: 1911–1961*. 2d ed. Venda Nova: Bertrand, 1984.

French, John D. "The Populist Gamble of Getúlio Vargas in 1945: Political and Ideological Transitions in Brazil." In *Latin America in the 1940s: War and Postwar Transitions*, ed. David Rock, 141–65. Berkeley: University of California Press, 1994.

Franco, Jean. *The Modern Culture of Latin America: Society and the Artist*. New York: Praeger, 1967.

Garcia, Nelson Jahr. *Estado Novo e propaganda política: a legitimação do estado autoritário perante as classes subalternas*. São Paulo: Edições Loyola, 1982.

García Canclini, Néstor. *Hybrid Cultures: Strategies for Entering and Leaving Modernity*. Minneapolis: University of Minnesota Press, 1995.

Garfield, Seth. " 'The Roots of a Plant that Today is Brazil': Indians and the Nation-State under the Brazilian Estado Novo." *Journal of Latin American Studies* 29 (1997): 747–68.

Gellner, Ernest. *Nations and Nationalism*. Oxford: Basil Blackwell, 1983.

Gertz, René. "Estado Novo: um inventário historiográfico." In *O Feixe: o autoritarismo como questão teórica e historiográfica*, 111–31. Rio de Janeiro: Jorge Zahar, 1991.

Gillis, John, ed. *Commemorations: The Politics of National Identity*. Princeton: Princeton University Press, 1994.

Gomes, Angela de Castro. *Essa gente do Rio: Modernismo e modernidade*. Rio de Janeiro: Editora Fundação Getúlio Vargas, 1999.

———. *História e historiadores*. Rio de Janeiro: Fundação Getúlio Vagas, 1996.

Gonçalves, José Reginaldo Santos. *A retórica da perda: os discursos do patrimônio cultural no Brasil*. Rio de Janeiro: Editora UFRJ/MinC/IPHAN, 1996.

Goulart, Silvana. *Sob a verdade oficial: ideologia, propaganda e censura no Estado Novo*. São Paulo: Marco Zero, 1990.

Grinberg, Piedade Epstein. *Ruben Navarro e a crítica da arte na década de 40 no Rio de Janeiro*. Master's thesis, Universidade Federal do Rio de Janeiro, 1996.

Guanabara, Brazil. Secretaria de Obras Públicas. *Rio de Janeiro em seus quatrocentos anos: formação e desenvolvimento da cidade*. Rio de Janeiro: Distribuidora Record, 1965.

Guimaraens, Cêça de. *Lucio Costa: um certo arquiteto em incerto e secular roteiro*. Rio de Janeiro: Relume-Dumará, 1996.

Guimarães, Manoel Luís Salgado. "Nação e Civilização nos Trópicos: O Instituto Histórico e Geográfico Brasileiro e o projeto de uma História Nacional." *Estudos Históricos* 1 (1988): 5–27.

Hale, Charles. "Political and Social Ideas." In *Latin America: Economy and Society, 1870–1930*, ed. Leslie Bethell, 225–99. New York: Cambridge University Press, 1989.

Hallewell, Lawrence. *Books in Brazil: A History of the Publishing Trade*. Metuchen, N.J.: Scarecrow Press, 1982.

Hardman, Francisco Foot. *Trem fantasma: a modernidade na selva*. São Paulo: Companhia das Letras, 1988.

Haussman, Fay, and Jerry Haar. *Education in Brazil*. Hamden, CT: Archon Books, 1978.

Hellwig, David, ed. *African-American Reflections on Brazil's Racial Paradise*. Philadelphia: Temple University Press, 1992.

Herkenhoff, Paulo. "The Jungle in Brazilian Modern Design." *Journal of Decorative and Propaganda Arts* 21 (1995): 238–59.

Hilton, Stanley. "The Overthrow of Getúlio Vargas in 1945: Diplomatic Intervention, Defense of Democracy, or Political Retribution?" *Hispanic American Historical Review* 67, no. 1 (February 1987): 1–38.

Hobsbawm, Eric. *Nations and Nationalism since 1780: Programme, Myth, Reality.* New York: Cambridge University Press, 1990.

Hobsbawm, Eric, and Terence Ranger. *The Invention of Tradition.* Canto ed. New York: Cambridge University Press, 1993.

Hollanda, Guy de. *Recursos educativos dos museus brasileiros.* Rio de Janeiro: Centro Brasileiro de Pesquisas Educacionais, 1958.

Holston, James. *The Modernist City: An Anthropological Critique of Brasília.* Chicago: The University of Chicago Press, 1989.

Hooper-Greenhill, Eilean. *Museums and the Shaping of Knowledge.* New York: Routledge, 1992.

Horta, José Silvério Baía. *O hino, o sermão, e a ordem do dia: e educação no Brasil (1930–1945).* Rio de Janeiro: Editora da UFRJ, 1994.

Hunter, Davidson James. *Culture Wars: The Struggle to Define America.* New York: Basic Books, 1991.

Jacintho, Edgard. *Memória Oral.* Rio de Janeiro: Fundação Pró-Memória, 1983.

Jesus Paulo, Heloísa Helena de. "Aspectos da ação do DIP: a divulgação de censura e a censura de divulgação." *LPH/Revista de História* 1, no. 1 (1990): 90–104.

———. "O DIP e a Juventude: ideologia e propaganda estatal, 1939–1945." *Revista Brasileira da História* 7, no. 14 (March–August 1987): 99–113.

Johnson, Randal. "The Dynamics of the Brazilian Literary Field, 1930–1945." *Luso-Brazilian Review* 31, no. 2 (1994): 5–22.

———. *The Film Industry in Brazil: Culture and the State.* Pittsburgh: University of Pittsburgh Press, 1987.

———. "The Institutionalization of Brazilian Modernism." *Brasil/Brazil* 3, no. 4 (1990): 5–23.

———. "Regarding the Philanthropic Ogre: Cultural Policy in Brazil, 1930–45/1964–90." In *Constructing Culture and Power in Latin America,* ed. Daniel H. Levine, 311–56. Ann Arbor: University of Michigan Press, 1993.

Kamen, Michael. *Mystic Chords of Memory: The Transformation of Tradition in American Culture.* New York: Knopf, 1991.

Karp, Ivan, Christine Mullen Kreamer, and Steven D. Lavine, eds. *Museums and Communities: The Politics of Public Culture.* Washington, D.C.: Smithsonian Institution, 1992.

Karp, Ivan, and Steven D. Lavine, eds. *Exhibiting Cultures: The Poetics and Politics of Museum Display.* Washington, D.C.: Smithsonian Institution, 1991.

Kessel, Carlos. "Estilo, discurso, poder: arquitetura neocolonial no Brasil." *Revista Brasileira da História Social* 6 (1999): 65–94.

Lacerda, Aline Lopes de. " 'Obra Getuliana' ou como as imagens comemoram o regime." *Estudos Históricos* 7, no. 14 (1994): 241–63.

Lafetá, João Luiz. *1930: a crítica e o modernismo*. São Paulo: Duas Cidades, 1974.

Landes, Ruth. *The City of Women*. New York: Macmillan, 1947.

Lauerhauss Jr., Ludwig. *Getúlio Vargas e o triunfo do nacionalismo brasileiro*. Belo Horizonte: Editora Itatiaia, 1986.

———. "Who Was Getúlio Vargas? Theme and Variation in Brazilian Political Lore." *Journal of Latin American Lore* 5, no. 2 (1979): 273–90.

Lehmkuhl, Luciene. "Brasil: uma imagem em exposição" *Esboços* Universidade Federal de Santa Catarina, 2000.

Lemos, Carlos Alberto Cerqueira. *The Art of Brazil*. New York: Harper & Row, 1983.

Lenharo, Alcir. *Sacralização da política*. Campinas: Papirus; Editora da UNICAMP, 1986.

Lesser, Jeffrey. "Immigration and Shifting Concepts of National Identity in Brazil during the Vargas Era." *Luso-Brazilian Review* 31, no. 2 (1994): 27–48.

Levine, Robert. *Father of the Poor?: Vargas and His Era*. New York: Cambridge University Press, 1998.

———. *The Vargas Regime: The Critical Years, 1934–1938*. New York: Columbia University Press, 1970.

A lição de Rodrigo: In memoriam pelos amigos do DPHAN. Recife: Universidade Federal de Pernambuco, 1969.

Lima (Junior), Augusto de. *Vila Rica do Ouro Preto: síntese histórica e descritiva*. Belo Horizonte: n.p., 1957.

Lima, Evelyn F. Werneck. *Avenida Presidente Vargas: Uma drástica cirurgia*. Rio de Janeiro: Biblioteca Carioca, 1990.

Linenthal, Edward T., and Tom Engelhardt, eds. *History Wars: The Enola Gay and Other Battles for the American Past*. New York: Metropolitan Books, 1996.

Lissovsky, Mauricio, and Paulo Sergio Moraes de Sá, orgs. *Colunas da Educação: a construção do Ministério da Educação e Saúde*. Rio de Janeiro: MinC/IPHAN/ Fundação Getúlio Vargas/CPDOC, 1996.

Lopes, Maria Margaret. *O Brasil descobre a pesquisa científica: os museus e as ciências naturais no século XIX*. São Paulo: HUCITEC, 1997.

Lowenstein, Karl. *Brazil under Vargas*. New York: Macmillan, 1942.

Mainwaring, Scott. *The Catholic Church and Politics in Brazil, 1916–1985*. Stanford, CA: Stanford University Press, 1986.

Martins, Wilson. *The Modernist Idea: A Critical Survey of Brazilian Writing in the Twentieth Century*. New York: New York University Press, [1969] 1971.

Matta, Roberto da. "Antropologia da saudade." In *Conto de mentiroso: sete ensaios de antropologia brasileira*, 17–34. Rio de Janeiro: Rocco, 1993.

Maxwell, Kenneth. *Conflicts and Conspiracies: Brazil and Portugal, 1750–1808.* Cambridge: Cambridge University Press, 1973.

McCann, Bryan. *Thin Air and the Solid State: Radio, Culture and Politics in Brazil's Vargas Era.* Ph.D. dissertation. Yale University, 1999.

McCann, Frank. *The Brazilian-American Alliance, 1937–1945.* Princeton: Princeton University Press, 1973.

Melo, José Ignácio de. *Ação e imaginário de uma ditadura: controle, coerção, e propaganda política nos meios de comunicação durante o Estado Novo.* Master's thesis. Escola de Comunicações e Artes, Universidade de São Paulo, 1990.

Mendonça, Ana Rita. *Carmen Miranda foi a Washington.* Rio de Janeiro: Record, 1999.

Miceli, Sérgio. *Imagens negociadas: retratos da elite brasileira (1920–1940).* São Paulo: Companhia das Letras, 1996.

———. *Intelectuais e classe dirigente no Brasil, 1920–1945.* São Paulo: Difel, 1979.

———. *Poder, sexo e letras na República Velha (estudo clínico dos anatolianos).* São Paulo: Perspectiva, 1977.

Miceli, Sérgio, org. *Estado e cultura o Brasil.* São Paulo: Difel, 1984.

Milet, Vera. *A teimosia das pedras: um estudo sobre a preservação do patrimônio ambiental do Brasil.* Olinda: Prefeitura de Olinda, 1988.

Morais, Frederico. *Cronologia das artes plásticas no Rio de Janeiro, 1816–1994.* Rio de Janeiro: Topbooks, 1995.

Morse, Richard. *O espelho de Próspero.* São Paulo: Companhia das Letras, 1988.

———. "The Multiverse of Latin American Identity, c. 1920–1970." In *The Cambridge History of Latin America,* vol. X, ed. Leslie Bethell, 1–129. New York: Cambridge University Press, 1995.

———. *New World Soundings: Culture and Ideology in the Americas.* Baltimore, Md.: Johns Hopkins University Press, 1989.

Mota, Carlos Guilherme. *Ideologia da cultura brasileira: pontos de partida para uma revisão histórica.* São Paulo: Ática, 1977.

Motta, Lia. "A SPHAN em Ouro Preto." *Revista do Patrimônio Histórico e Artístico Nacional.* 22 (1987): 108–22.

Motta, Marly Silva da. *A nação faz 100 anos: a questão nacional no Centenário da Independência.* Rio de Janeiro: Editora da Fundação Getúlio Vargas/CPDOC, 1992.

Moura, Gerson, *O Tio Sam chega ao Brasil: a penetração cultual americana.* São Paulo: Brasilense, 1984.

Mourão, Rui. *A nova realidade do museu.* Ouro Preto: MinC/IPHAN/Museu da Inconfidência, 1994.

Naves, Rodrigo. *A forma difícil: ensaios sobre arte brasileira.* 2d ed. São Paulo: Ática, 1998.

Needell, Jeffrey. "The Domestic Civilizing Mission: The Cultural Role of the State in Brazil, 1808–1930." *Luso-Brazilian Review* 36, no. 1 (1999): 1–18.

———. "Identity, Race, Gender, and Modernity in the Origins of Gilberto Freyre's *Oeuvre.*" *American Historical Review* 100, no. 1 (February 1995): 51–77.

———. *A Tropical Belle Époque: Elite Culture in Turn-of-the-Century Rio de Janeiro.* Cambridge: Cambridge University Press, 1987.

Neves, Margarida de Souza. *Vitrines do Progresso.* Ph.D. dissertation. Pontífica Universidade Católica do Rio de Janeiro, 1986.

Nist, John. *The Modernist Movement in Brazil: A Literary Study.* Austin: University of Texas Press, 1967.

Nolan Jr., James, ed. *The American Culture Wars: Current Contests and Future Prospects.* Charlottesville: University of Virginia Press, 1996.

Nora, Pierre, ed. *Realms of Memory: Rethinking the French Past.* 3 vols. New York: Columbia University Press, 1996–1998.

Oliveira, Lúcia Lippi. *A Questão Nacional na Primeira República.* São Paulo: Brasilense, 1990.

———, ed. *Elite intelectual e debate político nos anos 30.* Rio de Janeiro: Editora da Fundação Getúlio Vargas, 1980.

Oliveira, Lúcia Lippi, Mônica Pimenta Velloso, and Angela Maria Castro Gomes. *Estado Novo: ideologia e poder.* Rio de Janeiro: Zahar Editores, 1982.

Ortiz, Renato. *Cultura brasileira e identidade nacional.* São Paulo: Brasilense, 1985.

Palmatary, Helen. "The Pottery of Marajó Island." *Transactions of the American Philosophical Society,* New Series 39, no. 3 (1949): 261–470.

Pandolfi, Dulce, org. *Repensando o Estado Novo.* Rio de Janeiro: Editora da Fundação Getúlio Vargas, 1999.

Paulo, Heloísa. *Estado Novo e propaganda em Portugal e no Brasil: o SPN/SNI e o DIP.* Coimbra: Livraria Minerva, 1994.

Pécaut, Daniel. *Os intelectuais e a política no Brasil: entre o povo e a nação.* Trans. Maria Júlia Goldwasser. São Paulo: Ática, [1989] 1990.

Pedrosa, Mário. *Acadêmicos e modernistas.* São Paulo: Editora da Universidade de São Paulo, 1998.

Pessavento, Sandra Jatahy. *Exposições universais: espetáculos da modernidade do século XIX.* São Paulo: HUCITEC, 1997.

Pierson, Donald. *Negroes in Brazil: A Study of Race Contact in Bahia.* Chicago: The University of Chicago Press, 1942.

Projeto de vitalização do patrimônio cultural no Brasil: uma trajetória. Brasília: Ministério da Educação e Cultura: SPHAN: Fundação Pró-Memória, 1980.

Raphael, Allison. *Samba and Social Control: Popular Culture and Racial Democracy in Rio de Janeiro.* Ph.D. dissertation. Columbia University, 1980.

A Revolução de 1930: Seminário internacional. Brasília: Editora da Universidade de Brasília, 1980.

Ribeiro, Irene. *Raul Lino: pensador nacionalista da arquitectura*. Oporto: Faculdade de Arquitectura da Universidade de Porto, 1994.

Ricardo, Cassiano. *Viagem no tempo e no espaço: Memórias*. Rio de Janeiro: José Olympio, 1970.

O Rio de Janeiro e sua arquitetura. Rio de Janeiro: Prefeitura da Cidade do Rio de Janeiro; RIOTUR, 1989.

Romanelli, Otaíza de Oliveira. *História da educação no Brasil (1930-1973)*. Petrópolis: Vozes, 1978.

Sala Jr., Dalton. "Mário de Andrade e o anteprojeto do Serviço do Patrimônio Artístico Nacional." *Revista do Instituto de Estudos Brasileiros* 31 (1990): 19-26.

―――. "O Serviço do Patrimônio Histórico e Artístico Nacional e a questão das reduções jesuíticas da Bacia do Prata: um capítulo da historiografia artística brasileira durante o Estado Novo (1937-1945)." *Estudos Ibero-Americanos* 15, no. 1 (1989): 245-57.

―――. "O Serviço do Patrimônio Histórico e Artístico Nacional: história oficial e Estado Novo." Unpublished ms., Departamento de Artes Plásticas da Escola de Comunicações da Universidade de São Paulo, 1988.

Santos, Myriam Sepulveda dos. "História, tempo e memória: um estudo sobre museus (à partir da observação feita no Museu Imperial e no Museu Histórico Nacional)." Unpublished ms., Instituto Universitário de Pesquisa do Rio de Janeiro, 1989.

Saroldi, Luiz Carlos, and Sonia Virgínia Moreira. *Rádio Nacional: o Brasil em sintonia*. Rio de Janeiro: FUNARTE, 1984.

Schneider, Ronald. *Order and Progress: A Political History of Brazil*. Boulder, Co: Westview Press, 1991.

Schwarcz, Lilia Mortiz. *As barbas do imperador*. São Paulo: Companhia das Letras, 1999.

―――. *O espetáculo das raças: cientistas, instituições e questão racial no Brasil, 1870-1930*. São Paulo: Companhia das Letras, 1993.

Schwartz, Jorge. *Vanguardas Latino-Americanas: Polêmicas, manifestos e textos críticos*. São Paulo: Editora da Universidade de São Paulo: Iluminuras, FAPESP, 1995.

Schwartzman, Simon. "O intelectual e o poder: a carreira política de Gustavo Capanema." In *A Revolução de 1930: Seminário internacional*, 365-97. Brasília: Editora da Universidade de Brasília, 1980.

Schwartzman, Simon, Helena Maria Bousquet Bomeny, and Vanda Maria Ribeiro Costa. *Tempos de Capanema*. Rio de Janeiro: Paz e Terra, 1984.

Sevcenko, Nicolau. *Literatura como missão: tensões sociais e criação cultural na Primeira República*. São Paulo: Brasilense, 1983.

————. *Orfeu extático na metrópole: São Paulo, sociedade e cultura nos frementes anos 20.* São Paulo: Companhia das Letras, 1992.

Severiano, Jairo. *Getúlio Vargas e a música popular.* Rio de Janeiro: Editora da Fundação Getúlio Vargas, 1983.

Silva, H. Pereira da. *Oswaldo Teixeira em 3ª dimensão: vida, obra e época.* Rio de Janeiro: Museu de Armas Ferriera da Cunha, 1975.

Silva, Suely Braga da. "O Instituto Nacional do Livro e a institucionalização de organismos culturais no Estado Novo (1937-1945): planos, idéias, e realizações." Master's thesis. Universidade Federal do Rio de Janeiro, 1992.

Silva Telles, Augusto da. "Neocolonial: la polémica de José Mariano." In *Arquitectura Neocolonial: América Latina, Caribe, Estados Unidos,* ed. Aracy Amaral. São Paulo: Memorial da América Latina; Fundo de Cultura Economica, 1994.

Skidmore, Thomas E. *Black into White: Race and Nationality in Brazilian Thought.* New York: Oxford University Press, 1974.

————. *Brazil: Five Centuries of Change.* New York: Oxford University Press, 1999.

————. *Politics in Brazil, 1930-1964: An Experiment in Democracy.* New York: Oxford University Press, 1967.

Sodré, Nelson Wernick. *Síntese de história da cultura brasileira.* Rio de Janeiro: Civilização Brasileira, 1970.

Sommer, Doris. *Foundational Fictions: The National Romances of Latin America.* Berkeley: University of California Press, 1991.

Souza, Carlos Roberto de. *Catálogo: Filmes produzidos pelo INCE.* Rio de Janeiro: Fundação do Cinema Brasileiro, 1990.

Stam, Robert. *Tropical Multiculturalism: A Comparative History of Race in Brazilian Cinema and Culture.* Durham, N.C.: Duke University Press, 1997.

Stepan, Alfred. *The Military in Politics: Changing Patterns in Brazil.* Princeton, N.J.: Princeton University Press, 1971.

Stepan, Nancy Leys. *The Hour of Eugenics: Race, Gender, and Nation in Latin America.* Ithaca: Cornell University Press, 1991.

Taunay, Afonso de E. *A Missão Artística de 1816.* Brasília: Editora Universidade de Brasília, [1912] 1983.

Telles, Antonio A. Queiroz. *Tombamento e seu regime jurídico.* São Paulo: Revista dos Tribunais, 1992.

Thomaz, Omar Ribeiro. "Do saber colonial ao luso-tropicalismo: 'Raça' e 'Nação' nas primeiras décadas do Salazarismo." In *Raça, ciência, e sociedade,* ed. Marcos Chor Maio and Ricardo Ventura Santos, Rio de Janeiro: FIOCRUZ, 1996. 85-106.

Thomaz, Omar Ribeiro, and Waldemar Bernini Lichtenthäler. "O mundo que o português criou." In *Entre o Mito e a História: O V Centenário do Descobrimento da América,* ed. Paula Montero, 291-335. Petrópolis: Vozes, 1996.

Topik, Steven. "Where Is the Coffee? Coffee and Brazilian Identity." *Luso-Brazilian Review* 30, no. 2 (1999): 87–92.

Tota, Antonio Pedro. *A locomotiva no ar: rádio e modernidade em São Paulo, 1924–1934.* São Paulo: PW; Secretaria de Estado da Cultura, 1990.

————. *Samba de legitimidade.* Master's thesis. Universidade de São Paulo, 1980.

Velloso, Mônica Pimenta. *Os intelectuais e a política cultural do Estado Novo.* Rio de Janeiro: Fundação Getúlio Vargas/CPDOC, 1987.

————. *Modernismo no Rio: Turunas e Quixotes.* Rio de Janeiro: Editora Fundação Getúlio Vargas, 1996.

Vilhena, Luís Rodolfo. *Projeto e missão: o movimento folclórico brasileiro, 1947–1964.* Rio de Janeiro: Fundação Getúlio Vargas Editora/Ministério da Cultura, FUNARTE, 1997.

Williams, Daryle. *"Ad perpetuam rei memoriam:* The Vargas Regime and Brazil's National Historical Patrimony, 1930–1945." *Luso-Brazilian Review* 31, no. 2 (1994): 45–75.

————. "Gustavo Capanema, Ministro de Cultura." In *Capanema: o ministro e seu ministério.,* ed. Angela Castro Gomes, 251–69. Rio de Janeiro: Fundação Getúlio Vargas: São Francisco, 2000.

————. "Sobre patronos, heróis, e visitantes: O Museu Histórico Nacional, 1930–1960." *Anais do Museu Histórico Nacional* 29 (1997): 141–86.

Winz, Antônio Pimentel. *História da Casa do Trem.* Rio de Janeiro: Museu Histórico Nacional, 1962.

Wirth, John D. *Minas Gerais in the Brazilian Federation, 1889–1937.* Stanford: Stanford University Press, 1977.

————. "*Tenentismo* in the Brazilian Revolution of 1930." *Hispanic American Historical Review* 44, no. 2 (May 1964): 161–79.

————. *The Politics of Brazilian Development, 1930–1954.* Stanford: Stanford University Press, 1970.

Wood, Marcus. *Blind Memory: Visual Representations of Slavery in England and America, 1780–1865,* 215–91. London: Routledge, 2000.

Zillio, Carlos. *A quarela do Brasil: a questão da identidade da arte brasileira.* 2d ed. Rio de Janeiro: Relume-Dumará, 1997.

————. "A modernidade efêmera: anos 80 na Academia." In *180 anos de Escola de Belas Artes.* Anis do Seminário EBA 180. Rio de Janeiro: Universidade Federal do Rio de Janeiro, 1996.

Index

Daryle Williams is Associate Professor of History at the
University of Maryland.

Library of Congress Cataloging-in-Publication Data
Williams, Daryle.
Culture wars in Brazil : the first Vargas regime, 1930-1945 /
Daryle Williams.
p. cm.
Includes bibliographical references and index.
ISBN 0-8223-2708-2 (cloth : alk. paper) —
ISBN 0-8223-2719-8 (pbk. : alk. paper)
1. Brazil—Politics and government—1930-1945.   2. Politics
and culture—Brazil—History—20th century.   3. Brazil—
Cultural policy.   4. Vargas, Getûlio, 1883-1954.
I. Title.
F2538 .W55   2001
981.06'1—dc21   2001018769